POPULIST CONSTITUTIONALISM AND ILLIBERAL DEMOCRACIES

POPULIST CONSTITUTIONALISM AND ILLIBERAL DEMOCRACIES

Between Constitutional Imagination, Normative Entrenchment and Political Reality

Edited by
Martin Belov

INTERSENTIA

Cambridge – Antwerp – Chicago

Intersentia Ltd
8 Wellington Mews
Wellington Street | Cambridge
CB1 1HW | United Kingdom
Tel: +44 1223 736 170
Email: mail@intersentia.co.uk
www.intersentia.com | www.intersentia.co.uk

Distribution for the UK and
Rest of the World (incl. Eastern Europe)
NBN International
1 Deltic Avenue, Rooksley
Milton Keynes MK13 8LD
United Kingdom
Tel: +44 1752 202 301 | Fax: +44 1752 202 331
Email: orders@nbninternational.com

Distribution for Europe
Lefebvre Sarrut Belgium NV
Hoogstraat 139/6
1000 Brussels
Belgium
Tel: +32 (0)800 39 067
Email: mail@intersentia.be

Distribution for the USA and Canada
Independent Publishers Group
Order Department
814 North Franklin Street
Chicago, IL 60610
USA
Tel: +1 800 888 4741 (toll free) | Fax: +1 312 337 5985
Email: orders@ipgbook.com

Populist Constitutionalism and Illiberal Democracies. Between Constitutional Imagination, Normative Entrenchment and Political Reality

ISBN 978-1-83970-060-6
D/2021/7849/7
NUR 820

British Library Cataloguing in Publication Data. A catalogue record for this book is available from the British Library.

To My Wife Teodora with Love and Admiration

CONTENTS

PART VI. THE SPREAD OF POPULISM AND ILLIBERAL DEMOCRACY IN EUROPE

LIST OF CONTRIBUTORS

Martin Belov, Dr., is Professor in Constitutional and Comparative Constitutional Law at the University of Sofia 'St. Kliment Ohridski', Bulgaria. He is also Vice Dean of the Faculty of Law and is responsible for international relations and digitalisation of the education and scientific activities in the Faculty. He has been a visiting professor at many European universities, a project researcher at the Max-Planck Institute for European Legal History, Frankfurt am Main, Germany (2010–2012) and a visiting researcher at the Institute for Federalism, Fribourg, Switzerland (2014). He has published 18 books and more than 80 scientific papers.

Agnieszka Bień-Kacała is Professor in the Department of Constitutional Law, Faculty of Law and Administration at Nicolaus Copernicus University in Toruń, Poland. Her monograph on the sources of law was recognised as the best dissertation by the Chief of the Sejm Chancellery and the journal *Sejm Review* in 2014. Since 2015, she has been focusing on illiberal constitutionalism and has published, together with Professor Tímea Drinóczi, several works on this topic. Their newest co-edited book is *Rule of Law, Common Values, and Illiberal Constitutionalism* (Routledge, 2021).

Paul Blokker is Associate Professor at the University of Bologna, Italy, and a research coordinator at Charles University, Prague, Czech Republic. He is co-editor of the journals *Social Imaginaries* and *European Cultural and Political Sociology*. His most recent book (with Laura Guercio) is *Sociologia dei diritti umani* (Mondadori, 2020).

Monica Bonini is Associate Professor at the Università degli Studi di Milano-Bicocca, Italy. There, she is a member of several scientific committees, including the PhD committee, and teaches public law, communication law and policy and banking law. She is a visiting professor at the University of Konstanz, Germany, where she delivers courses on Italian constitutional law. Her research interests include public law, comparative constitutional law and EU law. Professor Bonini has numerous publications in the above-mentioned scientific fields and is a member of many research groups in these fields.

Carlo Alberto Ciaralli is PhD in Constitutional Law and Post-Doctoral Research Fellow at the University 'G. d'Annunzio' of Chieti-Pescara, Italy. He obtained the international Master of Studies at the European Law and Governance School (ELGS) and is the author of several papers published in national and international scientific journals and reviews. His research topics concern the Italian and Spanish regional financial autonomy, the crisis of political parties and representative democracy in a time of globalisation and the rise of populism in Europe.

Eoin Daly is a lecturer in law at the National University of Ireland, Galway. His research focuses on the intersection between political theory and constitutional law, particularly republicanism, judicial review, Rousseau, secularism and France. He is the author of *Rousseau's Constitutionalism: Austerity and Republican Freedom* (2017) and *Religion, Law and the Irish State* (2012), as well as co-author of *The Political Theory of the Irish Constitution* (2015).

Gianmario Demuro (PhD in Public Law, Florence, Italy) is Full Professor of Constitutional Law in the Department of Law, University of Cagliari, Italy. He was Adjunct Professor at John Marshal Law School, Chicago, USA, where he taught EU regulation and governance (1999–2019). His research focuses on political systems, constitutional conventions, human rights and multilevel constitutionalism; in the field of human rights he co-edited W.BT. Mock and G. Demuro (eds), *Human Rights in Europe. Commentary on the Charter of Fundamental Rights of the European Union* (Carolina Academic Press, 2010).

Tímea Drinóczi is Professor in the Department of Constitutional Law at the Faculty of Law, University of Pécs, Hungary. She has been a visiting professor in several European universities, served as a professor at the Kenyatta University School of Law, Nairobi, Kenya (2018–2019) and regularly invited as an expert by OSCE ODIHR. Her research interests cover comparative constitutional change, illiberal constitutionalism, constitutional identity and the quality of legislation. Her newest co-edited book with Agnieszka Bień-Kacała is *Rule of Law, Common Values, and Illiberal Constitutionalism* (Routledge, 2021).

Wojciech Engelking is a PhD candidate at the University of Warsaw, Poland. His main areas of research are Carl Schmitt, Leo Strauss, states of exception and the relationship between law and literature. He was a research fellow at Mainz University, Germany, Tel Aviv University, Israel, and Université Paris 1 Panthéon-Sorbonne, France. His works have been published in *History of European Ideas*, *Law, Culture and the Humanities* and *Państwo i Prawo*. He is also a novelist and columnist of the Polish edition of *Newsweek*.

Angela Di Gregorio is Full Professor of Public Comparative Law at the University of Milano, Italy. Her research interests include transition to democracy, democratic deterioration, constitutional justice, transitional justice and academic freedom. She is a member of many Italian and international lawyer's associations and is Editor-in-Chief of the journal *Nuovi Autoritarismi e Democrazie* (New Authoritarian Regimes and Democracies).

Marcin Kilanowski is Professor of Law at Nicolaus Copernicus University in Toruń, Poland. After completing his studies and research in philosophy and law at Nicolaus Copernicus University, Utrecht University, the Netherlands, Oxford University, UK, and Harvard University, USA, he was a visiting researcher and a visiting scholar at Freie Universität, Germany, The Institute for Social Research at Johann Wolfgang Goethe-Universität, Germany, Harvard University and Science-Po Ecole de Droit in Paris. Besides his previous work as a law tutor at Harvard College, teaching assistant at the Institute of Global Law and Policy at Harvard Law School and present work at Nicolaus Copernicus University, he worked as a member of the Prime Minister of Poland Working Group on Corporate Social Responsibility and in various ministries. His research focuses on the development of democracy, civil society, human rights and global governance.

Zoltán Pozsár-Szentmiklósy is Associate Professor of Constitutional Law at the ELTE Eötvös Loránd University, Budapest, Hungary. He is a member of the Advisory Board of the ICON-S CEE Chapter. He is a regular co-author of the Hungarian report of the annual Global Review of Constitutional Law, and author and co-author of chapters published in international volumes on the current challenges related to the separation of powers and constitutional adjudication. In his current research, he focuses on alternative interpretations of the separation of powers.

Przemyslaw Tacik is Assistant Professor at the Institute of European Studies of the Jagiellonian University of Kraków, Poland. A philosopher, lawyer and sociologist by education, he holds PhDs in philosophy (2014) and international law (2016). In his academic work he combines both philosophical and legal perspectives, attempting to approach them from an interdisciplinary angle. His main fields of interest are international law, human rights law and EU law. He has authored three books: *Sociology of Zygmunt Bauman* (2012, in Polish), *The Freedom of Lights. Edmond Jabès and Jewish Philosophy of Modernity* (2019) and *The Accession of the European Union to the European Convention on Human Rights* (2017, in Polish), over 40 articles and one translation of a poetry volume (from French to Polish).

Anna Tarnowska, Dr. hab., is Assistant Professor in the Department of History of Legal and Political Thought and German Law at the Nicolaus Copernicus University in Toruń, Poland. Her main fields of interest are history of public law in Poland and in Germany, history of modern constitutionalism and history of administration and state structures. She was a member of an international group conducting research in the frames of the European Research Council Advanced Grant 'Reconsidering Constitutional Formation', headed by Professor Ulrike Müssig (University of Passau, Germany, 2014–2018). Since 2017, Dr Tarnowska has been involved as a head of project in the National Science Centre grant: Legislative delegation in a representative democracy (program OPUS 11).

Zoltan J. Toth, Dr., graduated in law from the University of Szeged, Hungary, in 2002. Since 2002, he has been working in the Faculty of Law at Károli Gáspár University, Budapest. He is also currently serving as a chief counsellor to the Constitutional Court of Hungary. Previously, his main research topic was the matter of capital punishment; now he studies the theoretical and practical aspects of constitutional adjudication and the issue of statutory interpretation. Altogether, he has published 14 books as author or co-author; the latest one is the monograph *Changing Attitudes Towards the Death Penalty: Hungary's Renewed Support for Capital Punishment* (Palgrave Macmillan, 2020).

Julia Wesołowska is a PhD candidate in the Department of Philosophy of Law and Legal Ethics of Jagiellonian University in Kraków, Poland. Her main research interests concern legal philosophy and legal realism: her work centres on the interactions between law and emotions (especially in tort law), as well as the relationships between law and religion. She is working on a dissertation concerning the legal and philosophical concept of harm and is conducting a research project funded by the National Science Centre of Poland concerning Polish courts' evaluation of emotional distress (2019).

Wojciech Włoch, PhD in philosophy (2012) and law (2017), is an assistant in the Department of Constitutional Law, Nicolaus Copernicus University in Toruń, Poland. His research interests focus on the philosophical and theoretical aspects of constitutional law. As part of his theoretical research, he studies I. Kant's thought and post-Kantian tradition, and investigates the concepts of democracy, constitution and the rule of law. In the field of legal research, he has used philosophical concepts to analyse legal phenomena. He is the Scientific Editor of the fifth volume of the Polish edition of collected works by I. Kant and author of the monograph on Kant's philosophy of law. His last book (2018) is devoted to the concept of constitution in the doctrines of H. Kelsen and J. Rawls and their importance for understanding the essence of the democratic system.

INTRODUCTION

Martin BELOV

We are living on the edge of epochs. Our societies are stretched between our heritage from the past and the demands of the future, which has so brutally and swiftly entered into our seemingly well established and carefully maintained constitutional and political orders. And now, having faced the demons from the past – especially the ones ravaging the Interwar period – which have been reborn as visions from the near future, we must admit that we are in a deep crisis. A crisis which is overwhelming and has a multitude of manifestations on institutional and normative levels, on the socio-political playground and in the mindset of the people forming their constitutional imagination. This is at once a crisis of constitutionalism, representative democracy, party democracy and liberal-democratic constitutionalism. A crisis that challenges globalisation, open statehood, constitutionalisation of international and European law and internationalisation of constitutional law. Furthermore, we are facing severe criticism on international human rights' regimes, and on rule-of-law-providing institutions detached from immediate democratic control, such as the courts and the administration.

This is a crisis with multiple dimensions, which are mutually reinforcing themselves thus pushing our constitutional civilisation to the edge of disaster and self-destruction. Key constitutional principles, paradigms and doctrines are put under severe pressure from forces stemming from both within and outside the domestic constitutional and political system. The institutional design seems rather outdated to give a proper response to the contemporary political, economic and social challenges to which it is exposed. The civil societies are imploding. Human rights are massively violated. Constitutional empowerment is used in unpredictable ways, producing mass disavowal of traditional politics and deep cracks in established normative ideologies.

In addition, there are objective determinants of the crisis. The most important of them are the information technology (IT) revolution, the rise of importance of new-media-producing populism, fake news, infodemics[1] and the severe turbulences in the neoliberal world order, questioning not only neoliberal globalisation – itself a problematic phenomenon – but also the very foundations of the post-World War II international law architecture of peace, political and economic interaction. New technologies are not paralleled by new political morals, adequate skills for democratic coexistence in the context of the global information society or reasonable and novel constitutional infrastructure.

The spread of the COVID-19 pandemic gave new impetus to populist leaders, as well as to seemingly democratic politicians, to severely limit human rights and infringe constitutional principles in an unprecedented manner, scale and intensity. Thus, the COVID-19 pandemic, in combination with massive infodemics, triggered by various sources and players, jointly produce some of the effects of a world war. This poisonous combination has a tremendously negative effect on already fragile and destabilised liberal democracies in 2020.

Western constitutional civilisation at the end of the second decade of the 21st century resembles the elephants going to die alone in despair. The French writer Michel Houellebecq has compared Europe to a boxer who had to lie down on the playground after a knock-down, but unreasonably tried to get up and fight again in the next round. Indeed, what else can we do but stand up, reconsider the foundations of our constitutional orders, adjust our political systems and their constitutional frames to the daring demands of a post-modern world and, thus, stay in the game? Otherwise, not only liberal-democratic constitutionalism, but Western civilisation itself, is in danger.

Yet, the crisis is also a chance. It is a chance for deep reform – for the reassessment of outdated constitutional infrastructure and inadequate political routines. It is a chance for resurrection of our spiritual socio-political home: Western constitutional civilisation.

One of the most striking phenomena in recent decades is the tremendous rise of different variants of non-traditional constitutional and political orders which are more or less radically departing from our traditional understanding of representative constitutional democracy.

[1] Infodemics consists of the exorbitant spread of information containing both real, partially manipulated and fake news. Infodemics is a metaphor for the global explosion of information capable of destabilising the constitutional order due to the massive manipulation of the public opinion. Hence, infodemics is a pandemic of distorted information capable of inducing mass panic, mass distrust in the established order and mass disinformation via the flooding of information.

The first quarter of a century after the fall of the Berlin wall has been time of immense prosperity for liberal democracy. Some authors, such as Francis Fukuyama, even unreasonably believed in the 'liberal end of history'. Authoritarian and totalitarian orders were falling apart one after the other. Even those regimes which proved more resilient demonstrated a desire to modernise in the direction of liberal constitutional democracy, adopting, at least formally, Western constitutional design.

Indeed, this has been the form of hidden cultural imperialism led by the West and especially by the United States (US) and the European Union (EU). It was, rather, a formal process, which did not really change authoritarian seeds, practices and especially mentalities which were deeply rooted in a multitude of political systems. Thus, constitutionalisation and globalisation were mostly Western export products. And the West was so deeply blind to believe that it could impose the first entirely global constitutional civilisation, thus making global constitutionalism possible.

However, many non-Western political systems seemed sufficiently resilient and preserved their authoritarian and definitely illiberal and even anti-liberal outlook. Peripheral European jurisdictions, usually labelled as 'democracies in transition', showed increasing trends for democratic backsliding. Moreover, even established and traditional democracies proved to be very much exposed to the temptation to experiment with less liberal and less democratic – or even overtly populist and authoritarian – models.

In Europe, the formal preservation of liberal-democratic consensus on the EU level has been paralleled by a steady trend towards the establishment of semi-authoritarian, populist and illiberal regimes. Indeed, the EU did not do much to prevent this trend. In fact, the EU was granting indulgence to overt or hidden national authoritarian leaders promoting populist constitutionalism for the sake of their support for EU policies – or at least self-restraint from overt revolts against the status quo.

Hence, the last decade, especially the period after the 2009 financial crisis, is characterised by deep and profound changes in constitutional design and constitutional politics in both the Global North and Global South and in both the European East and European West. We have witnessed the mushrooming of intermediate forms usually labelled in constitutional and political theory and in the public discourse as 'illiberal democracies', 'authoritarian constitutionalism', 'populist constitutionalism' and 'revolutionary constitutionalism'. Authoritarianism, populism and political radicalism and extremism are no longer exotic remnants of a shameful past. They are the present reality – and they have the potential to become an important and even a predominating model in the near future.

Against this rather toxic and pitiful background, this book offers insightful research into the roots of radicalism, populism and populist and illiberal constitutionalism. The analysis explores the intellectual foundations of these phenomena, entrenched in normative ideologies, normative beliefs and political anthropology. It analyses their institutional and normative background, as well as their performance in socio-political practice. The book devotes special attention to the intellectual impact of illiberalism and populism on social and political imaginaries. Thus, the contributors to the book take into account not only the purely legal, but also the socio-legal and intellectual, dimensions of radical versions of democracy, as well as the blossoming of forms of populism, illiberalism and authoritarianism.

The book is not a biased 'black-and-white' judgement on populist and radical constitutionalism. It is not a moralising enterprise devoted to imposing political verdicts on 'bad' and 'wrong' forms of constitutional practices, institutions and mindsets. The book admits the deep problems – both conceptual and pragmatic – of contemporary liberal democracy. It tries to go deep beneath the surface of formal liberal-democratic consensus, which has been formative in recent decades, and expose the weaknesses of the still predominant model of democracy. However, this is done in conjunction with a critical assessment of the threats to freedom, rule of law and democracy created by the rising of authoritarianism in its different forms and manifestations.

To a certain extent, we are in the same situation as the Interwar constitutionalists and political scholars, who were challenged to give a swift response to the immense growth of authoritarian and totalitarian regimes. Moreover, I believe we are witnessing the end of the Second Belle Époque, which lasted for a number of decades after the fall of the Berlin wall. Thus, serious and unprejudiced research on the roots of radicalism, extremism, populism and illiberalism is a glaring need of our time.

Sound scientific analysis also requires feasible and coherent intellectual and conceptual foundations. Thus, a book like this must be grounded on impeccable logic of research and must pose important and acute research questions.

This is of particular importance in the context of booming and mushrooming of literature on illiberalism, populism, populist and illiberal constitutionalism, as well as the democratic backsliding which we have been witnessing in the last few years. In fact, this is a revival of the interest in the reversed transition from democracy to authoritarianism which was also typical in the Interwar period. However, there are also many new issues enriching the discussion, especially with regard to the impact of the IT revolution on the rise of populism and the deconstruction of liberal-democratic representative democracy.

This edited volume is based on the following logic. The book opens with Part I, which is devoted to republican constitutionalism and, more precisely, to the role of the people in radical democracy. This part discusses the radical democratic foundations of our democracies, the radical democratic legacy enshrined in particular in the principle of popular sovereignty and the preconditions for improvement of the shortcomings of the current democratic model, which will allow for enhancement of the quality of democratic engagement and for the establishment of more solidaristic, cohesive and enlightened society.

In Eoin Daly's chapter, he reassesses 'the ambiguous figure of the "legislator" – or "lawgiver" – in relation to problems of revolution and political founding'. He explores the role of the lawgiver, which is usually understood 'as compensating for the people's apparent incapacity for political reason, or perhaps, even for political action, before it has yet formed political consciousness'. In contrast, the author argues that 'the lawgiver, at least in Rousseau's thought, responds not to a specifically epistemic deficit, but rather to the moral perils of popular action – and specifically the moral perils of an heroic role, a peril from which the people is relieved by the lawgiver's providential intervention'.

Daly focuses on several conceptual premises in radical democratic theory and particularly on the theory of Jean-Jacques Rousseau: the incapacity of the people as a founding agent; the moral perils of political founding; and the relationship between political action and natural harmony. Last, but not least, Daly contrasts Rousseau's theory with 'Robespierre's political "melodrama"'.

In the next chapter, Marcin Kilanowski tries to provide conceptual solutions for the cracks and fractures of democracy in times of illiberalism and populism. He finds such fractures in increased empowerment of the people in the context of participatory and deliberative democracy. Kilanowski builds his arguments on the conceptual paradigms offered by Roberto Mangabeira Unger and John Dewey. Kilanowski suggests that we need to create a more solidary society based on civic engagement and political education in order to overcome, in his views, the problematic solipsism of the individual based on rigid separation between 'public' and 'private'.

Before exploring the degrading of radical into populist democracy in Part III, Part II offers thorough reassessment of some of the key constitutional principles in times of democratic ruptures. Thus, while Part I is focused on popular sovereignty, Part II deconstructs the rule of law and democracy in the context of rising populism and explores the impact of authoritarian tendencies on these basic constitutional principles.

Part II opens with a chapter written by Zoltán Pozsár-Szentmiklósy. The author offers critical and original research on a phenomenon which he defines as the 'invisible separation of powers'. He explores the impact of the invisible separation of powers on controlling populist constitutionalism, illiberal democracies and emergent semi-authoritarian orders. Hence, Pozsár-Szentmiklósy reconsiders the classical principle of the separation of powers, providing insights into informal constitutional amendments, unconstitutional constitutional amendments and national referenda as elements of the new power dynamics, polycentrism and control in the context of rising populist and illiberal constitutionalism.

The author defends his theses against three important case-studies of the functioning of the invisible separation of powers in Hungary, Moldova and Romania. The focus on 'instable democracies', 'recent democracies', 'democracies in transition' and 'emergent illiberal democracies' is properly justified by Pozsár-Szentmiklósy, who believes that the effects of the invisible separation of powers is most important precisely in countries where the 'visible' and traditional separation of powers do not have a long and established tradition.

In the following chapter, Zoltan J. Toth provides a critical deconstruction of the relationship between rule of law and democracy in the age of the crisis of liberal constitutional democracy. He thoroughly and systematically defines the concepts of rule of law and democracy, with all properties and elements typical of these two pillars of modern liberal democracy. Subsequently, Toth explores the synergy and tensions among democracy, popular sovereignty and the rule of law in the constitutional court's practice, looking for their reconciliation in the current context of the democratic crisis.

Part III, as already mentioned, provides insightful research into the crisis of contemporary democracy and its impact on the renaissance of populist constitutionalism. Among the issues discussed in Part III, one should mention the degeneration of contemporary democracies and its conceptualisation within the framework of a new phenomenology of constitutional transition and its conceptual boundaries; the questioning of the constitutionality of populism against the background of rule of law and democracy; and the impact of populist constitutional revolution, its consequences for the EU legal order and its impact on Western liberal democracies.

Angela Di Gregorio, in her chapter, defines the problem of the degeneration of contemporary democracies and systematically assesses the methodology used for its research. She presents the key issues in contemporary research – especially on constitutional theory of democracy and transitology[2] – and outlines the doctrines and theoretical viewpoints on authoritarian constitutionalism, populist constitutionalism and illiberal democracies. She explores the degeneration of contemporary democracies as a trigger of a new phenomenology of constitutional transition and classifies the 'degraded' democracies as an intermediate form between democracy and authoritarianism. Finally, she focuses on the crisis of liberal democracy and various meanings of the words 'democracy' and 'constitutionalism'.

What is populism constitutional, and what are its conceptual and constitutional dimensions and manifestations? This is the provocative question raised by Gianmario Demuro in his chapter. Demuro explores the tension among populism and constitutionalism and parliamentary democracy. He offers a study on populism as an ideology that is fundamental for illiberal democracies.

The chapter written by Carlo Alberto Ciaralli is devoted to the problem of the challenges that the ongoing rise of populism and illiberal constitutionalism poses to Western liberal democracies. Ciaralli even defines this phenomenon as populist legal revolution. The chapter opens with brief outline of the rise of populism in Europe. Furthermore, the author argues a counter-position and makes comparison between the European technocratic democracy and populist direct democracy. He believes that populism is a 'stress test' for the European legal order and convincingly explains why. The chapter finishes with a case-study of Italy as an example of the rise of populism and its main features in the context of established Western democracy.

---

2 Transitology is specific branch of comparative constitutional law and political theory exploring the transition of the constitutional orders and political systems from one form of government or political regime to another. The emphasis of transitological studies in the 1990s has mostly been on the transition from authoritarianism (especially communism and the Soviet style of government) to liberal democracy. However, nowadays the focus shifts to the emergent illiberal democracies and 'soft' authoritarian regimes replacing fragile 'democracies in transition'.

It has already been mentioned that this edited volume has the task of exploring not only the institutional and purely legal dimension of populist constitutionalism and illiberal democracy, but also of analysing the socio-legal and intellectual (imaginary, emotional and anthropological) dimensions of the researched phenomenon. Hence, Part IV explores populist constitutionalism from the viewpoint of emotions and constitutional imagination. It engages in the ongoing debate on the impact of populism on constituent power, especially as viewed through the prism of constitutional imagination, and offers an account of anti-constitutional populism on the basis of the 'law and emotions' research paradigm.

Paul Blokker, in his chapter, explores the intersection of populism, constituent power and constitutional imagination. Blokker starts by defining the concept of populist constitutionalism, which was actually proposed by him in several key scientific papers published in recent years. He builds upon his research in order to offer novel analysis of the counter-position between popular sovereignty and global legalism. He then explores the significance of constituent power for populists. In this regard, he joins an implicit dialogue on popular sovereignty, constituent power and populism led by several contributors to this volume.

The engagement of the author with the problem of constitutional imagination deserves particular attention. More precisely, Blokker provides an insightful analysis of revolutionary and populist constitutional imagination, forming what he defines as 'populist imaginary'. He further develops his analysis, concentrating it on legal resentment and populist understandings of the law.

The emotional-imaginary approach to populism is continued in the next chapter, in which Julia Wesołowska explores anti-constitutional populism from the viewpoint of law and emotions. The author briefly outlines the role of the affective-emotional side of law. She analyses the myth of irrationality, asking the question: are constitutions devoid of emotions? She explores whether the problem in the context of rising populism is that we have too many emotions – or perhaps, that we do not have the *right* emotions.

Populism and illiberal democracies thrive in times of crisis. They benefit from the instability of society and the fragility of its democratic constitutional order. In 2020, a massive and unprecedented crisis hit the world in the form of the shock of the COVID-19 pandemic. Part V therefore provides critical analysis of the political regimes established during the COVID-19 pandemic. It explores the impact of this pandemic on constitutionalism and democracy. Special attention is devoted to the use of fear politics in the context of a global pandemic as justification for limitations of freedom and fundamental human rights. The COVID-19 pandemic is explored as an important factor in the already steady trend of downgrading the quality of democracy, as well as the deconstruction and replacement of democracy with authoritarianism based on fear, dependency and oppression.

In the next chapter, I define the concept and features of COVID-19 constitutionalism. Subsequently, I explore the impact of COVID-19 on constitutionalism, constitutional principles and human rights. I devote special attention to fear and fear politics in constitutional law. I attempt to explore the interrelation between populism, illiberalism and the reformulation of normalcy, raising the question of whether stigmatisation and war rhetoric is part of the 'new normal'. I analyse the ways in which fear is encoded in contemporary constitutionalism through fear politics. In doing so, I research the personalisation of fear and the subject of fear politics; the messages of fear which forming the content of fear politics; and the places of stigma serving as the locus of fear politics. Finally, I raise the issue of the emergence of the new paternalistic state – 'the health Leviathan'.

The chapter by Tímea Drinóczi and Agnieszka Bień-Kacała is devoted to democracy and human rights in illiberal constitutionalism. The authors argue that the historical trajectories, value orientation and emotional profiles of Hungary and Poland have facilitated the creation and consolidation of illiberal constitutionalism. They outline several typical elements of illiberal constitutionalism: illiberal legality; illiberal democracy; and the reduced protection of human rights. According to the authors, until the spring of 2020 neither Hungary nor Poland had constituted an authoritarian regime. However, Drinóczi and Bień-Kacała believe that the COVID-19 crisis could serve as the factor that will accelerate the tendency towards overt authoritarianism. The authors show how the COVID-19 pandemic regime is destroying the remnants of democracy and rule of law in Poland and Hungary.

Finally, Part VI provides a range of case studies exemplifying some of the most visible regimes based on illiberal and populist constitutionalism. The selection of cases – Italy, Poland and Russia – offers a broad perspective on the different methods for the establishment of illiberal democracies. It provides insightful analysis into the preconditions for populism, as well as shedding light on its most significant forms and consequences.

Monica Bonini explores the roots and current tendencies of populism in Italy. She outlines the swirl of Italian constitutional history between the extremities of democracy, populism and authoritarianism. Bonini defines the role of people and democracy in the Italian constitution, while outlining the main factors for misuse of this role for the sake of the populist causes in Italy.

Przemyslaw Tacik proposes the novel and insightful concept of 'revolution without a revolution', which he uses for topical analysis of Polish constitutional order. In fact, Tacik demonstrates the main features and strengths of his theory of 'revolution without a revolution' on the basis of the Polish anti-liberal and populist experiment. The author convincingly demonstrates that populist constitutional revolution is also possible without explicit constitutional reform, thus contrasting the case of Poland to that of Hungary.

Agnieszka Bień-Kacała, Anna Tarnowska and Wojciech Włoch explore representative democracy in the times of populism. The authors present the case of the Polish parliament and its deficiencies with regard to delegation, representation and legitimacy. They explore how the 'chain of delegation' is constructed and the significance of deliberations and discussions for the representativeness of the Polish Sejm. The authors also demonstrate how the chain of delegation can be disrupted.

Finally, in the concluding chapter of the volume, Wojciech Engelking traces back the roots and guises of legal populism in Russia. He discovers them in the *Narodniki*, statism and legalism of soviet law and the political theology of Ivan Ilyin.

PART I

REPUBLICAN CONSTITUTIONALISM: THE ROLE OF PEOPLE IN RADICAL DEMOCRACY

THE PEOPLE AND THE LAWGIVER IN POLITICAL FOUNDINGS

Eoin Daly

1. INTRODUCTION

This chapter reassesses the ambiguous figure of the 'legislator' – or 'lawgiver' – in relation to problems of revolution and political founding. In short, the role of the lawgiver has been understood primarily as that of bestowing a constitution and thus, a political identity upon a people that – owing to never having constituted itself as a political unity – had no capacity to grant this to itself. Thus, the role of the lawgiver is to heroically and providentially break a cycle of seeming impossibility in political time: the apparent impossibility, that is, of a people successfully forming *itself* as a political identity or political unity. It is a rather awkward and discomfiting role, but a seemingly essential one that accounts for the temporal and conceptual paradoxes of political founding. In this chapter, however, I reassess, specifically, the peculiar quality of the people's incapacity or unsuitability, for which the lawgiver is understood as a response. The lawgiver's role has typically been understood as compensating for the people's apparent incapacity for political *reason*, or perhaps even for political action, before it has yet formed political consciousness. I argue instead that the lawgiver, at least in Rousseau's thought, responds not to a specifically epistemic deficit, but rather, to the *moral* perils of popular action – and specifically the moral perils of a heroic role, a peril from which the people is relieved by the lawgiver's providential intervention. Unlike other republican thinkers – and especially his acolyte Robespierre – Rousseau rejects the image of political freedom as being realised in the life of political action, because he sees this as inconsistent with well-ordered harmony as a normative standard given by 'nature'. Political heroism, ultimately, is a potentially potent source of moral corruption and *amour-propre*.

Therefore, the seemingly heroic and miraculous role of the lawgiver is not to compensate the people's epistemic incapacities, but rather, to relieve the people of the moral burdens of political action and political heroism. Accordingly, these insights invite a reappraisal of the limits of the people's role as a revolutionary agent. In particular, the relationship between the people and the lawgiver can be understood in terms of a dichotomy of *action* and *will* – with the role of the lawgiver being to relieve the people of the moral burdens of political action, and the modest role of the people – at least in the Rousseauan schema – being to *will* the constitution as the general framework of social life.

2. THE INCAPACITY OF THE PEOPLE AS A FOUNDING AGENT

The need for a lawgiver arises from the apparent incapacity – at least the relative incapacity – of the people as a constituent or founding agent. The lawgiver can be understood, roughly speaking, as the historical, even heroic figure who endows a nascent people with a set of founding laws, or simply a constitution. And the need for a lawgiver arises from the apparent incapacity of the people itself to do just this. For Rousseau, this problem arises partly from a paradox of political temporality: when the people has not already lived under a republican constitution, it has not gained the civic skills and knowledge to found a state. Indeed, paradoxically, it is not yet formed as a people without a constitution, but it cannot legitimately give itself a constitution without first constituting itself as a people, something that would presuppose a constitutional form of its own. The challenge for the lawgiver is that since political institutions do not yet exist, there is not yet any political consciousness, nor is there any sense of citizenship to utilise or exploit. The paradox, as Rousseau puts it, is that 'men would have to be prior to laws what they ought to become by means of them'.[1] It is this cycle of paradox that the lawgiver breaks, performing a sort of heroic historical intervention – often seen as vaguely miraculous – that allows political time to start, so to speak. It is, as Rousseau puts it, an 'office, which sets up the Republic, [but] nowhere enters into its constitution'.[2]

Therefore, it seems – from a surface reading of Rousseau at least – that the need for the lawgiver arises, on the one hand, from the people's *incapacity*. Moreover, on the other hand, it seems this incapacity is understood as specifically either *practical* or *epistemic* in nature – simply, the people lack the skills and knowledge to found a state or to give themselves fundamental laws. Thus, Rousseau asks: 'How can a blind multitude, which often does not know what it wills, because it rarely knows what is good for it, carry out for itself so great and difficult an endeavour as a system of legislation?'[3] In short, the need for the lawgiver then arises from the apparent incapacity of the people to spontaneously exercise the kind of judgement needed to give itself a constitution or political form. Indeed, in the actual work of the lawgiver, there is a large element of what might be termed as prudential reasoning – the political reasoning of statecraft – and particularly in assessing the suitability of a given people for a republican constitution. Thus, Rousseau says:

> … [the] general objects of every good legislative system need modifying in every country in accordance with the local situation and the temper of the inhabitants; and these circumstances should determine, in each case, the particular system of institutions which is best, not perhaps in itself, but for the State for which it is destined.[4]

3. THE MORAL PERILS OF POLITICAL FOUNDING

As we have seen, it is true that to a great extent Rousseau believes the people incapable – in a practical and epistemic sense – of founding a state and granting themselves a constitution. However, the aim of this chapter is partly to show that Rousseau, in particular, wishes to deny the 'people'

1 J.J. Rousseau, *Du Contrat Social: Principes de Droit Politique*, ENAG, Paris 1998/1762, Book II, Chapter 7.
2 *Ibid.*
3 *Ibid.*, Book II, Chapter 6.
4 *Ibid.*, Book II, Chapter 11.

a genuinely foundational or constituent role for quite a different – and possibly a more important – reason: specifically, because he understands the task of political founding, and the audacity or heroism it requires, as being inconsistent with the tranquillity or harmony, modelled on the order of nature, that he understands as being essential to restoring man's happiness and freedom in the post-lapsarian social world.

This suggestion may seem counter-intuitive, because Rousseau is a republican and is ostensibly therefore associated with a tradition which sees political freedom, for the citizenry, as being realised in the life of political action, whether this be understood in the Machiavellian sense of vigilance against elite oppression, or in the Arendtian sense of performative self-realisation in the public realm. And in turn, it seems, the act of political founding appears quintessentially as a source of political freedom and legitimacy, as well as an expression of popular virtue. Rousseau, after all, builds his political theory around the central premise of popular sovereignty, surely expressed in the establishment of the state itself.

However, a closer reading of Rousseau's works reveals a clear disavowal of any such classical-republican vision of political *action*, as being either a privileged form of human flourishing, for individuals, or as constitutive of freedom, for the people taken collectively. Rather, what is striking about Rousseau's writing on Poland, Geneva and especially Corsica is that he envisages a social order in which the people will have relatively little involvement in *politics*, whether in the Machiavellian, Arisotelian or Arendtian sense. Far from realising their freedom through virtuous, vigilant or performative action – directed at whatever end – he instead envisages the people as realising happiness and freedom in a life of relative peaceability and tranquillity that, it has been suggested, mirrors or emulates the order of nature itself. In works like *Constitutional Plan for Corsica*, in particular, Rousseau envisages a peaceable, agrarian social order – with citizens devoted to the rhythms of work – that leaves little room for the contingency and cut-and-thrust of political life. While he implores the Poles to 'cultivate your fields … and have no other care',[5] equally he advises the Corsicans to confine administration to a 'small number' of 'enlightened' citizens (*éclairés*)[6] – thus advocating, again, a model of citizenship that is removed from the cut-and-thrust of

---

5 J.J. Rousseau, 'Considerations on the Government of Poland', in F. Watkins (ed.), *Jean-Jacques Rousseau: Political Writings*, Thomas Yelsen, New York 1953, Chapter 11, p. 373.

6 J.J. Rousseau, *Projet de Constitution pour la Corse*, Nautilus, Paris 2000, p. 35. (French-English translations are my own).

political action. The Corsicans are to live a *quiet* life; his constitution, he says, will cause them to 'love the rural life (*vie champêtre*) [and] the work it brings … such that they will never want to leave it'; Rousseau exalts 'the equality, the simplicity of rustic life' from which, stems a 'contentment in his state which makes man peaceful, and a love of the homeland'.[7] There is little sense, therefore, of citizens being made or fulfilled in political *action*. On the one hand, Rousseau simply does not see early modern peoples as being fit for such heroics. Addressing the Genevans in *Letters from the Mountain*, he writes:

> Ancient people are no longer a model for modern ones; they are too alien to them in every respect. You above all, Genevans, keep your place … You are neither Romans, nor Spartans; you are not even Athenians … You are Merchants, Artisans, Bourgeois … always occupied with their private interests, with their work … Not being idle as ancient peoples were, you cannot ceaselessly occupy yourself with the Government as they did.[8]

Indeed, in contrast with the life of action, Rousseau seemingly prefers to base citizenship upon *labour* – upon a life that is, in Arendt's description, defined by cyclical and continuously exhaustible efforts spent on 'the maintenance of life.'[9] Rousseau identifies this life with a certain dignity and happiness, whereas Arendt suggests that the ancients associated it, instead, with servility, seeing this as inferior to the recognition and valour men obtained in the public realm.

Thus Rousseau arguably envisages a social order that mimics the order of nature, an order where freedom is realised partly through the dissolution of contingency and instability itself, and his vision of citizenship aims, seemingly, to dissolve the very circumstances that other republicans conceptualise as being essential to political freedom – the confrontation of *fortuna*, the instability of political form in time, and so on – that 'world of mutability' upon which, in the classical and humanist depictions, men impose 'order and glory', in the Machiavellian spirit, using their 'skill and courage'. Far from this image, the main political role of the people, a people of peasants and artisans, is to *legislate* the general will – in the sense of

---

7 *Ibid.*, p. 31.

8 J.J. Rousseau, 'Letters Written from the Mountain' in C. Kelly, and E. Grace (eds), *Letter to Beaumont, Letters Written from the Mountain, and Related Writings*, Dartmouth College Press, Dartmouth 2001, p. 96.

9 See H. Arendt, *The Human Condition*, Chicago University Press, Chicago 1958, Chapters 11–16.

approving fundamental laws – and not to *act*, where popular action, is seen in this sense not only as unrealistic, but also as a source of disharmony and discord.

It is this ambivalence about the people's suitability as a political *actor*, in turn, that explains the necessity of the lawgiver. Whereas the people is confined to the role of legislating, as opposed to governing, *within* the constituted order of the state, similarly, the people cannot be the actor that truly founds or constitutes the state. The role of political founding is a heroic one, which is precisely why, in Rousseau's schema, it is a morally dangerous role that must be divested to a lawgiver – a figure who Walzer, after all, describes as having 'heroic dress'.[10]

It is revealing, in this respect, that while Rousseau cites Moses as an exemplary lawgiver, he notes that: 'out of [a] wandering and servile horde Moses had *the audacity to create a body politic*, a free people'.[11] The reference to audacity is revealing, because it helps to emphasise the logic of creative action in the task of political founding and to emphasise how the people's incapacity is not simply one of political knowledge of competence, but rather, a question of unsuitability to fulfil this world-historic role. This has a certain mysterious, almost miraculous character that suggests an element of heroic action for which the people is simply unsuited. In a similar passage, Rousseau repeats this language of audacity:

> … he who dares to undertake the making of a people's institutions ought to feel himself capable, so to speak, of changing human nature, of transforming each individual, who is by himself a complete and solitary whole, into part of a greater whole from which he in a manner receives his life and being; of altering man's constitution for the purpose of strengthening it; and of substituting a partial and moral existence for the physical and independent existence nature has conferred on us all.[12]

It is the lawgiver, in Lindahl's wording, who 'seizes the initiative' to alter political temporality,[13] who 'restarts time',[14] effecting a 'transmundane'

---

10 M. Walzer, 'Philosophy and Democracy' (1981) *Political Theory* 379, 384.

11 Rousseau, above n. 5, Chapter 2, p. 91.

12 Rousseau, above n. 1, Book II, Chapter 11.

13 H. Lindahl, 'Constituent Power and Reflexive Identity: Towards an Ontology of Collective Selfhood' in M. Loughlin and N. Walker (eds), *The Paradox of Constitutionalism: Constituent Power and Constitutional Form*, Oxford University Press, Oxford 2008, p. 22.

14 C. Frost, 'Summoning Sovereignty: Constituent Power and Poetic Prophecy in Ireland's 1916 Proclamation of the Republic' (2017) 24 *Constellations* 76, 77.

event in a secularised version of 'rectilinear' time,[15] and thus becoming the historical actor the people cannot and must not themselves aspire to become.

4. POLITICAL ACTION AND NATURAL HARMONY

But why, specifically, does Rousseau understand the role of heroic political actor as not only being beyond the people's capacities, but also as being morally perilous – as being inconsistent with the goodness and harmony of nature? Why, in other words, is the revolutionary role a morally hazardous one in this specific sense?

On the one hand, there are familiar concerns about the morality of popular action, of the mob's propensity for violence, its unaccountability and caprice, and so on. On the other hand, Rousseau is an outlier in the republican canon, because he is ambivalent as to the political promise of conflict and contestation. Whereas 'Machiavelli grounds constituent power on the conflictual force of the free multitude',[16] Rousseau by comparison is sceptical of popular combativity, based primarily on a fear that such discord will undermine the order and harmony which, as we will see, he models on the providential order of nature itself. Again, more specifically, Rousseau has peculiar concerns, however, about the corrupting effects of *amour-propre* – that form of self-love consummated in external recognition. Arguably, he applies this concern, indirectly at least, to the corruptibility that is latent in any possible role for the people as a heroic actor, particularly in the revolutionary process of political foundations.

Political founding is indeed quintessentially a type of political *action*, defined by creativity and improvisation, entailing the creation of a new political form in the absence of an existing norm – of something that is not only new and unauthorised, but that is also unlegislated for. And in the Arendtian sense, this type of political action is a site of self-disclosure and self-actualisation, of performative virtuosity, of the sort that she associates with positive political freedom – freedom-in-action.[17] For Arendt, furthermore, it is crucially the presence of an audience – the element of virtuosity and the leaving of one's mark, so to speak – that makes political

15 H. Arendt, *On Revolution*, Penguin, London and New York 1963, p. 170.

16 F. Del Luchesse, 'Machiavelli and constituent power: The revolutionary foundation of modern political thought' (2017) 16 *European Journal of Political Theory* 3, 6.

17 Arendt, above n. 9, Chapters 11–16.

action freedom-giving. But for Rousseau, it is precisely this same element of recognition, and therefore of *distinction*, that inflames man's *amour-propre* and drives a corrupting vanity and pride. The same aspect of politics that Arendt identifies as freedom-giving – the 'space of appearances' that men use to gain an 'audience [for] their virtuosity' – is itself, for Rousseau, the source of its artifice and corruptibility. And it is precisely this kind of role, in turn – especially a role in world-historical drama – that arguably disrupts the well-ordered existence, consistent with natural harmony, that Rousseau envisages for the Corsicans, Poles and Genevans. As we have seen, he juxtaposes the cyclical and benign order of nature with the caprice and tumult of political life, seen as a source both of disharmony and corruption.

In short, then, Rousseau rejects the republican idea of political action as emancipatory, precisely because he understands it as a corruptible site of distinction and self-display that is inconsistent with natural goodness. Thus, the problem is not merely that the people are too diffuse or uncoordinated to rise to this role of revolutionary actor, but rather, that such a role risks corrupting their virtue and destroying their happiness. Indeed Rousseau so strongly emphasises the *ritual* life of austere republican peoples largely, it seems, because ritual – despite its performative and theatrical aspects – absorbs and dissolves the individuating and self-revelatory qualities of political heroism and action: in ritual, the individual is neither distinguished nor effaced, but harmoniously absorbed: in Rousseau's ritualism, Strong suggests, 'the effect of the gaiety is to lose all sense of self-consciousness in the revelry of one's public identity'.

Crucially, then, Rousseau arguably juxtaposes freedom not only with domination, in the sense of subjection to an arbitrary will, but also with disorder or disharmony, with the disequilibrium of man's powers and desires that Rousseau identifies as the chief ill of socialised man. Thus it has been argued that despites ostensibly rejecting 'nature' and natural rights in favour of a fully socialised man, Rousseau's social contract in fact aims to restore, in political society, the 'calm repose' of original or 'natural' man – to maintain his psychic equilibrium, to hold his powers and desires in harmony. Thus 'the state of nature provided the setting for a model of the good life … it presented the conditions to which any form of the good life must conform'.[18] Scott argues that life in Rousseau's republic, expressed as the impersonal rule of the general will, places citizens in a

---

18 R. Douglass, *Rousseau and Hobbes: Nature, Free Will and the Passions*, Oxford University Press, Oxford 2016, p. 59.

similar position, in relation to the polity, as man is originally positioned in relation to nature. This it restores 'our original position as well-ordered beings within the divine or natural whole, a whole ordered by law'.[19] This arises by subjecting man to a will that, unlike capricious private wills, he can identity as his own. The rule of the general will does not restore nature, but rather emulates or redeems it. And this conception of the republican polity, and of its relation to nature as a normative standard, helps explain the oddly peaceable, almost apolitical vision of citizenship that Rousseau advocates. He rejects the classic vision of the political life – defined by the confrontation of contingency – precisely because of this commitment to a social order that emulates the order of nature, because of his commitment to stability and harmony over disorder and contingency – viewing politics itself as a site not only of contingency, but of dangerous vanity and desire.

Thus while Machiavelli and Arendt envisage citizenship as flourishing and coming alive in an unstable world of *fortuna* and disorder, Rousseau, as Shklar observed, envisages exactly the opposite – to hold contingency itself in check, to stabilise the social world so as to allow citizens to exist in a social order modelled on the order of nature itself. This explains his commitment to agrarianism in particular, because the agrarian life will hold ambition and desire in check: his Corsican constitution in particular, aims to 'make [the people] love its [agrarian] occupation ... to make it the general happiness of their life, and to limit their ambitions to it.'[20] The cyclicality and toil of agriculture, in Corsica and Poland, stand in vivid contrast with the tumultuous life of political action. And while Rousseau rejects urbanity as a source of vice, correspondingly this can itself be interpreted as dissolving the spatial and spectatorial dimension of Arendtian politics, as dissolving the space of appearances and thus the 'public' sphere wholesale, with citizens, in contrast with the ancients, retreating to the ordered and virtuous life of private toil.

It must be noted that Rousseau does, in fact acknowledge a role in revolutionary action for the Corsican people, in particular, in overthrowing Genoese rule. But he is apprehensive about this role and sees it as being temporally confined at the advent of the republic, as an aberration borne of necessity. He acknowledges popular heroism, but it is temporary and exceptional and must give way to the harmonious tranquillity of the

---

19 J. Scott, 'Politics as the Imitation of the Divine in Rousseau's "Social Contract"' (1994) 26 *Polity* 473, 479.

20 Rousseau, above n. 6, p. 51.

post-revolutionary republic. Rousseau portrays the Corsicans as having exercised a kind of valour, and Machiavellian *virtù*, in having cast off Genoese rule at an opportune moment, and encourages them to exploit their fortuitous geographical position to maintain their freedom, since the island's topography and relative isolation allows some hope for an autarkical republic to be maintained But this very Machiavellian *virtù*, exercised at a moment of liberation, is strangely at odds with the kind of virtuous existence, the quietness and order, envisaged in normal times. In a revealing passage, Rousseau warns: 'one must not count on the lively (*vif*) but short-lived enthusiasm following the recovery of liberty. Popular heroism is a moment of ardour (*fougue*), followed by lethargy (*langueur*) and relaxation (*relâchement*). One must found a people's liberty on its way of being, not on its passions.'[21] What is striking here, in contrast with Machiavelli and Arendt in particular, is Rousseau's understanding of popular action or popular heroism as a kind of temporal aberration which, if pursued as a general template or model, becomes a recipe for instability and discord.

Thus the role of the lawgiver, accordingly, is to relieve the people of this moral burden, to assume the role of *action* in place of the people, and to leave the people to *legislate* – understood as an exercise of will, not of action – within the constitutional parameters of the state accordingly established. And indeed, this division of political labour is replicated within the constituted order of the state, with the people taking a relatively minimal political role, being called up to consider and revise 'legislation' in the sense of fundamental laws, but not to govern, whether in the sense of executive power or, what would now be understood as and routine legislative power.[22] This confounds a commonplace association of Rousseau's thought with something akin to democratic absolutism.

Of course, legislating itself might appear as a creative or audacious task. But whereas the Rousseuauan people 'legislates' – an ostensibly political and creative craft – Rousseau's understanding of legislation seems much closer to that which Arendt associates with the ancient Greeks – a conception of legislating as a pre-political activity, akin to 'the builder of the city wall, who … had to finish his work before political activity could begin.'[23] By legislating, the people neither constitute the

---

21 *Ibid.*, p. 88.

22 For discussion, see P. Steinberger, 'Hobbes, Rousseau and the Modern Conception of the State' (2008) 70 *The Journal of Politics* 595.

23 Arendt, above n. 9, p. 194.

state nor actually exercise any faculties of rule, but rather *wills* the general framework of social life. Indeed Rousseau tells the Genevans that 'once the Constitution of the state has taken a fixed and stable form, your [legislative] functions are finished'.[24] Sovereignty, he says, is a 'power that *wills*', and government, a 'power that *acts*', and the sovereign should not assume governmental power.[25] Tuck argues that in distinguishing between 'sovereignty' and 'government' in this way – and by confining sovereignty to an approximation of constituent power – Rousseau 'permitted the reappearance of democracy in the modern world', where 'citizens simply could [no longer] give … time and attention to government'. Thus 'citizens could all be true legislators in fundamental matters but leave less fundamental ones to their agents'.[26]

It is important, also, that whereas Rousseau envisages the people as legislating only fundamental laws, rather than 'legislation' in its broad modern sense, furthermore he in fact envisages the people arguably as only approving or ratifying such fundamental laws, rather than an initiating or devising them – despite sometimes using the language of authorship.[27] And this relatively passive role stands in sharp contrast with various republican conceptualisations of political action, associated with natality, rupture and improvisation in the face of contingency and instability. The legislator appears, as Fireside puts it, as an 'historical quirk'; his role is the essence of natality in politics, as the novel or unexpected. The people's role in constitution-making and constitutional revision must be conceptually distinguished from the genuinely founding act, the extraordinary intervention through which the political order is posited – a role which is assumed instead by the lawgiver. And far from the merely technical or procedural aspect of constitution-making, the lawgiver's role is essentially *creative*, because its work is not only the constitution of the state but of the people itself, through the deployment of ritual and symbolic devices that alchemise a sense of peoplehood that endures over time and stabilises the republican polity.

---

24 Rousseau, above n. 8, p. 340.

25 *Ibid.*, pp. 302–04.

26 R. Tuck, 'Democratic sovereignty and democratic government' in R. Bourke and Q. Skinner (eds), *Popular Sovereignty in Historical Context*, Cambridge University Press, Cambridge 2016, p. 141.

27 There has been some debate however, as to whether Rousseau's sovereign itself proposes laws. See E. Putterman, 'Rousseau on the people as legislative gatekeepers, not framers' (2005) 99 *American Political Science Review* 145; J.T. Scott, 'Rousseau's Anti-Agenda-Setting Agenda and Contemporary Democratic Theory' (2005) 99 *The American Political Science Review* 137.

5. A CONTRAST WITH ROBESPIERRE'S POLITICAL 'MELODRAMA'

These insights of Rousseau, concerning the necessity of the lawgiver, invite a reappraisal of the popular role, and of its limits, in contexts of revolution and political founding. Whereas most sceptical accounts of popular agency in a revolutionary or constituent moment will focus either on the capacity of the people, its accountability, or of the potentially diffuse and chaotic structure of its action, Rousseau invites consideration of its disruptive and disharmonising effects for republican social life. Counter-intuitively, he offers, on the one hand a quintessentially *modern* understanding of popular capacities generally, telling the Genevans, as we have seen, that they cannot emulate the heroic actions of ancient peoples – and so they must realise a different kind of freedom, one consistent with the largely private orientation of the moderns. And on the other hand, the corrupting or destabilising effect of popular political action lies in exactly the same features that other republicans have thought of as being emancipatory: particularly its performative or self-revelatory character, which is liable to inflame *amour-propre* and disrupt the harmonious co-existence of an austere peasant citizenry. Regarding the question of revolution, this is decisive because Rousseau is effectively led to reject what John McCormick, inspired by Machiavelli, has described as 'republican existentialism' – a vision in which a citizenry 'spiritedly reacts and hopefully adapts to the vagaries of politics'.[28]

In this respect, Rousseau can, counterintuitively, be usefully contrasted with his most famous and notorious political disciple – Maximilien Robespierre. Most debate contrasting the two figures has centred on the question of whether Robespierre's predilection for political violence and popular/populist absolutism finds any justification or basis in those political theories of Rousseau to which he enthusiastically subscribed. But there has been less analysis of their contrasting understandings of the moral dimensions of political action and its effect on popular virtues.[29]

---

28 J. McCormick, 'Pocock, Machiavelli and Political Contingency in Foreign Affairs: Republican Existentialism Outside (and Within) the City' (2017) 43 *History of European Ideas* 171, 173.

29 C. Blum, *Rousseau and the Republic of Virtue; The Language of Politics in the French Revolution,* Cornell University Press, Ithaca 1986; J. Swenson, *On Jean-Jacques Rousseau: Considered as One of the First Authors of the Revolution,* Stanford University Press, Stanford 2000; D. Edelstein, *The Terror of Natural Right: Republicanism, the Cult of Nature, and the French Revolution,* Chicago University Press, Chicago 2009.

As I have argued, on the one hand, the need for the lawgiver in Rousseau's theory arises largely from his concern to safeguard the people from the moral pitfalls of political heroism or political action – based precisely on his sense of the capacity of world-heroic endeavours both to inflame *amour-propre* and destabilise the citizenry's psychic harmony. Robespierre, on the other hand, can be understood as appealing to popular heroism – indeed, as centring the whole of his political thought around it – as an extension of what has been described as a peculiar, contemporary ideal of 'sentimentalism', understood as an imperative of effusive and unmediated sentimental expression as a mark of authenticity and legitimacy. On the one hand, various scholars have noted a peculiar strain of sentimentalist literary tropes in the 1780s and 1790s which, for individuals, emphasised unmediated sentimental expression as a hallmark of virtue. Thus the rhetorical interventions made in the various political assemblies leading to, and following the republican revolution of 1792 are marked by ostentatious performances of emotional sincerity, and of personal identification with the elevating emotions of the revolutionary cause – with Robespierre's own rhetorical interventions, reportedly moving men to tears, having been aimed at eliciting the appropriate emotional responses in imitation of the familiar literary or theatrical *tableau*.[30]

On the other hand, Andress in particular has argued that this sentimentalist imperative, for individuals, was extended and projected by the Jacobins and Robespierre onto the revolutionary 'people' conceptualised as a single collective agent. Robespierre, witnessing, modelling and eliciting popular emotional reactions to revolutionary events, conceptualises the people 'toward a sense of their collective moral and sentimental heroism.'[31] Thus whereas for the sentimentalism of Robespierre, 'truth is always to be found in feelings'[32] – and verified in their authentic, performative expression – for Rousseau, by contrast, the public exhibition or performance of sentimental authenticity is, as I have argued, likely to be a source of corrupted distinction for individuals, and an expression of inflamed *amour-propre*. Indeed politics in general, for Rousseau, is an arena where men seek power, in particular, through command of discourse, through sophistry and insincerity.

---

30 D. Andress, 'Jacobinism as Heroic Narrative: Understanding the Terror as the Experience of Melodrama' (2014) 5 *French History and Civilisation* 6, 18.

31 D. Andress, 'Living the Revolutionary Melodrama: Robespierre's Sensibility and the Construction of Political Commitment in the French Revolution' (2011) *Representations* 103, 107.

32 *Ibid.*, 108.

Thus while Rousseau fears the corrupting effects of popular action or popular heroism, Robespierre actively elicits the morally elevating effects of melodramatic heroism to grant the people a central role – rhetorically at least – not as a legitimating agent but as a world-historical *actor* and *hero*. This can be identified, on the one hand, in his approval of 'terror', understood not only as an expression of virtue and justice in revolutionary contexts, but as a 'spring' – as corresponding to a logic of action, in the Arendtian sense. Thus Robespierre implores the people to 'subdue by terror the enemies of liberty, and you will be right, *as founders of the Republic*'.[33]

On the other hand, Rousseau's scepticism of popular heroic action is arguably borne out in a 'terrorist' revolutionary experience in which such representations or constructions of popular heroism engendered a spiral of corrupted, self-righteous conceit for those projecting or identifying themselves in the people's martyrdom against a despotic enemy. Because Robespierre conceived of the people as a singular collective identity, 'its perilous status as a melodramatic victim was something he could identify with, and [so] he rapidly came to imagine himself as a defender of popular honour, dignity, and life itself.'[34] Indeed Andress notes that in his own writings, Robespierre expresses 'melodramatic form of sentimental identification' – and projects these onto the people as a constructed agent. Thus 'Jacobin identity' was 'a story written around certain tropes – victimization, heroic suffering … – which licensed [educated men] to write themselves into the story as its heroes and, indeed, to act out that role in a self-consciously theatrical public sphere.'[35] In this 'conception of political experience as melodrama' there is, Andress points out, 'always a suffering hero to be singled out'.[36] The peril of such a politics of authentic sentimentalism is, in Arendt's description, that sentiments 'become "mere appearances" behind which, again other, ulterior motives may lurk, such as hypocrisy and deceit' – which 'made Robespierre and his followers, once they had equated virtue with the qualities of the heart, see intrigue and calumny, treachery and hypocrisy everywhere.'[37] Thus 'the reign of virtue was bound to be at worst the rule of hypocrisy, and at best the never-ending fight to ferret out the hypocrites … the demand that everybody

---

33 Speech of 5 February 1784, cited in R. Bienvenu, *The Ninth of Thermidor: The Fall of Robespierre*, Oxford University Press, Oxford 1970, p. 49; emphasis added.

34 Andress, above n. 31, p. 109.

35 Andress, above n. 30, p. 7.

36 Andress, above n. 30, p. 19.

37 Arendt, above, n. 15, p. 96.

display in public his innermost motivation, since it actually demands the impossible, transforms all actors into hypocrites; the moment the display of motives begins, hypocrisy begins to poison all human relations.'[38] Thus a politics of authentic sentimentalism led to a 'hunt for hypocrisy', which descended into chaos because it was 'boundless by nature'.[39]

From the Rousseauan perspective, in turn, this vortex of heroism and martyrdom both destabilises the austere tranquillity of the republican citizenry as envisaged in Rousseau's depictions, while correspondingly providing a dangerous resource for heroic revolutionary individuals projecting their own sense of martyrdom onto, and identifying with, the mythologised people. But crucially, it is also the result of conceiving republican virtue as something to be exercised in a public 'space of appearances', where the hypocrisy of speech and sentiment undermine the possibility of social harmony.

It is arguably this kind of conceited moralism, and all of its corrupting effects, which Rousseau wishes to guard against in entrusting the lawgiver, instead, with the political qualities of 'daring' and 'audacity' and so on. Significantly, indeed the lawgiver, in founding the polity and people, is entrusted not only with a task of 'reason', but also one of 'persuasion', the kind of emotive endeavour that poses moral perils in the Rousseauan schema. Tellingly, indeed, Rousseau notes that the lawgiver's challenge, is 'how [it is] possible *to move the hearts of men*' – or to create 'the souls on which appropriate legislation will take hold.'[40] It is precisely this emotive endeavour which Rousseau assigns to the lawgiver because it is considered so unsuitable and dangerous for the people itself.

In another dimension, the self-conscious sentimentalism of communal revolutionary experiences that Robespierre invokes – ('all eyes were wet with tears, intoxicated sentiment was everywhere')[41] – evoke Rousseau's description of the moral hypocrisy of the bourgeois theatre, of the self-conscious and self-congratulatory qualities of emotional experience in a context of theatrical spectatorship.[42] Whereas Robespierre and the Jacobins

---

38 Arendt, above, n. 15, p. 96.

39 Arendt, above, n. 15, p. 96.

40 Rousseau, above n. 5, Chapter 2, p. 89.

41 W.H. Sewell, 'Historical Events as Transformations of Structures: Inventing Revolution at the Bastille' (1996) 25 *Theory and Society* 854–55, cited in Andress, above n. 30, p. 109.

42 J.J. Rousseau, *Lettre à d'Alembert* (1758); See A. Bloom, C. Butterworth and C. Kelly (eds), *Rousseau: Letter to d'Alembert and Writings for the Theatre*, University Press of New England, Dartmouth 2004.

championed the public expression of emotional sincerity an inoculation against moral hypocrisy – with the capacity for emotional authenticity laid transparent and accountable to a scrutinising public audience – Rousseau arguably adopts a more pessimistic, and correspondingly a more *austere* stance in relegating citizenship and civic virtue to an essentially private realm, to the harmonious rhythms of nature, agriculture and work, where man's psychic harmony remains unthreatened by the allure of self-revelation and self-validation in something like the Arendtian public realm, in the 'space of appearances' where mutual recognition affords men subjecthood and freedom. Whereas 'sentimentalism', in the French revolutionary setting 'nurtured a cultural expectation of the performance of a 'natural' sincerity through emotional excess', Rousseau, by contrast, was wary not simply of moral hypocrisy but of the performativity of emotional sincerity itself, as seen in his incisive critique of the theatre in *Letter to d'Alembert*. Whereas Jacobinism evokes the 'cliché of the radical republican as a man of feeling', Rousseau, despite his own preoccupation with sentiment and emotion, eschewed any centring of citizenship on expressive sentimentalism, favouring instead the more austere expressions of communal identity – of folk ritual and especially work – in which individual expressivity and self-distinction are largely dissolved.

In this vein, melodrama – specifically the sentimentalist melodrama that has been identified in the Jacobin narrative of the French revolution – can be conceptualised both as a conservative device, or reaction to upheaval, but also as an instrument for the theatrical unsettling of existing sensibilities – something that clearly in tension with Rousseau's vision of autarkic social harmony, contrasted with the confrontational or tumultuous class relations in the Machiavellian image. Far from contingency, mutability and melodramatic confrontation, indeed, Shklar argued that Rousseau's social vision is essentially 'an effort to prevent change'.[43] Thus the Jacobin propensity for performative melodrama, conceived as a source both of political energy and legitimation, can usefully be contrasted with Rousseau's ambivalence towards the insatiability and excitability of the bourgeois, excited and inflamed by frippery and novelty, a vortex of destructive covetousness and desire in juxtaposition with the stoic clam of the austere peasant. Indeed in conspicuous contrast with the Jacobin vista of political melodrama,

---

[43] J. Shklar, *Men and Citizens: A Study of Rousseau's Social Theory*, Cambridge University Press, Cambridge 1985, p. 181.

Rousseau suggests that 'true pleasure' is 'simple and quiet (*paisible*), it loves silence and contemplation (*recueillement*)'.[44]

6. CONCLUSION

The role of the lawgiver, then, can usefully be understood as a cautionary substitute or safeguard against the possible perils of positing a constructed popular agent as an heroic actors on a world-historical stage – as a figure who relieves the people of the moral perils of political melodrama, of the corrupting effects of self-revelatory posturing, and so on. The question that arises, then, is not so much whether or not the lawgiver himself is not subject to the same moral perils, of corrupted egotism and so on, but rather to emphasise that the lawgiver is simply a presupposition, a providential historical figure whose anomalous, almost alchemic power serve to absorb and neutralise this moral hazard in the successful foundations of a republic.

[44] Rousseau, above n. 6, p. 77.

RADICAL DEMOCRACY AND REVOLUTIONARY REFORM

Looking for Solutions in Times of Democratic Disruption

Marcin KILANOWSKI*

1. INTRODUCTION

In 1968, a large portion of society within the West challenged the capitalist regime and its coercive social and political structure. It was apparent to the protesters that their so called 'freedom' was a form of serfdom. Those opposing were looking toward the East with a desire to live in a state in which education was free; women were equal with men in rights and in access to jobs; where segregation did not exist; and where the means of production were owned by the whole of society.

In 1968, however, many in the East were also opposing the communist regime. They were challenging the system in which there was almost always only one political party to which one could belong – with one acceptable view; a system of the censorship of private letters, academic lectures and

* This chapter is a developed version of argumentation presented in *Ku społeczeństwu obywatelskiemu. Czego dziś może nas nauczyć pragmatyzm?* Kultura i Edukacja, Nr 1/2017, pp. 50–62.

newspapers; a system where there was no free speech; where people often had nothing to eat or could not heat their houses; and a system where members of the political opposition (including priests) were imprisoned, tortured or killed. Marxism-Leninism was the only appropriate message – the true message – that the class struggle was inevitable and had to end with the eradication of the ruling class. No one was able to question that.[1]

Now, in the 21st century, we talk of the 20th century as the century of ideologies, as if the 21st century is free of them.[2] However, one ideology prevails: that of the democratic capitalist state as the only feasible model for the organisation of society, politics and the economy.[3] One can, of course, say that there is an alternative to this and this is the social democratic state, but in the current century the social democratic goals have changed so dramatically that it is hard to distinguish them from the capitalist goals. This is why we often hear that the political left and political right are not so different anymore and that the distinction no longer even matters.[4] Roberto Unger calls such social democracy just a more humane version of capitalist democracy – a nicer, humanised project of the political right, with its support for the free market economy, based on tax and transfer, and support for investment in debt instead of production.[5] One could say that the problem with both forms of democracy is that they no longer have their own agendas or their own distinct political projects, and this is evident when they reach for each other's tools when problems appear.[6]

---

1 T. Snyder, *Bloodlands: Europe Between Hitler and Stalin*, Basic Books, New York 2012; A. Applebaum, *Iron Curtain: The Crushing of Eastern Europe, 1944–1956*, Anchor Books, New York 2013.

2 See the new introduction by Daniel Bell to his 1962 book *The End of Ideology*: D. Bell, *The End of Ideology: On the Exhaustion of Political Ideas in the Fifties*, Harvard University Press, Cambridge 2000.

3 On that ideology and its consequences, see: T. Piketty, *Capital in the Twenty-First Century*, Harvard University Press, Cambridge 2017; T. Piketty, *Capital and Ideology*, Harvard University Press, Cambridge 2020.

4 From general analysis present in daily news to specific studies. See: J. Daley, 'There's no such thing as Left and Right any more – can we all agree on that?' in *The Telegraph*, 10.10.2015; C. Sartwell, 'The Left-Right Political Spectrum Is Bogus' in *The Atlantic*, 20.06.2014; F. Ross, 'Beyond left and right": the new partisan politics of welfare' (2000) 13 *Governance* 2, 155–83.

5 R.M. Unger, *The Self Awakened. Pragmatism Unbound*, Harvard University Press, Cambridge 2009, pp. 118–19, 200–01.

6 See: cutting social spending by social democratic governments, or nationalisation and governmental intervention by right wing governments in times of crisis. For more detailed studies, see: B. Bremer, 'The missing left? Economic crisis and the

2. THE PEOPLE

What can be done in these circumstances? Is there a possibility for a better life than both systems, in theory, have aimed for? Is there the possibility of more freedom and opportunities for personal growth? What means should be used to bring these possibilities to reality? It seems that we may answer these questions if, at the very beginning, we understand what the main problems were with the performance of those past ideologies that were promising more freedom and more equality.

The crucial issue against which people were demonstrating in 1968 was the abuse of power – the corruption of the mind of those in power by the power they had under their command.[7] Their increasing wealth and privileges, as well as their detachment from understanding the needs of ordinary people, were key factors in the dissatisfaction and later rage. One could still try to defend the systems, arguing that perception of the problems was just a matter of interpretation of facts. But it is hard to blur the issue when one looks at the real corruption that was widely present. No ideology mattered when there was a substantive amount of money that was given to the decision makers (in whatever form).[8] Political parties functioned like most of the corporations. They served only their own interests, or the interests of some members, and not their constituencies.

If the above was the case, then one important lesson can be learned: that any good idea – any social, political or economic agenda – can be jeopardised if those who are taking it forward, or those who replace them, again abuse their power and become corrupted and detached from the people. But the past reality is also our own. Today's reality is not better. We observe huge inequalities, political parties' power games and the rise

---

programmatic response of social democratic parties in Europe' (2018) 24 *Party Politics* 1, 23–38; P. English, M.T. Grasso and B. Buraczynska, 'Convergence on crisis? Comparing Labour and Conservative Party framing of the economic crisis in Britain, 2008–14' (2016) 44 *Politics & Policy* 3, 577–603; J. Callaghan, *The Retreat of Social Democracy*, Manchester University Press, Manchester, New York 2000.

7 Z. Brzeziński, *The Grand Failure. The Birth and Death of Communism in the Twentieth Century*, MacDonald, London 1989.

8 C.A. Schwartz, 'Corruption and Political Development in the U. S. S. R.' (1979) 11 *Comparative Politics* 4, 425–43; W. Sandholtz and R. Taagepera, 'Corruption, Culture, and Communism' (2005) 15 *International Review of Sociology* 1, 109–31; M.S. Konstantin, *USSR: The Corrupt Society: The Secret World of Soviet Capitalism*, Simon & Schuster, New York 1982; N. Hammerstein, *Die Deutsche Forschungsgemeinschaft in der Weimarer Republik und im Dritten Reich; Wissenschaftspolitik in Republik und Diktatur, 1920–1945*, C.H. Beck, Munich 1999.

of corporate power.[9] Furthermore, today, politicians are detached from the people.[10] To overcome such a situation, it is necessary to propose an agenda that will strengthen those that are most vulnerable – the people. Unfortunately, the problem that we face in our democracies at present is the lack of an agent that could propose such a reform of our democratic system as would ensure that power will not be re-abused and that the project of a better life, of a 'larger life', as Unger would call it, for the people, will not be jeopardised.[11] In these circumstances, one can ask: why not consider the people themselves as the agents of change?[12]

'The people' today to a large extent are no longer a class of people determined by the form of labour they perform in a work place. There is no longer a class or race of people that was born to govern. They are the people who, to a large extent, have political rights and who, by constant participation in the market space, became employees and owners of the means of production (also by being shareholders). When looking back, we can say that the times for the superior treatment of the territory of the state and of the government formed by the ruling party or the coalition of parties is the 'song of the past'. It seems that now is the time for acknowledging the people and their role in shaping the future and in governing change.[13] The goal could be to empower the people and so

---

9 On the aforementioned issues, see, *inter alia*: B. Milanovic, *Global Inequality: A New Approach for the Age of Globalization*, Harvard University Press, Cambridge 2016; T. Baldwin, *Ctrl Alt Delete: How Politics and the Media Crashed Our Democracy*, Hurst & Company, London 2018; A. Winkler, *We the Corporations: How American Businesses Won Their Civil Rights*, Liveright Publishing Corporation, New York and London 2018.

10 For the account of that, see, *inter alia*: R. Parker, *Here, the People Rule, A Constitutional Populist Manifesto*, Harvard University Press, Cambridge 1998; L. Lessig, *They Don't Represent US*, Dey Street Books, New York 2019.

11 R.M. Unger, *The Religion of the Future*, Harvard University Press, Cambridge 2014, p. 135.

12 This approach is especially valued in the postcolonial context. See: D.B. Knight, 'Territory and People or People and Territory? Thoughts on Postcolonial Self-Determination' (1985) *International Political Science Review*, 248–72.

13 The people are the third element characterising a state in international law. The territory and the government are the other two. For more on a traditional view, see: M.R. Fowler and J.M. Bunck, 'What Constitutes the Sovereign State?' (1996) 22 *Review of International Studies* 4, 381–404; In light of growing concern about the people and the multicultural character of our communities, there is a need to move toward a state form that institutionalises polycentricity, heterogeneity and plurality. See: R. Axtmann, 'The State of the State: The Model of the Modern State and Its Contemporary Transformation' (2004) 25 *International Political Science Review/Revue internationale de science politique* 3, 259–79.

perhaps change the direction of the social and political evolution. It could allow the freeing of the energy – of the potential – that exists within the people. It could lead to a change of the one-sided mode of institutional modification: from a limited top-down approach to a broader, bottom-up approach, as Unger suggests.[14]

With this in mind, we can address the need for the establishment of the project for a social, institutional or economic reform that will allow for the establishment of conditions for a 'larger life' for the people.[15] Unger argues that the path should not lead through a revolution that immediately changes one system for another, nor through reform that is based on the old system, but instead, through revolutionary reform, when a gradual change of the present social, institutional and many other arrangements is undertaken. This revolutionary reform can also be described as a gradual redesign.[16] The question that follows is: what should we do first? This question has already been asked during the times of the Great Depression, and it was answered by John Dewey – just as it is asked and answered by Roberto Mangabeira Unger today. That answer is: we should build a strong civil society and develop social solidarity to strengthen the legitimacy of the democratic system.[17]

3. TOWARDS CIVIL SOCIETY

It can be striking for us today that – when so little divides us – there is still so much that separates us from each other. We observe the fragility of social cohesion and witness the degradation of social capital, even though some say that our religious beliefs as well as material conditions

---

14 R.M. Unger, *The Left Alternative*, Verso, New York 2009, pp. 52–63. We can observe how important such an approach is in the process of European integration or in the case of climate governance. See: I. Melnykovska and R. Schweickert, 'Bottom-up or top-down: what drives the convergence of Ukraine's institutions towards European standards?' (2008) 8 *Southern European and Black Sea Studies* 4, 445–68; See also: M.A. Schreurs, 'From the Bottom Up: Local and Subnational Climate Change Politics' (2008) 17 *The Journal of Environment & Development* 4, https://doi.org/10.1177/1070496508326432; J. Dirix, W. Peeters, J. Eyckmans, P.T. Jones and S. Sterckx, 'Strengthening bottom-up and top-down climate governance' (2013) 13 *Climate Policy* 3, 363–83.

15 R.M. Unger, *The Self Awakened*, p. 253.

16 R.M. Unger, *The Religion of the Future*, pp. 326–28.

17 How important is civil society for democratic legitimacy, see, for example: J. Greenwood, 'Organized civil society and democratic legitimacy in the European Union' (2007) 37 *British Journal of Political Science* 2, 333–57.

or differences in political rights no longer divide us.[18] In light of critical observations, one can say that there is a need to reconcile people with each other – to establish bonds between us – and that we need to establish civil society. The need to establish such bonds was one of the main ideas present in the pragmatism of John Dewey, who was trying to respond to political crisis and the Great Depression. It is present today in the work of Roberto Unger, who is trying to respond to the socio-political and economic crisis within our democracies. In this text, I will focus on the proposition of John Dewey and Roberto Unger as the most far-reaching.

When trying to establish a well-functioning civil society, we have to ask ourselves a few crucial questions. These questions include: how can Western individualism be combined with the values of community and social solidarity? What are the necessary conditions for freedom and solidarity among people? I believe that answering these questions is an important step towards dealing appropriately with the issues of developing civil society and strengthening social integration today. To answer these questions, it is worthwhile to turn to the pragmatic thought of John Dewey, mentioned above, which is the base for his vision of radical democracy, as well as to the discourse of Roberto Unger, one of the leading voices calling for revolutionary reform today. It is important to understand the role of the individual in the community – to understand that we act as part of a society, in a network of mutual relations and that our personal well-being cannot be fully realised if it is not also a part of the community's well-being.[19] Such an understanding leads us, as Dewey pointed out, to a rejection of the classical, abstract, sharp distinction between the individual and the community. In reality, what we have is a give-and-take relation in which both the individual and the community affect each other.[20] Acknowledging the irreducible interdependencies existing between the individual and the community helps us to perceive the organic identity of their interests. He argues that understanding the interdependencies that exist between us and others,

---

18 On fragility of social cohesion and how much still divides us in Western democracies see, S.F. Schram, *The Return of Ordinary Capitalism: Neoliberalism, Precarity, Occupy*, Oxford University Press, Oxford 2015; C.H. Guilluy, *Twilight of the Elites: Prosperity, the Periphery, and the Future of France*, Yale University Press, New Haven and London 2019.

19 J. Dewey, 'Ethics', in J.A. Boydston (ed.), *Collected Works of John Dewey. The Later Works: 1925–1953*, Southern Illinois Press, Carbondale-Edwardsville 1991, 7, 298.

20 J. Dewey, 'Individualism, Old and New', in Boydston (ed.), above n. 19, 5:75; J. Dewey, 'Liberalism and the Social Action', in Boydston (ed.), above n. 19, 11:52.

in the light of the consequences of our actions, makes us more aware that the barrier between us (classically termed as between the self and the other) is relative. Just as we cannot divide means and goals when the former are themselves goals – that is, the results of other activities caused by specific motives – we also cannot delineate the differentiation between the individual and the other, because we begin and end in others, and vice versa.[21]

In the light of the above – by focusing on everyday experiences and not following philosophical abstractions – we should understand that the individual is a social being from the very beginning, and that he or she is a part of the community, or in other words, of the public.[22] We can go further and say that there should be no sharp distinction between the private and the public.[23] We should understand that our private actions have an impact on the possibility of the growth of others, just as the actions of others have an impact on our individual growth. In other words, private and public are also entangled. Because of this, we should act with the consciousness that everything that contributes to the development of ourselves also contributes to the development of the community. There is no way to profit individually in the long run if not through making sure that the community is also profiting. With this comes responsibility. Our understanding of this responsibility comes with the recognition of mutual interdependence. What has so far been only understood as private is also public. In these circumstances, actions are no longer conducted only for our own good; they should also be carried out for the good of the community, which is part of one's own being – one's private sphere.[24] By broadening our consciousness of the community and of the role of the public in our own life, we are becoming part of the people being responsible for one another.

Dewey calls our attention to the fact that what we need is a new understanding of the position of the individual in democratic society and an understanding of the role of the community. Such an observation is very much the rejection of the old individual–community and private–public dichotomy and will allow us to present a perspective which can help us to overcome an existing worldview based on these two crucial dichotomies and other reductive cognitive attitudes which do not take into account

21 J. Dewey, 'Ethics', in Boydston (ed.), above n. 19, 7:350.
22 J. Dewey, 'Individualism, Old and New', in Boydston (ed.), above n. 19, 5: 121.
23 J. Dewey, 'The Public and its Problems', in Boydston (ed.), above n. 19, 2: 332.
24 J. Dewey, 'The Public and its Problems', in Boydston (ed.), above n. 19, 2: 328.

the full range of dependencies that exist among us. It can help us to introduce new social and political attitudes with the aim of overcoming the controversy: is it the individual or the community that must win over the other? After the rejection of sharp dichotomies, it should be possible to do away with formulations in which either social goals take precedence over the individual, or individual goals assume importance over social imperatives. The new perspective could solve various controversies which have arisen within liberalism and communitarianism by overcoming dualistic divisions for the perception of mutual relations in which the individual and the community exist.[25]

The new perspective can be of enormous importance for the formation of the previously mentioned civil society and social solidarity – which we have yet to achieve, even though so much has been said about it.[26] We can call it a change of the language game, of public philosophy, of worldview – and a change of consciousness. We can call it redefinition and redesigning. All these descriptions refer to the same issue: that we have to 'leave behind' what we have now, to the extent that it does not allow us to reach for a greater life for everybody, nor does it allow us to create a civil society. This will be possible by getting rid of the old, abstract dichotomies that are constraining us from building a well-functioning civil society. Those that use them draw lines and divide people from each other. But we can challenge such an abstract basis and – in doing so – challenge the present, all-encompassing ideology of capitalist democracy or capitalist democracy with a human face (social democracy), as Unger argues.[27] This is especially important today when we face certain obstacles to taking a democratic project further and when the goal of more freedom and opportunities for personal growth or self-development for all has not been achieved.

So far, we do not have a developed consciousness that will allow us to perceive the network of mutual relations that bonds us with others.

---

25 There are examples of the research that already takes such a direction: B. Singer, 'Reconciling liberalism and communitarianism' in B. Singer (ed.), *Pragmatism, Rights and Democracy*, New York University Press, New York 1999; K. Baynes, 'The Liberal/Communitarian Controversy and Communicative Ethics' in D. Rasmussen (ed.), *Universalism vs. Communitarianism, Contemporary Debates in Ethics*, The MIT Press, Cambridge 1995.

26 Some scholars are pointing out that we are even losing what we have gained so far, see: J. Gerhards, H. Lengfeld, Z. Ignácz, F.K. Kley and M. Priem, *European Solidarity in Times of Crisis: Insights from a Thirteen-Country Survey*, Routledge, New York 2019.

27 R.M. Unger, *False Necessity: Anti-necessitarian Social Theory in the Service of Radical Democracy*, Verso, New York 2004, pp. 390–91.

We still operate on the basis of the abstract notion of individuality and community – of what is private and what is public.[28] We also function on the basis of the understanding of the notion of freedom, as it would be the only value that needs to be protected.[29] Furthermore, we create legal regulations that only occasionally refer to our needs and that frequently divide us or constrain us from further development as individuals and as a community.[30] What we need is to overcome all these obstacles by developing appropriate skills: that is, the ability to solve problems and, most importantly, be critical. We can shape these developed abilities and strengthen them through education.

4. EDUCATION

We can ask why so little has been done so far to make our education appropriate. In the past, there were many critics of the educational system, among them also Dewey.[31] There are others today, including Unger.[32] They all criticise the system for not teaching critical thinking. The system mostly teaches how to memorise and repeat. At best, it teaches how to argue without any further assessment of what the consequences will be if they are put to work. The art of arguing and challenging is the goal in itself, even though the issues discussed are not ultimately resolved, or are merely partially resolved. Organising education in this way does not allow us to develop the abilities to deal with the problems 'on the ground' or to deal with them in a complex way. We are taught old truths and that there is true

---

28 This issue is indicated not only by philosophers, but also by legal doctrine, which analyses the legitimacy of applying a strict division between private law entities and public law entities. See: H. Muir-Watt, 'Private International Law Beyond the Schism' (2011) 2 *Transnational Legal Theory* 3, 347–428; H. Muir-Watt, 'Conflicts of laws unbounded: the case for a legal-pluralist revival' (2016) 7 *Transnational Legal Theory* 3, 313–53.

29 In practice that leads to works that present abstract understanding of the notion of freedom, see: M. Freedman, *Capitalism and Freedom*, The University of Chicago Press, Cambridge 1962.

30 See: M.A. Glendon, *Rights Talk: The Impoverishment of Political Discourse*, The Free Press, New York 1991.

31 J. Dewey, 'Democracy and Education', in J.A. Boydston (ed.), *Collected Works of John Dewey. The Middle Works: 1899–1924*, Southern Illinois Press, Carbondale-Edwardsville 1991, 9.

32 Unger represents a critical approach rooted in the Critical Legal Studies tradition. For other examples, see: D. Kennedy, *Legal Education and the Reproduction of Hierarchy: A Polemic Against the System*, New York University Press, New York 2007.

knowledge that we should possess. Applying such knowledge and such old truths leads to the appearance of unforeseen consequences, because the conditions in which we live are changing, and applying solutions that are often outdated leads to failures. By applying them, we miss the chance to create positive outcomes.[33] When the consequences are not those that we were hoping to achieve, we often blame the situation, not ourselves.[34] We do not see that we were the origin of the problem and that we were not prepared to deal with the challenging situation in front of us. Our understanding that we have knowledge and truth on our side immunised us from thinking that we were making mistakes, from challenging our own thinking and from listening to others with different points of view. The problem is that most of the time we do not recognise that truth and knowledge are contextual, at least not our truth and knowledge.[35] As Dewey and Unger would say, all of this is a consequence of the educational system that created our understanding, of which we are certain that it is correct.[36] Instead, Dewey argues, we need a critical approach which will allow us to criticise what we see and do.[37] We should learn about the fallibility of our knowledge and about taking other points of view into consideration and should try to experiment with new approaches. When we are aware of the fallibility of knowledge, of course we can still say that our goal is to gain 'better knowledge', but only if we are conscious that our understanding is shaped by our limitations in fully grasping the changing processes in the world. We should be aware that we make mistakes while dealing with various problems and that our 'knowledge' should always be under revision.

Adding to what Dewey said, we do not need the old laws of necessity, but instead, we should learn just one: the 'law of shifting considerations'. Having that law as a basis for our thinking and acting would allow us to focus on multiple approaches to particular problems. It would allow us to consider critically various propositions and respond to situations, keeping

---

33 R.M. Unger, *Knowledge Economy*, Verso, New York 2019, pp. 93–101.

34 For an example of the analysis showing the mechanism of such thinking and its impact on legal actions and social policy, see: J. Hanson and K. Hanson, 'The Blame Frame: Justifying (Racial) Injustice in America' (2006) 2 *Harvard Civil Rights Civil Liberties Law Review* 41, 413–80.

35 R.M. Unger, *Knowledge Economy*, pp. 117–20.

36 J. Dewey, 'Challenge to Liberal Thought', in Boydston (ed.), above n. 19, 15:273; R.M. Unger, *Democracy Realized: The Progressive Alternative*, Verso, New York 2001, pp. 10–16.

37 J. Dewey, 'Reconstruction in Philosophy and Essays', in Boydston (ed.), above n. 19, 12:198.

in mind that doing so is not the end and that we might not be right. This is also what Unger argues for.[38]

In light of this, we can say that students should not be taught that everything is good or evil, that one can be only a hero and that the other is only a monster.[39] We should know that our description of others may not be right – that it might be biased or contextual, depending on the situation. That will allow us not to close our eyes to other possibilities when trying to understand and act in a given situation. We will avoid being trapped by our own perspective. What is right and wrong is often unclear; furthermore, defining someone as a victim and the other as an oppressor might, instead of helping, create another problem.[40] Thus, we should be taught how to be open to other points of view, because they may be pointing to something that we had previously not considered. Moreover, as Dewey would suggest, we should teach students how to be aware of the consequences of our actions for others and also for us, by showing that the division between us and others is an abstract one.[41] We are created by – and we live in – a network of various relations.[42] As Unger adds, we should understand our role in shaping such relations and feel responsible for them.[43] Of course, being part of these relations does not meant that we cannot secure our individuality at the same time. And there is no way out. We should stop rationalising existing inequalities by looking for whom is to blame, and we should instead think about how to change a situation that might be harmful also to ourselves. These should be the goals for a life-long education. In short, we should be taught how to develop our critical thinking, our openness toward others, our understanding that we are composed of various relations and the ability to revise our knowledge. Taken together, this will lay a foundation that can help us to get closer to reaching the goal of changing the present conditions for the better.

Through abovementioned education, it should be possible to awaken imagination and energy in people which could push them toward

---

38 R.M. Unger, *The Self Awakened*, pp. 135–36, 160–62.

39 This is why Habermas, whose thinking is rooted in pragmatic tradition and in John Dewey's thought, argues in *Philosophy in times of terror* that we should not look for heroes, see: G. Borradori, *Philosophy in times of terror. Conversations with Jürgen Habermas and Jacques Derrida*, The University of Chicago Press, Chicago 2008, p. 43.

40 See M. Koskenniemi, 'Between Impunity and Show Trial' (2002) 6 *Max Planck Yearbook of United Nations Law* 1, 1–32.

41 J. Dewey, 'Democracy and Education', in Boydston (ed.), above n. 31, 9: 105.

42 J. Dewey, 'Liberalism and the Social Action', in Boydston (ed.), above n. 19, 11: 40.

43 R.M. Unger, *The Left Alternative*, pp. 140–41, 159–60.

engagement in the public sphere and different forms of cooperation.[44] We should replace our desire to reach for ultimate truth and certainty, which should not be questioned, and redesign our educational system not to be centred on such issues. Every 'truth' or every view should be taught in reference to another to show existing differences. Such an education would be based on the free exchange of ideas. It would allow the development of an individual personality based on the value of interaction and communication with others. Such a personality could be a good basis for building civil society centred on common critical engagement – on sharing convictions and needs. In doing so, we would be growing closer to each other, becoming more responsible for each other and eventually closer to establishing social solidarity.

5. INSTITUTIONS

To establish the system described above, we need to create the additional favourable conditions for individual development and self-realisation, which are indispensable in shaping individual and social well-being through growth.[45] Such a goal could be reached with the achievement of appropriate changes at the level of social, legal and political institutions. These changes should, of course, rely strongly on previously discussed changes in the educational system, allowing people to develop imaginative and critical competences to take an active role in making changes possible through public deliberation and civic participation.[46]

Social, legal and political institutions play a crucial role in establishing conditions for change. They should play a further role, by creating the conditions for people's involvement. Praising people's participation in decision-making processes and their individual responsibility and capacity for critical thinking does not mean that individuals should now be totally responsible for their choices. That would take away the responsibility of the state or legal institutions for the outcomes of their decisions. The idea of empowering people – by making them the decision-makers and rendering them responsible for their actions – could be abused by those who will still be making decisions in the background (as it is

---

44 R.M. Unger, *The Self Awakened*, pp. 175–79.

45 *Ibid.*, p. 160.

46 This public deliberation requires necessary formal preconditions, as was well explained by Habermas, see: J. Habermas, *The Theory of Communicative Action*, vol. 1 & vol. 2, Polity Press, Oxford 1991.

abused now).[47] We often hear that 'we have what we wanted', because power politics runs according to our choices expressed during elections, but such voices do not recognise how legal and institutional arrangements constrain our perception of the situation and our decisions.[48] Because of that, the responsibility of the individual should not be perceived as being detached from the context in which people live. And the context is, to a significant extent, an institutional one. We live in a certain social and institutional setting that shapes our life, our perceptions, our habits and our biases.[49] Precisely because of these circumstances we should reshape our thinking about the usefulness of the individual–community dichotomy and the private–public dichotomy, as well as that of individuals–institutions, which function as the basis for legal and political institutions.

As to the institutions – educational, legal, political – the basic criterion underlying their existence should be concerned with the degree to which these institutions work toward the development of individual potential and allow for individual growth. These institutions should not be concerned about their own eternal existence, and the protection of such institutions can often be harmful in the new circumstances. When the institutions start to serve only themselves or to preserve an outdated social or legal model, then it is the time to change them, as Unger argues.[50] We can also add that this also includes present economic institutions.

Initially, it is hard to imagine that economic institutions could be interested in changes in our understanding of what is private and what is public; where the responsibilities and freedoms of the individual or the state lie; and where the responsibility of economic institutions is. For example, corporations would say – most of the time – that in today's world, it is the responsibility of the state, through the system of taxation and transference, to pass some of the wealth produced to those who were not successful, or to finance the system of the reproduction of 'knowledge' to maintain that order in society which protects the very institutions

---

47 For the study of such abuse see: D. Kennedy, *A World of Struggle: How Power, Law, and Expertise Shape Global Political Economy*, Princeton University Press, New Haven 2016.

48 See the classical studies by Judith Shklar: J. Shklar, *Legalism*, Harvard University Press, Cambridge 1964.

49 J. Dewey, 'A Common Faith', in Boydston (ed.), above n. 19, 9: 57–58; R.M. Unger, *False Necessity*, pp. 432–36.

50 R.M. Unger, *Free Trade Reimagined: The World Division of Labor and the Method of Economics*, Princeton University Press, New Haven 2010, pp. 25–44.

it produced. In the 'Western world' in which there are typically no caps on executive compensation, where corporations are even receiving the right to freedom of speech and where – according to Friedman's teaching – they have no responsibility for the public sphere, it is hard to imagine that those who profit from such arrangements would like to see changes other than those leading to more profits for some (i.e. themselves).[51] They will say that they believe in progress, change and the growth of individuals in the world of free and equal opportunities and that, in their opinion, we already have such a world.[52] The general message is that increasing differences in wealth among the people are just a matter of personal choice – of not enough hard work – but that can change with time if individuals work hard and accumulate capital from generation to generation.

In such circumstances, it is hard to imagine that there is a possibility of changing the direction of the development of our societies without reshaping the institutions and the basis on which they rest. Getting rid of the sharp divisions between the dichotomies that I have mentioned and reducing the limited understanding of the terms that we use by tying them down to the real-life experience of the people seems to be the way to allow us to perceive that there is not just one way to achieve 'growth' and 'progress'. It might be possible to see that growth and progress can be achieved when shareholder primacy is not only a smoke screen for the unrestrained activities of business and when stakeholder interests are also a point of concern.[53] Ultimately, the intellectual growth of the people is the most important factor, as well as the use of their great potentialities, which should start to matter now, and not in some distant future.

6. CONCLUDING REMARKS

In many of his works, Unger argues that today's social and political order are not solid or stable. Even our democratic order, which I was referring

---

51 On CEO compensation, see: S. Clifford, *The CEO Pay Machine: How It Trashes America and How to Stop It*, Penguin Random House, New York 2017. On the right of free speech for corporations, see: *Citizens United v. Federal Election Commission*, 558 U.S. 310 (2010).

52 See: M. Friedman, 'The Social Responsibility of Business Is to Increase Its Profits' in W.C. Zimmerli, M. Holzinger and K. Richter (eds), *Corporate Ethics and Corporate Governance*, Springer, Berlin and Heidelberg 2007.

53 See: O. Hart and L. Zingales, 'Companies Should Maximize Shareholder Welfare Not Market Value' (August 2017) ECGI Working Paper Series in Finance, Working Paper N° 521/2017.

to in this chapter (like that in Europe or in the United States), faces challenges that may undermine its base.[54] It is Dewey and Unger who point out that without the right preparation to face these challenges – through responsible, open-minded participation in the public sphere and deliberation – it is possible that instead of having some sort of possibility of steering the growth of our societies and having an impact on political and economic reform, the evolving situations will steer us. If this happens, we will be left behind, unable to grasp and handle new and different situations.

We should not wait for social theory to come up with all-encompassing propositions for change. We should look more to who we are and to our needs (which are changing) – to come down from the level of abstraction and refer to the potential in us that is constrained by the present arrangements, by the language based on sharp dichotomies and by use of categories understood in too abstract of a way. According to Unger's project of revolutionary reform, the goal is a larger life in a civil society, which is undeveloped today in terms of its identity and the goals it sets up for itself. The goals can be achieved by means of changes in language and institutional arrangements – and especially through redesigning the education system. The goal should be to shape a more appropriate understanding of the world and our place in it – to deal more effectively and critically with the contemporary problems that we are facing in our democracies. Our problems, as Dewey has already pointed out, are not proof that democracy is not the appropriate political form: the fact that we did not attain the ideals should not be a reason to turn back. For Dewey, democracy is not a goal, but a means by which we can create conditions for everyone to participate in the process of forming civil society and institutions allowing for social inclusion and solidarity. In other words, democracy is here an idea of life in itself, based on communication and the free exchange of ideas.[55] Dewey calls such democracy 'radical democracy' – radical not in its outcomes, but in its method.

We should be aware that the achievement of civil society and social solidarity – which is equally important for Dewey's radical democracy and for Unger's revolutionary reform – is dependent upon the extent

54 See: Y. Mounk, *The People vs. Democracy: Why Our Freedom Is in Danger and How to Save It*, Harvard University Press, Cambridge 2018; S. Levitsky and D. Ziblatt, *How Democracies Die*, Crown, New York 2018.

55 J. Dewey, 'Creative Democracy – The Task Before Us', in Boydston (ed.), above n. 19,14:227.

to which the individual is free and has the chance of individual growth and the opportunity to perceive the numerous relations which bind him/her to others. Furthermore, with a change of language – overcoming the use of sharp dichotomies – we can broaden our consciousness about our place in the societies or communities in which we live, as well as our role in them, when achieving individual goals. The goal of achieving social solidarity will also require leaving behind old abstract concepts of class, race and nationality. Instead of forming ideological bases for our perspectives, it would require us to direct our attention – with the attitude of openness toward others – towards real, concrete needs and to create formal conditions for working out reasonable solutions while addressing different problems in a cooperative effort, without giving up our individuality. Only then will our democracies be able to develop to such a point that they can disseminate the ideas of democracy based on civil society and individual freedom, understood as reaching agreements in a cooperative and responsible way.

PART II

REASSESSING CONSTITUTIONAL PRINCIPLES IN TIMES OF DEMOCRATIC RUPTURES

THE INVISIBLE SEPARATION OF POWERS AND THE CONTROL OF THE CENTRAL POLITICAL POWER

Lessons from Hungary, Moldova and Romania

Zoltán Pozsár-Szentmiklósy

1. LEGAL INSTITUTIONS AND PROCEDURES AFFECTING THE SEPARATION OF POWERS

The classic principle of the separation of powers is – from time to time – the subject of reconsideration. It has been demonstrated that there are no clear definitions of the doctrine in legal literature[1] and it 'has not been

1 M.J.C. Vile, *Constitutionalism and the Separation of Powers*, 2nd ed., Liberty Fund, Indianapolis 1998, p. 13.

wholly reproduced in the institutional architecture of any modern state'.[2] Moreover, new social and political phenomena generate new challenges to constitutional law and call for new interpretations of the separation of powers. New approaches to the doctrine in most of the cases focus on selected aspects of the relations and activities of state organs (e.g. the doctrine as a set of principles; the interdependency and cooperation of the branches of government; taking new powers into consideration alongside the traditional ones; focusing on the vertical separation of powers between the constituent power and the constituted powers; etc.). However, none of these various aspects are exclusive, and their significance depends on the particularities of the legal dispute in question. On the other hand, both the classic and new approaches to the doctrine seem to focus on the same function: setting limits for the exercise of the central (majoritarian) political power. Focusing on this function, the doctrine can be taken as a broad, complex frame of interpretation.

The diversity of concepts and interpretations of the separation of powers leads to the argument that when examining the proper functioning of this principle, not only the institutional design of state institutions and their formal powers shall be taken into consideration. The first hypothesis of this chapter is that a number of legal institutions, procedures and doctrines have primary functions which are not explicitly related to the system of the separation of powers, but which have a significant (secondary) impact on the relations of state organs, especially on the room for manoeuvring of the majoritarian political power. Certain factors can limit the sphere of action of state organs, especially the majoritarian political power. Such factors include: tools of direct democracy (e.g. citizens' initiatives, referenda initiated by a minority); internal limits of the legislative power (e.g. open debate, supermajority requirements); the application of certain doctrines developed in constitutional interpretation (e.g. informal constitutional amendments, the basic structure doctrine); judicial enforcement of political rights (e.g. the right to vote, the freedom of expression, the freedom of assembly); as well as certain norms of and actions performed under international legal orders (e.g. dispute resolution before international fora). If we accept the limitation of the exercise of the central (majoritarian) political power as the basic function of the doctrine, these effects can be taken into consideration within the

---

[2] E. Carolan, *The New Separation of Powers. A Theory for the Modern State*, Oxford University Press, Oxford and New York 2009, p. 18.

complex frame of the separation of powers as control mechanisms – as 'invisible checks and balances'. Therefore, as the secondary effects of these legal institutions, procedures and doctrines can be interrelated, which can also be conceptualised as an 'invisible layer' of the system of separation of powers. Of course, the central political power can react to the limiting effect of these institutions: counteractions are not necessary, but they are likely to occur.

According to the second hypothesis of this chapter, the secondary effect of these legal institutions, procedures and doctrines on the limitation of the central political power could be more significant in countries where the state practice – based on the classic constitutional principles (including the separation of powers) – has no long-standing tradition. Moreover, in times of constitutional or governmental crises, these effects could be even more powerful. In other words, if the core components of the system of the separated powers – formal checks and balances – do not function properly, it is worth examining whether other legal tools could play a role in limiting the central political power.

What is the benefit of the conceptualisation of the 'invisible separation of powers'? First, taking into consideration this 'invisible side' of the system of the separation of powers supports the more accurate analysis of the state of separated powers in a given country, which can lead to more precise findings. Second, it offers a fresh perspective for the detailed comparison of certain legal institutions in the practice of given countries. Third, the exercise of certain political rights and competences of state organs can attain more weight in light of their effects on the central majoritarian political power – an aspect which can be taken into consideration in daily practice.

2. THEORY AND PRACTICE

The literature on the doctrine of separation of powers is immense, with contributions from a number of brilliant authors. In this chapter, I do not intend to analyse in detail the classic concepts of the doctrine, its critiques or its alternative interpretations. Instead, I aim to clarify the function of the separation of powers as a common basis of the old and new theories. Then, I will briefly summarise some alternative interpretations of the doctrine to demonstrate that the separation of powers can function as a broad frame of interpretation and a frame for the invisible layer of the separation of powers, as well.

Those legal institutions, procedures and doctrines which can be evaluated within this frame have also been extensively analysed in legal literature and have been the subjects of productive debates. This chapter does not focus on the details of these debates, but rather, it intends to highlight those functions of the legal institutions in question which could have an effect on the room for manoeuvring of the central political power. These theoretical aspects of the research hypotheses will be discussed in the first part of the chapter.

In the second part of the chapter, short case studies illustrate some practical aspects of the concept. The cases will be selected from three countries: Hungary, the Republic of Moldova and Romania. Every country fits the second hypothesis, that is, of not having a long-standing tradition of functioning based on the principle of the separation of powers. Moreover, these countries have experienced various governmental and constitutional crises in recent decades – a circumstance which could strengthen the secondary effect of the examined legal institutions. Every case study focuses on a different legal institution (doctrine) which has some remarkable specialities in the given legal system.

The concluding part of the chapter briefly evaluates the case studies in light of the previously discussed theoretical questions and assumptions. Based on these, the concept of the invisible separation of powers can be clarified, alongside the conditions related to further research.

3. THE SEPARATION OF POWERS AS A COMPLEX SYSTEM

Taking the classic principle of the separation of powers as a broad frame of interpretation is not new in constitutional scholarship. The antique concepts of mixed government, the early idea of the functional separation of powers, the writings of Locke and the theory of Montesquieu and its influence on the 'architects' of the American and French revolutions all have contributed to our knowledge in this regard.[3]

M.J.C. Vile's attempt to describe the particularities of the 'pure doctrine' have received the most attention in contemporary constitutional scholarship. According to him, the doctrine has three elements: the

---

[3] For a detailed analysis of the development of the idea, see: J.S. Martinez, 'Horizontal Structuring' in M. Rosenfeld and A. Sajó (eds), *The Oxford Handbook of Comparative Constitutional Law*, Oxford University Press, Oxford and New York 2012, pp. 548–52.

'separation of agencies' (separation of branches) – namely, establishing 'autonomous centres of power' that are capable to develop an 'institutional interest'; the distinction between the three specific functions of government (legislative, executive and judicial functions); and the separation of persons ('the three branches of government shall be composed of quite separate and distinct groups of people, with no overlapping membership').[4] Vile himself depicted the pure doctrine as 'an ideal for an extreme separation of powers', capable of various modifications.[5] Accordingly, his approach has served as a point of reference for critiques and for alternative analyses of the doctrine.

Some scholars argue that the pure doctrine is not sufficiently precise to describe the functioning of the present governmental systems (i.e. the relations of state organs form a more diverse and sophisticated picture). Giovanni Bognetti argues that the global creation of a contemporary 'interventionist' state calls for a new, social model of the separation (division) of powers. According to this model, five fundamental functions of the state can be separated: the governing power; the legislature; the public administration; the judiciary; and the court, 'that is the ultimate guardian of the constitutions'.[6] Bognetti considers that the governing power – which is political in its nature – has to be strong, efficient and personified.

Eoin Carolan builds up his analysis on the basis of the 'tripartite theory' and emphasises the difference between the formal and the functionalist approaches to the doctrine.[7] He clearly demonstrates that neither the formal nor the functionalist approaches clarify the aim supported by the separation of powers, while different state organs can follow different aims in this regard.[8] According to him, the 'tripartite theory' cannot describe precisely the functioning of contemporary (administrative) states. Carolan suggests a focus on the autonomy and participation of citizens and their role in building up legitimacy for the exercise of power of state organs. In his view, the different state organs (governmental branches) shall support different interests of the citizens.[9]

Christoph Möllers is critical of the classic and contemporary analyses of the separation of powers, as in the majority of these cases, the concept

---

4 Vile, above n. 1. pp. 17–18.
5 *Ibid.*, p. 21.
6 G. Bognetti, *Dividing Powers. A Theory of the Separation of Powers* (A. Baraggia and L.P. Vanoni, English eds; K. Bailey trans), Wolters Kluwer Cedam, Milan 2017, pp. 3, 26.
7 Carolan, above n. 2, pp. 22, 25.
8 *Ibid.*, p. 38.
9 *Ibid.*, pp. 127–36.

is underdeveloped, or too much attention is given to the position of one particular branch of government. Similarly to Carolan, Möllers suggests a focus on the legitimacy of state power.[10] In his view, democratic states shall recognise and protect both the individual and the democratic (communal) autonomy, as the expression of these is the source of legitimacy. The activity of the legislative branch is related to democratic autonomy, and the judiciary is linked to individual autonomy, while the executive branch plays a kind of a mediation role between these prongs.[11]

Jeremy Waldron calls to our attention the fact that 'the separation of powers does not operate alone as a canonical principle of constitutionalism'.[12] By referring to the United States (US) constitutional system, he claims that the separation of powers is composed of a set of principles: the separation of functions of government; the division of power in order to prevent the concentration of too much political power; and checks and balances and bicameralism and federalism.[13] Waldron also emphasises an interesting correlation between the separation of powers and the rule of law principle. According to him, the rule of law requires all government actions to be articulated in stages which 'offer multiple points of access, participation, and internalization'.[14] Functions of government, namely, law-making at the general level, actions of government based on the authorisation of the law and the adjudication in individual cases are all parts of this processes – which is why the functioning of the rule of law principle requires the separation of powers.[15]

Aileen Kavanagh emphasises that the classic 'one branch – one function' approach is heavily problematic, as every governmental branch exercises to some extent functions which belong to other branches. She differentiates between the 'positive' and the 'negative' side of the separation of powers, as the former relates to the creation of constitutional organs, while the latter aims for the prevention of the abuse of power.[16] Kavanagh argues for a reconstructed view of the pure doctrine, which recognises that the

---

10 C. Möllers, *The Three Branches: A Comparative Model of Separation of Powers*, Oxford University Press, Oxford and New York 2013, p. 13.

11 *Ibid.*, pp. 80–106.

12 J. Waldron, 'Separation of Powers in Thought and Practice' (2013) 54 *British Columba Law Review* 2, 438.

13 *Ibid.*, 438.

14 *Ibid.*, 458.

15 *Ibid.*, 459–66.

16 A. Kavanagh, 'The Constitutional Separation of Powers' in D. Dyzenhaus and M. Thorburn (eds), *Philosophical Foundations of Constitutional Law*, Oxford University Press, Oxford and New York, 2016, pp. 230–34.

branches of government 'are independent from one another, [but] they are also interdependent in various, subtle ways'; therefore, 'the branches must take account of each other's actions and work together in partnership'.[17]

Every approach to the principle of the separation of powers highlighted above refers to selected aspects which have special relevance in the relations and activities of state organs. None of these various aspects are exclusive, and the significance of these depends on the particularities of the legal dispute in question. Moreover, many of these aspects can be jointly taken into consideration. As a consequence, it is more appropriate to depart from the pure doctrine, as well as from its alternatives to some extent, and take the concept of the separation of powers as a complex system which has different dimensions, levels and layers (e.g. cooperation, legitimacy) and which is interdependent of other principles (e.g. the doctrine as a set of principles, its relation with the rule of law).

There is another relevant aspect which is rarely discussed in scholar works: the function of the doctrine itself. The classic (Montesquian) and simplified understanding of the function of the doctrine can be summarised as 'a bulwark against the abuse of state power and the threat of tyranny'.[18] If one considers the constitutional values to protect when preventing tyranny, in classic interpretations, two interrelated principles come to light: 'limited government' and 'individual liberty'.[19] However, the picture can be even more diverse. Alongside the prevention of tyranny, Carolan points to other aims that can be served by the doctrine: securing a balance between institutions; ensuring that law is made in the public interest; enhancing efficiency; preventing partiality and self-interest; ensuring objectivity and generality in the creation of laws; and allowing elected officials to supervise the actions of executive officials. Moreover, that there can be an overlap between these objectives, and the individual's support of these always depends on personal perceptions and preferences.[20] However, all these additional aims – together with the general purpose of the prevention of tyranny and the underlying constitutional values of limited government and individual liberty – are related to the exercise of the political power. This particularity deserves special attention.

The difference between motivations which determine the activity of political branches and the judicial branch ('the least dangerous branch')

---

17 *Ibid.*, pp. 235, 237.
18 Kavanagh, above n. 16, p. 221.
19 Vile, above n. 1, pp. 12, 15.
20 Carolan, above n. 2, pp. 27–28, 128–36.

is widely accepted in legal scholarship.[21] In a very similar vein, Carolan reminds us that in reality, there is a separation between the judiciary and the 'political organs'.[22] Möllers describes the separation of powers principle as an instrument of constituting and restraining political power.[23] Waldron is more straightforward when stating that the division of powers (as an element of the set of principles which constitute the separation of powers) is needed to avoid 'excessive concentrations of political power'.[24] In this regard, Waldron also refers to the ability of people 'to confront political power in a differentiated way'.[25] All these arguments – alongside the specific aims associated with the doctrine – support the conclusion that controlling and limiting political power (especially majoritarian, central political power) is a core particularity of the separation of powers.

At this point, it is worth focusing on the first hypothesis of this chapter. Certain legal institutions, procedures and doctrines, which are not part of the classic frame of the separation of agencies, functions and persons, could similarly support the aforementioned core particularity of the doctrine (limiting central political power). If the separation of powers is considered as a complex system, these legal institutions, procedures and doctrines can also affect its proper functioning.

In the next section, I briefly focus on the particularities of three institutions (doctrines) which could limit the room for manoeuvring of the central political power and which are included in the case studies to be discussed in the latter half of this chapter: informal constitutional amendments; unconstitutional constitutional amendments; and national referenda.

3.1. INFORMAL CONSTITUTIONAL AMENDMENTS

Informal constitutional amendments are related to the general term of constitutional change; however, their meaning can be identified more precisely: the change of the meaning of a constitution as a result of a

---

21 See A. Bickel: *The least dangerous branch: the Supreme Court at the bar of politics*, Yale University Press, New Haven 1986.
22 Carolan, above n. 2, p. 26.
23 Möllers, above n. 10, p. 10.
24 Waldron, above n. 12, p. 433.
25 *Ibid.*, p. 466.

non-formal procedure.[26] In the majority of cases, this occurs by way judicial interpretation of fora (constitutional courts or supreme courts) which can issue authentic interpretations of the constitution.

Xenophon Contiades and Alkmene Fotiadu call our attention to the diversity of the possible interactions between the judicial forum entitled to issue authentic interpretations and the constitution-amending power: namely, the court can amend informally the text of the constitution on its own, however, it often happens that the court only signals the possible new meaning of the constitution, which leads to the formal amendment of the document, due to the cooperative action of the constitution-amending power. It also can happen that the constitution-amending power counteracts the interpretation of the court by way of over-constitutionalisation.[27] Moreover, it is not only the constitutional court or the supreme courts which can pass informal constitutional amendments; instead, the legislative and the executive powers can do so, as well (by building up a practice which is in contradiction with the provisions of the constitution).

Those informal constitutional amendments can be considered as part of the 'invisible layer' of the system of separation of powers, which are linked to a non-political organ (in most of the cases, the constitutional court or the supreme court), which is not authorised to enact formal amendments to the constitution. In that case, an informal constitutional amendment can have the function of limiting the room for manoeuvre of the formal constitution-amending power (a political power).

3.2. UNCONSTITUTIONAL CONSTITUTIONAL AMENDMENTS

The doctrine of unconstitutional constitutional amendments[28] is developing increasing amounts of influence in jurisdictions around the world.[29] The term seemingly refers to a paradox; however, if one

[26] See R. Albert, 'How Unwritten Norms Change Written Constitutions' (2015) 38 *Dublin University Law Journal* 2, 389.

[27] X. Contiades and A. Fontiadou, 'Models of Constitutional Change' in X. Contiades (ed.), *Engineering Constitutional Change. A Comparative Perspective on Europe, Canada and the USA*, Routledge, London and New York 2013, pp. 423–24.

[28] See K. Gözler, *Judicial Review of Constitutional Amendments*, Ekin Press, Bursa 2008.

[29] For a recent overview in the countries of Europe see: M. Hein: 'Do Constitutional Entrenchment Clauses Matter? Constitutional Review of Constitutional Amendments in Europe' (2020) 18 *International Journal of Constitutional Law* 1, 78–110.

differentiates between the constituent power and the constitution-amending power as a constituted power, the substantive examination of a constitutional amendment can take place. In those countries where the constitution includes an eternity clause, such an examination can have a strong textual basis.[30] However, even in the case of eternity clauses, the standard of review shall be clarified.

Yaniv Roznai offers significant arguments related to this debate in his monograph.[31] Roznai differentiates between primary (constituent) and secondary (constitution-amending) powers[32] – the latter being a *sui generis* power which has certain explicit and implicit limits. The implicit limits can be described by foundational structuralism, a concept which is close to the basic structure doctrine.[33] Based on these limits, the judicial review of constitutional amendments can be justified, on different grounds: the separation of powers; the core function of judicial activity; the primacy of the constitution; and the possible failures of political decision-making processes. As for the separation of powers argument, Roznai highlights its vertical dimension, based on the difference in the hierarchical status of the primary and secondary powers.[34]

Based on the above arguments, the judicial review on constitutional amendments can be analysed within the complex frame of the separation of powers. In such cases, the judicial forum can act as counterbalance against the excessive use of power by the secondary (constitution-amending) power.

3.3. NATIONAL REFERENDA

Classic constitutional theory does not refer to referendum as a prerequisite for the constitutional and democratic functioning of the state. While this instrument is used quite frequently in constitutional democracies,[35] there

---

30 Aharon Barak is of the opinion that eternal clauses do not play a key role in this regard. See: A. Barak, 'Unconstitutional Constitutional Amendments' (2011) 44 *Israeli Law Review*, 322.

31 Y. Roznai, *Unconstitional Constitutional Amendments. The Limits if Amendment Powers*, Oxford University Press, Oxford and New York 2017.

32 Roznai, above n. 31, p. 11.

33 Roznai, above n. 31, pp. 141–44.

34 *Ibid.*, n. 30, pp. 180–86.

35 See L. Morel, 'Referendum' in M. Rosenfeld and A. Sajó (eds), *The Oxford Handbook of Comparative Constitutional Law*, Oxford University Press, Oxford and New York 2012, p. 521.

are also countries with remarkable constitutional history and practice where referenda are not available to the citizens.[36]

National referenda can be classified based on many aspects. The most important of these is the subject who initiates the direct decision-making process of the people. From this perspective, Silvano Moeckli differentiates between the notions of minority direct democracy and plebiscitary direct democracy. When exercising minority direct democracy, citizens or a minority group of members of parliament can pose a question to the political community against the will of the majority. On the contrary, when exercising plebiscitary direct democracy, the political majority organises a referendum in a question on which it could otherwise reach a final decision on its own.[37]

This distinction has special relevance from the perspective of the separation of powers: minority direct democracy (national referenda initiated by a political minority) can be considered as a direct counterbalance against the central majoritarian political power. On the other hand, pure manifestations of plebiscitary direct democracy (majoritarian initiatives of national referenda) can hardly have such a limiting effect. On the contrary, manifestations of plebiscitary direct democracy often strengthens the position of the central political power. Moreover, there also can be national referenda which are manifestations of conflicts between state organs or governmental branches (e.g. the recall of elected office-holders), which also fit into the concept of invisible separation of powers.

4. CASE STUDIES

Three Central and Eastern European countries – Hungary, Moldova and Romania – offer illustrative, but different examples of the functioning of the above described legal institutions within the complex system of the separation of powers.

---

36 According to the database of the International Institute for Democracy and Electoral Assistance (IDEA), 64% of 188 countries use optional referendums at national level. See International Institute for Democracy and Electoral Assistance, *Optional Referendum in the World*, 17.08.2015, http://www.idea.int/news-media/media/optional-referendum-world, last accessed 08.12.2020.

37 See S. Moeckli, 'Direct democracy and political participation from a cross-national perspective' in T. Zittel and D. Fuchs (eds), *Participatory Democracy and Political Participation: Can Participatory Engineering Bring Citizens Back In?* Routledge, Abingdon 2007, p. 107.

Each country began to function as a rule-of-law-based constitutional democracy after the 1989 transition period,[38] and therefore, building up the constitutional system based on the separation of powers was a new project. Accordingly, it is worthwhile to examine these countries, taking into consideration the second hypothesis of this chapter: institutions of the 'invisible' layer of the separation of powers could have stronger effects when institutional checks and balances are not stable.

The governmental structure of these countries is different from each other and seemingly has not changed in the past 30 years. Based on historical traditions and on the regulation of the Federal Republic of Germany as a model, the Hungarian governmental system was built up as a parliamentary democracy, with a stable government and the prime minister as the key figure (so called 'chancellor democracy'). The governmental structure of the Republic of Moldova followed the new governmental structures of its neighbouring countries (Romania, Russia, Ukraine), the semi-presidential system. In Romania, the newly constructed semi-presidential system followed the model of the Fifth French Republic.

However, the governmental structures cannot be considered as unchanged in the recent history of these countries. In Hungary, the 1989 revision of the constitution introduced the British type of parliamentarism,[39] which was later (in 1990) substituted by the German model of chancellor democracy.[40] The first period of this governmental structure was marked by intensive debates between the president (the head of the state) and the prime minister, as both claimed control of the executive power.[41] The new constitution, the Fundamental Law (2011), did not change this governmental structure; however, the position of the government became stronger. In the Republic of Moldova, after introducing the semi-presidential governmental system, a national referendum was organised in 1999 on the possibility of having a presidential governmental system, while a 2000 amendment to the constitution took an opposite direction and introduced a parliamentary system of government.[42] As this

---

38 In the Republic of Moldova, this period is also the beginning of the sovereign statehood, as previously the country was part of the Soviet Union.

39 Act XXXI of 1989 on the Amendment to the Constitution.

40 Introduced by Act XL of 1990 on the Amendment to the Constitution.

41 For an overview of the first period of the Hungarian constitutional democracy, see L. Sólyom, 'The Hungarian Constitutional Court and Social Change' (1994) 19 *Yale Law Journal* 1.

42 For an overview of the development of the Moldovan Constitutional system, see: V. Puscas, 'Dezvoltarea constitutionala a Republicii Moldova. 20 de ani de la adoptarea Constiutiei' (2014) *Revista Institutului National al Justitiei* 2.

system proved to be unstable, the Constitutional Court later annulled the respective amendment to the constitution (2016), and therefore, since then, the governmental system can again be described as semi-presidential. Romanian politics is marked by frequent cohabitation periods (2005–8, 2012–14, 2017–19), with alternating conflicting and cooperation periods between the directly elected president (the head of the state) and the prime minister, supported by the parliamentary majority.[43] Therefore, in practice, in Romania there are shifts from semi-presidential to parliamentary governmental systems, and vice versa.

As a consequence, it can be argued that the relative permanency of these governmental systems is combined with periods of instability. Governmental and constitutional crises have also occurred in these countries in the past 30 years.

In the case of Hungary, the first and longest-lasting crisis is linked to 2006. After the parliamentary elections, the newly re-elected prime minister gave a speech to his fellow members of parliament (MPs; members of the faction of the governing party) in a closed meeting. In his speech, the prime minister declared that the government lied in the campaign related to the budgetary data, which is why he claimed the support of fellow MPs for the prospective and inevitable austerity measures. The speech was recorded, leaked and caused long-lasting protests and riots. As a consequence, public support for and trust in governmental institutions was lost, and some governmental institutions could even not function properly in the absence of elected leaders. This crisis lasted until the *de facto* resignation (formally a motion of no confidence) of the prime minister (2009).[44]

The second constitutional crisis in Hungary relates the unilateral enactment of the Fundamental Law by the governing majority (2011), as well as the previous legislative steps intended to change the composition and competence of the Constitutional Court to end the mandate of leaders of independent state organs (e.g. Supreme Court, ombudsman, etc.). The conflict between the government, parliamentary majority and independent state organs – which also invited the attention of international fora – formally ended with the enactment of the Fourth Amendment to the Fundamental Law, which over-constitutionalised some of the former

43 For an overview, see: B. Dima, 'The European models of semi-presidentialism: the peculiarity of Romania's post-communist system of government' (2014) *Romanian Journal of Comparative Law* 1.

44 See E. Palonen, 'Transition to Crisis in Hungary: Whistle-Blowing on the Naked Emperor' (2012) 40 *Policy & Politics* 5, 928–954.

decisions of the Constitutional Court, which had been subjects of former debates.[45]

In the recent history of the Republic of Moldova, two constitutional crises can be mentioned. In the period between 2000–10, as a result of the constitutional amendment which introduced the parliamentary form of government and the indirect election of the president, in the absence of the required majority, the legislature could not elect a president for more terms. As a consequence, interim presidents were in office for longer periods, while Parliament was dissolved and early elections were called (2000, 2009, 2010).[46] In 2019, a long-lasting political, governmental crisis (in which the parties in the newly elected parliament were not able to form a coalition) transformed into a one-week constitutional crisis. During this week, the Constitutional Court suspended the president from office, the interim president dissolved the Parliament and two governments were formed at the same time. Finally, due to international diplomatic measures, the newly formed government, the formerly suspended president and the Parliament remained in office, while all members of the Constitutional Courts resigned.[47]

As mentioned earlier, Romanian politics has been heavily marked by conflicts related to cohabitation periods in the previous 30 years. One of the longest-lasting political and governmental crises, the 2012–14 period, can be described as a constitutional crisis as well, as the conflict between the president and the prime minister put the proper functioning of independent state institutions at risk (i.e. the Constitutional Court, the ombudsperson and several judicial organs).[48] In this period, the president was suspended from office by the parliamentary majority, while the related national referendum on his recall was not valid, as the participation of citizens did not reach the required quorum. At a certain point, the president and the prime minister entered into a private contract in which

---

45 See European Commission for Democracy through Law (Venice Commission), *'Opinion on the Fourth Amendment to the Fundamental Law of Hungary'* Opinion 720/2013 (2013).

46 See Decision 7 of 2016 of the Constitutional Court of Moldova, 04.03.2016.

47 See Z. Pozsár-Szentmiklósy, 'The hyper-judicialisation of politics of Moldova: Opportunities for constitutional reform', *constitutionnet.org*, http://constitutionnet.org/news/hyper-judicialisation-politics-moldova-opportunities-constitutional-reform, last accessed 23.06.2020.

48 See B. Iancu, 'Separation of Powers and the Rule of Law in Romania: the Crisis in Concepts and Contexts' in A. von Bogdandy and P. Sonnevend (eds), *Constitutional Crisis in the European Constitutional Area. Theory, Law and Politics in Hungary and Romania*, Hart Publishing, Oxford 2015.

they mutually interpreted the competences of the two offices related to the exercise of the executive power.

Those legal institutions which – according to the above-described first hypothesis – can be considered as part of the 'invisible layer' of the complex system of separation of powers, are present in these countries and are related to considerable practice. It is worth mentioning that the regulation on direct democracy (especially national referenda), and the concepts which function as safeguards against the abuse of the constitution-amending power (i.e. informal constitutional amendments, unconstitutional constitutional amendments) are unique in these countries, at least from certain perspectives.

In Hungary, the national referendum plays no role in the constitution-making or constitution-amending processes. Moreover, the Fundamental Law itself prohibits organising national referenda in topics which are subjects of regulation of the constitution.[49] Both in Moldova and Romania, the constitution prescribes that draft constitutional amendments have to be submitted to Parliament together with the preliminary opinion of the Constitutional Court.[50] It is also unique that in both Moldova and Romania, the impeachment procedure of the president is followed by a national referendum (recall).[51] Contrary to the constitutions of Moldova and Romania, the Hungarian Fundamental Law does not contain any eternity clause, but the Constitutional Court has explicit authorisation for the procedural review of constitutional amendments.[52]

In the following case studies, the practice related to the legal institutions (doctrines) examined is not compared in the case of the three countries. The case studies rather function as three distinct illustrations of the research hypotheses.

4.1. INFORMAL CONSTITUTIONAL AMENDMENTS IN HUNGARY

In Hungary, the transition from the state-socialist period to constitutional democracy was marked by peaceful negotiations at the so-called

49 Fundamental Law of Hungary, Article 8, para. (3), a.
50 Constitution of the Republic of Moldova, Article 141, para. (2); Constitution of Romania, Article 146, a.
51 Constitution of the Republic of Moldova, Article 89, para. (3); Constitution of Romania, Article 95, para. (3).
52 Fundamental Law of Hungary, Article 24, para. (5).

'National Roundtable', where the Hungarian Worker's Socialist Party (the state party), the opposition political movements and civic organisations[53] were present. The minimal intention of the members of the roundtable was to reach a compromise in the conditions of organising free elections, while their decisions were formally enacted by the (one-party) Parliament.[54] However, as a result of the roundtable discussions, the formal, comprehensive amendment to the 1949 Constitution, which entered into force on 23 October 1989, produced a new constitutional system, which was in line with the basic constitutional principles. After the first free elections (Spring 1990) and the consecutive elections, for various reasons, none of the elected National Assemblies created a new constitution; therefore, the provisional '1989 Constitution' was in force for 21 years.

The Fundamental Law – the new constitution of Hungary – was enacted in 2011 and entered into force on 1 January 2012. In the National Assembly elected in 2010, the governing Fidesz-KDNP coalition[55] had a two-thirds majority. The Fundamental Law was enacted with the unilateral votes of representatives of the governing parties, according to the procedure prescribed in the 1989 Constitution, which required the two-thirds majority support of all MPs.[56] The provisions of the Fundamental Law related to constitutional amendments were identical to those of the 1989 Constitution. Neither the 1989 Constitution nor the 2011 Fundamental Law contained eternity clauses, while the amendment procedure required the support of the two-thirds majority of all MPs.[57] As a consequence, it can be argued that both constitutions were relatively unstable and were easy to amend.

In the absence of eternity clauses as textual bases, the doctrine of unconstitutional constitutional amendment was not explicitly present in the jurisdiction of the Hungarian Constitutional Court. However, the Court expressed its opinion on this theoretical problem several times: according to its general approach, supported until 2010, the amendment to the constitution cannot be reviewed after becoming part of it.[58]

---

53 The majority of these had strong relations with the state party; however, the organisations did not play a significant role in the transition process.

54 For a detailed analysis, see: A. Bozóki, *The Roundtable Talks of 1989. The Genesys of Hungarian Democracy*, CEU Press, Budapest 2002.

55 'Alliance of Free Democrats' (Fidesz) and 'Christian Democratic Party' (KDNP).

56 Constitution of the Republic of Hungary (1989), Article 24, para. (3).

57 Fundamental Law of Hungary, Article S, para. (2).

58 Explained for the first time in Resolution 293/B/1994. The first president of the Constitutional Court (1990–99), later president (head of the state, 2005–10)

On the other hand, informal constitutional amendments – even not explicitly – were present in the practice of the Hungarian Constitutional Court. Since the beginning of its functioning (1990), the Court interpreted the constitution in such a way which altered its meaning in nine cases all together. These interpretations were often tacitly accepted by the legislature and by the constitutional amendment power (the National Assembly in its capacity to amend the Constitution with two-thirds majority votes of its members); in other cases, the constitutional amendment power reacted with over-constitutionalisation. There are also, however, examples of the formal inclusion of these interpretations into text of the constitution.[59]

The case of the Transitory Provisions to the Fundamental Law (2011) is an illustrative example both of the problem of unconstitutional constitutional amendments and informal constitutional amendments. As the former doctrine is not accepted by the majority of scholars or the Constitutional Court itself, this case will be presented below from the perspective of informal constitutional amendments.

The Fundamental Law, which was proclaimed on 25 April 2011, contained a provision which prescribed that the transitory provisions related to it have to be enacted in a separate legal act, in a procedure which is identical to the enactment of the Fundamental Law itself.[60] The National Assembly enacted the Transitory Provisions on 31 December 2011. This legal act declared itself to be part of the Fundamental Law, while the constitution did not clarify the legal status of the Transitory Provisions. It is important to note that this document led to intensive political debates for two reasons: it contained political declarations which strengthened the politically exclusive, unilateral nature of the Fundamental Law, as well as provisions which over-constitutionalised the former decisions of the Constitutional Court. Soon after its enactment, the ombudsman turned to the Constitutional Court, initiating the posterior norm control of the Transitory Provisions.

The principle of separation of powers was mentioned in the motion of the ombudsman, as well. According to this argument, when the legislature

---

expressed that in his opinion the above approach does not exclude the examination of constitutional amendments from the procedural perspective, as in the absence of the appropriate procedure, an amendment cannot be considered as part of the constitution. See: L. Sólyom, *Az alkotmánybíráskodás kezdetei Magyarországon*, Osiris, Budapest 2001, p. 277.

59 For a detailed analysis, see: T. Drinóczi, F. Gárdos-Orosz and Z. Pozsár-Szentmiklósy, 'Formal and Informal Constitutional Amendment in Hungary' (2019) MTA Law Working Papers 18.

60 The Fundamental Law of Hungary (25 April 2011), Closing provisions, 3.

includes in the Transitory Provisions a piece of legislation which was previously found unconstitutional by the Constitutional Court, it weakens the proper functioning of constitutional adjudication and the separation of powers.

In the reasoning of its decision,[61] the Constitutional Court emphasised the requirement of the 'unity of the constitution' as a new constitutional concept. As this concept can function as a normative requirement related to the text of the constitution, it can be considered as an informal constitutional amendment. According to this concept, all norms of constitutional rank shall be included in a single written legal document.[62] Moreover, the constitution can only contain provisions which are connected to its function. As a consequence, the Transitory Provisions, which contain norms of a transitory nature as well as other norms, cannot be considered as part of the Fundamental Law. The Constitutional Court declared the provisions included in this legal act unconstitutional, with retroactive effect. It is worth noting that the majority opinion of the decision did not refer explicitly to the principle of the separation of powers or the theoretical difference between the constituting power and the constitution-amending power.

From the perspective of the functioning of the invisible separation of powers, it also important to refer to the following interactions between the constitution-amending power and the Constitutional Court, in relation to this case.

One of the main arguments the ombudsman expressed in his motion was the uncertain legal position of the Transitory Provisions: its 'self-legitimising' nature. During the time when the Constitutional Court examined the case, the National Assembly – with the intention of weakening the argument expressed in the motion of the ombudsman – in the First Amendment to the Fundamental Law (18 June 2012) supplemented the text of the Fundamental Law by declaring explicitly that the Transitory Provisions are part of it.

The Fourth Amendment to the Fundamental Law (25 March 2013), enacted after the publishing of the decision of the Constitutional Court,

---

61 Decision 45/2012. (XII. 29.) CC.

62 In his critical analysis on the decision, Zoltán Szente calls attention to the fact that in the case of many constitutional democracies, the written constitution is not included in a single document, rather, in more constitutional letters. See: Z. Szente, '*Az Alkotmánybíróság döntése Magyarország Alaptörvényének Átmeneti rendelkezései alkotmányosságáról. Az Alaptörvény integritása és az alkotmányozó hatalom korlátai*' (2013) JeMa 2 p. 17.

was a more direct reaction to this case. With this amendment, the National Assembly incorporated into the text of the Fundamental Law those provisions of the Transitory Provisions which were declared unconstitutional by the Constitutional Court. Ironically, the reasoning of the draft legislative proposal expressed that the National Assembly included all provisions of the Transitory Provisions to the Fundamental Law with the aim to comply with the requirements expressed by the Court. Moreover, the Fourth Amendment contained a new provision which can also be considered as a reaction to the decision of the Court. According to this provision, the Constitutional Court can review the fulfilment of procedural requirements related to the enactment of constitutional amendments, but only in the form of *ex ante* (preliminary) review, or within a short deadline after enactment. The wording of the provision in question excludes the possibility of substantive review of constitutional amendments.[63]

Alongside the above-expressed reactions to the decision of the Constitutional Court, the Fourth Amendment contained a rather symbolic and more general pressure on the Constitutional Court: all decisions of the Court which were published before the entering into force of the Fundamental Law were repealed.[64]

As a consequence, the informal constitutional amendment of the Constitutional Court (i.e. the requirement of the unity of the constitution) can be considered as part of the complex system of the separation of powers (belonging to its invisible layer) for the following reasons: (a) the legal question at its basis (the enactment and legal nature of the Transitory Provisions) is explicitly related to the functioning of the separation of powers (as mentioned in the ombudsman's motion); (b) the informal constitutional amendment limited the room for manoeuvre of the central political power (by setting the requirement of the unity of the constitution against its actions); (c) the decision of the Court lead to the counter-action of the constitution-amending power (initially by the enactment of the First Amendment, which created the constitutional basis for the Transitory Provisions); and lastly, (d) as an extreme counter-action, by the enactment of the Fourth Amendment, the constitutional-amending power nullified the limiting effect of the decision of the Constitutional Court and even modified its capacity to control the constitution-amending power.

---

63 'The Constitutional Court may review the Fundamental Law or the amendment of the Fundamental Law only in relation to the procedural requirements laid down in the Fundamental Law for making and promulgating it.' Fundamental Law of Hungary, Article 24, para. (5).

64 Fundamental Law of Hungary, Closing and miscellaneous provisions 5.

As a result, the position of the central political power was significantly strengthened, and the effect of informal constitutional amendments as part of the invisible checks and balances was neutralised.

4.2. UNCONSTITUTIONAL CONSTITUTIONAL AMENDMENTS IN MOLDOVA

The Republic of Moldova became an independent country after the collapse of the Soviet Union. The period of modern statehood officially began with the adoption of the Declaration of Independence by the Parliament of Moldova on 27 August 1991. The country's new constitution was adopted on 28 July 1994.

The Constitution prescribes: (a) substantive; (b) procedural; and (c) temporal constraints related to constitutional amendments. Similar to eternity clauses of other constitutions, the Constitution contains – as a substantive constraint – a general prohibition of amendments that infringe on fundamental rights and their safeguards. In the case of amendments that affect the sovereignty, independence and unity of the state, as well as its 'permanent neutrality', a special amendment procedure (different from the regular procedure) is prescribed, namely, a national referendum and the majority vote of the registered voters. As a temporal limit, the proposals for constitutional amendments may be passed six months after their initiation at the earliest and one year after their initiation at the latest.[65]

Taking into consideration the above-presented constraints, the regular procedure for the amendment of the Constitution can be initiated by 200,000 voters, one-third of the members of Parliament or the government. The advisory opinion of the Constitutional Court on the draft amendment is a necessary condition for the submission of the proposal to the Parliament. Constitutional amendments can pass in Parliament with the support of a two-thirds majority of MPs.[66]

Since the beginning of its activity, the Constitutional Court has reviewed draft constitutional amendments in 39 cases (*ex ante*), and the constitution has been amended successfully ten times. In these cases, the Constitutional Court examined procedural and substantive requirements related to constitutional amendments prescribed in the constitution. However, the most influential case related to the doctrine of unconstitutional

---

65 Constitution of the Republic of Moldova, Article 142, para. 2, Article 143, para. 1–2.

66 Constitution of the Republic of Moldova, Article 141, para. 1–2, Article 143, para. 1.

constitutional amendment – presented below – was the singular *ex post* review of a constitutional amendment which resulted in the modification of the text of the Constitution of Moldova.

The case[67] originated with a motion for posterior norm-control, submitted by 18 MPs in 2015. The claim challenged the provisions of the law that amended the Constitution in 2000,[68] which prescribed the election of the president (the head of the state) by a three-fifths majority of MPs. The petitioners based their motion on both formal and substantive arguments: on the one hand, questioning the procedure related to the enactment of the amendment; and on the other hand, arguing that the substance of the amendment is in contradiction with the rule of law principle.

As mentioned above, in the period between the enactment of the amendment to the constitution (2000) and the submission of the motion of MPs for posterior norm control (2015), there thrice occurred a situation in which Parliament failed to elect a president as the required majority was not met. Therefore, the Parliament was dissolved, and early parliamentary elections took place (2000, 2009, 2010). On the whole, this period can be characterised by instability of the political and the governmental system.

In its decision,[69] on the formal ground, the Court declared that it is competent to examine the constitutionality of a law amending the constitution, as the basic law accords it the general competence of reviewing the constitutionality of laws, as well as the specific capacity to deliver its opinion on the initiatives to amend the constitution.

The Court also made an important statement by declaring that 'no amendment of the Constitution shall disturb the harmony of the Constitution or the harmony of values enshrined in the Constitution'.[70] Accordingly, the Court declared that the provisions of the constitution make up a harmonious system. The Court referred to harmony as 'the unity of matter and the balance of values enshrined in the Constitution'.[71]

---

67 Some observations related to this case were made in a paper co-authored with Yaniv Roznai. See: Z. Pozsár-Szentmiklósy and Y. Roznai, 'The Timing of Judicial Review of Constitutional Amendments – Towards a "Time Sensivity Test" Following the Moldovan Constitutional Court's Decision on the Modality of Electing the President' in S. Ranchordás and Y. Roznai (eds), *Time, Law and Change. An Interdisciplinary Study*, Hart, Oxford, London, New York 2019.

68 Law 1115-XIV of 5 July 2000.

69 Decision 7 of 2016 of the Constitutional Court of Moldova, 04.03.2016. (See above n. 46.)

70 *Ibid.*, 75.

71 *Ibid.*, 67.

According to the Court, this unity implies a ban on the adoption of legislative measures (including constitutional amendments) that would lead to conflicts between state organs and cause institutional deadlocks. The Court emphasised that: 'almost all political and institutional stalemates in the Republic of Moldova are related to the modified provisions referring to the procedure to elect the President and the mechanism to dissolve the Parliament'. These provisions lead to 'a rupture' of the constitutional unity as these failed to 'secure the normal functioning of the presidential institute', as the Parliament could not elect compromise candidates, and, accordingly, political and institutional deadlocks occurred.[72]

According to the Court, the harmony of the provisions of the Constitution was also challenged by the fact that – due to the stalemates described above – the Speaker of the Parliament occupied multiple offices when acting as an interim president. Such a situation is in contradiction with the principle of the separation of powers, also taking into consideration that the office of the interim president may be exercised for an unlimited period of time. The Court reached the conclusion of the unconstitutionality of the challenged provisions based on the unbalanced position of constitutional institutions, which includes potential conflicts among them, and can also be described by the 'imperfect system of government' generated by the constitutional reform.[73]

The significance of the decision is twofold: it was the first – and a unique – decision in the constitutional practice of Republic of Moldova when the Constitutional Court exercised *ex post* review of a constitutional amendment. Moreover, the decision is unique from the comparative perspective as well, taking into consideration that the decision on the unconstitutionality of the constitutional amendment was made 16 years after its enactment – a topic worthy of distinct analysis from the perspective of time.[74]

The constitution-amending power did not react directly to the decision of the Constitutional Court for several reasons. The composition of the Parliament was fragmented, and therefore, there was no constitution-amending majority which could stand against the decision of the Court. On the other hand, the major parties had a political interest in ending the period marked by governmental instability, and the direct election of the president also had public support. As a consequence, the

---

72 *Ibid.*, 180, 184, 192.

73 *Ibid.*, 207.

74 See Pozsár-Szentmiklósy and Roznai, above n. 67, pp. 161–65.

text of the constitution was changed according to the decision of the Constitutional Court, and its former provisions on the direct election of the president again came into force. The Parliament also reacted in a cooperative manner, as it formulated an expert committee to produce the draft amendment of the Electoral Code. This draft was also examined by international organisations,[75] and the Parliament later enacted the respective amendment to the Electoral Code.[76]

At this point, some conclusive remarks can be made. First, the major question which was at the basis of the case before the Court was not only related to the governmental structure, but also to the system of the separated powers: state organs did not function in a balanced manner, according to one of the normative requirements of the doctrine. Second, the Constitutional Court extensively limited the room for manoeuvre of the constitution-amending power by declaring its own competence for the *ex post* review of constitutional amendments and by setting the standard of harmony of the provisions of the constitution as a substantive limitation for previous and future amendments. Lastly, the decision of the Court did not lead to counteractions from the central political power; rather, it strengthened institutional stability of the separated powers.

As a result, the position of the central political power was limited, and the doctrine of unconstitutional constitutional amendment as part of invisible checks and balances functioned efficiently.

4.3. NATIONAL REFERENDA IN ROMANIA

The Constitution of Romania, enacted by the Constituent Assembly formed after the transition (21 November 1991), can be considered as a rigid constitution which contains both procedural and substantive limitations related to constitutional amendments.

The amendment to the constitution can be initiated by the president (based on the proposal of the government), by one-fourth of the MPs or senators, as well as by 500,000 citizens. The amendment has to pass both chambers in Parliament (the Senate and the House of Representatives), with a two-thirds majority in each house. If there is no agreement between

75 See European Commission for Democracy through Law (Venice Commission) – Office for Democratic Institutions and Human Rights (OSCE / ODIHE), '*Draft joint opinion on the draft law on changes to the Electoral Code*' Opinion 848/2016 (2016).

76 Act 147 of 2016 on the amendment of the Electoral Code of 1381-XIII of 1997.

the two houses, both houses have to come to a decision in a joint session, with a three-fourths majority. After the parliamentary resolution, the amendment has to be confirmed by a national referendum, as well.[77] In a similar fashion to the Republic of Moldova, the Constitutional Court has a significant role in the amendment process: its preliminary opinion is required for the initiation of the amendment. The Constitutional Court examines the procedural requirements and the substance of the proposed amendment, as well as its compliance with the provisions of the constitution protected by the eternity clause.[78]

The eternity clause of the Constitution sets two types of substantive limitations for constitutional amendments: certain, enumerated constitutional values cannot be subjects of constitutional amendments;[79] and at the general level, there could no amendments which would lead to the suppression of the citizens' fundamental rights and freedoms, or the safeguards thereof.[80]

Since the enactment of the Constitution, only one successful amendment has been enacted – related to the planned integration of the country into the European Union (EU; 2003).[81]

Direct democracy – and especially national referenda – play a significant role in the Romanian constitutional system. As mentioned above, a national referendum is required for the passing of amendments to the constitution. In other cases, the directly elected president (a key figure of the executive power in the Romanian semi-presidential governmental system) can initiate national referenda by way of 'turning to the people in issues of national importance'. Moreover, national referenda can be used in a unique way: if the Parliament suspends (temporarily removes) the president from office, as part of the impeachment procedure, a national referendum has to be organised on the recall of the directly elected President.

In the past 30 years, all forms of national referenda have been exercised: there were two national referenda on amendments to

---

77 Constitution of Romania, Articles 150–51.

78 Constitution of Romania, Article 146. See also B. Selejan-Gutan, 'Informal Constitutional Changes in Romania' (2015) 1 *Romanian Journal of Comparative Law* 35–53.

79 The national, independent, unitary and indivisible character of the Romanian State, the republican form of government, territorial integrity, independence of justice, political pluralism and official language. Constitution of Romania, Article 152, para. (1).

80 Constitution of Romania, Article 152, para. (2).

81 Law 429/2003 on the Amendment to the Constitution.

the Constitution;[82] three on questions of national interest, initiated by the President;[83] and two on the recall of the President.[84] In this section, I will briefly analyse the 2012 national referendum on the recall of the head of the state from the perspective of the separation of powers.

Then-President Traian Basescu was elected by direct popular vote for his second term in 2009. However, in 2012, the government supported by the president's party (the Democratic Liberal Party) was dismissed due to a motion of censure which passed in Parliament. As a consequence, in early May 2012, a new government was formed, led by Victor Ponta, supported by the Social Democratic Party and its allies. This cohabitation period was marked by intensive conflicts between the president and the prime minister, which transformed the political crisis into a constitutional crisis, as the proper functioning of constitutional organs was also at risk.[85] According to the provisions of the constitution, in case of having committed grave acts infringing upon constitutional provisions, the President of Romania may be suspended from office by the Chamber of Deputies and the Senate, in joint sitting.[86] In July 2012, the Parliament made such a decision and turned to the Constitutional Court for its advisory opinion, in accordance with the provisions of the constitution.

The parliamentary resolution on the suspension of the president from office argued that the role the president played in reality in the governmental system was not in accordance with his 'mediation role' prescribed in the constitution, for various reasons: when the former government was in office, the president has announced governmental actions in more cases in the name of the government, in absence of a formal governmental decision; he called on the government to by-pass the Parliament; he heavily criticised judicial decisions; and he also put the Constitutional Court under pressure in his public statements.

In the Constitutional Court's opinion,[87] the first issue (announcing governmental actions in the absence of formal decisions of the government) could be considered as an infringement upon constitutional provisions and therefore as a legitimate cause for suspension from office. The other cases mentioned in the parliamentary resolution were not found to be problematic by the Court.

---

82 18–19.10.2003, 6–7.10.2018.

83 25.11.2007, 22.11.2009, 26.05.2019.

84 19.05.2007, 29.07.2012.

85 See Iancu, above n. 48.

86 Constitution of Romania, Article 95, para. (1).

87 Opinion no. 1 of 6.07.2012 on the suspension from office of President Traian Basescu.

According to the provisions of the constitution, after suspension from office, the national referendum was organised on the recall of the president. However, although the vast majority of the votes were in favour of recalling the president (87.55%), the result was not valid, as only 46.15% of the voters cast valid votes, and the required quorum prescribed in law[88] (participation of the majority of the voters) was not met. As a consequence, the president remained in office. Later in 2012, after the parliamentary elections in December and the formation of the second Ponta Government, the political and constitutional crisis was consolidated to some extent.

It is important to note that the government took legislative actions in order to influence the result of the referendum on the recall. With a special legislative act, an 'urgency decision' made an exception from the general 'quorum requirement' related to national referenda prescribed by law (participation of the majority of the voters on the referendum): according to this legislative act, in the case of recalls, the quorum requirement would not have to be met.[89] The Parliament later confirmed the content of this piece of legislation and added an additional provision, by extending the opening hours of the polling stations.

Based on the motion of a minority group of MPs, the Constitutional Court declared that – according to the principle of people's sovereignty – the will of the people can only be precisely identified if the majority of the voters express their opinion via referendum, and therefore, the exception rule included in the urgency decision is unconstitutional.[90] Accordingly, the exception rule was not applied during this referendum.

In this case, the national referendum had a significant impact on the state of the separation of powers, as well. First, the basic political conflict related to cohabitation has transformed into a deep constitutional crisis; therefore, the balance between the separated powers was threatened. Second, the referendum on the recall (organised after the suspension of the President from office) was a potentially effective measure to limit the room for manoeuvre of one organ of the central political powers (i.e. the president) based on the initiative of another political organ (i.e. the government and the parliamentary majority). Third, this is further highlighted by the fact that legislative steps were taken in order influence

88 Act 2000/3 on the organisation of referenda.

89 Urgency decision no. 41/2012 on the amendment of Act 3/2000 on the organisation of referenda.

90 Decision 731/2012 CC.

the result of the referendum. Lastly, however, a formal institution of the system of institutional checks and balances (the exercise of competence of the Constitutional Court) neutralised that influence.

It is important to add that in this case, direct democracy and the institution of national referendum did not function in its 'pure' form – it was not a tool of minority direct democracy[91] capable of limiting central political (majoritarian) powers in every case. It was rather a manifestation of an 'intra-branch' conflict within the executive power branch. In that regard, the national referendum, as part of the 'invisible checks and balances', played a role in the stabilisation of the state of the separated powers.

5. CONCLUSIONS

In the cases discussed above, the effect of the institutions and doctrines related to the 'invisible layer' of the system of the separation of powers led to different results. In the case of Hungary, the constitution-amending power strengthened its position by neutralising the limiting effect of the informal constitutional amendment of the Constitutional Court. On the contrary, in the case of Moldova, the decision of the Constitutional Court on unconstitutional constitutional amendments successfully limited the room for manoeuvre of the constitution-amending power. In the case of Romania, the national referendum on the recall of the president led to a more balanced relationship of state organs belonging to the executive power. One can add that every case was directly connected to a governmental or constitutional crisis in which the classic checks and balances were insufficient to produce a balanced relationship of the separated powers.

These different experiences illustrate that the effect of those legal institutions, procedures and doctrines which can be considered as part of the 'invisible layer' of the separation of powers is not unilateral. As a result of possible counteractions, the room for manoeuvring of the central political body of power is not limited in every case; rather, it can balance or even strengthen its position. However, the existence of counteractions of the central political power demonstrate that (according to the first hypothesis of this chapter) the examined institutions can operate within the complex frame of the separation of powers. Further research is needed to extend the analysis to the whole practice related to these institutions

91 See Moeckli, above n. 37.

in the selected countries,[92] based on the same methodology. The second hypothesis of the chapter (i.e. the stronger effect of these institutions, procedures and doctrines in countries where the state practice, based on the classic concept of separation of powers, has no long-standing tradition) can be comprehensively verified in the future based on comparative analysis, extending the research to constitutional democracies where the functioning of the principle of separation of powers covers a much longer period.

92 As mentioned above, in the 1990–2020 period, in the practice of the Hungarian Constitutional Court, nine informal constitutional amendments can be identified; in the case of Moldova, the Constitutional Court (alongside the case discussed above) issued preliminary opinions on constitutional amendments in 39 cases, while in Romania, seven national referenda were organised (including the case discussed above). Moreover, every discussed institution and doctrine is present in the practice of all three selected countries, as well as other institutions and procedures which can be considered as part of the 'invisible layer' of the separated powers (e.g. citizens' initiatives, supermajority requirements, judicial enforcement of political rights, norms of and actions performed under international legal orders).

RULE OF LAW vs. DEMOCRACY

With Special Regard to the Case of Hungary

Zoltan J. Toth*

1. INTRODUCTION

The term 'democracy' has essentially two main meanings, or two possible contents, despite the growing inflation of the descriptors attached to it. From among them, the practical importance of 'direct democracy' – deriving from the ancient Hellas – has been gradually declining (even in its official form), and, as a main rule, democracy is present in modern society as 'representative democracy' (wherever it exists at all). However, whichever form is mentioned, it cannot be enforced exclusively, and the need to implement it cannot be absolutised; the majority cannot do everything against the minority members of the political community just because they are more numerous. Enforcing the decisions and the will of

* The present chapter was written and the underlying research was carried out with the support of the Bolyai János Scholarship of the Hungarian Academy of Sciences.

the majority is limited by what is called the requirements of the rule of law; however, the term 'rule of law' is just as diffuse and complex as the term 'democracy' itself.

In fact, the term 'rule of law' has by now become the ace of trumps in political philosophical thinking – besides democracy – and has turned from the subject matter of scientific analysis into a part of the political discourse. Its implementation – or the lack thereof – may serve as the basis for the legal, political and even moral evaluation of a political system. However, it is used so often and for so many things that it takes significant effort to free this term from the non-immanent meanings that have been superposed onto it over recent decades and to separate them from the former meaning. These efforts are made even more difficult by the fact that the content of this phrase is not at all constant – but it gains new and more appropriate meanings, with special regard to substantive considerations beyond the formal aspects. For this reason, it is not possible to pinpoint the contents of this term. The researcher can only try to detect its 'core': the range of meaning without which the rule of law does not exist today.

My main proposition is that democracy and the rule of law (no matter how we define them) are, in fact, not independent of each other; we cannot talk about 'real' political democracy in the absence of certain criteria of the rule of law.

2. MEANINGS OF THE 'RULE OF LAW'

The term 'rule of law' is used by many people today, but it is difficult to clarify its meaning. Like all other 'fashionable' terms, rule of law also becomes devalued, and it is constantly given new meanings (as old ones are sloughed off). It is therefore impossible to accurately define its content (just as it is generally hard to objectively decide on conceptual problems). However, as this term exists and is in frequent use, we should somehow try to define the meaning of the rule of law and explore the eventual differences in the current word usage by ensuring that its meaning is not too wide – that is, there should be a truly specific range of meaning that enables us to talk about it sensibly, distinguishing it from other, similarly diffuse meanings.[1] Below, we attempt to do so.

---

1 Many times, constitutionality is used as a synonym for the rule of law. Accordingly, constitutionality is a requirement towards states in terms of form and content.

Historically, the rule of law[2] (*Rechtsstaat*)[3] meant two basic things. Initially, the term covered the *formal rule of law* at the end of the 18th and into the 19th century. Once the requirements of the Enlightenment became clear, it became a *de facto* necessity for the upcoming nation-states and for the developing capitalist economy to terminate the injustices of absolutism in the given country and to ensure that people can match their actions to the laws (i.e. to the legal expectations). The main requirement

---

In reality, constitutionality is partly a narrower and partly a wider term than the rule of law, and these two expressions should not be exchanged or used as synonyms. The Hungarian public law science divides the criteria for the contents of constitutionality in three major lines. One line says that the 'principles of constitutionality' are: the principle of democracy, the principle of pluralism, the principle of the rule of law and the principle of the separation of powers {cf. L. Trócsányi: 'Grounds' [Alaptanok], pp. 67–75, in L. Trócsányi and B. Schanda (eds), *Introduction into the constitutional law [Bevezetés az alkotmányjogba]*, HVG-ORAC, 2012, pp. 19–75}, according to the other line: 'the requirements of constitutionality' are: the principle of popular sovereignty and popular representation, the principle of separating and balancing the branches of powers, the rule of laws, establishing the state of the rule of law, the principle of equal rights and the declaration of human rights {cf. I. Kukorelli (ed.), *Constitutional theory I. Basic concepts, constitutional institutions [Alkotmánytan I. Alapfogalmak, alkotmányos intézmények]*, Osiris, Budapest 2007, pp. 29–31}; according to the third line, the 'the principles of constitution' are: the principle of state sovereignty, the principle of democracy, the principle of the rule of law (also including the separation of powers and legal security) and the principle of market economy (cf. J. Petrétei, *Hungarian constitutional law I. [Magyar alkotmányjog I.]*, Dialog Campus, 2002. pp. 85–106; basically, the division is the same in the later works of József Petrétei, following the enactment of the Fundamental Law, with the difference that he generally talks about 'the principles of economic order' instead of the principle of market economy, also including other second-generation rights and state purposes in addition to the principle of market economy that are not specified in the Fundamental Law *expressis verbis* but which are actually included implicitly; cf. J. Petrétei, *Hungary's constitutional law I. Grounding, constitutional institutions [Magyarország alkotmányjoga I. Alapvetés, alkotmányos intézmények]*, Kodifikátor Foundation, Pécs 2013, pp. 71–98, and J. Petrétei and T. Péter: *Bases of Hungary's constitutional law [Magyarország alkotmányjogának alapjai]*, Kodifikátor Foundation, Pécs 2013, pp. 31–35.) However, despite the fact that there can be different ways of classification, basically each case specifies the need to actually enforce the same content aspects.

2 The term 'rule of law' is attached to the name of Charles I (cf. Sz. Péter and T. Péter, *The theory of the rule of law [A jogállamiság jogelmélete]*, Napvilág, Budapest 2004, p. 230).

3 The term *Rechtsstaat* was (probably) first used by Robert von Mohl. [cf. F. Neumann, 'Rule of law and sovereignty' [Jogállamiság és szuverenitás], in T. Péter (ed.), *An anthology from the literature of the Rule of Law and the Rechtsstaat [Joguralom és jogállam. Antológia a Rule of Law és a Rechtsstaat irodalmának köréből]*, ELTE, 1995, p. 232. Originally: F. Neumann, *The Rule of Law. Political Theory and the Legal System in Modern Society*, Berg Publishers, Oxford 1986.] For the formal concept of the term see also: K. János: *Constitutional democracy [Alkotmányos demokrácia]*, Indok, 2000, p. 108.

for this was to introduce a predictable legal order, with rules streamlined for consistency, which everyone can learn, follow and rely upon. This purely formal system of criteria contained expectations like the chance to learn the legal regulations. This means that state-made rules have to be, at the very least, made public. (This did not happen everywhere even in the 18th century.)[4] These formal criteria also covered the requirement that changes made too quickly have to be avoided; legal regulations have to be clear and easy-to-understand; these rules must actually be enforced, etc. The formal rule of law meant that state bodies could not proceed either against the laws (*contra legem*) or without the laws, that is, without a statutory basis (*praeter legem*). Thus, the key point was predictability, namely, that clear and unambiguous laws should be enforced in a manner that can be pre-planned.

The following concepts belonged, and still belong, to the formal rule of law:

1. *rejecting the open inequality of rights and a sovereign legislator above the laws and recognising the state that is bound by law*: the state (i.e. the legislator) is also bound by law; the legal norms also cover the legislator (i.e. the state itself), after creating the laws the state is subject to the laws just as any other entity;
2. *legal security, which means that the laws*
   a. *are proclaimed publicly and can be accessed* by anyone in advance *and in due course, and*
   b. *must be clear and easy to understand* for the addressees ('clear norms'): the legislator must create norms that are clear to people and have accurate contents, where the addressees (the obligors and obligees of the provisions of law) can learn with relative accuracy when the state law enforcement bodies recognise their conduct as lawful;
   c. *they should not change quickly* (the changes can be followed) as well as

[4] For example, judges in the Italian city-states were instructed through secret decrees; France ran the legal institute of the *lettre de cachet*, which also covered the French absolute monarchy's subsequent legislative right depending on individual considerations and aimed at specific matters. The latter, for instance, included the possibility for the monarch 'to terminate a prosecution or, without relying on the judges, convict or imprison an individual without a trial and without even an offence having been committed'; C. Elliott, *French Criminal Law*, Routledge, New York 2011, p. 5.

d. *the prohibition of legislation with a retroactive effect:*[5] with some exceptions, the state cannot regulate life events that have already occurred or were fulfilled upon the introduction of the law i.e. legislation is permitted if it does not prescribe more adverse conditions than the current ones for any involved legal subject, except for the state (thus, Section 2(1) of Act CXXX of 2010 on law-making says that 'laws may not establish obligations, make obligations more onerous, withdraw or restrict right, or declare any conduct to be illegal with respect to the period prior to their entry into force', that is, retroactive legislation is permitted if it only provides rights to all persons involved, or exempts them from obligations or liabilities and this does not make the situation of another natural or legal person more onerous);
e. *the requirement of sufficient preparation time*: the legal subjects not only required to learn the relevant rules in time, but sufficient time must be provided to them for adapting to these rules and to provide the conditions of law-abiding conduct;
f. *protection of the acquired rights*: legal relationships that are fulfilled shall be left untouched;
g. *protection of confidence*: rights arising in the future but which are also permanently prevailing in the present can only be limited with regard to the future, with regard to the fact that the legislator should respect the reasons for establishing that legal regulation (e.g. concluding a permanent contract), furthermore, that the rights arising in this manner should not be vacated in the future either;[6]

---

5 In the case of a retroactive effect, the legal regulation shall also be applied for the legal facts and legal relationships arising before promulgating the legal regulation. The retroactive effect can be: (a) *full retroactive effect*: if the legal regulation must also be applied for facts already taken place and legal relationships closed upon the promulgation; (b) *partial retroactive effect*: if the legal regulation must also be applied – in the period preceding the promulgation – for legal relationships arising before the promulgation and still in progress upon the promulgation. It is *not* a retroactive effect if the legal regulation must be applied for legal relationships arising before the promulgation and still in progress upon the promulgation only for the period after the promulgation.

6 In the interpretation of the Constitutional Court: 'The requirement of confidence protection attached to legal security may set a limit to [...] intervention by the legislator into the existing, permanent legal regulations. Confidence protection is a well-founded expectation – protected by law – towards the unchanged survival of a legal regulation (i.e. it should remain in effect). The Constitutional Court considers from case to case the borderline between the freedom of the legislator and the

3. *legitimacy*, i.e. that
   a. *the right is proclaimed in legal sources issued in an appropriate form*[7] and
   b. *these should cover all addressees specified in a normative manner.*

However, this formal rule of law – achieved through the theory of Hans Kelsen, who was widely acknowledged during the era of *formal* approach to the rule of law – was heavily criticised in the 19th century and especially between the two world wars. Later – after World War II – it became evident to everyone that it could not be maintained in itself because, for instance, even Nazi Germany could be treated as a state governed by the 'rule of law', at least in its merely formal sense: life and death were controlled by norms that were created in a proper procedural order and with proper authorisation and that were (more or less) known to the public. Jews, Gypsies and homosexuals were detained in camps and later killed, and mentally ill individuals were sterilised, *inter alia*, based on publicly proclaimed and clear norms. Thus, in this sense, Nazi brutalities were committed under the predictable circumstances of the 'rule of law'.[8] For this reason, there was already clear consensus after World War II that the term 'rule of law' had to be properly defined, even regardless of the well-known formula by Radbruch.[9]

---

addressees' interest in the permanence and the predictability of the legal regulations, examining whether the disadvantage suffered by the legal subjects as a result of change in the laws justifies to establish that it is contrary to the Fundamental Law based on the violation of legal security.' {3061/2017. (III. 31.) Resolution of the Constitutional Court, Reasons [13]}.

7 In this sense, 'legitimacy' is a guarantee not only in terms of form, but *also* in terms of content, as constitutional rules are in place for statutory contents, which *also* serve the rule of law in terms of content.

8 Stalin's communist (state socialist, Bolshevist) system was not even a 'rule of law' in this formal sense, as their state bodies also violated their own norms. Although the text of Stalin's (Bukharin's) constitution of 1936 was regarded as very modern at that time and contained all the rights that they found necessary to guarantee in the developed world, none of these declared norms were enforced. Constitutionality was only a Potemkin phenomenon, and the system ignored it day by day. (For the Stalinist Bukharin Constitution of 1936, see: E. Kriza, 'From utopia to dystopia? Bukharin and the Soviet Constitution of 1936' in K.-M. Simonsen and J.S. Kjærgård (eds), *Discursive Framings of Human Rights: Negotiating agency and victimhood*, Routledge, New York 2017, pp. 79–93.)

9 G. Radbruch, 'Gesetzliches Unrecht und übergesetzliches Recht', *Süddeutsche Juristen-Zeitung*, Jahrg. 1, Nr. 5 (August 1946), pp. 105–08. The formula is as follows (in the original language, that is, German): 'Der Konflikt zwischen der Gerechtigkeit und der Rechtssicherheit dürfte dahin zu lösen sein, daß das positive, durch Satzung und Macht gesicherte Recht auch dann den Vorrang hat, wenn es inhaltlich ungerecht

The material rule of law includes the following elements:

1. *all requirements of the formal rule of law* as a basic condition;
2. *considering the violation of any right on the merits, by judges* – who are independent, impartial and unbiased both in their status and in their judging work and who are only subject to the laws – also including the judicial review of the unlawful acts of public administrative bodies, that is, public administrative adjudication;[10]
3. *protecting human rights;*
4. *equality of rights;*[11]
5. *pluralism*:
   a. in a narrower sense: the mere existence of pluralism (the functioning of competing parties operating under equal public law conditions),
   b. in a wider sense: the existence of free elections held in regular periods, based on general and equal, active and passive voting

und unzweckmäßig ist, es sei denn, daß der Widerspruch des positiven Gesetzes zur Gerechtigkeit ein so unerträgliches Maß erreicht, daß das Gesetz als >>unrichtiges Recht<< der Gerechtigkeit zu weichen hat'. In English: 'The conflict between justice and the reliability of the law should be solved in favor of the positive law, law enacted by proper authority and power, even in cases where it is unjust in terms of content and purpose, except for cases where the discrepancy between the positive law and justice reaches a level so unbearable that the statute has to make way for justice because it has to be considered "erroneous law"'. (See, e.g.: J. Hage, 'Philosophy of Law', in J. Hage, A. Waltermann and B. Akkermans (eds), *Introduction to Law*, 2nd ed., Springer, 2017, pp. 359–82, p. 376.)

10 The existence of public administrative justice is independent from the existence of separate public administrative courts; it is also implemented if this rule-of-law function is performed by ordinary (e.g. civil) courts.

11 The material requirement of equal rights is more than the purely formal requirement that the laws should cover all normatively specified addressees, namely because the latter still allows for the laws to treat differently persons whose relevant attributes are identical, which means discrimination (i.e. it only requires that the law should not make any difference between the addressees, but it does not expect that everybody with similar, relevant attributes should be an addressee of the law), while equal rights already prohibit the laws from making selections among the addressees if such a selection has no reasonable cause that can be morally defended. It is to be noted that some opinions in the legal literature say that human rights arise from the principle of equal rights in itself, so these human rights do not have to be considered as a separate part of the material rule of law; thus, according to János Kis: 'several other classical human rights derive from the principle of equality before the law, thus the political equality of religions, the prohibition of attaching the holding of office to birth or financial position etc.'. K. János: *Do we have human rights? [Vannak-e emberi jogaink?]*, Dialogues Européens, Paris 1988, pp. 158–59.

rights and on previously defined rules providing a result representing the citizens' will;
6. *the division of powers;*
7. *democracy (and democratic legitimacy)*, that is, basic decisions should be made by the majority of the legislative body elected by the people as a whole or operating with the participation of the people as a whole, and all decisions by the public power can be traced back (directly or indirectly) to the people's majority will. This latter relationship will be dealt with later.

3. THE DEFINITION AND THE CONTENT OF DEMOCRACY

Democracy is a Greek word, meaning the power (*kratos*) of people (*demos*).[12] However, the expression the 'people's power' actually says very little about the form of state organisation or about the manner in which power is practised in the political system. Another problem is that the established democracies are very different, and numerous states call themselves 'democratic' even though the true enforcement of the people's interests can be called into question – or is actually missing from these systems. The term 'democracy' has become the jolly joker of political self-reflection by now, as essentially all existing states lay claim to the descriptor of 'democracy'. It can also be argued that there is a political consensus claiming that democracy is something inherently good,[13] and therefore, some regimes also try to define themselves as democratic which are, in fact, very far from the requirements of democracy. There are three questions related to the *substantive* problem of democracy. First, what are the content requirements that make a regime democratic? The second and

---

12 See, e.g.: V. Laopodis, 'DEMOS: Democratic evaluation of multiple options in society', in J. Berleur and D. Whitehouse (eds), *An Ethical Global Information Society. IFIP – The International Federation for Information Processing*, Springer, Boston 1997, pp. 318–29, p. 319. This term was first used by Herodotus, who was amongst those, according to most scholars, who praised Athenian democracy. J.N. Davie, 'Herodotus and Aristophanes on Monarchy' (1979) 26 *Greece & Rome*, 162. For the opposite view, see e.g.: P.A. Stadter, 'Herodotus and the Athenian "arche"' *Annali della Scuola Normale Superiore di Pisa. Classe di Lettere e Filosofia*, Serie III, Vol. 22, No. 3, 1992, p. 784.

13 Cf.: A. Schedler and R. Sarsfield, 'Democrats with adjectives: Linking direct and indirect measures of democratic support' (2007) 46 *European Journal of Political Research* 639.

third essential questions (which are related to each other) are whether the *actual* (truly existing) attributes of 'implemented democracies' lead to anything with regard to the democracy's normative (i.e. *prescriptive*) concept (i.e. what *should* be the features of the political systems that have the ground to call themselves 'democratic'), and vice versa: to what extent can existing democracies be held accountable for the normative requirements.

These questions are much more difficult to answer than what would follow from the literal interpretation of the term ('people's power'). It is certain that *all democratic systems must be recognised by the people, and the political groups that are currently on power must be authorised by the people to exercise this power.* It can also be said that *the legitimacy of exercising power in a democratic way comes from the people.*

However, this still does not get us closer to differentiating real democracies from 'false democracies', since both public speech and the political-philosophical literature mention numerous types of democracies. It is difficult to discern among the multitude of definitions which ones feature the true content of the people's power and which ones merely camouflage and hide the non-democratic features of the exercise of power. Thus, in addition to the term 'democracy' without adjectives, the following expressions are also used: direct democracy; electoral democracy; representative democracy; indirect democracy; participation democracy; self-governing democracy; assembly democracy; referendum democracy; electronic democracy; constitutional democracy; liberal democracy; social democracy; Christian democracy; egalitarian democracy; consensus democracy; majority democracy; limited democracy; deliberative democracy; consociational democracy; and, moreover, 'people's democracy'[14] and 'illiberal democracy'.[15] These dimensions partly exclude each

14 In the state socialist era, in fact, democracy did not exist at all. For instance, in Hungary, until 1985 citizens could vote for only one candidate [only a state-run social organisation named Patriotic People's Front (Hazafias Népfront) could nominate], so there was no real active and passive suffrage.

15 This term was invented by Fareed Zakaria, who used this expression for semi-democratic countries, mainly and originally for those in Latin America, Central Asia and for Russia. See: F. Zakaria, *The Future of Freedom. Illiberal Democracy at Home and Abroad*, W. W. Norton, New York and London 2007, particularly pp. 23 and 89–118.) 'Illiberal', virtually, is a privative suffix and a democracy cannot be 'illiberal'. In fact, the Hungarian government no longer uses this word, it uses the term 'Christian democracy' instead. As Francis Fukuyama pointed out, in an 'illiberal' system, 'democratic majorities do not necessarily feel themselves bound to respect universal human rights'; F. Fukuyama, '30 Years of World Politics: What Has Changed?' (2020)

other and are partly orthogonal – that is, they overlap and co-exist (and in some cases, they concretely reject the essence of democracy, where the qualifying adjective is actually a privative suffix); thus, it is complicated to orientate in this chaos of terms.

One of the most essential problems with *defining* democracy is what the term 'people' means. Fortunately, there is already a consensus today in this regard. Thus, *people* are – in terms of democratic decision-making – the *same as the political nation, that is, the community of citizens who also have the right to vote* (except for the natural reasons for exclusion [minor age, incapacity for other reasons, persons imprisoned through a final court decision for committing a crime and/or prohibited from public affairs]).

4. THE CONTENT ELEMENTS OF DEMOCRACY

However, *people are not a simple tool for legitimacy* that one can nominally refer to, but they are a community of citizens who can actually enforce their will. As the people's will is not given once and for all, *an institutional guarantee must be provided for people to change their will*, that is, to express (and enforce) their intention to think differently about public affairs or about the representatives of public affairs. Only those states, political regimes or political interest-articulation mechanisms can be called democracy where *people have a real opportunity to enforce their current will.* This is served by *regular assemblies, votes* and – in the case of a representative democracy – *regular elections* in public affairs. Thus, in this regard, the requirements of the rule of law and democracy coincide. There is no 'people's power' in terms of content, and therefore the concept of democracy cannot be implemented where – upon the first election – the citizens waived their right to have a say in public matters and to control (or periodically change) the political stakeholders, or where this was prevented by those who gained power once.

Furthermore, the term 'democracy' implies the *decision* itself. *Political democracy means the democracy of decision-making* in all of its existing forms, that is, direct choice from among alternative action models, rules and programmes (e.g. via referendum) or indirect choice from among competing political forces (parties, politicians) that are able to make the

31 *Journal of Democracy* 1, 13 – therefore, a genuine democracy, either in Eastern Europe or anywhere else, cannot be illiberal. For the relationship between the rule of law – and, within it, human rights protection – and democracy, see section 5.

relevant decisions. Whether the members of a political community vote directly about a proposal or indirectly about politicians judging the future proposals (representatives), *they always make a decision: they select from the possible, incurring possibilities* and decide which model or rule to employ (in direct democracy) or who should later vote about the same questions (indirect democracy). People have different interests and values, namely, they have different opinions about certain social problems to be solved or political questions to be decided because of their life situation or selected moral views (furthermore, due to their other values, prejudices, preferences, attitudes, educations or world views). Therefore, they have different views about what is good, correct or expedient with regard to certain issues. As a result, *there is always a conflict of interests or values among the members of political communities*, and they have to find a political solution in this situation of conflicting interests or values. Thus, a decision always has to be made about the dilemmas that arise in society, which means that a certain standpoint will succeed after the decision (the given rule will be introduced, and the given programme will be implemented), and the alternative solutions will not be carried out.

Of course, it is also theoretically possible that there are no interest or value conflicts in a society – that the members of society always think the same about certain issues. However, apart from the fact that such a political society has never existed anywhere in the world thus far, it is also to be noted that if there were such a community, there would be no need for decision-making at all, as there would be no dilemmas to decide on. We can talk about a choice between options, that is, about a *decision only if such options exist* and there are people who support or favour them; *if views, opinions and wills were in perfect harmony in a society, there would be no need for politics and for a political system*, and within this, there would be no need for any (not even democratic) interest articulations and decision-making mechanisms. However, a perfect harmony of interests and values has never been realised anywhere, and it is not even possible; therefore, there is a need for choice among different wills. If this is true, then *all democracies can only be majority democracies* (i.e. the decision is ultimately made by the majority, or by the majority of representatives elected by the majority).[16] Therefore, in what follows, we always talk about democracy in this sense.

16 Sartori draws the attention to the fact that the majority principle is a modern invention, and it does not date back to the Greeks, but only to Locke (based on the precedence of monk communities) – similarly to secret voting or to the principle of representation.

This is how the term of consensus-based democracy becomes content-less, as it says that anything can only be accepted if there is consensus between the members of society. Deliberative democracy is partly emptied in the same way – at least in terms of its conceptual definitions, which seek to continue deliberation until the proponents of one position persuade the proponents of the other position through their arguments.[17] *Deliberation* is a process thought to be ideal by the supporters of this type of democracy whereby the representatives of originally different standpoints try to convince each other through logical arguments and make a compromise that is ultimately acceptable to everybody. If the only acceptable result of deliberation is the jointly worked-out, discussed and compromise-based solution, it already complies with the concept of consensus-based democracy (and what was said about it losing its content will also apply for deliberative democracy). If, on the other hand, deliberation (i.e. rational debate over the proposals) can also come to an end without specifying the objectively appropriate standpoint that is uniformly accepted by everybody, and voting is still ultimately held in order to solve the problem,[18] it (i.e. this type of deliberative democracy) does not differ from the majority interpretation of democracy (namely, because some kind of debate also precedes the decision in the classical approaches of majority decision-making), as the dilemma is solved in the same way through a majority decision.

The term of *deliberative democracy* was developed by Joseph M. Bessette for negotiation- and argument-based political decision-making in 1980;[19] he still accepted that deliberation can be concluded without a

---

Cf. G. Sartori, *Democracy [Demokrácia]*, Osiris, 1999, p. 80. Originally: G. Sartori, *Democrazia: cosa è*, Rizzoli, Milano 1993.

17 According to Jon Elster, deliberation is decision-making based on the debate of free and equal citizens. J. Elster, 'Introduction' in J. Elster (ed.), *Deliberative Democracy*, Cambridge University Press, Cambridge 1998, p. 1. Deliberation simultaneously refers to the discussion itself and to the exchange of information that is required for it, thus implying the necessity to share rational considerations with each other and to take them into account upon the final decision.

18 Thus, e.g. Joshua Cohen says that the goal of deliberation is consensus (therefore, we have to be open to convincing counter-arguments against our own standpoint), still it may happen that no arguments will be accepted based on a consensus – and finally voting must be held (based on some majority principle). J. Cohen, 'Deliberation and Democratic Legitimacy' in J. Bohman and W. Rehg (eds), *Deliberative Democracy. Essays on Reason and Politics*, MIT Press, Cambridge MA and London 1997, p. 75.

19 Cf. J.M. Bessette, 'Deliberative Democracy: The Majority Principle in Republican Government' in R.A. Goldwin and W.A. Schambra (eds), *How democratic is the*

result (at which point, it has to be started again, or votes have to be cast). However, some of the later theories already tried to work out mechanisms that facilitate finding the only objectively right solution.

The majority concept of democracy, however, does not exclude that the will of the majority should not be enforced without any limits; the majority will can, of course, be limited if it does not satisfy a value aspect that is important to society (thus specifically some criterion of the rule of law). This issue will be covered later in detail; for now, we only note that *these limits are laid down in all political (and legal) systems in advance and they prevent the unlimited enforcement of the majority will based on objective aspects* and simultaneously ensure that the democratic decision-making system is maintained in the long run. In this sense, democracy and the rule of law do not (necessarily) contradict, but they are much more similar categories that supplement, presuppose and strengthen each other. This also means that *today's modern democracies are necessarily constitutional democracies*, that is, decision-making is based on previously laid down, constitutional rules that serve the people's real interests as against certain short-term interests. Thus, as a basic condition, constitutional democracies *do not allow for the people to permanently waive power, to terminate the limits to power, to ignore basic human rights or to introduce (openly discriminative) regulations contradicting the minimalist, formal concept of equal rights. Constitutional democracies are also liberal democracies*, as the requirement of recognising human rights, limiting power and providing equal rights (as well as free elections based on the general voting right) are achievements of the liberal ideology.[20] This is also true if some theories also emphasise other aspects in addition to interiorising classical liberal values. For example, similarly, social democracy is nothing else but the demand – within the institutional framework deriving from liberalism – that the state should lay a greater emphasis on material equality and on social rights. We do not deal with the various adjectives of democracy (liberal democracy, social democracy, Christian democracy, etc.) which are used unfortunately more and more frequently in public life on a party political basis in order to deliberately slander and stigmatise the opposing political power – as this does not have any scientific/professional aspect.

---

constitution? American Enterprise Institute for Public Policy Research, Washington D.C. 1980, pp. 102–16.

20 Cf. Sartori, above n. 16, p. 18.

5. DEMOCRACY, THE RULE OF LAW AND THE CONSTITUTIONAL COURT'S PRACTICE

The criteria of the material rule of law are ultimately enforced in most legal systems by the constitutional court (or by another body with similar functions), which also means that the purely majority concept of democracy cannot be enforced without limits. The question is what legitimates this body to overrule the decisions of the parliament, which was elected by the majority of the people (or, equally, to overrule the people's will) and to annul parliamentary laws (or simply 'not to apply them' without annulment, like e.g. in the United States). To put it in another way: how far does democracy stretch, and from whence can it be limited with reference to the material principles and values of the rule of law?

The starting point is *that enforcing the people's will is the main rule in democracy*. Of course, the 'will' of the whole people (understood in terms of psychology) is an illusion, and so it is that a unified, consensus-based standpoint could be worked out among the members of society. People's interests and values are different, and therefore their standpoints are, evidently, also different in various social issues. The *criteria of the rule of law* do not operate as a 'qualitative filter' in that they *do not prevent the enactment of laws that are bad, ineffective, dysfunctional or even counter-productive*. It is often said that 'the people cannot be wrong' or 'the people are always right'; however, this should not mean that the people always make correct, scientifically verified, consistent and well considered decisions, but that the *people have the right to make a mistake*, that is, the people's will also has priority if the people make an inexpedient or wrong decision.

5.1. THE RULE-OF-LAW-BASED SELF-DEFENCE OF DEMOCRACY

Bearing in mind the above-mentioned considerations, democratic legitimacy must be accepted as a starting point. However, *the 'people's will' cannot be enforced without limits*. A decision that makes it impossible to enforce democracy in the future sets an evident barrier to democratic decision-making. It is therefore clear that the self-defence mechanism of democracy can never let the extreme case happen where democracy would liquidate itself (e.g. a referendum about cancelling regular elections cannot be permitted). This, however, no longer depends on democracy, but *on the rule of law, which prohibits certain things based on their content even if they were supported by most citizens* (via single, all-decisive and irrevocable voting). This does not just prevent the termination of democracy (e.g. the institution of elections), but it also covers all material value aspects that would violate equal rights – which is accepted by democracy as a value – the human rights that also set a foundation for people's civil rights and the right for political participation, as well as all the principles ensuring their organisational conditions and institutional guarantees (separation of powers, the judicial review of laws/constitutional court practice, etc.). *A real democracy is possible only on a content basis; it is guaranteed by the criteria of the rule of law.* In that regard, the constitutional court practice has had a prioritised role since the middle of the 20th century.

5.2. DEMOCRACY AND THE CONSTITUTIONAL COURT'S PRACTICE

The main assertion I am defending here is that in fact, *the constitutional court practice – in its consolidated form – is not against the idea of democracy at all. Actually, the existence of the constitutional court practice can be a security for real democracy.*

Hans Kelsen, who worked out the modern, European, centralised constitutional court practice,[21] faced criticism of the court review of legal regulations, basically focusing on two aspects. On the one hand, it was argued that the constitutional court practice is against parliamentary sovereignty. On the other hand, critics argued that is also against the separation of powers (this latter aspect is not covered here in detail).[22]

---

[21] Kelsen – as state chancellor Karl Renner's consultant – succeeded in seeing that the constitutional court and constitutional court practice were established in Austria in 1920. Cf. K. von Beyme, 'Judicial review' [Alkotmánybíráskodás] in P. Paczolay (ed.), *Constitutional adjudication – constitutional interpretation [Alkotmánybíráskodás – alkotmányértelmezés]*, Rejtjel, 2003, p. 119. Originally in: *America as a model. The impact of American democracy in the world*, Palgrave Macmillan, 1987, pp. 85–109.

[22] Cf. P. Paczolay, 'Constitutional adjudication on the border of politics and law' [Alkotmánybíráskodás a politika és jog határán] in P. Paczolay (ed.), *Constitutional adjudication – constitutional interpretation [Alkotmánybíráskodás – alkotmányértelmezés]*, Rejtjel, 2003, p. 16; L. Favoreu, Az alkotmánybíróságok, in: P. Paczolay, *Constitutional adjudication – constitutional interpretation [Alkotmánybíráskodás – alkotmányértelmezés]*, Rejtjel, 2003, p. 58. In the original language: L. Favoreu, *Les Cours constitutionelles*, Presses Universitaires de France, Paris 1992, pp. 1–105.

Kelsen's answer to the first criticism was that parliamentary sovereignty is only a sub-type of the principle of popular sovereignty; furthermore, as the goal is to trace back to the people's will not only one single branch of power, but the operation of the whole state order, *popular sovereignty* is therefore not provided by parliamentary sovereignty, but basically by state sovereignty, *the operation of the branches of power based on the people's will, where no single organisation can enjoy priority* compared to other state organisations providing for popular sovereignty. In this situation, *it is the very task of the constitutional court to limit the eventual violation to popular sovereignty by the parliament*: just as courts and public administration are subject to the laws, the *parliament is also subject to the constitution, and it may carry out legislation work only within the framework of the constitution.* As can be seen, the procedure of the legislative body is bound by the constitution and by the constitutional court enforcing the constitutional provisions exactly with a view to popular sovereignty and democracy (where the point is to create compromise between the majority and the minorities and, thus, to promote social peace). The task of the constitutional court is to enforce the provisions of the constitution as against laws and decrees (and to terminate anti-constitutional norms), to resolve disputes over scope and competence (also based on the constitution) as well as to protect the minority, that is, to prevent the tyranny of the majority.[23]

Christopher Wolfe stated that three responses can be offered to the criticism claiming that judicial review is antidemocratic. The criticism essentially relates to the American decentralised judicial activities, but can be extended to all types of constitutional court practice. The advocates of constitutional court practice can prove with these answers that the institution of judicial norm review is not antidemocratic; on the contrary, it expressly promotes the enforcement of democracy. Accordingly: '*(1) the basic goals of the Court are democratic, (2) the judges are ultimately subjected to the control of the public will, (3) the modern judicial power was legitimated by tacit approval*'.[24] From among these, the most important is Wolfe's first argument about the democratic nature of judicial goals.

Therefore, as far as the democratic goals of constitutional court practice mentioned by Wolfe are concerned, this argument only legitimates

23 Cf. Paczolay, above n. 22, pp. 16–17; Favoreu, above n. 22, pp. 58–59.

24 C. Wolfe, 'Judicial review and democracy' [Alkotmánybíráskodás és demokrácia], in: P. Paczolay (ed.), *Constitutional adjudication – constitutional interpretation [Alkotmánybíráskodás – alkotmányértelmezés]*, Rejtjel, 2003, p. 129. Originally in C. Wolfe, *Judicial activism. Bulwark of freedom or precarious security?* Brooks/Cole Publishing Company, California 1991, pp. 49–71.

certain constitutional court procedures in cases that are especially important for articulating democratic political interests. Thus, for example, *if legislation deprived some people of political rights or changed these political rights* (e.g. the right to vote or the rules of the election procedure) *in such a way that it does not provide everybody with equal opportunities* to select political decision-makers, *it would injure the principle of democracy itself, as well as the decision-making process based on the opportunity of equal participation.* As this correction cannot be expected from the corrupted legislative majority because democracy must, in fact, be protected *from them*, this task can only be carried out by an entity which has no political responsibility and which is outside the political system taken in a narrow sense (and this task should actually be carried out for the sake of democracy and in order to enforce the real public will). Similarly, *if certain basic human rights are endangered, such as the freedom of speech (also including the freedom of assembly), people will not obtain the relevant information that helps them to take decisions expressing their real will* when selecting the future members of legislation. Democracy is also injured directly if the opportunity to access information is limited by prohibiting the freedom of speech of the persons possessing the information. The principle of democracy also provides the opportunity that everybody's interest should appear upon decision-making. All decisions have some losers, and all legislative decisions are injurious to some people – to those whose opinions or interests were in the minority in the given debate. This does not injure democracy as long as these minorities change from time to time, that is, there is a real chance that the person who was once in the minority will someday belong to the majority on certain other issues. *If, however, there are* 'separated and isolated' *minority groups always consisting of the same persons who are losers in all decisions, and they are systematically suppressed by the majority, they will not be members of society or participants in political decision-making with equal rights or at an equal rank. The suppression of such homogeneous minorities can also be prevented by operating a body that is outside the legislation.*[25]

Tamás Győrfi, on the one hand, also highlights the aforementioned principle that democracy can only be realised if the legal system considers the voters (based on Dworkin's formula) as 'persons of equal dignity',[26]

---

25 Cf. Wolfe, above n. 24, pp. 129–32.

26 Cf. R. Dworkin, *Taking Rights Seriously*, Harvard University Press, Cambridge MA 1977, p. 370. The same principle also appeared in the initial practice of the Hungarian Constitutional Court: 'The prohibition of discrimination means that the law must treat everybody equally (as persons with equal dignity), i.e. the basic right of human

that is, an equal opportunity is provided for anyone to belong to a majority and minority position from time to time instead of a homogeneous majority enforcing its will against a homogeneous minority.[27] On the other hand, he also draws the attention to the fact that – according to those who regard constitutional court practice as democratic – *the concept of purely majority democracy does not consider the intensity of preferences at all*: 'it violates the principle of equal treatment as it prefers the weak preferences of the smallest possible majority over the strong preferences of the largest possible minority'.[28] On another instance, Győrfi presents the standpoint of those who are in favour of constitutional court practice by claiming that (what he calls 'procedural') democracy purely based on the majority principle is (or may also be) incorrect in terms of contents as 'the procedural concept is insensitive to both the correctness of the reasons supporting preferences and the distribution of the burdens of the decision'.[29] In fact, Győrfi himself would also transfer the consideration of content arguments to the legislator; in his opinion, this is required by the principle of 'equal care and respect'.[30]

5.3. THE RELATIONSHIP BETWEEN DEMOCRACY, PEOPLE'S SOVEREIGNTY AND CONSTITUTIONAL COURT PRACTICE IN HUNGARY

If we project the issue at hand to the case of Hungary, the earlier question of what authorises the Constitutional Court to overrule the decisions of the political legislative body elected by the people (parliamentary laws) can be given three different answers. This is besides and in addition to what is set forth in the previous part of this chapter. Each answer (both together

dignity cannot be injured, and the aspects of dividing rights and benefits must be determined with the same respect and care, by considering individual aspects at the same rate'. 9/1990. CC Resolution, ABH 1990, pp. 46, 48.

27 Cf. T. Győrfi, 'Democracy' [Demokrácia], in P. Takács, I.H. Szilágyi and B. Fekete, *State theory. Chapters and lectures on the general theory of the state [Államelmélet. Fejezetek és előadások az állam általános elmélete köréből]*, Szent István Társulat, Budapest 2012, pp. 379–80.

28 Cf. Győrfi, above n. 27, p. 380.

29 T. Győrfi, 'Limitations on majority decision-making and constitutional adjudication' [A többségi döntés korlátai és az alkotmánybíráskodás], in A. Jakab and A. Körösényi (eds), *Constitution in Hungary and elsewhere. Political science and constitutional law approaches [Alkotmányozás Magyarországon és máshol. Politikatudományi és alkotmányjogi megközelítések]*, MTA TK PTI, 2012, p. 42.

30 Győrfi, above n. 29, pp. 54–55.

and separately) verifies that *the authorisation for constitutional court practice is not contrary to the requirement of democratic legitimacy.*

The *requirement of democratic legitimacy says that* in a democratic political and legal system built on the idea of people's sovereignty, *no public authority decision can be made if it does not come directly or indirectly from the community of citizens*, that is, if its ultimate source is not the people. Accordingly, *it must be ensured that each public authority decision* (either individual or general, i.e. normative) *can be traced back to the original decision of the voting citizens*, and this is where it must derive from, in one or more steps. By concentrating expressly on the current Hungarian situation (but also maintaining the need for the general authenticity of the statements), the three justifications are as follows:[31] first of all, the *members of the Constitutional Court*, having the power to annul laws, are

---

31 In addition, there is also a fourth answer that does not start out from the requirement of democratic legitimacy, but from the philosophical interpretation of the term 'majority'. Alexis de Tocqueville was the first to analyse – after his two trips to America as early as in 1840 – the opportunity of the judicial review of laws by checking how it contributes to preventing the 'tyranny of the majority'. (A. de Tocqueville, *Democracy in America*, The Lawbook Exchange, Clark, New Jersey 2003.) It is evident that basically the will of the majority must be enforced against the minority in a democracy; however, de Tocqueville says that it is wrong to identify the majority as the majority of a *country*, namely because the main laws (the laws of justice) were created by the *majority of whole mankind*. If the laws of the people's majority are against the general laws of the majority of mankind, then the latter must be enforced. If only the majority of one nation expresses its will, this still does not imply the absolute validity of the law. If a larger nation can tyrannise a smaller one, or a person with large power can tyrannise people under them, similarly the majority of a nation can also suppress the minority with the laws created by it. And this, being the 'tyranny of the majority' can and must be prevented. In de Tocqueville's words: 'A general law – which bears the name of Justice – has been made and sanctioned, not only by a majority of this or that people, but by a majority of mankind. The rights of every people are consequently confined within the limits of what is just. A nation may be considered in the light of a jury which is empowered to represent society at large, and to apply the great and general law of Justice. Ought such a jury, which represents society to have more power than the society in which the laws it applies originate?' (A. de Tocqueville, *Democracy in America*, The Lawbook Exchange, Clark, New Jersey 2003, p. 240.) This is the very reason why the majority of a given country cannot create *any* norm or cannot give constitutional authorisation to create *any* norm without violating the content-related requirements of the rule of law. For example, by quoting the opinion of the Venice Commission dated June 2013, Imre Vörös wrote the following: 'Creating or modifying the constitution (…) *is not an arithmetical issue*, i.e. not a quantitative opportunity that automatically derives from the 2/3 parliamentary majority (…)'. I. Vörös, 'Outline of the nature of fundamental rights after the Fourth and Fifth Amendments to the Fundamental Law of Hungary' [Vázlat az alapvető jogok természetéről az Alaptörvény negyedik és ötödik módosítása után], *Fundamentum*, Vol. 3, 2013, p. 60.

elected in Hungary by the same body, that is, the parliament (National Assembly), which also makes the laws. When electing constitutional judges, *the same indirect (presumed) people's will is enforced as upon adopting laws.* If the constitutional judges are elected by the National Assembly and it authorises them to carry out the constitutional review of the laws, then *there is* democratic legitimacy behind the constitutional court practice (just as behind, e.g. the president of the republic and any of his/her decisions or actions). It is true, however, that this legitimacy is not direct, that is, it is not the people (their majority) who decide about the contents of the decisions of the Constitutional Court,[32] but the majority of constitutional judges. However, the same is also true of the laws: their contents are not decided directly by the voting citizens, but only by the majority of the representatives elected by them. Only the referendum has a *direct* democratic legitimacy in Hungary, and all other contents reflect the people's will only *indirectly*. Of course, it cannot be said that both analysed activities (legislation and constitutional court practice) would have *the same* indirect democratic legitimacy: while the content of Constitutional Court resolutions goes through double mediation calculated from the people's will (the democratic legitimacy of these resolutions is doubly indirect, as the resolutions are made by constitutional judges elected by parliamentary representatives who are elected by the people), the content of laws goes through only single mediation calculated from the people's will (the democratic legitimacy of the laws is indirect only once, as the decisions are made by the parliamentary representatives elected by the people). However, since legitimacy is only indirect in both cases (although at a different rate), we can say that there is a difference between the democratic legitimacy of constitutional court practice (resolutions of the Constitutional Court) and legislation (adopted laws). The difference, however, is not *qualitative* (e.g. between a referendum and parliamentary legislation), only *quantitative*, that is, gradual.

Second, looking at the requirement of democratic legitimacy based on the *legal source* used for the decision, we can produce an even stronger argument that verifies the constitutional court practice serving the protection of human rights in an even more plausible manner: namely, because the *legitimacy basis* of the *constitution* (the Fundamental Law in Hungary, used as a measure for judging laws) is clearly *stronger than the legitimacy basis of the laws that can be overruled.* While the constitution

32 Similarly: people do not decide about many other aspects, either, e.g. presidential pardon, reports of the State Audit Office, ombudsman recommendations, etc.

is adopted in any legal system in the form of a special procedure and/or with a qualified majority (in Hungary with the two-thirds majority of all parliamentary representatives) and amendment is also possible at the same rate, adopting most laws only requires a simple majority (i.e. more than half) of the parliamentary representatives who are present and have a quorum. However, the two-thirds majority of the attending parliamentary representatives is also enough for cardinal laws, and a two-thirds vote of all representatives is not required. As the legitimacy basis of the resolutions made by the Constitutional Court is stronger than that of the National Assembly acting as a simple legislator (the human/constitutional rights are protected by a majority of representatives – as well as by the constitution adopted by this majority – who were elected by a larger majority of the citizens compared to the majority that passed the laws), *the constitutional court practice does not violate – on the contrary, it serves – the requirement of democratic legitimacy.*

Third, we can also talk about the *actual* enforcement of the requirement of democratic legitimacy (taken in a sociological sense) in the case of legislation only if the governing political forces – having gained parliamentary majority – *do exactly and only what they promised to the citizens in their election programme.* The reason is that the voting citizens (ideally) vote for a political force based on its election programme and promises, and thus the democratic authorisation of the parliamentary majority is attached to the promises and programme points with which the given parties acquired the votes necessary for parliamentary majority. Anything that they do without, or contrary to, such a promise, and anything that they fail to do despite their promises violates the requirement of democratic legitimacy. As this has not yet happened anywhere (and it is not even possible in full),[33] *the democratic legitimacy of legislation is not only indirect, but it is also necessarily partial* (to a smaller or larger extent).

All in all, it can be said that regardless of the vagueness the content of the terms '*rule of law*' and '*human rights*', it is *necessary to enforce them* – at least to a minimum extent – *in all legal systems.* One of the most effective ways to do so is enforcement by the constitutional court (constitutional judges), even if this system has only existed for fewer than two centuries. *As these rights can be violated in the most dangerous manner exactly by the*

33 There are always unforeseeable problems that arise and require an *ad hoc* decision, and, for this reason, some of the former promises cannot be fulfilled or it would not be expedient to fulfill them.

majority and by the legislative body meant to represent them (but at least consisting of politicians elected by the majority), *it is therefore not only verifiable but also necessary that* – in the spirit of justice but in a manner prescribed by the statutory law and by the constitution forming a part of it – *an authorised body (or bodies)* (in Hungary, the Constitutional Court) *can review and cancel* (or at least ignore, like in the United States) *these laws in order to prevent the evolvement of a 'tyrannical majority'.*

PART III

POPULIST CONSTITUTIONALISM: DEMOCRACY IN CRISIS

THE DEGENERATION OF CONTEMPORARY DEMOCRACIES AS A NEW PHENOMENOLOGY OF CONSTITUTIONAL TRANSITION

Angela Di Gregorio

1. DEFINITIONS AND METHODOLOGICAL PROBLEMS

The crisis of democracy and the crisis of constitutionalism have been discussed for at least ten years, and the discussion has taken on dramatic tones in the recent epidemiological emergency, adding new profiles and elements to the subject.[1] It is a methodologically complex issue, both from

[1] Although the worldwide adoption of emergency measures to face the Covid-19 pandemic has given rise to a specific, and particularly rich, doctrinal debate, this aspect will not be examined in this contribution. Emergency law and the constitutional architecture of emergency powers produce derogations temporally limited to the complete exercise of fundamental rights in order to protect individuals and public health, considered to be a priority. However, anxiety about the subsistence of the democratic structure is inevitable when such dangerous precedents, which reduce

the point of view of definitions and from the perspective of the disciplinary approach, since it is dealt with by different disciplines.

In the last 30 years, reflections on the 'intermediate' forms of political systems have been frequent. However, those who spoke of 'other' democracies or 'imperfect' or 'uncertain' democracies in the 1990s and 2000s referred to countries of recent democratisation, and often even in cultural contexts distant from Western ones.[2] Conversely, the most recent debate, which can be dated to the period immediately following the great economic crisis of the first decade of the 2000s (and the explosion of globalisation), goes beyond the 'culturally different' systems affecting the same Western hemisphere.

It is not easy to put these categories in order, both because of terminological difficulties[3] and because of the addition of positions with different cultural imprints. I am referring not only to the necessary synergy

---

the distance between democratic and non-democratic systems, are created and more quickly impel hybrid cases into the bed of autocracy.

2 L. Mezzetti, *Le democrazie incerte. Transizioni costituzionali e consolidamento della democrazia in Europa orientale, Africa, America latina, Asia*, Giappichelli, Torino 2000; A. Di Giovine and S. Sicardi (eds), *Democrazie imperfette*, Giappichelli, Torino 2005.

3 The definitions proposed by scholars are the most disparate. The categories mix together, linking the historical opposition between 'liberal democracy' and other forms of democracy (socialist or popular, Jacobin, direct, etc.) to the more recent opposition between 'mature' or 'stabilised' democracies and 'imperfect' or 'young' democracies, still different from merely 'electoral' democracies (the category most used by political scientists). Today, we need to add the reference to 'sovereign' or 'illiberal' democracy. On the concepts of democracy in constitutional and political theory, see the classics: P. Biscaretti Di Ruffia, 'Democrazia' in AA VV., *Enciclopedia del Diritto*, XII, Giuffrè, Milano 1964; C. Mortati, *Le forme di governo*, Cedam, Padova 1973, p. 354; N. Bobbio, 'Democrazia' in N. Bobbio, N. Matteucci and G. Pasquino (eds), *Dizionario di politica*, Tea, Torino 1990, p. 293; G. De Vergottini, *Diritto costituzionale comparato*, Cedam, Padova 1999, p. 132. A summary of the different positions can be found in A. Di Gregorio, 'I fenomeni di degenerazione delle democrazie contemporanee: qualche spunto di riflessione sullo sfondo delle contrapposizioni dottrinali' (2019) *Nuovi Autoritarismi e Democrazie (NAD)* 2, 2 ss. On sovereign democracy: P. Casula, 'Sovereign Democracy, Populism, and Depoliticization in Russia' (2013) *Problems of Post-Communism* 60, 3. As for illiberal democracy, it is well known that Fareed Zakaria was the first author to introduce the label into political science discourse in 1997; F. Zakaria, 'The Rise of Illiberal Democracy' (1997) 76 *Foreign Affairs* 6. This was done in a context different from the one in which the term has been taken up in the last few years, that is, in Orbán's renowned speech of 2014; A. Di Gregorio, 'L'Ungheria e i valori europei: un matrimonio impossibile' (2018) *Rassegna parlamentare* 2, pp. 2 ss. Please also refer to Y. Mounk, *The People Versus Democracy: Why Our Freedom Is in Danger and How to Save It*, Harvard University Press, Harvard 2018.

between different disciplines of social sciences (constitutional law, political science, sociology), but above all to the different cultural approach of European legal doctrine compared, for example, to that of the United States, where the strand of studies on non-liberal constitutionalism is rather dated.

The reference to hybrid, spurious or intermediate political systems is generally used critically by constitutionalists to deny the possibility of a degenerate form of constitutional democracy (be it illiberal democracy or illiberal constitutionalism): the traditional approach of constitutional law or comparative law studies, which is 'Western-centric', generally denies dignity to these conceptual categories. A greater sensitivity to less rigid interpretations can be found in research on non-Western political systems that highlight the peculiar transformations that constitutional models of liberal origin undergo when they are exported or imposed in contexts different from those in which they historically originated.[4] Similarly, a propensity for a less static view of the traditional classifications of regimes – and a greater habit of thinking about contaminations between different forms – can be found in studies on the transition to democracy.

These are not new debates, but questions that periodically resurface in the reasoning of constitutional law scholars when the traditional instruments of the discipline appear insufficient to interpret the contemporary evolution of political systems. The research on degenerate forms of democracy and 'non-liberal' constitutionalisms therefore proposes conceptual hypotheses that are only apparently new. The same category of illiberal democracy is not new, having already been hypothesised by the Italian political scientist Giovanni Sartori in the 1950s.[5]

2. THE DOCTRINE ON ILLIBERAL CONSTITUTIONALISM AND DEMOCRACY

Before focusing on my personal interpretation of the intermediate systems, it is useful to reconstruct the most recent debate on the degeneration of

---

4 Mezzetti, *Le democrazie incerte. Transizioni costituzionali e consolidamento della democrazia in Europa orientale, Africa, America latina, Asia*, above n. 2; D. Amirante (ed.), *«Altre» democrazie. Problemi e prospettive del consolidamento democratico nel sub-continente indiano*, FrancoAngeli, Milano 2010; M. Ganino, 'Appunti e spunti per una ricerca di diritto costituzionale su paesi "altri"' in AA.VV., *Alle frontiere del diritto costituzionale. Scritti in onore di Valerio Onida*, Giuffrè, Milano 2011.

5 G. Sartori, *Democrazia e definizioni*, il Mulino, Bologna 1957, p. 228.

democracies, in which one can identify three doctrinal macro strands. The first two such strands are focused on the constitutional aspect of this degeneration (authoritarian constitutionalism and populist constitutionalism), and the third, mainly of a political nature, refers to illiberal democracies. In all three cases, they are studies of outdated origin that have seen a recent rereading or evolution.

The most recent debate on 'populist constitutionalism' and 'authoritarian constitutionalism' is partly linked to the contrast developed in Anglo-Saxon doctrine between political/popular constitutionalism and legal/judicial constitutionalism.[6] The first type of constitutionalism is seen as a 'democratic' and original version of constitutionalism, as opposed to 'legal constitutionalism', characterised by the predominance of the courts to the detriment of popular participation. The debate began in the 1990s with the use of the term 'populist constitutionalism' and then continued in the first decade of the 2000s with the use of the term 'popular/political constitutionalism' within a broad criticism of liberal/legal constitutionalism, which ended up proposing new, alternative forms of constitutionalism.[7] However, the criticism of judicial activism by the jurists at Yale (Balkin, Amar, Ackermann) and Harvard (Parker and Tushnet) intervened in a particular historical moment, to oppose a conservative Supreme Court.

Among the main contributions on authoritarian constitutionalism is that of one of the supporters of popular constitutionalism, Harvard jurist Mark Tushnet, who introduced the hypothesis of different forms of constitutionalism compared to liberal constitutionalism.[8] These would be intermediate situations between authoritarianism and democracy in which the constitutional mechanisms of the liberal democracies are

---

6 See: L. Kramer, 'Popular Constitutionalism' (2004) 92 *California Law Review* 4; M. Tushnet, 'Popular Constitutionalism as political law' (2006) *Chicago-Kent Law Review* 81; R. Bellamy, *Political Constitutionalism*, Cambridge University Press, Cambridge 2007; R. Bellamy, 'Constitutionalism' (2019) *Encyclopaedia Britannica*, www.britannica.com/topic/constitutionalism, last accessed 30.05.2020. On legalist constitutionalism, see also J.N. Shklar, *Legalism. Law, Morals and Political Trials*, Cambridge, Harvard University Press 1964.

7 J.M. Balkin, 'Populism and Progressivism as Constitutional Categories' (1991) *Yale Law Journal* 104; R.D. Parker, '"Here, the people rule": A constitutional populist manifesto' (1993) 27 *Valparaiso University Law Review* 3. For a broad analysis of the U.S. debate, see L. Corso, 'What does Populism have to do with Constitutional Law? Discussing Populist Constitutionalism and Its Assumptions' (2014) *Rivista di filosofia del diritto* 2.

8 M. Tushnet, 'Authoritarian Constitutionalism' in T. Ginsburg and A. Simpser (eds), *Constitutions in Authoritarian Regimes*, Cambridge University Press, New York 2014; M. Tushnet, 'Authoritarian Constitutionalism' (2015) 100 *Cornell Law Review* 2.

formally placed in a context of attenuated pluralism and strong social control. He distinguishes three variants of non-liberal constitutionalism: 'absolutist constitutionalism' (corresponding to the enlightened sovereign); 'rule-of-law constitutionalism' (an intermediate, imperfect form of constitutionalism in which there would be the rule of law – understood, however, in a formal sense – but not the liberal content of rights; this includes countries such as Hungary and Venezuela); and 'authoritarian constitutionalism' (in which freedoms of liberal origin would be protected 'at an intermediate level' and elections would be reasonably free and competitive; the main example is that of Singapore).

In Tushnet's conception, rule of law constitutionalism could in some cases coincide with 'illiberal democracies'.[9] This is a different approach from that of the European institutions which, on the other hand, see in Hungary and Poland precisely a crisis of the rule of law, but they understand this principle so broadly as to identify it with the form of a democratic-liberal state.[10]

The German scholar Gunter Frankenberg also uses the category of authoritarian constitutionalism. However, he does not make a clear distinction between authoritarianism and authoritarian constitutionalism, considering the latter as a modern form of authoritarianism and attributing certain of its characteristics to some consolidated democracies, as well.[11]

Some authors also speak of authoritarian constitutionalism with reference to the responses of the European Union to the economic crises of recent years and the consequent sacrifice of one of the fundamental components of the democratic-pluralist model of state, namely, the social model. In this case, we even speak of 'authoritarian liberalism' as

---

9 Hungary and Venezuela are also described as cases of abusive constitutionalism: D. Landau, 'Abusive constitutionalism' (2013) *UC Davis Law Review* 47. On abusive constitutionalism and on the distorted use of borrowing, see also R. Dixon and D. Landau, '1989–2019: From democratic to abusive constitutional borrowing' (2019) 17 *International Journal of Constitutional Law* 2. K.L. Scheppele speaks of *autocratic legalism*: 'Autocratic Legalism' (2018) *University of Chicago Law Review* 85.

10 See, for instance, the Venice Commission's *Rule of Law Check-list*: www.venice.coe.int/webforms/documents/default.aspx?pdffile=CDL-AD(2016)007-e, last accessed 23.09.2020.

11 G. Frankenberg, 'Authoritarian Constitutionalism – Coming to Terms with Modernity's Dreams and Demons', Faculty of law Research Paper No. 3/2018, Goethe Universität. The author also takes into consideration the authoritarian elements present in liberal democracies, such as the concentration of powers in the hands of the executive in the event of states of crisis or emergency, which would then be exacerbated in authoritarian constitutionalism.

a variant of authoritarian constitutionalism.[12] This reconstruction, which at times seems too criticical, has the merit, however, of focusing on two important aspects: on the one hand, the similarities between today's crisis of liberalism, with its constitutional consequences, and the situation in Weimar in the 1930s;[13] and on the other hand, the shortcomings of liberal democracies that favour the illiberal degeneration discussed here. The emergence of new political proposals, either from the point of view of the insertion of a certain amount of non-liberal elements and therefore the strengthening of the plebiscitary aspect of political consensus, or in the form of a communitarian (tribe versus people), familial and sovereignist/nationalist reading of the community of reference, represents a natural reaction to ordoliberalism or neoliberalism, especially in contexts of greater institutional fragility.

As far as the literature on populist constitutionalism is concerned, the interest on this topic is not new to political theory and philosophy. In fact, the term populist constitutionalism was used both at the beginning of the American debate mentioned above and by Latin American scholars, where constitutional populism is an 'ancient' way of challenging the liberal narrative that has its roots in the period between the two world wars.[14] Recent contributions on the theme of populist constitutionalism are numerous,[15] since this is not always considered in

---

12 M.A. Wilkinson, 'Authoritarian liberalism as authoritarian constitutionalism' in H.A. García and G. Frankenberg (eds), *Authoritarian Constitutionalism. Comparative Analysis and Critique*, Edward Elgar Publishing, Cheltenham 2019, pp. 317 ss. Also, R.H. Pildes, 'The Inherent Authoritarianism in Democratic Regimes' in A. Sajo (ed.), *Out of and Into Authoritarian Law*, Kluwer Law International, New York 2003.

13 This analogy, which in Weimar's example identifies the first historical case of degeneration of a liberal democracy, has been noted by several authors, including G. Allegri, 'Pluralismo solidale, innovazione sociale e processi federali per un nuovo garantismo costituzionale' in G. Allegri, A. Sterpa and N. Viceconte (eds), *Questioni costituzionali al tempo del populismo e del sovranismo*, Editoriale scientifica, Napoli 2019, p. 53. The term authoritarian liberalism was coined at that time by Hermann Heller (and was supported in Weimar Germany by Carl Schmitt's ideas). Also Polanyi (K. Polanyi, *Origins of our time. The great transformation*, Farrar & Rinehart, New York 1944, London 1954) notes that the authoritarian-liberal reaction to the economic crisis in the interwar period (fear of the people, of social democracy, of labour democracy, etc.) would have been a drain on democracy, thereby weakening its capacity for resistance to Nazism and Fascism.

14 C.M. Herrera, 'Le populisme constitutionnel' (2018) *Annuaire International de Justice Constitutionnelle* XXXIV, p. 702. E. Laclau, *La raison populiste*, Seuil, Paris 2008.

15 See for instance the special issues of a series of journals: *International Journal of Constitutional Law* (2019 17 2, 'Symposium: Public Law and the New Populism');

a negative way, especially with reference to certain variants that are made to bring about greater popular participation and policies of inclusion of the disadvantaged classes (as is the case of the initial constitutional transformations in Venezuela, Ecuador and Bolivia in so-called 'leftist' populisms). The conservative attitude is instead present above all in the European version, where populist politicians claim to have a monopoly on representation with antipluralist rhetoric (Hungary). The constitutionalism of the populist forces therefore becomes – depending on the case – an instrument of transformation of the constitutional system once their power has been consolidated in order to remain more stable,[16] or a challenge to liberal constitutionalism to correct its neo-liberalist and elitist distortions/deviances.[17]

European Constitutional Law Review (2019 15 3, special section on 'Populism and Constitutionalism'); *German Law Journal* (2019 20 2–3, Double Special Issue on 'Populism and Constitutionalism'); *Annuaire International de Justice Constitutionnelle* (XXXIV 2018 'Peuple, populisme et démocratie–Regards croisés'); *Questione giustizia* (2019 1 'Populismo e diritto').

16 D. Landau, 'Populist Constitutions' (2018) *The University of Chicago Law Review* 85. Landau points out three features of populist constitutionalism: deconstruction of the existing political system, ideological criticism of the shortcomings of the previous constitutional system and consolidation of the power of new populist leaders. G. Martinico, 'Fra mimetismo e parassitismo. Brevi considerazioni a proposito del complesso rapporto tra populismo e costituzionalismo' (2019) *Questione giustizia* 1, 74 ss. disputes the validity of populist constitutionalism and believes that populism distorts the values of constitutional democracies by producing a 'conceptual emptying of the categories proper to constitutionalism', thus adhering to the prevailing position that considers the term 'constitutionalism' to be non-adjectivable. See also L. Corrias, 'Populism in a Constitutional Key: Constituent Power, Popular Sovereignty and Constitutional Identity' (2016) *European Constitutional Law Review* 12, for the tripartition of contents of populist constitutionalism (nature of the constituent power; purpose of popular sovereignty; and constitutional identity). According to this author, populists (both right and left-wing) do not reject constitutional discourse, but propose alternatives to liberal constitutionalism, re-evaluate revolutionary roots and constituent power and enhance the identity vision of the community.

17 Herrera, *Le populisme constitutionnel*, above n. 14, with reference above all to the Argentine case where constitutional populism has historically led to an expansion of citizenship (or social rights) not in a judicial but political way. See also P. Blokker, 'Il costituzionalismo populista' in M. Anselmi, P. Blokker and N. Urbinati (eds), *Populismo di lotta e di governo*, Fondazione Feltrinelli, Milano 2018, p. 55, which, detecting in the left-winged populism a more acceptable version from the political and constitutional point of view, points out that this criticises the legal and elitist constitutionalism in favour of the participation of citizens in the constitutional policy. Also Corso, 'What does Populism have to do with Constitutional Law? Discussing Populist Constitutionalism and Its Assumptions', above n. 7, which seems to evaluate populist constitutionalism positively.

With specific reference to the label 'illiberal democracy', as a concept that divides the two components of post-war constitutional democracy, the conceptual approach depends on the starting point chosen for observation. The term generates confusion because it is used to refer indifferently to regimes that have suffered a decline in their democratic characteristics starting from positions of democratic stability (such as Hungary and Poland) and regimes that have always combined democratic and authoritarian elements (Russia, Turkey, Singapore).[18] Thus, one can refer to an authoritarian state that is democratising; to a liberal democracy that is deteriorating; or to a mixed system that has been stabilised for some time. Precisely because it applies to very different contexts, the term 'illiberal democracy' loses scientific credibility. For purist constitutionalists, illiberal democracy would be nothing more than 'an authoritarian regime in the process of emerging or consolidating',[19] i.e. a pure illiberal regime of a different intensity from the totalitarian one.[20]

3. THE DEGENERATION OF CONTEMPORARY DEMOCRACIES AS A NEW PHENOMENOLOGY OF CONSTITUTIONAL TRANSITION

Until a few years ago, the topic of the transition to democracy predominated, having created a real tradition of 'transitological' studies,

---

18 T.G. Daly, 'The Democratic Recession and the "New" Public Law: Toward Systematic Analysis', *International Journal of Constitutional Law Blog*, 22.04.2016; T.G. Daly, 'Illiberal Democracy: Pinning Down a Problematic Term', International Association of Constitutional Law (IACL) World Congress, Seoul, June 2018. For Pech and Scheppele, Hungary and Poland should be qualified as 'majoritarian autocracies'; L. Pech and K.L. Scheppele, 'Poland and the European Commission, Part I: A Dialogue of the Deaf?', *Verfassungsblog*, 03.01.2017; Puddington speaks of 'modern authoritarianism' (A. Puddington, 'Breaking Down Democracy: Goals, Strategies, and Methods of Modern Authoritarians' *Freedom House*, June 2017, https://freedomhouse.org/sites/default/files/June2017_FH_Report_Breaking_Down_Democracy.pdf, last accessed 26.09.2020). Referring to countries of Central and Eastern Europe, see B. Bugarić, 'Central Europe's descent into autocracy: a constitutional analysis of authoritarian populism' (2019) 17 *International Journal of Constitutional Law* 2, speaks of a 'diminished' form of democracy pervaded by strong authoritarian elements and therefore potentially a stand-alone form of constitutionalism.

19 X. Philippe, 'La légitimation constitutionnelle des démocratures' (2019) *Pouvoirs* 2, 35–37.

20 C. Pinelli, 'Illiberal regimes in the perspective of comparative constitutionalism' (2017) *Rivista di Diritti Comparati* 1, 7–9.

especially in the field of political science.[21] In the subsequent period, between the end of the 1990s and the middle of the first decade of the 2000s, when the moment of transition came to an end, the awareness that for a not inconsiderable number of countries it was difficult to identify a real transition to democratic consolidation – despite the apparent integration into supranational organisations, with the relative certification of democratic maturity – took over.[22]

In that phase, the adjectives 'imperfect' and 'uncertain' were used to designate this limited kind of democracy, with a different perspective, however, from today's reference to illiberal or populist democracies, as they referred to hypotheses of 'frozen' transitions.[23] At that time, the reference to these forms constituted a useful label with which to remove oneself from the paradigm of democratic transition, which should have had a limited time horizon. The terms and concepts used then seem similar to those used today, but the assumptions and starting points are different.

First of all, the main point of reference was that of established democracies, which these imperfect forms approached with varying degrees of approximation. Secondly, the imperfection was configured considering a precise starting point – that of the authoritarian or socialist system (or, in any case, of a regime not in accordance with the canons of liberal constitutionalism), from which the relative country had emancipated itself through a regime change. Thirdly, the reference to democracy included a precise indicator of value, assuming that it was a

21 See the classic study of G. O'Donnell, L. Whitehead and P.C. Schmitter (eds), *Transitions from Authoritarian Rule: Tentative Conclusions about Uncertain Democracies*, Johns Hopkins University Press, Baltimore and London 1986. Also J. Linz and A. Stepan, *Problems of Democratic Transition and Consolidation*, Johns Hopkins Press, Baltimore and London 1996; P.C. Schmitter, 'Reflections on "Transitology" – Before and After' in D.M. Brinks, M. Leiras and S. Mainwaring (eds), *Reflections on uneven democracies: the legacy of Guillermo O'Donnell*, Johns Hopkins University Press, Baltimore 2014.

22 On the concepts of transition and paradigm, and on their demystification, see I. Michel, 'Le paradigme de la transition: chronique d'une fine annonceé. Le cas de l'Europe centrale et orientale' (2006) *Revue d'études politiques et constitutionnelles Est-Européennes* Numéro spéciale. Also T. Carothers, 'The end of the transition paradigm' (2002) 13 *Journal of Democracy* 1.

23 For instance, see M. Volpi, 'La diffusione della democrazia e i suoi limiti' in Di Giovine and Sicardi (eds), *Democrazie imperfette*, above n. 2, foreshadowed a possible degradation of some 'imperfect' democracies (young, recently democratised, with no cultural background and in unfavourable contexts) towards semi-authoritarian impaired systems.

liberal and constitutional democracy. The imperfections and uncertainties thus stemmed from a contextual situation, although they were not always clearly perceived as provisional (to the point of being a stable intermediate hypothesis).[24]

Today's reference to different forms of democracy, with a preference for the label of 'illiberal' democracies, is made in a different political and cultural context to resurrect a happy and unconscious intuition of Zakaria of 1997 and to follow Orbán's theorisation of the famous speech of 2014.[25] These are phenomena of constitutional decay, regression or degeneration that not only concern countries of recent democratisation, but also extend to 'consolidated' democracies where the re-emergence of populist political phenomena enriches the discussion on the different constitutional models.

4. 'DEGRADED' DEMOCRACIES AS AN INTERMEDIATE HYPOTHESIS BETWEEN DEMOCRACY AND AUTHORITARIANISM

If we accept the hypothesis of an intermediate category ('degraded' or 'degenerate' democracy), we have to greatly reduce the size of the class in terms of path, duration and starting point. It is therefore necessary to identify the characteristics that – from a constitutional point of view – cause individuals to speak of a degraded democracy. These characteristics consist of a series of indicators of constitutional transformation, the presence of which reveals, in some countries, a path contrary to that experienced a few years earlier. However, a condition of democratic consolidation is taken as a starting point. This aspect is important in order to circumscribe the case studies, so as to avoid excessive trivialisation of the phenomenon. The cases of constitutional regression refer to those countries in which a certain maturation of the institutions of liberal democracy, albeit recent, had been reached and not to those in which there has been a deepening of an already semi-authoritarian or hybrid political regime.[26] This research

---

24 On this point, see A. Di Giovine, 'Forme di Stato' in L. Pegoraro (ed.), *Glossario di Diritto pubblico comparato*, Carocci, Roma 2009, p. 147, which distinguishes among mature democracies, imperfect democracies and undemocratic states.

25 M.F. Plattner, 'Illiberal democracy and the struggle on the right' (2019) 30 *Journal of Democracy* 1.

26 A. Huq and T. Ginsburg, 'How to Lose a Constitutional Democracy' (2018) *University of Chicago Law Review* 78 distinguish between *authoritarian reversion*, intended

is in contrast to the previous 'transitological' strand, even though it could be considered as a new form of authoritarian transition.[27]

The identification of an intermediate typology of degenerate democracy must necessarily refer to circumscribed cases that meet at least three basic criteria: an initial condition of democratic stability; the deterioration of certain requirements of liberal-democratic constitutionalism;[28] and the stabilisation of a hybrid system. The analysis must also be of medium or long term nature so as to verify the existence of the characteristics identified. It could include, as a context element, the democratic conditioning of the main supranational organisations. In fact, we speak of 'rule of law backsliding' with reference to the preventive and/or sanctioning paths of the European institutions (in particular, the Commission).[29] The relationship between the internal and European dimensions is further justified by the conditionality of international organisations, and in particular the European Union, which some consider to be the last possible remedy for the decay of democracies.[30] But from a different point of view, the European institutions would not be a solution, but instead, would be a cause for degenerative processes. This is due to the exasperation

as a rapid transition to an authoritarian system (*coup d'état*, proclamation of an emergency, etc.), which was more widespread in the past (Weimar, Thailand, Mali, Mauritania, etc.), and *constitutional retrogression*, as an incremental deterioration of liberal democracy through the simultaneous worsening of the three essential predicates of democracy (competitive elections; right to speak and association; rule of law), which is a much more widespread path in the contemporary era (Hungary, Poland, Venezuela, Turkey, Ukraine, Russia, etc.).

27 On the difference between the transition to democracy (a complex process of cooperation and competition involving a large number of independent agents) and the transition to authoritarianism (which can be performed by a small group that is compact and hierarchically structured, like a military *junta*), refer to Schmitter, 'Reflections', above n. 21.

28 In particular, the rule of law and, consequently, the separation of powers, the weakening of the majority counter-powers, starting from the courts (Please refer to A. Di Gregorio, 'Constitutional Courts in the Context of Constitutional Regression. Some Comparative Remarks' in M. Belov (ed.), *Courts, Politics, and Constitutional Law*, Routledge, London 2019); modification/amendment and replacement of the constitution, or the emptying or derogation of the constitution in order to neutralise the system of checks and balances provided for by it.

29 L. Pech and D. Kochenov, *Strengthening the Rule of Law Within the European Union: Diagnoses, Recommendations, and What to Avoid*, Policy Brief, European Commission, June 2019.

30 A. Von Bogdandy and L.D. Spieker, 'Countering the Judicial Silencing of Critics: Article 2 TEU Values, Reverse Solange, and the Responsibilities of National Judges' (2019) *European Constitutional Law Review*.

of liberalist and technocratic elements and the absence of genuine popular involvement.[31]

Having limited, in the way indicated above, the field of investigation, which is based especially on the two fundamental aspects of these new forms – namely, the starting point and duration, as well as the characteristics of the degenerative process –, the analysis in the European context can only refer to the cases of Hungary and Poland. It is therefore considered wrong to identify a generalised democratic recession in post-communist countries as the result of failed democratisation. Not all these countries had reached full democratic maturity, while others were not affected by the phenomenon of constitutional regression.[32]

Hungary and Poland were forerunners of democratic change – an example for neighbouring countries. They have experienced numerous transitions in history and have civil societies that are still vibrant and participate in European culture. It is therefore reasonable to consider the degenerations taking place in the two countries as a manifestation of an intermediate category and not of a sure descent towards authoritarianism (in which case there would be no hope of recovery).

5. CRISIS OF LIBERAL DEMOCRACY AND VARIOUS MEANINGS OF 'DEMOCRACY' AND 'CONSTITUTIONALISM'

Debates on the degeneration and/or transformation of democratic-constitutional models, on the identification of intermediate typologies and on the most suitable terminology to identify them – carried out with a multidisciplinary approach[33] – are useful tools to reflect on the defects

---

31 D. Kosař, J. Baroš and P. Dufek, 'The Twin Challenges to Separation of Powers in Central Europe: Technocratic Governance and Populism' (2019) 15 *European Constitutional Law Review* 3.

32 For a more extensive analysis of the region, refer to A. Di Gregorio (ed.), *The Constitutional Systems of Central-Eastern, Baltic and Balkan Europe*, Eleven International Publishing, The Hague 2019. It should be remembered that Zakaria himself, in his 1997 essay, considered the democratic transition of the Central European countries to be successful since they had gone through the same phase of 'liberalisation without democracy' as other European countries in the 19th century. In fact, the Austro-Hungarian Empire in which they were inserted responded to the classic model of liberal-autocracy. These countries were therefore not considered by Zakaria in the ranks of illiberal democracies, with the exception of Slovakia.

33 On the praise of multi-disciplinarity as a characteristic feature of global constitutionalism, see A.F. Lang jr., M. Kumm, A. Wiener, J. Tully and M. Poiares Maduro,

and limitations of traditional liberal democracies in the era of economic globalisation and pandemic, as well as in order to introduce antibodies to avoid their destruction.

First of all, two trends can be observed that allow us to mitigate the pessimism prevailing in the crisis of the model of constitutional democracy. On the one hand, a slow but progressive retreat from the populist and demagogic wave,[34] since these forces, while grasping the discomfort caused by the errors of Western constitutional democracies (including the EU system), in terms of limiting popular participation and bureaucratic technicalism and neo-liberalism, on the other hand, have not been able to provide an alternative model of coexistence with guarantees of pluralism and inclusion. The second trend is the affirmation of the values of constitutionalism in non-Euro-Atlantic geographical areas. This latter development leads to a shift away from the identification between the West and constitutionalism which, although historically founded, today gives way to an extension of the mechanisms and values of constitutionalism at a global level.[35] These values, in the history of Western countries, have also gone through different phases with periods of negation (restoration, fascism, etc.) and continue to coexist today with non-democratic values which are the expression of different cultures.[36]

'Interdisciplinarity: Challenges and opportunities' (2013) 2 *Global Constitutionalism* 1. The fundamental contribution of interdisciplinarity to understand the 'global public law' developed after 1989 is at the basis of the reasoning of T. Ginsburg, 'Thirty years after the fall: An academic perspective' (2019) 17 *International Journal of Constitutional Law* 2, according to which precisely the interdisciplinary turn in social sciences of the last 30 years would have allowed the flourishing of comparative constitutional law studies in the US.

34 See the results of the 2019 European Parliamentary elections, even before the victory in the 2017 presidential elections in France, the change of government alliances in Italy in August 2019, the non-plebiscite result of the Polish elections in October 2019 and the presence of a series of internal and external counterweights, the crisis of Latin American populism, etc.

35 Quite optimistic is the position of M. Kumm, J. Havercroft, J. Dunoff and A. Wiener, 'Editorial. The end of "the West" and the future of global constitutionalism' (2017) 6 *Global Constitutionalism* 1, according to which the crisis or decline of the West – as a category of the cold and post-colonial war – would not entail an analogous crisis of Western ideology (liberal and constitutional ideas produced by the 18th-century revolutions).

36 On this more extensively, see D. Kennedy 'Authoritarian constitutionalism in liberal democracies' in García and Frankenberg (eds), *Authoritarian Constitutionalism. Comparative Analysis and Critique*, above n. 12, pp. 161 ss. distinguishing between authoritarian and republican (progressive) elements in liberal democracies, noting how progressive traditions are lacking in countries that accessed this model later, as in Latin America and Eastern Europe, where authoritarian elements, much more deeply

To avoid further degeneration, however, it is not sufficient to go back to the past. Although there are important signs of the end of the populist wave, what has happened nevertheless reinforces the need to move on to a new season of constitutionalism. The extension of the geographical scope of the rules of constitutionalism to areas further away from Western culture (Asia, Latin America and Africa) entails a reformulation. The salvation of constitutionalism does not lie in taking refuge in anachronistic ivory towers, but in its re-founding with the contribution of different cultural elements and the restoration of social content and values of solidarity. The method by which to recover the attractiveness of the liberal democratic system does not consist of more courts and more guarantees,[37] but of more society (understood as participation and social rights).

Another caveat concerns the meaning of the terms 'democracy' and 'constitutionalism', which continue to undergo diversification. But while the semantic differentiation of democracy is historically known, constitutionalism is not so diversified, although it has also received multiple adjectives in the doctrine.[38] Twentieth-century European constitutionalism, as it had developed by the end of the First World War – but above all, by the end of the Second World War – is different from that of its 18th-century origins and represents a typology in its own right that during the last 30 years has undergone further transformations, which have not always been positively perceived. This is with reference to two developments: on the one hand, excessive jurisdictionalisation (too much power of the courts; too much emphasis on individual rights; too many unrepresentative, technical, elitist institutional counterbalance

---

rooted, remained on the surface and managed to emerge easily. See also R.H. Pildes, 'The Inherent Authoritarianism in Democratic Regimes' in A. Sajo (ed.), *Out of and Into Authoritarian Law*, Kluwer Law International, New York 2003.

37 Among others, B. Randazzo, 'Populismo e diritto. Dialogando con Enrico Scoditti' (2019) *Questione Giustizia* 1, 70, warns against the risks of judicial populism and considers populisms to be a symptom of the 'crisis of democratic systems overwhelmed by globalization' and not just 'mere forms of regression of Western civilization'. See also K. Ragnarsson, 'The counter-majoritarian difficulty in a neoliberal world: Socio-economic rights and deference in post-2008 austerity cases' (2019) 8 *Global Constitutionalism* 3.

38 Frankenberg, *Authoritarian Constitutionalism – Coming to Terms with Modernity's Dreams and Demons*, above n. 12, distinguishes four types of regimes: liberal constitutionalism; democratic constitutionalism; authoritarian constitutionalism; and authoritarianism. With the expansion over the last century, constitutionalism underwent several metamorphoses in Europe, Latin America, Africa and Asia, experiencing a wide range of constitutional 'scaffolds' (liberal, illiberal and a-liberal).

mechanisms); on the other hand, to remain in Europe, the not entirely happy combinations of democratic conditionality and economic integration into the Community model.[39] In the first case, the participatory element has been sacrificed too much (also because of the crisis of intermediate bodies) and in the other case, the social element has been excessively sacrificed. But both are essential to constitutionalism, which in its European version and in the version disseminated to other parts of the world in the successive waves of democratisation has been enriched by new demands (such as community and environmental democratisation in Africa and Latin America). The sacrifice of the social and solidarity element has weighed particularly heavily on post-communist countries, fuelling a populist policy of recovering the paternalistic and welfare elements erased by Euro-community technicalism.

Democracy and constitutionalism are no longer monolithic phenomena. Consequently, that simplifying dichotomy which seemed to be established, between democratic and autocratic models of state, is rediscovered complexity, with the appearance of intermediate forms which, although difficult to insert in precise typologies, are nevertheless characterised by a sufficient degree of stability. This dynamism of political regimes, far from rendering the efforts of comparative doctrine useless, reveals even more the need for a multidisciplinary investigation.

The worldwide emergence of the coronavirus has tested the stability of different regimes that often responded to the crisis with measures on the edge of constitutional legality. This blurred the border between democracies and autocracies, giving rise to heated debates on the legitimacy and limits of emergency instruments, with further food for thought on the different methods used to manage the emergency and on the quality of the democratic system. Once the emergency is over, we will have to deal with the veil that these exceptional instruments have placed on the (false) sharpness of democracies. Furthermore, we will be called to rethink the purism of certain theories in accordance with a post-global world scenario, in which dangers are much more insidious than traditional wars or natural emergencies.

---

39 To which are added the distortions on the principle of separation of powers reported by Kosař, Baroš and Dufek, 'The Twin Challenges to Separation of Powers in Central Europe: Technocratic Governance and Populism', above n. 31.

BETWEEN LAW AND REVOLUTION

Is Populism Constitutional?

Gianmario Demuro

1. INTRODUCTION

Populism can be revolutionary, because a prescriptive conception of democracy is not able to rule our globalised world and economy. Therefore, the question that populism tries to answer is: how can we represent the people, left alone to face the uncertain economic and social relationships that are the by-products of the globalized economy?

In D. Rodrik's opinion, for example, we find this strong root:

> I do not claim that globalization was the only force at play – nor necessarily even the most important one. Changes in technology, rise of winner-take-all markets, erosion of labor-market protections, and decline of norms restricting pay differentials all have played their part. These developments are not entirely independent from globalization, insofar as they both fostered globalization and were reinforced by it. But neither can they be reduced to it. Nevertheless, economic history and economic theory both give us strong reasons to believe that advanced stages of globalization are prone to populist backlash.[1]

---

1 D. Rodrik, 'Populism and the economics of globalization' (2018) *Journal of International Business Policy* 2.

The impact of globalisation is different in every part of the world, and we therefore have a variety of populist movements. However, we are witnessing the predominance of right-wing populism in the current wave. This brand of populism emphasises a cultural cleavage: the national, ethnic, religious or cultural identity of the 'people' against outside groups who allegedly pose a threat to the popular will. In the United States (US), Donald Trump has at various points demonised the Mexicans, Chinese and Muslims. In Europe, right-wing populists portray Muslim immigrants, minority groups (Roma or Jews) and the faceless bureaucrats of Brussels as the 'other'.

An alternative type of populism revolves around a largely economic cleavage between the wealthy groups who control the economy and define its rules and the lower-income groups without access to power.[2] The calculation of the distance between the people and the power is explored by F. Sureau: 'It is hard to live, especially as a conscious citizen, in a world that seems to escape both organizing reason and political action'.[3]

Populism therefore grows where society is under pressure; where the welfare state is under pressure; and where traditional democracy is unable to give a simple answer to a complicated question: 'Populism considers that the representative system and democracy in general are structurally corrupted by politicians and that the only real form of democracy would be the appeal to the people, i.e. the referendum'.[4]

The above-mentioned is the social, political and constitutional context described 20 years ago by C.R. Sunstein, who writes:

> In a free society, those who want to avoid general interest intermediaries are certainly permitted to do so. No government Agency compels adults to read or watch. Nonetheless, a central democratic goal is to ensure a large measure of social integration – not merely of racial groups, but across multiple lines, in a way that broadens sympathies and enriches human life.[5]

In this disrupted society, which Sunstein calls 'a balcanized society',[6] 'the deepest message offered by populism' is: 'You are not alone',[7] and this

---

2 *Ibid.*, 10.

3 See F. Sureau, *Sans la Liberté*, Gallimard, Paris 2019, p. 27.

4 P. Rosanvallon, *Penser le populisme*, in *La vie des idèes*. Collège de France, September 2011.

5 C.R. Sunstein, *Republic.com*, Princeton University Press, Princeton and Harvard 2001, p. 196.

6 *Ibid.*, p. 199.

7 M. Ferraresi, *Solitudine*, Einaudi, Torino 2020.

ideology can easily constitute a political party programme that set an apparently simple agenda.

This explains why the most accurate studies are in the field of political science, and also why these studies demonstrate that populism is a programmatically inaccurate and ambiguous term[8] and a type of programmatic rhetoric that tries to reveal its traits in political programs such as, for example, what happened in Italy during the first year of the legislature in 2018.[9]

Finally, certain individuals consider populism to be an attitude or a posture that pretends to represent 'the people' directly, without any other parties' mediation. For example, Y.W. Muller states that:

> Populism, I contend, is a profoundly illiberal and, in the end, directly undemocratic understanding of representative democracy. It has an inner logic which makes both the claims and the actions of populists hang together in a particular way; and by both their claims and their actions can we tell them, that is to say, populists.[10]

Thus, the narrative of every populist party makes it possible for the people to have the illusion of making 'direct' political decisions, because they are taken 'directly' by those who will suffer them, such as, for example, the idea that the borders of the territory of the state can stop global migration.[11] In fact, populism is:

> ... an ideology that consider society to be ultimately separated into two homogeneous and antagonistic groups, the pure people versus the corrupt elite, and which argues that politics should be an expression of the volonté générale (general will) of the people.[12]

---

8 Y. Mény and Y. Surel, 'The Constitutive Ambiguity of Populism' in Y. Mény and Y. Surel (eds), *Democracies and the populist challenge*, Palgrave, London 2002, pp. 1 ss.

9 G. Martinico, *Il diritto costituzionale come speranza. Secessione, democrazia e populismo alla luce delle Reference Re Secession of Quebec*, Giappichelli, Torino 2019, pp. 113 ff.

10 Y.W. Müller, 'The People must be extracted from within the people. Reflections on populism', (2014) 21 *Constellations* 4, 484.

11 C.S. Maier, *Once Within Borders. Territories of Power, Wealth, and Belonging since 1500*, The President and Fellows of Harvard College, Harvard University Press, Cambridge, Massachusetts 2016, p. 7 ff.

12 C. Mudde, *An Ideational approach*, in C. Rovira Kaltwasser, P.A. Taggart, P. Ochoa Espejo and P. Ostiguy (eds), *The Oxford Handbook of Populism*, Oxford University Press, Oxford 2017, p. 29.

Following this ideology of populism, politics is not intermediation, but a direct representation of what the people demand, which must be respected as a sort of political arithmetic,[13] because political science and big data analysts know that political parties control the people; they intimately know the nature of the people, as well as what the people demand and what the people need.[14] In other words, I control you, so I know what you want; in order to know what you want, I have to control you, and we know that globalism affects you as a part of the people.[15]

We can certainly say that this idea – which represents the basis of the European Alliance of Sovereign Parties, currently the fifth group in the European Parliament – has failed. Sovereign parties failed to go beyond a representation that is incapable of affecting European policies. It would therefore seem that the European dimension prevailed over the aspiration of national politics to replace it. In the French elections, the 'Macron doctrine' brought the European dimension into the national debate, and this choice undoubtedly favoured the concentration of electoral themes on the defence of the European solidarity constraint.[16]

In that context, this chapter will discuss whether different versions of a populist doctrine can affect the common, shared idea of the European constitutional law traditions – that is, the European dimension of national politics as a series of weights and counterweights that exist as a common constitutional rule of law.

Therefore, the representation of European solidarity, even in a context of tension between budget deficits and social rights which are laboriously financed, holds up despite the most dangerous form of sovereignty carried out by the so-called *Visegrad* countries, which continue to support the aporia of illiberal democracies, which are completely removed from the European constitutional identity. The European themes therefore hold up both in the dimension of the national debate and in the European dimension, because they circularly strengthen the bonds of solidarity

---

13 During the Glorious Revolution, in William Petty's time, the political arithmetic was represented by the territorial partition in D. Runciman, *Cosi finisce la democrazia*, Bollati boringhieri, Torino 2019, italian translation of D. Runciman *How Democracy Ends*, Profile Books London 2018, p. 128.

14 D. Runciman, *ibid.*

15 Y. Algan, E. Beasley and M. Foucault, *Les Origines du Populism*, Seuil, Paris 2019.

16 G. Pallaver, M.Gehler and M. Cau (eds), *Populism, Populists, and the Crisis of Political Parties: A Comparison of Italy, Austria, and Germany 1990–2015*, Bologna Il Mulino, Duncker/Humboldt 2018.

between the countries that have signed onto them. From this perspective, a European debate can begin on how this burgeoning link can be translated into inclusive public policies. If this national dimension of the European constraint does not find an outlet in concrete public policies, this will be the moment in which it will be difficult to overcome the simplifications of sovereignty.

2. POPULISM vs. CONSTITUTIONALISM AND PARLIAMENTARY DEMOCRACY

Populism and constitutionalism are facing each other in a final battle for democracy. An attempt is being made to make people believe that the supporters of liberal democracy are accomplices of elites who vote against the people they represent, while the populist and illiberal forces defend a people (not represented by them) that the elites have betrayed. According to populist ideology, elites are against 'the have-nots':[17] growing inequality is 'the engine of populism',[18] fitted with the ideology of national identity that, for some, is the result of the global economy within the EU.

For the economist T. Piketty,

> All European leaders ... bear their share of responsibility. The free movement of capital, goods and services, without collective regulation, without a common fiscal or social policy, works above all to the benefit of the richest and most mobile, and hurts the most disadvantaged and the most vulnerable.[19]

Therefore, the rise of populism in European countries is the political response to the social and fiscal dumping.

From this point of view, the Hungarian reaction during the vote of the European Parliament in 2018 on violations of the European Charter of Human Rights and European value is summed up by Prime Minister

---

17 R. Inglehart and P. Norris, *Trump, Brexit and the Rise of Populism: Economic Have Nots and Cultural Backlash*, Harvard Kennedy School, John F. Kennedy School of Government, 2016.

18 Runciman, above n. 13, p. 72.

19 T. Pikkety, 'Social-fédéralisme contre national-liberalisme', in *Le Monde*, 10.02.2020.

Viktor Orban's statement. Orban declared that the European Parliament would vote against the Hungarian People:

> I know that my speech here today will not manage to change your opinion. Still I've come here today because you are not going to condemn a government but a country as well as a nation. You are going to denounce Hungary, which has been a member of the family of Christian European nations for thousand years.[20]

The populist ideology frames this counter-position as a battle between the 'European Parliament and Hungary':

> You're going to condemn Hungary that contributed to the great history of Europe with hard work and shed its blood when needed. You're going to denounce Hungary that rebelled and took to arms against the biggest army of the world the Soviet Army and shed its blood for freedom and democracy. And when time came opened its borders to fellow eastern German friends Hungary has fought its battles for freedom and democracy and I stand here today and see those are the ones to accuse Hungary who inherited democracy who did not have to take personal risks in order to obtain liberty.[21]

In his final statement, Orban announces that:

> … whatever your decision will be Hungary will not accede to this blackmailing Hungary will protect its borders stop illegal migration and will defend its rights if needed. We will stand up to you too. We stand ready for the elections next May where people can decide on the future of Europe and reconstituted democracy to European politics.[22]

This produced a negative climate in the run-up to the European elections, which have increasingly been polarised on the issues of the sharing or rejection of European values. However, such values should be shared by all Member States. The values written in Article 2 of the Treaty on the Union (which have never, to date, been subject to a vote of Parliamentary censure) range from constitutional democracy to the rule of law, and

---

20 Debate on the situation in Hungary: Statement by Viktor ORBÁN, Hungarian Prime Minister (15:31–15:39), 11 September 2018, https://multimedia.europarl.europa.eu/en/debate-on-the-situation-in-hungary-statement-by-viktor-orbn-hungarian-prime-minister-1531_I160027-V_v.

21 *Ibid.*

22 *Ibid.*

from the separation of powers to the respect of fundamental rights. Therefore, traditional parties and coalitions that participated in the European elections had the courage to call for a vote to remove the risk that our liberal democracies could turn into illiberal democracies. The term 'illiberal democracies' usually implies democracies where only the majority is aware of what is right for a country. Moreover, illiberal democracies are systems with limited freedom of press and manifestation of thought. It is those institutions that eliminate the counterweights exercised by autonomous powers – from the judiciary to central banks – and it is those majorities that change constitutions to keep illiberal power in place.

In a recent article in *El Pais*, Muller clarify this core populist understanding of duty:

> Orbán and other potential autocrats claim to be the authentic representatives of a homogeneous people, but if they gain power, they will not hesitate to reject pluralism and trample on the rights of minorities. Sociologist Olivier Royad says Christianity is a question of tribal belonging, with no relation to beliefs or ethical behaviour. As the bishop of Szeged, who is aligned with Orbán, said: "In Europe, even atheists are Christians. What interests them is not Christianity but Christianity, understood as a civilization inherently hostile to Islam.[23]

Illiberal democracies are not democracies – instead, they are the opposite of the very *idea* of democracy.[24] For this reason, the greatest effort to be made, on the part of all and not just by the political parties, will be to accept the fact that liberal democracies live in the constraints of recognition of values that are universal or, at least for Europeans, supranational.

It is a question of rethinking an undoubtedly fundamental theme; as Hannah Arendt pointed out, the recognition of the other is the basis of a political life.[25] But we can also take up the idea that the origins of democracy can be traced back to personal autonomy: we are democratic because we are free. From this point of view, European studies should bring back the debate on whether democracy begins in self-determination, in the subsidiarity principle or in the transparency of self-government.

---

23 J.-W. Müller, *Democracia cristiana o democracia illiberal?* in *El Pais* 09.02.2020, p. 13.

24 Y. Mounk, *The People vs. Democracy*, Harvard University Press, Cambridge Massachusetts 2018.

25 H. Arendt, *The Human Condition*, 2nd ed., The University of Chicago Press, Chicago and London 1998.

This is to argue against the current debate which, conversely, seems to bring us back to Max Weber's ideas expressed in *Economics and Society.* According to Weber, the perfect model of democracy is that of the city-state, in that conceptual models are the borders that define democracy.[26] The idea of the border is under stress by the opposite model of global democratic governance which is, by definition, without borders: sovereignty is still 'defined as the supreme authority within a territory', but 'a territory is a set of geographical coordinates projected onto the world of atoms; the state is no more a given feature of the natural world than a centimetre or a country club'.[27]

Today, in the digital economy, which has been made possible due to technological advancement, we can use different words – for example, *cyber-sovereignty* or, even better, *cyber-subsidiarity*[28] – to react to the idea of the tyranny of state sovereignty and reinforce the notion that democracy exists only if it is open and recognises minorities.

More than ten years of financial crisis seem to have facilitated the restoration of nationalism and protectionism in the global economy. Thus, if we want to defend representative democracy, we must start from a democracy of proximity, which is inscribed in the concept of responsible autonomy. We have to return again to the rule of law, deriving from the courts, and the sovereignty of the Parliament, which can fight the aforementioned 'growing inequalities' which are the base of populism. If we want to 'restore democracy',[29] as Stiglitz writes, we must start from an 'open city ethic', as Sennet calls it, where one can live with others in a framework that is proposed by the ethical dimension of the city.[30]

The debate on Europe could originate not from the Member States but rather from the pluralism of cities, where every city and every citizen brings us back to the assumption of responsibility of those who self-govern. Recalling collective responsibility is useful in remembering that illiberal democracy is not so much the result of a polemic of its opponents, but

---

26 M. Weber, 'Economy and Society. An outline of interpretive sociology' in G. Roth and G. Wittich (eds), University of California Press, Berkeley 1978.

27 J.G. Allen and R.M. Lastra, 'Border Problems: Mapping the Third Border' (2020) *The Modern Law Review* 9.

28 *Ibid.*, p. 13.

29 J. Stiglitz, *People, Power and Profits: Progressive Capitalism for the Age of Discontent*, Penguin Books, New York 2019, Part 2, Chapter 8.

30 R. Sennet, *Building* and *Dwelling. Ethics for the City*, Ferrar, Strauss and Giroux, New York 2018, p. 293.

rather, a proud self-definition among those who propose it as a response to open democracy.

3. POPULISM AS AN IDEOLOGY PROLIFERATES IN ILLIBERAL DEMOCRACIES

Some authors suggest 'strengthening democratic institutions within states' because 'it constitutes the only possibility of democratic control over the power delegated to transnational decision-making bodies. Democratic controls would help prevent delegation from actually becoming a permanent and total transfer of control'.[31] If we start with the ideological definition of populism, we find completely different definitions of the same phenomenon. As M. Naim writes:

> The essence of the populist recipe is to undermine the checks and balances that limit populists' power and hold them accountable. The common wisdom used to be that populists tended to succeed in countries where institutions were too weak to contain them, or where citizens believed that 'all politicians were the same' and nothing could be worse than what they had. But the success of populist politicians in some European countries and the United States shows that even mature democracies are no guarantee against populism.[32]

But the most clear and open definition is the 'ideanational' definition developed by Mudde: 'populism *is* essentially a set of ideas-whether or not they constitute an ideology or "only" a discourse ... connected to an essential struggle between the "good people" and the "corrupt elite". So, there is certainly a relationship between populism and nationalism in every single area of the world, but populism is essentially "a set of ideas"'.[33] Therefore, how can an ideology affect and change constitutional rules? Is populism able to change the prescriptive rules of a formal constitution?

---

31 R.A. Dahl, 'Efficiency of the "versus" effective citizenship order: a dilemma of democracy', Dahl-Ferrara-Haberle, New-Rusconi, in M. Luciani (ed.), *Democracy at the end of the century*, Laterza, Bari 1994, p. 22.

32 M. Naim, *How to be a populist. Power and populism in a new world*, in Ipsos MORI Social Research Institute's Understanding Society – *Beyond Populism*, 2017, https://www.ipsos.com/sites/default/files/2017-07/Understanding_society-beyond_populism-2017.pdf, p. 20.

33 Mudde, above n. 12, p. 42.

Populism is the opposite of the constitutional liberal tradition, as P. Norris and R. Ingelhart write:

> Cosmopolitan ideas emphasizing open borders and open societies are combined with Liberal values which challenge the authoritarian component of populism, emphasizing the importance of horizontal checks and balances in the institutions of representative democracy, protection of minority, participation through elections and membership of political parties, tolerance of social, intellectual, and political diversity, the process of pluralistic bargaining and compromise, the contribution of scientific expertise for rational policymaking, and the post-war architecture of global governance and international cooperation. Social liberalism is also linked with support for equal rights for women and minorities, flexible rather than fixed gender roles, fluid gender identities and LGBT rights, environmental protection, and secular rather than religious values.[34]

Norris and Ingelhart also argue that the theory of the 'cultural backlash' as the heart of rising populism has significant consequences:

> If the cultural backlash argument is essentially correct, then this has significant implications; the growing generational gap in Western societies is likely to heighten the salience of the cultural cleavage in party politics in future, irrespective of any improvements in the underlying economic conditions or any potential slowdown in globalization. The orthogonal pull of cultural politics generates tensions and divisions within mainstream parties, as well as allowing new opportunities for populist leaders on the left and right to mobilize electoral support, although it still remains challenging for populist parties to build an organizational base and to sustain any temporary breakthroughs if they enter government coalitions and become part of the establishment. The net result is that Western societies face more unpredictable contests, anti-establishment populist challenges to the legitimacy of liberal democracy, and potential disruptions to long-established patterns of party competition.[35]

Therefore, in the following section, we will discuss whether the idea that a constitutional democracy can only be a polyarchy is still commonly held.[36]

---

34 Inglehart and Norris, above n. 17, pp. 7–8.

35 *Ibid.*, p. 31.

36 R.A. Dahl, *Polyarchy, participation and opposition*, Yale University Press, New Haven, CT 1971; G. Pasquino, *Minima politica. Sei Lezioni di Democrazia*, Utet, Torino 2020.

4. CONCLUSION: EUROPEAN CONSTITUTIONAL IDENTITY HAS TO LIMIT POPULISM WITHIN THE INTERNAL STATE

As P. Rosanvallon writes:

> ... democracy cannot be reduced to a system of decision-making. Democracy is a regime of the general will, which is built over time. It is the fact of elaborating a project, a collective history, and not simply of saying yes or no, or of choosing a person. Democracy is not simply a regime of instantaneous decision, but it is the expression of a will in history. That is why its modes of expression and its voices must also be multiplied and made permanent. But not only in terms of increasing the number of votes, but also in terms of citizen involvement. By multiplying the modalities of a permanent democracy. For example, by subjecting those in power to increased surveillance, more frequent accountability, forms of control, and forms of judgement. The citizen cannot expect to be behind every decision, but he can participate in a collective power of control, surveillance, judgment, permanent evaluation of the established powers.[37]

Consequently, sovereign populism can be considered as an infringement of the constitutional identity of every state, and different versions of *populism* can affect constitutional law. The European dimension of the national rule of law means that a series of weights and counterweights exist in electoral appointments, functioning as European constraints to discussions of concrete problems.

The representation of European solidarity, therefore – even in a context of tension between budget deficits and social rights which are laboriously financed – holds up despite the most dangerous form of sovereignty. It continues to support the aporia of illiberal democracies – completely remote from the core of European constitutional identity. If the national dimension of the European constraint does not find an outlet in concrete public policies, this will be the moment in which it will be difficult to beat the simplifications of illiberal democracies.

---

[37] Rosanvallon, above n. 4.

EUROPEAN CONSTITUTIONAL ORDER AND POPULIST LEGAL REVOLUTION

A Challenge for Western Liberal Democracies

Carlo Alberto CIARALLI

1. THE RISE OF POPULISM IN EUROPE

Populism is the most important political phenomenon of our times. Particularly in Europe, populism has produced relevant effects on institutions and on social and political approaches to contemporary challenges.[1] The 'popular proliferation' of the populist cultural vision of society clearly denotes that the populist approach is 'hegemonic' in today's societies.[2]

---

1 A significant study about the origins of the populist phenomenon in a comparative perspective (with particular reference to the United States and European experiences) is offered by N. URBINATI, 'Democracy and Populism' (1998) 5 *Constellations* 1, 110–24. On this topic, see also K.P. MILLER, 'Constraining Populism: The Real Challenge of Initiative Reform' (2001) *Santa Clara Law Review* 41, 1037–84; D. STOCKEMER (ed.), *Populism Around the World. A Comparative Perspective*, Springer, Cham 2019.

2 On the rise of 'populist ideology' and its hegemonic spread in Western societies see, among others, E. LACLAU, *On Populist Reason*, Verso, London 2005; M. ROODUIJN, S.L. DE LANGE and W. VAN DER BRUG, 'A populist Zeitgeist? Programmatic

The theoretical and academic debate about the populist phenomenon is related to the correct categorisation of this political factor.[3] With reference to the pure textual data, the first impression is that of a political phenomenon that places the people at the centre of its own ideological approach. In this way, in a well-known 1966 essay, the Italian academic scholar Giovanni Sartori was the first to argue the thesis of the 'anti-system party', understood as a political and social force organised in a political party that places itself in a radical antagonism to the national and supranational economic, social and political framework (i.e. political order).[4]

However, in recent times, a classic academic definition of populism (that has become a usual analytical starting point among the scholars) is advanced by Cas Mudde, according to which populism must be identified as 'an ideology that considers society to be ultimately separated into two homogeneous and antagonistic groups, "the pure people" versus "the corrupt elite", and which argues that politics should be an expression of the *volonté générale* (general will) of the people'.[5] We are talking about a real one 'barrier axiom', based on a rigid (Manichean) division between

---

contagion by populist parties in Western Europe' (2014) 20 *Party politics* 4, 563–74; Y. Stavrakakis, 'Populism and Hegemony', in C. Rovira Kaltwasser, P. Taggart, P. Ochoa Espejo and P. Ostiguy (eds), *The Oxford Handbook of Populism*, Oxford University Press, Oxford 2017, pp. 536–53; T. Lochocki, *The Rise of Populism in Western Europe*, Springer, Cham 2018.

3 With reference to the correct categorisation of contemporary populist phenomenon see, among others, C. Rovira Kaltwasser, 'The ambivalence of populism: threat and corrective for democracy' (2012) 19 *Democratization* 2, 184–208; B. Moffitt and S. Tormey, 'Rethinking Populism: Politics, Mediatisation and Political Style' (2014) *Political Studies* 62, 381–97; H. Kriesi, 'Populism. Concepts and conditions for its rise in Europe' (2015) *Comunicazione politica* 2, 175–93; P. Aslanidis, 'Is Populism an Ideology? Refutation and a New Perspective' (2016) 64 *Political Studies* 1, 88–104; B. Bonikowski, 'Three Lessons of Contemporary Populism in Europe and the United States' (2016) 23 *The Brown Journal of World Affairs* 1, 9–24; N. Urbinati, 'Political Theory of Populism' (2019) *Annual Review of Political Sciences* 22, 111–27; R.R. Barr, 'Populism as a political strategy', in C. de la Torre (ed.), *The Routledge International Handbook of Global Populism*, Routledge, London and New York 2019, pp. 44–56; L. Bustikova and P. Guasti, 'The State as a Firm: Understanding the Autocratic Roots of Technocratic Populism' (2019) 33 *East European Politics and Societies and Cultures* 2, 302–30; M. Laruffa, 'The absolutist dream of democracies in crisis. The political culture inspiring soft and hard populism' (2019) *Politica e Società* 2, 269–82.

4 G. Sartori, 'European Political Parties: The Case of Polarized Pluralism', in J. La Palombara and M. Weiner (eds), *Political Parties and Political Development*, Princeton University Press, Princeton 1966, pp. 137–76. In this way, see also M. Canovan, *Populism*, Junction Books, London 1981.

5 C. Mudde, 'The Populist Zeitgeist' (2004) 39 *Government and Opposition* 4, 541–63, 543. With reference to the scientific classification of populist phenomenon, see J. Hopkin and M. Blyth, 'The Global Economics of European Populism: Growth Regimes and Party System Change in Europe' (2018) 54 *Government and Opposition* 2, 193–225.

'us' and 'them', *demos* and ruling elites, right and wrong, democratic and antidemocratic.[6] The 'barrier axiom' is a fundamental pillar in the populist rhetoric.[7] Populists need an enemy to attack – a political and social antagonist that has triggered the difficulties of society – and populists therefore propose themselves as the only political alternative which is legitimised by the people and capable of solving social issues. The only popular and political alternative, legitimised by the popular consensus.

In this framework, the academic debate has also focused on the relationship between the democratic form of government and populism, qualifying it in terms of 'democratic pathology' (liberal approach), the 'essential element of democracy' (radical approach) and the 'democratic ambivalence' (minimal approach).[8] With reference to the latter issue, the qualification of populism in terms of good or bad, natural or unnatural,

---

6 With regard to the methodology of this analysis, it is relevant to emphasise the original approach proposed by the academic sociologist Robert Jansen, which proposes a different analytical plan, based on the 'shift away from the problematic notion of "populism" and toward the concept of populist mobilization'. See, in this sense, R.S. Jansen, 'Populist Mobilization: A New Theoretical Approach to Populism' (2011) 29 *Sociological Theory* 2, 75–96.

7 With reference to the populist ideological and communicative strategies, a central role is played by the 'barrier axiom' between us and them – pure people and ruling corrupt elites. In this vein, see J.L. Cohen, 'Hollow parties and their movement-ization: The populist conundrum' (2019) 45 *Philosophy and Social Criticism* 9–10, 1084–1105.

8 With reference to the academic debate on this topic, see the remarkable analysis of Rovira Kaltwasser, above n. 3, 196–97. With reference to the relationship between democracy and populism (in terms of 'polyarchy'), taking inspiration from the analysis proposed by Dahl, focused on the models of 'political contestations' ('development of a system of political competition, which implies the possibility to oppose the government and to offer alternative points of view') and 'inclusiveness' ('denotes the breadth of the right to participate in the system of public contestation'), Rovira Kaltwasser argues that 'these two dimensions of polyarchy are crucial to analyse the ambivalent relationship between populism and democracy. From a theoretical point of view, there are good reasons to think that populism may well be a threat to public contestation, but under certain conditions it can also be a corrective to inclusiveness'. In this vein, but with a different meaning, see F. Carreira da Silva and M. Brito Vieira, 'Populism and the politics of redemption' (2018) 149 *Thesis Eleven* 1, 10–30, 16; they suggest that 'populism is an outgrowth of democracy and its logic cannot be understood apart from democracy's fundamental commitment to the principle of equality. To put it more simply, populism results from a paradox at the heart of democracy'. Regarding this point, a definitional 'third way' of populism is proposed by T.S. Pappas, 'Populist Democracies: Post-Authoritarian Greece and Post-Communist Hungary' (2014) 49 *Government and Opposition* 1, 1–23, 2, which defines populism as 'democratic illiberalism' because, in accordance with his suggestion, 'firstly, this definition is both adequate, since the characteristics it contains are enough to identify the referents and their boundaries, and it is parsimonious, since no accompanying property is included among the necessary, or defining, characteristics'.

us or them, is susceptible to ambiguity, misinterpretation and loss of the meaning and implications of this political phenomenon.[9]

First of all, populism is a global political phenomenon that can arise from the crisis of contemporary representative and liberal democracy, but it is not a distorting element of democracy or naturally present in it. It is a political, social, economic and legal phenomenon that has its own life. Secondly, in close connection with the latter point, populism (and its various political derivations) is not a phenomenon that is exclusive to the Western liberal democracies, but it can be born and develop under illiberal regimes[10] as well, as a reaction to the lack of freedom, democracy, civil and social rights generated by an authoritarian and illiberal national establishment.[11]

Populism, in this perspective, could be a 'good option' to counter illiberal governments in power and encourage a process of return to democracy.[12] In this sense, the populist approach in the framework of illiberal regimes refers to the need to save the democratic form of government and civic freedoms from autocratic elites and authoritarian regimes. In essence, based on a systematic investigation, it is relevant to emphasise that populism is an 'anti-ideological ideology', understood as a political and social model that expresses strong and clear ideological elements, but it is also based on the deep negation of traditional ideologies and politics.

---

9 In this framework, related to the different approaches on the relationship between populism and democracy, see in particular P. Blokker, 'Populist Nationalism, Anti-Europeanism, Post-nationalism, and the East-West Distinction' (2005) 6 *German Law Journal* 2, 371–89.

10 In accordance with the approach proposed by C. Pinelli, 'Illiberal regimes in the perspective of comparative constitutionalism' (2017) *Rivista di Diritti Comparati* 1, 3–15, 3, it can be argued that 'illiberal regimes are generally defined as regimes in which neither democracy nor fundamental rights are granted, and in which rule of law is substantially disregarded'.

11 In this way, see K.M. Roberts, 'Populism and Political Representation', in C. Lancaster and N. Van de Walle (eds), *The Oxford Handbook of the Politics of Development*, Oxford University Press, Oxford 2018, pp. 518–34. An original approach to the 'diarchic character' of contemporary populism is proposed by N. Urbinati, 'Populism and the Principle of Majority', in C. Rovira Kaltwasser, P. Taggart, P. Ochoa Espejo and P. Ostiguy (eds), *The Oxford Handbook of Populism*, Oxford University Press, Oxford 2017, pp. 572–88.

12 In this sense, G. Cerrina Feroni, 'Ripensare la democrazia rappresentativa. Aldilà del "mito" populista' (2019) *Osservatorio sulle Fonti* 2, 1–13, suggests that the populist phenomenon should not only be seen in a 'negative' perspective. In this regard, the author highlights that a 'democratic populism', in the framework of a 'mature democracy', could be an 'effective "tonic" for the constitutional state'. In opposition to the latter approach, see, among others, A. Mueller, 'The meaning of populism' (2019) 45 *Philosophy and Social Criticism* 9–10, 1025–57.

2. EUROPEAN TECHNOCRATIC DEMOCRACY AND POPULIST DIRECT DEMOCRACY

Some of the most relevant 'public enemies' of populist political movements and parties are the so-called 'technocrats', intended as unelected supranational entities that affect domestic political and economic policies and sovereignty. In this way, it is relevant to underline that the 'technocratic enemy' is not always clearly identified, given that – in accordance with the suggestion proposed by Thompson – 'elites are always rather vaguely specified: unaccountable Brussels bureaucrats, mainstream politicians, experts of various kinds, the traditional (i.e. liberal) media, the IMF and more besides'.[13] In accordance with the populist rhetoric, it is essential to evoke an enemy to the people, especially if that enemy is invisible or opaque, in order to channel social hatred towards their own electoral ends.

The populist approach disputes this shift of decision-making centres from national states to supranational institutions,[14] often not democratically elected, claiming (with demagogic speeches, as well) the need to bring back to the people effective decision-making power, through the tools of direct democracy.

The reference to the techniques and technicians of politics, authoritative or otherwise, produces the effect of increasing popular distaste for the establishment. In parallel, it also increases the moral and electoral support of populist political movements and parties.[15] Considering, for example, one of the most important institutions of the European Union, the European Central Bank (ECB),[16] Hopkin and Blyth argue that 'empirically,

---

13 See G.F. Thompson, 'Populisms and liberal democracy – business as usual?' (2017) 46 *Economy and Society*, 1, 43–59, 49.

14 On this topic, in accordance with the analysis proposed by H. Bang and D. Marsh, 'Populism: a major threat to democracy?' (2018) 39 *Policy Studies*, 3, 352–63, 357, the real challenge for Western democracies 'concerns how to govern beyond neoliberalism's depoliticizing technocracy, without falling prey to populism's repoliticized bureaucracy'.

15 In this vein, see the analysis of G. Rico, M. Guinjoan and E. Anduiza, 'The Emotional Underpinnings of Populism: How Anger and Fear Affect Populist Attitudes' (2017) 23 *Swiss Political Science Review* 4, 444–61.

16 An interesting analysis of the role and status of the European Central Bank is proposed by D. Howarth and P. Loedel, *The European Central Bank. The New European Leviathian?* Palgrave Macmillan, London 2005. On this topic, see, among others, M. Fratianni and H. Huang, 'Reputation, Central Bank Independence and the ECB' in P.L. Siklos (ed.), *Varieties of Monetary Reforms. Lessons and Experiences on the Road to Monetary Union*, Springer, Cham 1994; J. De Haan, 'The European Central Bank: Independence, Accountability and Strategy: A Review' (1997) 93 *Public Choice*

having an independent central bank means that politicians are no longer responsible for either creating or managing economic outcomes. As such, they cannot be held accountable for their effects'.[17] In this way, if political parties or national public institutions cannot be held responsible, becoming 'irresponsible' in the face of the most relevant legislative and economic policies,[18] including the policies implemented by the ECB, they will not even be able to claim the positive results obtained – showing, by contrast, that they are helpless when faced with political and economic processes which take place at a higher level than the national level.[19] In this way, taking a cue from the suggestion proposed by Fossum, it could be argued that 'representative democracies may find themselves increasingly enmeshed in a highly toxic mixture of market-oriented technocracy and extreme populism'.[20]

The contemporary European legal framework is based on the axiom of a 'partially secondary role' of the European Parliament in the legal architecture of the European Union. In the field of European legal governance, there are various institutions which are tasked with different missions, in a framework of mutual cooperation. This is the historic issue of the 'democratic deficit' in the EU's legal order. As is well known, the

---

3–4, 395–426; C. Zilioli and M. Selmayr, *The Law of the European Central Bank*, Hart, Oxford 2001; D. Ritleng (ed.), *Independence and Legitimacy in the Institutional System of the European Union*, Oxford University Press, Oxford 2016; A. Verdun, 'Political Leadership of the European Central Bank' (2017) 39 *Journal of European Integration* 2, 207–21; D. Curtin, 'Accountable independence of the European Central Bank: seeing the logics of transparency' (2017) 23 *European Law Journal* 1–2, 28–44.

17 Hopkin and Blyth, above n. 5, p. 204.

18 On this topic, taking a cue from the suggestions proposed by P. Mair, 'Political Opposition and the European Union' (2007) 42 *Government and Opposition* 1, 1–17, 13–14, it is correct to claim that 'Europe limits the capacities of national governments, and hence also the capacities of the parties in those governments, by reducing the range of policy instruments at their disposal and by limiting their policy repertoire'.

19 With reference to the 'usurpation' of decision-making power by technocratic elites, in accordance with the suggestion proposed by P. Aslanidis, 'Populism and Social Movements' in C. Rovira Kaltwasser, P. Taggart, P. Ochoa Espejo and P. Ostiguy (eds), *The Oxford Handbook of Populism*, Oxford University Press, Oxford 2017, pp. 305–325, 311, it can be argued that 'the populist frame offers a diagnosis of reality as problematic due to the usurpation of sovereign authority by "elites" suggesting that the "people" should mobilize to reclaim what is rightfully theirs'.

20 See J.E. Fossum, 'The crisis, a challenge to representative democracy in the European Union?' in J.E. Fossum and A.J. Menéndez (eds), *The European Union in crises or the European Union as crises?* Arena Centre for European Studies, Oslo 2014, pp. 637–660, 653. In this vein, see also E. Mavrozacharakis, 'Populism and Democracy: An Ambiguous Relationship' (2018) 7 *European Quarterly of Political Attitudes and Mentalities* 4, 19–35.

democratic deficit means that the directly representative institution of the *demos* at the European level is perceived as unable to truly influence economic and social processes. At the same time, the democratic deficit shows the image of a European Union essentially managed and governed by technicians, totally (or nearly) detached from the democratic and representative circuit and, consequently, not 'evaluable' in their work, in the field of electoral consensus,[21] that is, the cornerstone of Western representative democracies. Populism, in this sense, could also be interpreted as a new model of popular reaction to the excessive power of technique and technicians over politics and politicians. In this context, the physiological presence of unelected institutions is necessary to govern political and economic processes that take place above national levels, but it is also essential for a correct functioning of the system (i.e. that it be balanced by the role of representative politics).[22] In this sense, the current crisis of representative democracy is showing us once more that Europe must be capable of making decisions in a more effective and democratic way. We are not considering here (for thematic reasons) the historical problem of the appropriate legal definition of the nature of the EU,[23] which has not yet evolved (and may never evolve) into a well-defined federation of states, based on the US or German models.

---

21 With reference to the growth of populist electoral and social consensus in time of crisis of representative democracy (and democratic deficit in Western societies), it is relevant to underline the analysis proposed by A. Arato, 'How we got here? Transition failures, their causes and the populist interest in the Constitution' (2019) 45 *Philosophy and Social Criticism* 9–10, 1106–15.

22 See, in this vein, P. Magnette, 'Towards Accountable Independence? Parliamentary Controls of the European Central Bank and the Rise of a New Democratic Model' (2000) 6 *European Law Journal* 4, 326–40.

23 On this topic, see, among others, B. de Witte, 'The Pillar Structure and the Nature of the European Union: Greek Temple or French Gothic Cathedral?' in T. Heukels, N. Blokker and M. Brus (eds), *The European Union after Amsterdam: A Legal Analysis*, Kluwer Law International, The Hague 1998, pp. 51–68; J.W. de Zwaan, 'The Legal Personality of the European Communities and the European Union' (1999) *Netherlands Yearbook of International Law* 30, 75–113; M. Burgess, *Federalism and the European Union: The Building of Europe 1950–2000*, Routledge, London 2000; R.A. Wessel, 'Revisiting the International Legal Status of the EU' (2000) *European Foreign Affairs Review* 5, 507–37; P. Wagner, 'The Political Form of Europe, Europe as a Political Form' (2005) 80 *Thesis Eleven* 1, 47–73; F. Schorkopf, 'The European Union as An Association of Sovereign States: Karlsruhe's Ruling on the Treaty of Lisbon' (2009) 10 *German Law Journal* 8, 1219–40; N. Nugent, *The Government and Politics of the European Union*, Palgrave Macmillan, London 2010; J.H.H. Weiler, 'The Political and Legal Culture of European Integration: An Exploratory Essay' (2011) 9 *International Journal of Constitutional Law* 3–4, 678–94.

The phenomenon of populism, in accordance with the suggestion proposed by Bilancia, could be read as 'no more than the most evident output of the distance between the people and the intellectual aristocracy of the governing bodies'.[24] In the populists' theoretical approach, national parliaments are described as bodies incapable of giving real and concrete answers to the needs of the people. Substantially, the 'new' populist approach involves the re-emergence to more or less advanced forms of direct democracy – places where the people themselves decide, often without very transparent decision-making procedures.[25] In this way, authoritative academic scholars talk about an 'elective affinity' between populism and direct democracy.[26]

In any case, the continuous recall made by certain populist political forces to the instruments of direct democracy does not necessarily mean a clear divergence between populist voters[27] and non-populist voters.[28] The populist ideological approach is strongly oriented to the enhancement of the institutions of direct democracy[29] and, additionally, to the contraposition between *demos* and elites.[30]

---

24 See, in this sense, F. Bilancia, 'The constitutional dimension of democracy within a democratic society' (2019) 11 *Italian Journal of Public Law* 1, 8–21, 21.

25 In this vein, see in particular K. Sengul, 'Populism, democracy, political style and post-truth: issues for communication research' (2019) 5 *Communication Research and Practice* 1, 88–101. On the same topic, see also T. Aalberg, F. Esser, C. Reinemann, J. Strömbäck and C.H. de Vreese (eds), *Populist Political Communication in Europe*, Routledge, New York 2017.

26 C. Mudde and C. Rovira Kaltwasser, 'Populism' in M. Freeden and M. Stears (eds), *The Oxford Handbook of Political Ideologies*, Oxford University Press, Oxford 2013, pp. 494–512, 505. In this way, the authors argue that 'one of the practical consequences of the populist ideology is the promotion of strategies that are useful for enabling the putative will of the people. In fact, the adherents of populism criticize the establishment for their incapacity and/or disinterest in taking that will into account'.

27 For a remarkable empirical study related to the political attitude of young people voters (and their opinion of the populist political movements and parties), see G. Pollock, T. Brock and M. Ellison, 'Populism, ideology and contradiction: mapping young people's political views' (2015) 63 *The Sociological Review* 2, 141–66.

28 With regard to this point of analysis, see K. Jacobs, A. Akkerman and A. Zaslove, 'The voice of populist people? Referendum preferences, practices and populist attitudes' (2018) 53 *Acta Politica* 4, 517–41.

29 With reference to the theoretical model of direct democracy in the European constitutionalism framework, see, among others, M. Belov, 'Direct Democracy and European Integration' in S. Knezevic and M. Nastic (eds), *Globalisation and Law*, Faculty of Law–University of Niš, Niš 2017, pp. 19–36.

30 However, the constant reference of populist political movements and parties to forms of direct democracy does not always prove to be based on solid grounds. In this way, taking a cue from the analysis of C. Pinelli, 'The Populist Challenge to Constitutional Democracy' (2011) 7 *European Constitutional Law Review* 1, 5–16, 11, it can be

3. POPULISM AS A 'STRESS TEST' FOR THE EUROPEAN LEGAL ORDER

The populist phenomenon in the European Union is not only a political challenge for the European legal framework. The spread of this political model, with its destructive force, against the European 'ancient régime', begs some considerations about the cultural, economic and legal European framework.[31] The pressure exercised to achieve power by populist political movements and parties requires (when power is achieved) the profusion of every necessary effort to preserve the new *status quo*.[32]

In the populist institutional vision, it is possible to find the basis of an authentic constitutional theory, based on three fundamental elements, in accordance with the suggestion proposed by Corrias: 'constituent power, popular sovereignty and constitutional identity'.[33] These elements represent the populist legal approach to the institutions, the link between constitutional framework and political model.[34] Particularly, in the populist

---

argued that 'contemporary populist movements and parties are far from proposing alternative solutions to representation as practiced in constitutional democracies, nor necessarily favour the referendum, in spite of it frequently being believed as restoring democracy to the people. To the contrary, they regularly participate in elections and accept the rules of the representative system'. In this sense, see also F. Graef, 'Populists as Strangers: How the "politics of the extraordinary" challenges representative democracy in Europe' (2019) *Dahrendorf Forum Working Paper* 09, 1–19.

31 On this topic, see, among others, B. Crick, 'Populism, politics and democracy' (2005) 12 *Democratization* 5, 625–32; K. Abts and S. Rummens, 'Populism versus Democracy' (2007) *Political Studies* 55, 405–24; S. Chambers, 'Democracy and constitutional reform: Deliberative versus populist constitutionalism' (2019) 45 *Philosophy and Social Criticism* 9–10, 1116–31.

32 In this vein, taking a cue from the analysis proposed by K. Weyland, 'Populism: A Political-Strategic Approach' in C. Rovira Kaltwasser, P. Taggart, P. Ochoa Espejo and P. Ostiguy (eds), *The Oxford Handbook of Populism*, Oxford University Press, Oxford 2017, pp. 49–72, 55, it could be argued that 'populism is notorious for its twists and turns, driven by the opportunistic efforts of personalistic leaders to concentrate power and stay in office. The driving force behind populism is political, not ideological'. In the same sense, A. Batory, 'Populists in government? Hungary's system of national cooperation' (2016) 23 *Democratization* 2, 283–303, 292, claims that 'populism is normally thought of, and is defined by the populists themselves, as an anti-establishment, anti-elite force. This presents a fundamental paradox to populists: when presented with the responsibility of governing they are forced to become everything they told "the people" they hate'.

33 In this sense, see L. Corrias, 'Populism in a Constitutional Key: Constituent Power, Popular Sovereignty and Constitutional Identity' (2016) 12 *European Constitutional Law Review* 1, 6–26, 8.

34 In this way, see the remarkable analysis proposed by L. Corso, 'What does Populism have to do with Constitutional Law? Discussing Populist Constitutionalism and Its Assumptions' (2014) *Rivista di Filosofia del Diritto* 2, 443–69.

rhetoric, popular sovereignty is used to justify the continuous recall to the electoral moment and the strong criticism towards supranational and (or) nonelected institutions.

On a separate but related note, various empirical studies have shown us how the globalisation process has favoured the rise of populist political movements and parties (especially right-wing movements and parties).[35] In this way, some national states that have recently experienced the transition to democratic order have been shown to be more 'receptive' to the appeal of populist rhetoric, especially those who are facing the difficult transition from the socialist legal and economic system to liberal democracy (a transition which is, perhaps, too rapid and drastic for the legal and economic national frameworks)[36] and, by

35 It is relevant to underline the significant relationship among the progressive erosion of national sovereignty, the process of globalisation and the global rise of populism, given that, according to the theoretical approach of N. Walker, 'Sovereignty and Beyond: The Double Edge of External Constitutionalism' (2018) *Virginia Journal of International Law* 58, 799–820, 820, it could be said that 'populist leaders have been able to gain significant ideological traction before national audiences by warning of the erosion of national sovereignty in the face of the deracinated logic of cosmopolitanism'. On this topic, see also D.A. Smith, D.J. Solinger and S.C. Topik (eds), *States and Sovereignty in the Global Economy*, Routledge, London–New York 1999; W. Twining, *Globalisation and Legal Theory*, Cambridge University Press, Cambridge 2000; M. Troper, 'Sovereignty' in M. Rosenfeld and A. Sajò (eds), *The Oxford Handbook of Comparative Constitutional Law*, Oxford University Press, Oxford 2012, pp. 350–369; J.L. Cohen, *Globalization and Sovereignty. Rethinking Legality, Legitimacy and Constitutionalism*, Cambridge University Press, Cambridge 2012; L.E. Grinin, 'New Basics of State Order or Why do States Lose Their Sovereignty in the Age of Globalization' (2012) 3 *Journal of Globalization Studies* 1, 3–38; J. Westaway, 'Globalization, Sovereignty and Social Unrest' (2012) 5 *Journal of Politics and Law* 2, 132–39; R. Rawlings, P. Leyland and A. Young (eds), *Sovereignty and the Law. Domestic, European, and International Perspectives*, Oxford University Press, Oxford 2013; J. Agnew, *Globalization and Sovereignty. Beyond the Territorial Trap*, Rowman & Littlefield, Lanham 2017; T. Macdonald, 'Sovereignty, Democracy, and Global Political Legitimacy' in C. Brown and R. Eckersley (eds), *The Oxford Handbook of International Political Theory*, Oxford University Press, Oxford 2018, pp. 401–13.

36 In this sense, taking a cue from the analysis proposed by B. Stanley, 'Populism in Central and Eastern Europe', in C. Rovira Kaltwasser, P. Taggart, P. Ochoa Espejo and P. Ostiguy (eds), *The Oxford Handbook of Populism*, Oxford University Press, Oxford 2017, pp. 142–60, 143, it could be argued that 'the prevailing model of post-communist transition to democracy required the creation of a fully functioning capitalist economy, the building of liberal-democratic institutions, and the establishment and protection of the rights of the individual. As this model was imitative of globalization processes in Western Europe, it was logical to expect that it would exert a similar impact on social divides and their politicization by elites'.

contrast, those states which are in very difficult economic and financial conditions.[37]

The globalisation process has led to the gradual restatement of a self-regulated market approach, downgrading the national states to a marginal position on the world economic and financial stage.[38] The globalisation of Western markets has unquestionably played a prominent role in the rise of anti-system movements and parties.[39] In this sense, the costs for citizens have often been greater than the benefits (in terms of social legislation and daily life), giving a significant political space to the anti-system parties and movements, which required greater public regulation and an active position of the public sphere.

The risk for the constitutional democracy represented by the populist constitutional approach consists in the failure to recognise legal limits to the affirmation of its own political, social and institutional approach.[40] The progressive growth of populist parties is not a sporadic event or exclusively due to certain external circumstances to the national political systems.[41] Personalism, opportunism and strategic flexibility are therefore

---

37 In this vein, D. Swank and H.G. Betz, 'Globalization, the welfare state and right-wing populism in Western Europe' (2003) 1 *Socio-Economic Review* 2, 215–45. Relating to the rise of populist political movements and parties in Western Europe, see also T. Pauwels, *Populism in Western Europe: Comparing Belgium, Germany and the Netherlands*, Routledge, London and New York 2014.

38 With reference to this topic, the relationship between the globalisation process and the contemporary crisis of national states is a nodal point, given that, according to the suggestion proposed by J. Leaman, 'Reversing the neoliberal deformation of Europe' in J.E. Fossum and A.J. Menéndez (eds), *The European Union in crises or the European Union as crises?*, Arena Centre for European Studies, Oslo 2014, pp. 43–92, 64, it is correct to affirm that 'the role of the neoliberal state in the transformation of European and global capitalism is inherently contradictory, inasmuch as the executive decisions of key national administrations have involved a conscious self-marginalization, withdrawal from the responsibility of key allocatory functions within national and regional political economies'.

39 On this topic, see in particular M.E. Szatlach, 'European identity and populism' (2007) *Polish Political Science* 36, 69–90; C. Mudde, *Populist radical right parties in Europe*, Cambridge University Press, Cambridge 2007.

40 In this sense, according to the suggestion proposed by T. Fournier, 'From rhetoric to action, a constitutional analysis of populism' (2019) 20 *German Law Journal* 3, 362–81, 365, it can be argued that 'populist rhetoric is the use of political arguments aimed to convince a fictional majority that a constitutional democracy gives rise to a tyranny of minorities'.

41 In this sense, in accordance with the opinion proposed by Mudde, above n. 5, 561, it can be argued that 'to a large extent, populism draws its strength from the confused and often opportunistic democratic promises of the political elites. In this age of egalitarianism, the defence of the elitist aspects of liberal democracy becomes more and more like political suicide'.

essential characteristics of populist political movements and parties and their leading figures.

In this way, in order for a legal system to function correctly, mutual recognition is required between the political factions about their constitutional roles. If populist politics aims for the de-legitimisation of political antagonists (or 'enemies'), the same social pact that acts as the pivot of Western democratic society is questioned. If the social pact is broken, the consequences would be catastrophic for Western constitutional democracies and legal orders.

In this sense, one could speak of breaking the constitutional balance, to the point of reaching, as has sometimes happened, the 'authoritarian drift' of the state, even if covered by the democratic electoral process for the selection of the governmental majority.

4. ITALY AS A PECULIAR CASE STUDY OF POPULISM IN GOVERNMENT

The deep economic and financial crisis, the ambiguity about the soundness of Italian public debt and the entire national financial system, the widespread corruption, the effects of high unemployment levels, the end of the Berlusconi era and the technocratic governments, supported transversely by moderate right and left figures, have generated an intense distrust among Italian citizens towards the domestic political class. In this context of popular frustration, disappointment and distrust, populist ideas spread in Italian society as a reaction – often outraged and resentful – towards the ruling political class, which is perceived as too detached from social difficulties and as incapable of remedying them.

Starting from the 2013 political elections, the main Italian populist party of the time, the Five Stars Movement, came into the Italian Parliament with a relevant number of parliamentarians, placing itself as an alternative to the 'old' politics represented by the centre-right and centre-left coalitions.[42] Defining itself as a 'post-ideological' political

---

42 In this sense, the sentence uttered by the founder of the Five Stars Movement, Beppe Grillo, during an election rally will remain famous in the popular imaginary, in which he affirmed that the movement 'will open the parliament like a can of tuna'. This sentence, beyond the unusual language, symbolises the aim of the movement to completely undermine the party system, opening the parliament to transparency and legality (at that time, many members of parliament were subject to judicial investigations and there was talk of the 'Parliament of investigated and sentenced'.

movement, the Five Stars Movement spent five years in opposition to the national government, which was composed of the centre-left parties and a part of the old centre-right coalition, attacking every political and economic governmental measure with extreme vigour and invoking a change of national leadership, based on appeals to the popular vote; to political morality and uprightness against pervasive corruption; and to continuous consultation with its own voters through the Rousseau platform.[43] Initially, the Five Stars Movement supported the argument for Italy to exit from the single currency, opening the debate about the need for a popular referendum to decide on whether to remain or leave the European Union, whether to abandon the common currency and the need for a complete review of national and European regulations regarding common financial regulations and budgetary constraints.[44]

In parallel, another populist political movement has been renewed, born in the 1980s as an anti-unitary and federalist party, with a clear far-right political connotation, basing its political campaign on the safety of citizens and the opposition to perceived massive and illegal immigration. The new Lega (noticeably lacking the old word 'North') has quickly spread in the whole country, eventually becoming in the political elections of 2018 the greatest right-wing political force in Italy.[45]

2018 was the year of the coming into power of the two strong populist political movements in Italy (Lega and the Five Stars Movement), on the basis of a programmatic agreement that took place following the impasse that resulted from the parliamentary elections of 4 March 2018. In these national political elections, the arguments that dominated the political debates concerned European and national immigration policies, the relevant national public debt and the very high level of unemployment (especially

---

43 The 'Rousseau platform' is used by the Five Stars Movement in Italy to allow its members and militants to decide the political approach of the movement on individual measures or policies, by an electronic and secret voting procedure managed by a private company. For an analysis of the main features of the Five Stars Movement, see, among others, A. Pirro, 'The polyvalent populism of the 5 Star Movement' (2018) 26 *Journal of Contemporary European Studies* 4, 443–58; M. Bassini, 'Rise of populism and the Five Star Movement model: an Italian case study' (2019) 11 *Italian Journal of Public Law* 1, 302–33.

44 As is well known, Art. 75, para. 2 of the Italian Constitution prohibits the popular referendum 'for tax and budgetary laws, amnesty and indult, authorization to ratify international treaties'.

45 The name change from 'Lega Nord' to 'Lega' symbolises the change in the paradigm of political formation, aimed at also seeking electoral support also in southern Italy, leaving the 'northern border' where it was historically closed.

youth unemployment in the Southern regions of Italy).[46] The agreement between the two populist forces has produced the first populist government in Italy and the marginalisation of the Italian parties that support the actual European legal and political framework.[47] In Italy, the 'yellow-green' government has shocked international observers for its intense opposition to the EU, based on the request for greater flexibility in the public budget and the extreme firmness with reference to the migration phenomenon.

The Italian populist government resigned in August 2019, due to irreconcilable internal conflicts between the two coalition members, and it was replaced by a government headed by the same President of the Council of Ministries. However, it was composed of a populist movement (the Five Stars Movement) and a pro-European party, the Democratic Party, with a more conciliatory general approach towards European institutions and policies. The right-wing component of the old government (Lega) is now in opposition.

In actuality, the 'Italian anomaly' (with its contradictions, e.g. two populist movements that govern the nation with very different electoral bases) would seem to be in the process of being resolved with a restoration of a political bi-polarism. On the one side, there are the Five Stars Movement, the Democratic Party, the pro-Europe movements and the moderate Italian Left and, on the other side, Lega, the liberals, conservative parties, Eurosceptic movements and far-right parties.[48]

In this frame, the Five Stars Movement seems to have lost most of its anti-system profile. In parallel, the populist scenario seems to have moved to the extreme right in opposition to the government. The political keywords are the opposition to the migration policies, the European 'technocrats'

---

46 In this way, see L. Fazzi, 'Social work, exclusionary populism and xenophobia in Italy' (2015) 58 *International Social Work* 4, 595–605.

47 In accordance with the suggestion proposed by T. Boros, M. Freitas, G. Laki and E. Stetter, *State of Populism in Europe*, Foundation for European Progressive Studies, Brussels and Budapest 2018, p. 77, it could be argued that Lega and the Five Stars Movement 'are intensely Eurosceptic and their coalition agreement contains proposals that clearly run afoul of EU policies and Italy's obligations in the realm of fiscal policy (including budget balance and public debt) and asylum policy. Additionally, contrary to the austerity measures expected by the EU, the parties agreed on cutting taxes, amending the pension law and introducing a universal basic income'.

48 On this topic see, among others, M. Tarchi, 'Italy: the promised land of populism?' (2015) 7 *Contemporary Italian Politics* 3, 273–85; B. Verbeek and A. Zaslove, 'Italy: a case of mutating populism?' (2016) 23 *Democratization* 2, 304–23; L. Mosca and F. Tronconi, 'Beyond left and right: the eclectic populism of the Five Star Movement' (2019) 42 *West European Politics* 6, 1258–83.

and the domestic tax policies, defined as 'oppressive' for citizens. In this sense, with reference to the tax law, there is a clear liberal economic vision, balanced by a closed approach to supranational economic policies. As previously stated, it is evident that populism is capable of assuming theoretically contrasting positions in different fields, adapting the political approach to particular situations.

In any case, as of today, the polls indicate that there is a clear majority in favour of the right-wing populist and nationalist coalition, with the main political force (Lega) having more than 25% of the electoral consensus, and the traditional far-right parties holding close to 12%. The Five Stars Movement today would have 15% of the votes, compared to 33% of the last national political elections. In this way, the main Italian pro-European party, the Democratic Party, would also have only 20% of the electoral votes.

5. CONCLUDING REMARKS

After a systematic investigation of the populist phenomenon, several scholars have asserted the existence of a 'dark side' of populism. This dark side, in the opinion of Noble and Ottmann, concerns 'the appeal to a general will of the people against the elites can lead to the support of authoritarian tendencies and support of illiberal attacks on anyone who (allegedly) threatens the homogeneity of the people who have been defined outside the demos'.[49]

The issue of the rise of populist movements and parties (and their theoretical approaches) is particularly relevant in the European Union,[50]

---

49 C. Noble and G. Ottmann, 'National Populism and Social Work' (2018) 3 *Journal of Human Rights and Social Work* 3, 112–20, 113. In accordance with the suggestion proposed by M.A. Wilkinson, 'The Specter of Authoritarian Liberalism: Reflections on the Constitutional Crisis of the European Union' (2013) 14 *German Law Journal* 5, 527–60, 535, it is correct to affirm that 'what emerged in Europe, from a constitutional perspective, was a mixed regime, or a mixed commonwealth, combining elements of aristocracy, democracy, and technocracy, but whose central rationale was the safeguarding of nation-state democracy'. On this topic, see also N. Lacey, 'Populism and the Rule of Law' (2019) *Annual Review of Law and Social Science* 15, 79–96.

50 Relating to the recovery of public confidence at the cultural and social level by European institutions with respect to the populist challenge, see B. Bugaric, 'The two faces of populism: Between authoritarian and democratic populism' (2019) 20 *German Law Journal* 3, 390–400, 397, who highlights that 'the EU needs to regain credibility by delivering simple and palpable benefits, such as good salaries, decent pensions, high-quality social services, and high environmental standards'.

in which they are intensely structured at the continental level and capable of mobilising growing masses of the population against the institutions of the European Union (Euroscepticism) and the implementation of their policies.[51]

However, the analysis of the rise of populist political parties and movements has, by contrast, highlighted the current crisis of representative democracy.[52] Democratic governments are the most sensitive targets of populist rhetoric. The same form of liberal and democratic government of Western societies is a (potential) contributory factor in the proliferation process of the populist mode.[53] In this way, taking a cue from the suggestion proposed by Bugaric, it can be argued that 'the authoritarian populists not only attack policies that are based on core institutional pillars of this order but quite often also challenge the very foundations of liberal order as such'.[54]

In this way, it should be asserted that the liberal constitutions themselves are in a potentially dangerous situation, given that the experiences of populism in power show us that the purpose of populist political movements and parties is frequently to amend the national constitutions so as to weaken the system of institutional checks and balances between powers.[55]

---

51 With reference to this topic, an interesting suggestion is advanced by P. Taggart, 'Populism in Western Europe' in C. Rovira Kaltwasser, P. Taggart, P. Ochoa Espejo and P. Ostiguy (eds), *The Oxford Handbook of Populism*, Oxford University Press, Oxford 2017, pp. 249–64, 260, according to which 'the ubiquity of Euroskepticism in Western European populism is a testimony to the difficulty of constructing an integrated Europe. A complex, opaque, and distant political architecture has fed the populist distrust of the political institutions in general'.

52 In this vein, according to the suggestions of A. Dzur and C. Hendriks, 'Thick populism: democracy-enhancing popular participation' (2018) 39 *Policy Studies* 3, 334–51, 347, it could be argued that 'if populism represents a prominent new mode of "doing politics" then we contend that more consideration needs to be given, not just to the pathologies it poses to democracy, but also to its remedial offerings'.

53 In this sense, see the analysis of D. Kelly, 'Populism and the History of Popular Sovereignty' in C. Rovira Kaltwasser, P. Taggart, P. Ochoa Espejo and P. Ostiguy (eds), *The Oxford Handbook of Populism*, Oxford University Press, Oxford 2017, pp. 512–34.

54 B. Bugaric, 'Could Populism Be Good for Constitutional Democracy?' (2019) *Annual Review of Law and Social Science* 15, 41–58, 42.

55 With reference to the popular constituent power in a populist perspective, according to the analysis proposed by G. Halmai, 'Populism, authoritarianism and constitutionalism' (2019) 20 *German Law Journal* 3, 296–313, 306, it is relevant to note that 'unlike liberal constitutionalism, populists claim not only that the power to create a constitution belongs to the people alone, that is, that the people have a monopoly over the original or primary *pouvoir constituant*; but also the derivative or secondary constitutional amending power which for them means that the power of the people to amend the constitution is unlimited'.

The importance of safeguarding the principles of constitutional democracy involves the assurance of balanced powers that represents the real guarantee of liberal democracy.[56] In this regard, to stop the populist escalation in the European Union, it is necessary, first of all, to strengthen representative democracy and its 'intermediate bodies' (political parties;[57] trade unions; environmental, cultural and social associations) and, secondly, to ensure a greater proximity of national and supranational institutions to the voice and demands of *demos* – also through the enhancement of the constitutional means of direct democracy.[58] However, with reference to the latter, it is crucial to avoid the temptation to fall into populist political practices, always remembering the difference between popular demands and government exigencies.

Ultimately, in order to counter populist, nationalist and divisive tendencies, it is evident (but not obvious) that an increasing openness of national and supranational democratic institutions (and therefore of the general consciousness among the citizens about the importance of a modern, resilient and pluralist democracy[59]) and collective well-being coincides with lessened proliferation of the populist model.

---

56 In this sense, in accordance with the approach proposed by C. Mudde and C. Rovira Kaltwasser, 'Exclusionary vs. Inclusionary Populism: Comparing Contemporary Europe and Latin America' (2013) 48 *Government and Opposition* 2, 147–74, 168–169, it can be argued that 'populist forces might also refer to the idea of popular sovereignty with the aim of dismantling the checks and balances that are inherent to liberal democracy. In other words, the repoliticization of society that is fostered by all types of populist forces has an ambivalent impact on democracy'.

57 The importance of a truly competitive party system for the correct functioning of representative democracy structures is underlined by N.W. Barber, 'Populist leaders and political parties' (2019) 20 *German Law Journal* 2, 129–40. With reference to the importance of traditional parties in the legal and democratic order, it is relevant to emphasise the analysis of N. Urbinati, 'Liquid parties, dense populism' (2019) 45 *Philosophy and Social Criticism* 9–10, 1069–83.

58 On this topic, although it cannot be argued that a return to direct democracy is a viable solution, it seems necessary to recover a more popular dimension of national and supranational governance, given that, in accordance with the analysis of A. Batory and S. Svensson, 'The use and abuse of participatory governance by populist governments' (2019) 47 *Policy and Politics* 2, 227–44, 228, 'participatory governance has been advocated by many as a potential way to remedy a perceived alienation of voters from politics in western democracies – a sense of disillusionment with the political process that is said to fail to involve citizens in decisions affecting their own lives in a meaningful way'.

59 On this topic, see, among others, the analyses proposed by F. Bilancia, 'Constitutional Roots of Democracy' (2019) *Costituzionalismo.it* 3, 33–46.

PART IV

POPULIST CONSTITUTIONALISM FROM THE VIEWPOINT OF EMOTIONS AND CONSTITUTIONAL IMAGINATION

POPULISM, CONSTITUENT POWER AND CONSTITUTIONAL IMAGINATION

Paul Blokker

1. INTRODUCTION

Academic interest in the relationship between populist movements/parties and constitutions, as well as more broadly in the relationship between forms of populism, illiberalism and authoritarianism, on one hand, and (domestic and international) law and constitutionalism on the other, is rapidly increasing.[1] A significant part of the debate focuses on how to diagnose, and prevent, so-called 'backsliding' and on how to save constitutional democracy. There is, in this, much less engagement with the question of how populist movements might equally challenge core

[1] See, e.g. B. Bugaric and M. Tushnet, 'Populism and constitutionalism: an essay on definitions and their implications' (in press) *Cardozo Law Review*; W. Sadurski, *Poland's Constitutional Breakdown*, Oxford University Press, Oxford 2019; E. Posner, 'Liberal Internationalism and the Populist Backlash' (2017) 49 *Arizona State Law Journal* 795–819; D. Landau, 'Abusive constitutionalism' (2013) 47 *UCDL Rev.*, 189; W. Sadurski, 'How Democracy Dies (in Poland): A Case Study of Anti-Constitutional Populist Backsliding' (2018) No. 18/01 Sydney Law School Research Paper; W. Sadurski, 'Polish Constitutional Tribunal Under PiS: From an Activist Court, to a Paralysed Tribunal, to a Governmental Enabler' (2019) 11 *Hague Journal on the Rule of Law* 63–84; K.L. Scheppele, 'Autocratic Legalism' (2018) 85 *U. Chi. L. Rev.*, 545.

dimensions of taken-for-granted notions of constitutionalism and how they might reveal problematic dimensions.[2]

The general approach, often inspired by political science,[3] towards populism argues that it displays a friend–enemy logic in its political mobilisation of ordinary citizens; engages in the construction of a unified people; and criticises the liberal-democratic status quo in the people's name. Most analyses stress a strong tension between constitutional democracy and populism and understand the relationship predominantly as one in which the latter challenges and undermines the former. There is, however, relatively little attention paid to the critical potential of populism, not least in the way the populist challenge might expose problematic dimensions of liberal constitutional democracy. In other words, the self-reflexive dimension of the populist challenge is not taken up.[4]

The most prominent constitutional challenge posed by populism lies in its *constituent* thrust, that is, the propensity in many populist projects to significantly alter the constitutional order, generally understood as grounded in a form of 'liberal legalism',[5] into an alternative order, referred to as 'illiberal democracy', resulting from a conservative 'moral revolution'. A not frequently discussed, albeit crucial, dimension of the relation between populism and constitutionalism therefore regards populism's questioning of the fundamental 'spirit' of the liberal-democratic order. Studies on populism tend to overlook that the 'invocation of "the people" is not only a matter of bolstering mere political discourse, but of constitutional politics addressing the higher-ranking dimension of the legal and political community, the distribution of powers, and the overall design of rule-making and application'.[6] As Möller rightly claims, '[p]opulism does not

---

2 Cf. Z. Oklopcic, *Beyond the people: Social imaginary and constituent imagination*, Oxford University Press, Oxford 2018; M. Tushnet, 'Varieties of populism' (2019) 20 *German Law Journal* 3, 382–89; B. Bugaric and M. Tushnet, 'Populism and constitutionalism: an essay on definitions and their implications' (in press) *Cardozo Law Review*.

3 Cf. W. Sadurski, *Poland's Constitutional Breakdown*, Oxford University Press, Oxford 2019; K.L. Scheppele, 'Autocratic legalism' (2018) 85 *The University of Chicago Law Review* 2, 545–84.

4 For a partial exception, see K.L. Scheppele, 'The opportunism of populists and the defense of constitutional liberalism' (2019) 20 *German Law Journal* 3, 314–31. As Scheppele remarks, 'populism has become the obsessive focus of many of us academics precisely because the criticisms of liberal constitutionalism made by the populists hit us where we live' (p. 315).

5 J. Gray, *Two Faces of Liberalism*, Polity, Cambridge 1995; E.A. Posner, *The perils of global legalism*, The University of Chicago Press, Chicago 2009.

6 K. Möller, 'Popular Sovereignty, Populism and Deliberative Democracy' (2018) 42 *Philosophical Inquiry*, 17.

only refer to certain policy issues, but invokes "the people" as constituent power on which the political community relies'.[7] Different populisms draw on the 'multi-faceted character of foundational peoplehood' and in this, 'populists do not rely on a societal foundational force which checks and authorizes public institutions, but in fact can also turn the constitutional structure or the state against the "elites," supranational agreements, or economic powers'.[8] This constituent dimension in populism indicates how populist projects may question the foundations of liberal legalism and constitutionalism as such.

The reference to the 'spirit' of liberal constitutionalism above regards an under-appreciated dimension of constitutionalism, which is nevertheless of great relevance in manifestations of populism, and in particular with regard to the populist legal mind-set, which does not reject the law as such,[9] but rather, understands the role and the nature of law in a radically different manner from the post-World War II convention of modern constitutionalism, which is grounded in legal liberalism and anti-totalitarianism. In order to explore the dimension of the 'spirit' of constitutions, the notion of imaginary is of great utility in identifying how different political and legal actors imagine the constitutional order and the functioning of modern society. In other words, constitutionalism is not merely a rational technique of government, but it involves important imaginary and imaginative dimensions that allow it to function and render it legitimate vis-á-vis various 'constitutional interpreters'[10] and society at large. The imaginary dimension means, however, that constitutional orders can equally be imagined otherwise and, hence, that universalist pretensions – as particularly evident in liberal legalism[11] – may render liberal constitutionalism vulnerable to critique and alternative imaginations of human society, which depart from different, more particularistic (often nationalist) orientations.

In the chapter, I will first discuss the phenomenon of populist constitutionalism as a reaction to the post-WWII hegemonic model of anti-totalitarian liberal constitutionalism, as well as global legalism. Subsequently, I will explore the relationship between populism and

---

7 *Ibid.*

8 *Ibid.*, 17–18.

9 Cf. B. Bugaric and M. Tushnet, 'Populism and constitutionalism: an essay on definitions and their implications' (in press) *Cardozo Law Review*.

10 P. Häberle, 'Die offene Gesellschaft der Verfassungsinterpreten: Ein Beitrag zur pluralistischen und "prozessualen" Verfassungsinterpretation' (1975) 30 *JuristenZeitung* 10, 297–305.

11 Cf. J. Gray, *Two Faces of Liberalism*, Polity, Cambridge 1995.

constituent power. In the final part, I discuss the populist imaginary and mind-set as a negation of liberal legalism and the populist pretension of an alternative legal mind-set, grounded in the constituent power of the people.

2. POPULIST CONSTITUTIONALISM

In Europe, many of the current manifestations of populism can be related to the emergence of populist protest and anti-establishment movements from at least the 1980s and early 1990s onwards.[12] What is more, recently, Europe has witnessed populism's electoral and governmental weight, and in some cases – most conspicuously those of Hungary and Poland – the direct engagement of populist parties with constitutionalism.[13] In East-Central Europe, populism has to be related to post-communist transformation processes, in the struggle over the nature of transformation and the distinctive form of democracy to be institutionalised, while in Western Europe, populism can often be understood as a backlash against a distinctive (neo-)liberal, integrationist or post-national understanding of, and approach to, representative democracy. The post-national idea of democracy has been endorsed by domestic liberal forces as well as by international institutions (the European Union [EU], the Council of Europe). However, the liberal, constitutional-democratic model has always been faced with contestation by a variety of political forces, including nationalist and extremist actors. The novelty of recent years is that the liberal hegemony is increasingly seriously and structurally challenged by alternative, populist projects.[14]

The 'backlash' to the liberal democratic-constitutional model also means that the consensus on what has been variously referred to as 'liberal constitutionalism', 'legal constitutionalism' and 'new constitutionalism'

---

12 C. Mudde, 'The paradox of the anti-party party: Insights from the extreme right, (1996) 2 *Party Politics* 2, 265–76; P.A. Taguieff, 'Political science confronts populism: from a conceptual mirage to a real problem' (1995) *Telos* 103, 9–43; P Blokker, 'Populist Nationalism, Anti-Europeanism, Post-nationalism, and the East-West Distinction' (2005) 6 *German Law Journal* 2, 371.

13 Similar tendencies seem evident elsewhere, too; cf. P. Blokker, 'Populist Counter-Constitutionalism, Conservatism, and Legal Fundamentalism' (2019) 15 *European Constitutional Law Review* 3, 519–41; P. Blokker, 'Populist Understandings of the Law: A Conservative Backlash?' (forthcoming) *Participation and Conflict (PaCo)*.

14 Cf. J. Zielonka, *Counter-revolution: Liberal Europe in retreat*, Oxford University Press, Oxford 2018.

has waned, and that the latter is now openly contested. This also means that what around 1989 seemed natural and convincing in terms of constitutional choices has become much more problematic in the light of events since 2010. Perhaps it might even be argued that in some cases, the legal-constitutional model has been less 'natural' and more contested even at the start of the democratic transformation.[15]

While in the 1990s, the legal-constitutional model seemed to triumph, at the same time it became the object of increasing contestation and backlash. In 1989, the zeitgeist entailed – not least due to active promotion by international actors – a strong emphasis on a *legal-constitutional*[16] or *new constitutional* approach[17] to the building of democracy. Since WWII, the 'constitutional set-up of new democracies has increasingly relied upon the combination of four institutional features: dualist constitutional architecture, a codified bill of rights, judicial supremacy and the robust exercise of judicial review'.[18] This anti-totalitarian idea was applied equally in the context of transformation away from communism towards democracy. Indeed, many observers at the time claimed that post-communist constitution-making was about implementing well-tested designs, and any creative local input was mostly greeted with suspicion.[19] From the perspective of the globally predominant understanding of constitutionalism, the emphasis on legalism, legal continuity and the rule of law was instead related to a radical, binary view of legalism – that is, as an antidote to the 'ideological'[20] or 'contradictory'[21] socialist legality of the communist regimes. After 1989, the 'return' to constitutionalism

15 As, for instance, in the Polish case, see: E. Kowalewska, 'Competing visions of Constitutionalism in Post-Socialist Poland' ('New constitutionalism? New forms of democracy and rule of law beyond liberalism' conference, International Institute for the Sociology of Law, Oñati, Spain, July 2018); W. Sadurski, *Poland's Constitutional Breakdown*, Oxford University Press, Oxford 2019; for the Hungarian case, see: G. Halmai, 'Silence of transitional constitutions: The "invisible constitution" concept of the Hungarian Constitutional Court' (2018) 16 *International Journal of Constitutional Law* 3, 969.

16 A. Sajó and R. Uitz, *The Constitution of Freedom: An Introduction to Legal Constitutionalism*, Oxford University Press, Oxford 2017.

17 T. Győrfi, *Against the New Constitutionalism*, Edward Elgar, Cheltenham 2016.

18 *Ibid.*, 15.

19 Cf. J. Habermas, *Die nachholende revolution*, Suhrkamp, Frankfurt 1990.

20 S.A. Arjomand, 'Law, Political Reconstruction and Constitutional Politics' (2003) 18 *International Sociology* 1, 7.

21 J. Přibáň and W. Sadurski, 'The Role of Political Rights in the Democratization of Central and Eastern Europe' in W. Sadurski (ed.), *Political Rights under Stress in 21st Century Europe*, Oxford University Press, Oxford 2006.

and the rule of law or, at the very least, the rejection of the communist instrumentalisation of the law for political purposes, reconnected with this trend of 'new' constitutionalism. The internationally endorsed role of new constitutionalism – in East-Central Europe fortified through the institutions of the EU and the Council of Europe – was that of securing the transition to robust constitutional democratic orders.[22]

The legal-constitutional template – in its Kelsenian emphasis on independent apex courts[23] (à la the German Constitutional Court); significant forms of judicial review; extensive and entrenched rights catalogues; and a strong or even absolute separation between parliamentary politics and the constitutional order – was largely without historical precedent in the constitutional cultures in the region. Despite its alien, imported nature in most of the post-communist societies, this emphasis on written constitutions with an entrenched 'catalogue of rights' and a 'system of constitutional justice to defend those rights'[24] is unsurprising. Many perceived legalism, legal continuity and the rule of law as robust *antidotes* to the socialist legality of the communist regimes. The post-1989 'return' to constitutionalism and the rule of law constituted a strong rejection of the communist instrumentalisation of law for political ends, and legal constitutionalism was to secure the transition to robust constitutional democratic orders.

The promise of the anti-totalitarian constitutional model as a robust antidote has, however, not been able to hold in many East-Central Europe countries. It is equally showing signs of fatigue in the more so-called 'established' democracies (including Italy and the United Kingdom). In particular, in cases in which populist forces have engaged in *constituent action*, making significant changes to the existing constitutional order, such as in Hungary and Poland (with potentially similar tendencies elsewhere in the region, such as Slovenia[25]), the reaction to legal constitutionalism is highly evident. In distinctive ways, insights derived from these cases can help to shed light on the distinctive populist reaction to liberal legalism

---

22 B. Bugarič, 'A crisis of constitutional democracy in post-Communist Europe: "Lands in-between" democracy and authoritarianism' (2015) 13 *International Journal of Constitutional Law* 1, 219.

23 A. Stone Sweet, 'Constitutional Courts' in M. Rosenfeld and A. Sajó (eds), *The Oxford Handbook of Comparative Constitutional Law*, Oxford University Press, Oxford 2012.

24 A. Stone Sweet, 'Constitutions and Judicial Power' in D. Caramani (ed.), *Comparative Politics*, Oxford University Press, Oxford 2007, p. 219.

25 Cf. M. Avbelj and J. Letnar Černič, *The Impact of European Institutions on the Rule of Law and Democracy: Slovenia and Beyond*, Hart Publishing, Oxford 2020.

as well as on the potential trajectories that right-wing populists may take when firmly taking up the seats of governmental power.

3. CONSTITUENT POWER

What makes populism a constituent force? Why do populists show significant propensity towards changing the rules of the political game, when populism is mostly understood as a phenomenon *within* liberal democracy?[26] These questions are mostly ignored in current debates, both in those on populism and in those on constituent power. As John Grant has argued, 'studies of populism rarely mention constituent power despite its relevance to what populists say, while theorists of constituent power say little about populism, even though it seems like a form of politics open to embracing constituent power'.[27] That exploring and analysing this question is of great significance is attested by the same author: 'How can we face up to the serious problems that popular movements identify in existing liberal democratic politics without succumbing to authoritarian temptations that are common in recent manifestations of populism?'.[28]

Populism and constituent power show, however, important points of affinity, or – perhaps better – they exist 'on a continuum where both are mobile in the forms they take'.[29] Populism understands the popular will as the ultimate source of legitimacy, which needs to have primacy in the polity. Constituent power is a theory of foundational political power and locates this foundational power in popular sovereignty. Populism re-awakens the idea of constituent power; it understands constituent power as primary to constituted power, that is, the 'constitutional system that is put in place by a constituent act'.[30] As Luigi Corrias has also argued, constituent power is thus a key dimension in manifestations of populism. While the modernist constitutional – or legal-constitutional – order is predominantly grounded in the notions of preservation, stabilisation, careful management and the self-limitation of political power, thereby

26 M. Canovan, 'Trust the people! Populism and the two faces of democracy' (1999) 47 *Political studies* 1, 2–16; B. Arditi, *Politics on the Edges of Liberalism: Difference, Populism, Revolution, Agitation*, Edinburgh University Press, Edinburgh 2007.

27 J. Grant, 'Justifying Constituent Power in an Age of Populism' (2020) 52 *Polity* 1, 3–34, 3.

28 *Ibid.*, 4.

29 *Ibid.*, 5.

30 *Ibid.*, 3.

prioritising constituted powers, populism rejects such a view, which it understands as unduly constraining popular power.

The populist view of constituent power can be understood as a specific version of a revolutionary or democratic understanding of constitutionalism, in which the 'constituent power of the people is (almost) absolute and can be exercised directly in the polity'.[31] If the liberal or legal view of constitutionalism leans towards an emphasis on order and stability, the democratic, revolutionary understanding relates to constitutionalism as a vehicle of emancipation. One of the great dangers of the populist understanding of constituent power is that it tends to construct the 'people' – as the origin of this power – in a unitary, non-pluralist, non-social and exclusionary manner and, in this, as tending to fully occupy the vacuum of symbolic power, a crucial dimension of democracy as conceptualised by Claude Lefort.[32] If a key ambition of modern constitutionalism is to keep the space of power empty, populism has a strong tendency to significantly thwart this ambition, not least by instituting a strong type of populist leadership that actualises the abstract idea of the will of the people or the 'People-As-One' in a populist programme of governance.

The populist understanding of constituent power exalts the revolutionary, emancipatory dimensions of modern democracy, grounded in the idea of popular sovereignty, and contrasts this to the orderly view of liberal legalism, which shifts political power away from democratic politics towards the constituted, independent institutions of the law, which guard the existing order and resolve disputes on the basis of the law.[33] The 'great faith in the power of law and legal institutions to solve problems'[34] is questioned by populists, who emphasise populist political leadership in its stead. In this, the populist approach to law is related to a rejection of distinctive dimensions in the political imaginary which underpin modern constitutional democracy, based on the notion of control or rational 'mastery'.[35] The latter informs the crucial building blocks of liberal constitutional democracy, such as those of (legal) order, stability, legality and a separation of politics and law.

---

31 L. Corrias, 'Populism in a Constitutional Key: Constituent Power, Popular Sovereignty and Constitutional Identity', (2016) 12 *Eur. Const. L. Rev.* 6(11), 6–16.

32 Cf. A. Arato, *Post Sovereign Constitutional Making: Learning and Legitimacy*, Oxford University Press, Oxford 2016, pp. 269–70.

33 Cf. E.A. Posner, *The perils of global legalism*, The University of Chicago Press, Chicago 2009.

34 *Ibid.*, p. 16.

35 C. Castoriadis, *The imaginary institution of society*, MIT Press, Cambridge, Massachusetts 1997.

4. THE POPULIST IMAGINARY[36]

A discussion of populism in the context of imagination and constitutional imaginaries is of clear significance.[37] Such a view recognises how distinctive understandings of democracy and constitutionalism are grounded in particular modern political imaginaries (for instance, regarding post-national or sovereigntist views), and how prevalent or dominant understandings of constitutionalism and democracy – shared among various societies – may shift and change over time. A key dimension of shifting imaginaries in contemporary democracies is that of 'constitutional imaginaries'.[38] As argued above, in particular since WWII, a distinctive legal and constitutional imaginary constellation has taken hold, in which democratic regimes are perceived as principally grounded in non-political, juridical institutions, such as written constitutions and apex courts, which have the dual nature of 'taming' political passion and excessive power aspirations and of protecting individuals from the abuse of political power. As Timmerman and colleagues argue, focusing on the important dimension of universal human rights:

> ... since the middle of the twentieth century, a major shift in the social imaginaries has been underway: the rise of a *global human rights imaginary* that expands and transforms earlier imaginaries grounded in conceptions of the nation and nation state. Collective imaginaries today increasingly refer to the level of global society or the 'we' of a single human community. As expressed by the 1948 UN Universal Declaration of Human Rights, we imagine ourselves to be part of one humanity in which every human being, irrespective of his or her nationality, holds certain fundamental rights.[39]

This post-national, legal-liberal imaginary construct – grounded in universal human rights, constitutional democracy and mechanisms

---

[36] This section builds on P. Blokker, 'Political and Constitutional Imaginaries' in S. Adams and J. Smith (eds), *Social Imaginaries: Critical Interventions in a Paradigm-in-the-Making*, Rowman and Littlefield, Lanham, Maryland 2019.

[37] Cf. M. Loughlin, 'The constitutional imagination', (2015) 78 *The Modern Law Review* 1, 1–25; Z. Oklopcic, *Beyond the people: Social imaginary and constituent imagination*, Oxford University Press, Oxford 2018.

[38] Cf. O. Angeli, 'Global constitutionalism and constitutional imagination' (2017) 6 *Global Constitutionalism* 3, 359–76.

[39] C. Timmerman, G. Verschraegen, K. Hemmerechts and R. Willems, 'Europe and the Human Rights Imaginary' in: H. Alma and G. Vanheeswijck (eds), *Social Imaginaries in a Globalizing World*, De Gruyter, Berlin 2018, pp. 223–46; emphasis added.

of judicial review – has had remarkable success, as attested not least by the prominence of constitutional dimensions in the remarkable political transformations of post-communist societies in Central and Eastern Europe in the early 21st century. The post-WWII tendency towards legal constitutionalism and legal internationalism founds its ultimate triumph in the wake of the collapse of the Soviet empire, which led to great optimism about liberal democracy and a globalist legal liberalism.[40] Such a success seems now, however, to be rapidly diminishing. In the view of Koskenniemi, the current 'backlash' is not so much against international law as such, but against the 'project of international law and its ideological ambiance, especially in the form it received in the 1990s'.[41]

In recent years, one of the most significant threats to modern constitutional democracy, embedded in an international legal order, appears to be coming from the prominent resurgence of a populist approach to politics, becoming visible, *inter alia*, in recent instances of populists in government (as in the cases of, for instance, Hungary, Poland, Italy and the United States). Such populist governments frequently (attempt to) engage with constitutional reform and change from a 'revolutionary' perspective, heavily drawing on ideas of constituent power,[42] expressing intentions to re-construct the relations between domestic political orders and international institutions (Brexit is a clear example). Constituent power is employed as a means by which to redefine the domestic-constitutional order in populist-sovereigntist terms. In this regard, as Andrew Arato aptly notes, it is 'logical for populist governments to reach for the constituent power, and try to produce new documentary constitutions'.[43] In the words of Simone Chambers,

> ... contemporary populism has often progressed and gained ground through embracing and claiming ownership over national constitutions. Thus, constitutional reform has been the preferred means to consolidate the central authoritarian power in Hungary, Poland, Turkey and Venezuela. European and

---

40 Cf. M. Koskenniemi, 'International law and the far right: reflections on law and cynicism' (2019) Fourth T.M.C. Asser Lecture, p. 4.

41 M. Koskenniemi, 'International law and the far right: reflections on law and cynicism' (2019) Fourth T.M.C. Asser Lecture, pp. 3–4.

42 Cf. L. Corrias, 'Populism in a Constitutional Key: Constituent Power, Popular Sovereignty and Constitutional Identity' (2016) 12 *Eur. Const. L. Rev.* 6(11), 6–16.

43 A. Arato, 'How we got here? Transition Failures, their Causes, and the Populist Interest in the Constitution' (2019) 45 *Philosophy and Social Criticism* 9–10, 1106–15.

American populist movements have adopted a similar rhetoric even if they have not had a similar institutional success.[44]

In this, populism ought to be understood as both a rejection of the liberal-legal imaginary (in both the domestic and international sense) and as a political force of competition regarding the meaning, justification and realisation of constitutional democracy.[45] Populist engagement with constitutionalism is not least about an attempt to displace taken-for-granted meanings of what constitutions are. In offers, in this, a form of 'counter-constitutionalism',[46] in which national and popular sovereignty are frequently re-assessed as core dimensions, to the detriment of internationalist engagement and EU law.

The idea that constitutional law is to be understood as consisting of solid, stable and endurable institutional configurations, embedded in international and transnational legal regimes, is contrasted – and, in some cases, even displaced by – alternative, popular political imaginaries.[47] The 'cultural wars' and deeply divided societal positions regarding constitutional orders that affect many a constitutional order and norm in contemporary times (a case in point is Poland)[48] remind us of the crucial insight that legal and constitutional-democratic orders can only function as an integrative societal force when they are deeply imbued in social relations and the collective imagination.[49] Contemporary societies are affected by various forms of acceleration and fragmentation (not least as a result of economic processes), which may feed into manifestations of

---

44 S. Chambers, 'Afterword, Populist Constitutionalism v. Deliberative Constitutionalism'. in R. Levy et al. (eds), *The Cambridge Handbook of Deliberative Constitutionalism*, Cambridge University Press, Cambridge 2018, pp. 370–72, 370.

45 N. Urbinati, *Democracy Disfigured*, Harvard University Press, Cambridge, Massachusetts 2014.

46 K.L. Scheppele, 'The Social Lives of Constitutions', in: P. Blokker and C. Thornhill (eds), *Sociological Constitutionalism*, Cambridge University Press, Cambridge 2017, pp. 35–66.

47 Y. Ezrahi, *Imagined democracies, necessary political fictions*, Cambridge University Press, Cambridge 2012.

48 Cf. P. Blokker, 'Building democracy by legal means? The contestation of human rights and constitutionalism in East-Central Europe' (2020) 18 *Journal of Modern European History* 3, 335–51.

49 Cf. K.L. Scheppele, 'The Social Lives of Constitutions' in P. Blokker and C. Thornhill (eds), *Sociological Constitutionalism*, Cambridge University Press, Cambridge 2017, pp. 35–66; C. Taylor, *Modern social imaginaries*, Duke University Press, Durham/London 2004; R. Diaz-Bone, 'Institutionalist and methodological perspectives on law – Contributions of the economics of convention' (2015) *Historical Social Research/Historische Sozialforschung*, 23–41.

critique, resentment and backlash. The phenomena of societal acceleration and polarisation are producing major effects on the constitutional imaginary of order, stability and certainty, resulting in forms of disconnect between formal, legal institutions and wider society, as well as widespread sensations of powerlessness and (political and socio-economic) exclusion. As Loughlin and Dobner have argued with regard to liberal constitutionalism as an imaginary of order, stability and self-government, it is ironic to observe that the heydays of modern constitutionalism, that is, the 1990s and their aftermath, seem to be accompanied by the erosion of just such an imaginary:

> [T]his period of maturation of constitutionalism coincides with the erosion of some of the basic conditions on which those achievements have rested. Foremost amongst these conditions are those of statehood and a concept of democracy generated from the claim that 'we the people' are the authorising agents of the constitutional scheme. Constitutionalism is increasingly being challenged by political realities that effect multiple transgressions of the notion of democratic statehood. It is in this sense that constitutionalism can be understood to be entering a twilight zone.[50]

The core imaginary underpinnings of modern constitutional democracy, including popular sovereignty and democratic rule, are increasingly in tension with technocratic forms of international governance.[51] This global-legalist imaginary and its emphasis on international integration on the basis of the rule of legal experts is unconvincing to many, however. A prominent challenge is the right-wing, reactionary, populist 'backlash' 'against the rationalism and universalism that is often linked with internationalism and globalization as well as with the institutions of liberal-democratic politics – courts, bureaucracies, the media, political parties and processes, perhaps the idea of "liberal democracy" itself'.[52] This is, in effect, often described as a 'backlash', or what Madsen and colleagues refer to as 'extraordinary resistance', in which international legal institutions and their authority are criticised.[53]

---

50 P. Dobner and M. Loughlin (eds), *The twilight of constitutionalism?*, Oxford University Press, Oxford 2010, p. xi.

51 Cf. M. Koskenniemi, 'International law and the far right: reflections on law and cynicism' (2019) Fourth T.M.C. Asser Lecture.

52 M. Koskenniemi, 'International law and the far right: reflections on law and cynicism' (2019) Fourth T.M.C. Asser Lecture, p. 2.

53 M. Madsen, P. Cebulak and M. Wiebusch, 'Backlash against international courts: explaining the forms and patterns of resistance to international courts' (2018) 14 *International Journal of Law in Context* 2, 197–220.

While populism, in its different guises, tends to consist of a rejection of the legal-liberal imaginary of the post-war period, it simultaneously offers a claim to a different understanding, which purports to more intensely realise basic ingredients of democracy – in particular, *popular sovereignty* and *majority rule*.[54] A related question is therefore to what extent the emergence of a populist imaginary with important legal dimensions can be identified. Populist constitutionalism seems to be a rejection of the modern, legal and technocratic understanding of constitutionalism. It appears to constitute some kind of variant on a democratic understanding, grounded in undivided popular sovereignty. The relation between populism and constitutionalism might be understood by reference to a predominantly democratic imaginary, in contrast to a legalistic imaginary, as populism strongly rejects the liberal rule-of-law tradition – in particular, in its internationalist and post-sovereign version – and prioritises political and popular sovereignty.[55] Populism rejects the emphasis on the limitation of political power through legal norms and the subjection of power to higher norms as in legal constitutionalism, while it promotes a constitutional order that puts popular sovereignty and constituent power upfront. It denounces the rule of law and the constitutional state as vehicles that promote the interests of minorities (elites) against the well-being of the people and claims to build a new constitutional order that will promote the common good against partisan interests.

---

54 The thrust of my argument is similar to the likes of Jan-Werner Müller and Bojan Bugaric and Mark Tushnet in claiming that populists are not against institutions *per se*, but rather, they attempt to institutionalise their own populist political programme. Cf. J.W. Müller, 'Populism and Constitutionalism' in C.R. Kaltwasser et al. (eds), *The Oxford Handbook of Populism*, Oxford University Press, Oxford 2018; B. Bugaric and M. Tushnet, 'Populism and constitutionalism: an essay on definitions and their implications' (in press) *Cardozo Law Review*. I believe I differ from Müller, and am closer to Bugaric and Tushnet as well as Koskenniemi, in my acknowledgement of structural deficiencies in liberal constitutionalism, which in a distinct manner are taken up by populists.

55 L. Corrias, 'Populism in a Constitutional Key, Constituent Power, Popular Sovereignty and Constitutional Identity' (2016) 12 *European Constitutional Law Review* 1, 6–26. As Neil Walker states (N. Walker, 'Populism and constitutional tension' (2019) 17 *International Journal of Constitutional Law* 2, 515–35), a significant dimension of populism as a strain of our political and constitutional imaginary, and of our scholarly preoccupation with it, 'have to do with the relationship to an underlying tension within modern constitutionalism'.

5. POPULAR SOVEREIGNTY VERSUS GLOBAL LEGALISM

Populists tend to imagine political power in a distinctive manner, that is, as the expression of the will of a unified, common people. In this regard, populists are fundamentally modern in that they insist on an understanding of sovereignty that is strictly related to the nation-state. Indeed, populists 'frequently blame foreign influences and international institutions for the nation's problems'.[56] Political government means to govern in the name of an abstract, but simultaneously tangible, majority that corresponds to the distinctive, imagined features of a pure people (understood in clear contrast to a significant other, i.e. foreigners or international elites). As many observers have argued, following Lefort, for populists the people must be created or 'regenerated'.[57] As Jan-Werner Müller puts it:

> Populism, then, is not about a particular social base or a particular set of emotions or particular policies; rather, it is a particular *moralistic imagination of politics*, a way of perceiving the political world which opposes a morally pure and fully unified, but ultimately fictional, people to small minorities who are put outside the authentic people. In other words, the people are not really what prima facie appear as the people in its empirical entirety; rather, as Claude Lefort put it, first 'the people must be extracted from within the people'.[58]

Right-wing populists imagine a purely domestic or national people, which is put in strong opposition to the foreign, and is reified as a trans-historical subject. It also means that the 'global legalist project', which endorses the idea that 'people's loyalty should be to humanity as such rather than any particular tribe or national group', is strongly contested.[59] Populists equate this political subject with the political majority, understood as a durable and pre-political entity – which in right-wing, conservative populism takes

---

56 E. Posner, 'Liberal Internationalism and the Populist Backlash' (2017) 49 *Arizona State Law Journal* 795, 797.

57 Cf. A. Arato, *Post Sovereign Constitutional Making: Learning and Legitimacy*, Oxford University Press, Oxford 2016; J.W. Müller, '"The people must be extracted from within the people", Reflections on populism' (2014) 21 *Constellations* 4, 483–93.

58 J.W. Müller, '"The people must be extracted from within the people", Reflections on populism', (2014) 21 *Constellations* 4, 483–93, 485.

59 E. Posner, 'Liberal Internationalism and the Populist Backlash' (2017) 49 *Arizona State Law Journal* 795, 801.

the form of the nation.[60] As Eric A. Posner argues, in right-wing populism, the 'common theme is a challenge to the "establishment" or "elites" by outsiders on behalf of the common people, or, in some cases, by insiders who claim a mandate from the common people'.[61] The establishment is understood as 'corrupt', because it tends to show 'greater concern for foreigners or minorities than for the common citizen'.[62] The common people is hence not only in sharp contrast to the liberal understanding of the political majority as a mere temporary aggregate of individual citizens, but also in contrast to liberal internationalism, that is, globalist and cosmopolitan understandings of democracy, constitutionalism and the rule of law.

Populists therefore frequently mobilise against international institutions, international legal (human rights) regimes and global elites in the name of the common people, claiming that globalism and cosmopolitan forces are too distant from the common people; do not have a democratic mandate; and engage in abstract, technocratic governance in the name of the international elites themselves, ignoring the problems of the common people or nation.[63] Populists thus counter-position classical, national sovereignty to cosmopolitan views. A significant example of this in Europe is the argument of Paolo Becchi, an Italian philosopher close the populist Lega party, who criticises globalism and calls for a 'Europe of the Peoples' and a 'Charter of the Rights of the Peoples of Europe'.[64] The intent is clearly to favour national communities over any kind of post-national idea of community. As expressed in Article 1 of Becchi's Charter, the intent is 'inter-national' and not 'cosmopolitan':

> Art. 1 The European peoples recognize each other reciprocally as free and equal. The European peoples are the holders of their own rights, and as such autonomous and independent in relation to those [rights] attributed by international law to the states in which they live and to the individuals who make up these states.[65]

---

60 P. Blokker, 'Populist nationalism, anti-Europeanism, postnationalism, and the East-West distinction, (2005) 6 *German Law Journal*.

61 E. Posner, 'Liberal Internationalism and the Populist Backlash' (2017) 49 *Arizona State Law Journal* 795, 796.

62 *Ibid.*

63 *Ibid.*, 796–97.

64 P. Becchi, *Manifesto sovranista. Per la liberazione dei popoli europei*. Giubilei Regnani, Rome 2019, 16, 18–19.

65 *Ibid.*, 31.

Equally relevant is the 'cultural counter-revolution' of Orban and Kaczynski, not least directed against George Soros, the international (Hungarian-American) philanthropist and founded of the Open Society Foundation,[66] and in particular, against what Soros represents: a cosmopolitan, liberal internationalist view of universal human rights-based constitutional democracy, grounded in ideas of pluralism and minority rights.

6. LEGAL RESENTMENT OR POPULIST UNDERSTANDINGS OF THE LAW

The populist attitude to constitutions, and to law in general, is a critical attitude that I have labelled legal scepticism or 'legal resentment'.[67] With this notion, which is not dissimilar to Koskenniemi's understanding of the 'cynicism' of populists, I indicate the sceptical view of populists towards liberal understandings of the law, in particular those related to what Posner identifies as 'global legalism'.[68] The populists hence do not criticise law *tout court*, but rather a distinctive, liberal-internationalist or cosmopolitan understanding of law, human rights and constitutionalism. Koskenniemi describes this as a '*status anxiety*', which 'takes the form of a *cultural war* against the values and priorities associated with the "international" or the "global" that became dominant in the 1990s'.[69] Populist legal scepticism or legal resentment targets 'liberal legalism' or 'legal liberalism', that is, a distinctive liberal understanding of the law, or better still, a specific combination of liberalism and legalism.[70]

---

66 P. Krekó and Z. Enyedi, 'Explaining Eastern Europe: Orbán's Laboratory of Illiberalism' (2018) 29 *Journal of Democracy* 3, 39–51, 45.

67 P. Blokker, *New Democracies in Crisis? A Comparative Constitutional Study of the Czech Republic, Hungary, Poland, Romania and Slovakia*, Routledge, London/New York 2013.

68 E.A. Posner, *The perils of global legalism*, The University of Chicago Press, Chicago 2009.

69 M. Koskenniemi, 'International law and the far right: reflections on law and cynicism' (2019) Fourth T.M.C. Asser Lecture, p. 5; italics in original.

70 The populist vision dovetails with critical scholarly views of forms of liberalism. As John Gray has argued, '[c]urrent [liberal] orthodoxies treat the law as an accomplished fact. By passing over the political conditions that make the rule of law possible, the legalist liberalism that has prevailed over the past generation has been able to represent law as a free-standing institution. It has contrived to disregard that the institution of the law always depends on the power of the state' (J. Gray, *Two Faces of Liberalism*, Polity, Cambridge 1995, pp. 131–32).

Legal resentment refers to a critical, emotional stance towards liberal and legal constitutionalism,[71] and the latter's alleged juridification, de-politicisation and rational, technocratic formatting of society.[72] Legal resentment informs a distinctive populist reading of liberal constitutionalism and global legalism, that is, the post-WWII 'default design choice for political systems across Europe and North America', in the form of an internationally interdependent constitutionalism that 'typically hinges on a written constitution that includes an enumeration of individual rights, the existence of rights-based judicial review, a heightened threshold for constitutional amendment, a commitment to periodic democratic elections, and a commitment to the rule of law'.[73] The populists view the post-war practice and justification of liberal constitutionalism and the rule of law with scepticism, and their understanding in some ways follows the logic of what Hirschman has referred to as the 'perversity thesis',[74] that is, the idea that the liberal project achieves the opposite of what it promises. Rather than leading to a free society for all, the rule of law and liberal constitutionalism result in the dominance of distinctive groups in society and their 'oppressive' cosmopolitan, (neo-)liberal, individualist culture, to the detriment of large swaths of society, understood as the 'ordinary people' with their local culture and mores.

Populists of different ideological outlooks (right-wing, left-wing) share this critical, resentful attitude towards the liberal understanding and justification of the rule of law. A crucial dimension of legal resentment is a critical evaluation of the idea of the law as *non-political and neutral*. Post-1945 modern constitutionalism imagined order to be created through solid, independent constitutional institutions, such as international rights regimes, apex courts and entrenched constitutional rights. In the imagination of the promoters of this modern project,[75] the potentially violent consequences of irrational, passionate politics can be tamed by

---

71 For an extensive discussion of the debate on Law and Emotions with regard to populism, see Wesołowska in this volume.

72 M. Koskenniemi, 'International law and the far right: reflections on law and cynicism', (2019) Fourth T.M.C. Asser Lecture, p. 5.

73 T. Ginsburg, A. Huq and M. Versteeg, 'The Coming Demise of Liberal Constitutionalism' (2018) 85 *University of Chicago Law Review*, 239.

74 A.O. Hirschman, *The rhetoric of reaction*, Harvard University Press, Cambridge, Massachusetts 1991.

75 In Europe, for instance, the emergence of a liberal constitutional imaginary was related to the emergence of domestic (constitutional courts) as well as international juridical institutions, such as the European Court of Human Rights and later the European Court of Justice and, in the early 1990s, the Venice Commission or European Commission for Democracy Through Law.

means of a carefully designed constitutional framework, grounded in universalistic, rational principles. This move – normally understood as a key underpinning of constitutionalism – separates subjective, ideological politics from what is held to be the non-ideological, objective rules and procedures of constitutionalism.

For populists, possessing a sceptical mind-set, this move is exposed as a form of imagination in its own right, as well as a distinctive ideological position of a determined elite group, and hence it cannot be claimed to be non-social and non-ideological of origin. Populists criticise this move – of a strong separation between law, on the one hand, and politics and morality, on the other – in the name of a form of 'realism'. Populists not only stress that knowledge and power are closely interrelated, but go further in denouncing any knowledge other than their own as suspect. As Koskenniemi remarks, the 'cynicism of the far right lies in its having drawn from scepticism the conclusion that everything is corrupted, that knowledge and politics are types of deception carried out by "unaccountable elites" (of the academy) and the dark forces of the "deep state"'.[76] The populist understanding of the law denies the idea of a closed, self-sufficient and self-referential legal system, which imagines its own functioning through the specialist language of law. Populism emphasises instead the eternally political and hence partisan nature of the law (this could be ultimately understood as a critical, sociological move, exposing the historical, societal origins of the law). In the populist view, the law becomes inseparable from extra-legal sources, such as political power and the societal community, and is thus re-politicised.

A further relevant dimension is the evaluation of the *locus of sovereignty* in the populist narrative. In liberal understandings of democracy, sovereignty is related to the state and sovereignty is located in the legal system – and ultimately in the constitution. Liberals display an extraordinary trust in legal institutions and actors.

For liberals, the extraordinary, constituent power that emerges in the founding moment of liberal orders (at least, as imagined in the archetypal experiences of the American and French revolutions),[77] in which the popular will manifests itself, is channelled into the ordinary political and legal institutions of constitutional democracy. In contrast, populists clearly perceive this normalising or institutionalising of extraordinary power as

---

76 M. Koskenniemi, 'International law and the far right: reflections on law and cynicism' (2019) Fourth T.M.C. Asser Lecture, p. 31.

77 Cf. C. Taylor, *Modern social imaginaries*, Duke University Press, Durham/London 2004.

problematic, and reclaim popular sovereignty by situating sovereignty squarely in the 'nation' or the people. Populists hence seek to return to an archetypal, modern view of national, *political* sovereignty. In this, popular sovereignty and constituent capacity re-emerge in the populist political programme. Populists want to retrieve political sovereignty and, in order to do so, need to overcome the restrictions and limitations that the imaginary of the rule of law puts onto liberal political institutions and political forces, and institute popular sovereignty in a different way, allegedly bringing about 'real' popular sovereignty. The 'divided' sovereignty of liberalism, in the sense of a division of powers between state institutions, or post-sovereignty in the case of supranational integration, are therein rejected, while a re-centralisation and re-politicisation of sovereignty are pursued, which purportedly results in the actualisation of popular sovereignty.

Third, populists criticise the liberal understanding of the rule of law for its emphasis on individualism rather than collectivism, and hence its *eroding effect on unity*. The liberal rule of law erodes the collective, because it divides the polity (in its emphasis on political competition, different interests to be safeguarded and individual rights). It weakens its decision-making powers (through a hierarchy of legal rules and constraints) – and through its opening up of the polity to international influence (e.g. through its universalistic rationality and design and its disregard for local mores). Liberal individualism promotes a view of a pluralistic, 'civic' *demos* as the basis of the democratic polity, which is rejected by populists, in order to be replaced by a collectivist view which emphasises the belonging of the individual to a homogeneous community of either the *ethnos* or of the 'ordinary people'.[78] Constraints and rights become in some ways superfluous, as the law, as an expression of the populist rulers, is consistently promoting the best interests of those belonging to the nation. The liberal idea of the law can, in this, be understood as an obstacle to achieving individual freedom, as freedom is understood by populists as only possible as a collective endeavour.

The populist imaginary of constitutionalism clearly hinges on a democratic imaginary of the emancipation of the common people, in its promotion of collective self-government. But the way in which the populist imaginary informs constitutional practice and justification shows

78 Cf. L.A. Thio, 'Constitutionalism in Illiberal Polities' in M. Rosenfeld and A. Sajó (eds), *The Oxford Handbook of Comparative Constitutional Law*, Oxford University Press, Oxford 2012, pp. 133–52.

that it takes a one-sided and exclusionary – rather than an inclusionary and emancipatory – view towards constitutional democracy.[79] Populists share a tendency towards denouncing elite rule as detrimental to the common good, as potentially favouring partial interests and as separating the instituted political world from wider, societally held social imaginaries. It equally denounces the professed neutrality and rationality of the law as potentially resulting in inequality and exclusion. In populist constitutionalism, the actual engagement of (different groups of) citizens in society[80] is substituted by the idea of a united people, mobilised and represented by the populist leader. The main culprit is identified in corrupt elite rule, which simply needs to be replaced by a government for the people, but not necessarily *by* the people.

Populism criticises liberal constitutionalism and endorses an alternative constitutional solution, 'counter-constitution'[81] or 'constitutional counter-revolution',[82] which is, however, highly limited with regard to its democratic and *democratising* idea. Populist constitutionalism rejects the existing order because of its inequalities and injustices, but it often does so with the aim of restoring (an ideal of) a preceding, historical or cultural order. But one can equally identify a messianic, redemptive dimension, which

79 By comparison, a radical, left-wing, democratic approach to constitutionalism equally rejects the preceding order, or the existing order or status quo it agitates against, and wants to create a polity anew, eschewing any of the existing traditions. But democratic constitutionalism puts the rights of any individual and the idea of equality centre stage, against the corrupting and unequal implications of established traditions based on status and privilege. See C. Möllers, 'Pouvoir Constituant – Constitution – Constitutionalisation' in J. Bast and A. von Bogdandy (eds), *Principles of European Constitutional Law*, Hart Publishing, Oxford 2010; cf. S. Chambers, 'Afterword, Populist Constitutionalism v. Deliberative Constitutionalism' in R. Levy et al. (eds), *The Cambridge Handbook of Deliberative Constitutionalism*, Cambridge University Press, Cambridge 2018, pp. 370–72. In this, democratic constitutionalism targets liberal constitutionalism as potentially leading to inequality, as in the lack of possibilities for popular engagement with constitutional politics and norms, and in the emphasis on elitist, higher public reason. J. Colón-Ríos, *Weak Constitutionalism, Democratic Legitimacy and the Question of Constituent Power*, Routledge, London/New York 2012; J. Tully, *Public Philosophy in a New Key*, Cambridge University Press, Cambridge 2008.

80 As is argued in radical democratic approaches to constitutionalism in terms of the widening and deepening of possibilities of *de facto* citizen engagement with constitutional politics and norms.

81 K.L. Scheppele, 'The Social Lives of Constitutions' in P. Blokker and C. Thornhill (eds), *Sociological Constitutionalism*, Cambridge University Press, Cambridge 2017, pp. 35–66.

82 G. Halmai, 'The Rise and Fall of Constitutionalism in Hungary' in P. Blokker (ed.), *Constitutional Acceleration within the European Union and Beyond*, Routledge, London/New York 2017, pp. 215–31.

is future-oriented in that it aims to realising a pure, non-corrupted polity in the future (in the Polish case, e.g. in the form of a 'Fourth Republic'). Populism understands liberal democracy and the rule of law as a historical interruption and aberration. It rejects the idea of the legal-constitutional order because, according to populists, it produces or favours inequalities (e.g. between the haves and have-nots, between cosmopolitans and locals or between foreigners and nationals), as well as, more importantly, because it leads to the erosion of the historical nation. The hierarchy of the legal-constitutional order is not to be replaced by an inclusive, more universalistic order, but rather, by a return to, or realisation of, the past – that is, of a traditional order – based on 'natural' hierarchies related to ethnicity, family and tradition. Wolin's power imaginary also seems to be of some relevance here, in that populists claim a heroic mission against (age-old) enemies of the people, presented in a Manichean manner, thereby 'justifying a greater claim on society's resources, sacrifices by society's members, and challenges to the safeguards prescribed in the constitutional imaginary [the rule of law, division of powers, and so on]'.[83]

7. CONCLUDING REMARKS

The argument of this chapter has been that the relation between populism and constitutionalism ought to be approached from a historical and socio-cultural perspective, which emphasises the populist challenge to the distinctive post-WWII model of constitutional democracy, based on an anti-totalitarian and internationalist (or post-nationalist) understanding of constitutionalism, human rights and the rule of law. The contemporary populist approach to this post-WWII model is one of rejection, taking the form of a backlash against the post-war hegemony of liberal legalism and promoting a return to a classical modern idea of popular sovereignty, deeply grounded in the nation-state and in the rejection of post-national forms of integration. Rather than one-sidedly understanding the populist challenge as an indication of the 'end of civilization', this chapter calls for a more self-reflexive and self-critical stance, which recognises the problems in the cosmopolitan, liberal-legal model and attempts to overcome its shortcomings.

---

[83] S. Wolin, *Democracy Inc. Managed Democracy and the Specter of Inverted Totalitarianism*, Princeton University Press, Princeton 2008, p. 39.

LAW AND EMOTIONS

Insights for the Study of Anti-Constitutional Populism

Julia WESOŁOWSKA*

1. INTRODUCTION

In the modern political context, populism is often described as a deeply emotional rhetoric[1] connected with dissatisfaction with liberal constitutionalism due to its distance from the lives of 'ordinary people' and serving the interests of a narrow class.[2] This fuels the drive for a radical change in the political realm and legal policies. Populism seems to entail strong collective emotions, often leading to destructive aspirations, especially with regards to the concept of rule of law and observance of the constitution. While the emotional mechanisms of populism are often the subject of analysis for social scientists, and the mechanism in which populism affects law becomes the concern of jurisprudence, studies

* The writing of this chapter was funded by the National Science Centre, Poland according to Decision no. 2017/27/B/HS5/01053.

1 A. SCRIBANO, M.E. KORSTANJE and F.A.T. LOPEZ, *Populism and Postcolonialism*, Routledge, London 2019, p. 28.

2 P. BLOKKER, 'The Populist Assault on the Constitution' in P. BLOKKER and M. ANSELMI (eds), *Multiple populisms. Italy as democracy's mirror*, Routledge, London 2020.

connecting the threads are lacking. The triangular relation between populism, affect, and law is a curious ground for further exploration, which might produce new insights along each of these lines.

The goal of this chapter is to sketch out the connection between populism, emotions and the law in order to show how tools and insights offered by Law and Emotions scholarship (hereafter referred to as L&E) can be applied in the studies of contemporary populism. In other words, I ask: what does L&E bring to the table for populism studies? The chapter looks into the points of connection between populism and law and juxtaposes them with the achievements of the L&E movement. Law and legality is undoubtedly one of the lines by which the populist policies might be analysed. Populism may even be defined by its relationship to policies and to foundational legal acts.[3] But without also problematising it in terms of the affect, the links between populism and law may be still too opaque to take account of the phenomenon properly.

The populism I will refer to throughout this work is not to be modelled after any special country, but rather, is to be understood as an egregore of features that characterise this concept, especially in its authoritarian, anti-constitution variety.[4] This kind of populism manifests, *inter alia*, in envisioning constitutional law as protecting elite as opposed to mass interests, which in turn legitimises attacking it. It is also characterised by its scepticism towards conceptions of legality and rule of law, as well as constitution law and institutions in their current form.

For the purposes of this chapter, I will be focusing on the points of contact, that is, populist engagement with the law, and looking for the areas where the affective–legal connection is most pronounced. There, I draw from L&E scholarship in order to show the usefulness of using its methodology in the analysis of selected legal dimensions of populism. Building on these basic distinctions, I propose four problems which the perspective of L&E can address: firstly, I show how L&E's serious engagement with the affective – pigeonholed in public life – can provide an interdisciplinary addition to the study of populism and a method to propose practical solutions. Secondly, I present myths about emotions

---

3 G. Delledonne, G. Martinico, M. Monti and F. Pacini, 'Introduction: A Constitutional Viewpoint on Italian Populism' in G. Delledonne, G. Martinico, M. Monti and F. Pacini (eds), *Italian Populism and Constitutional Law*, Palgrave Macmillan, London 2020, pp. 1–9.

4 B. Bugaric, 'The Populist Backlash Against Europe: Why Only Alternative Economic and Social Policies Can Stop the Rise of Populism in Europe' in F. Bignami (ed.), *EU Law in Populist Times*, Cambridge University Press, Cambridge 2018, p. 485.

and irrationality that L&E has largely dispelled, but which studies of populism are yet to address. Thirdly, I demonstrate how L&E scholarship on the affective underpinnings of constitutionalism offers a fresh take on populisms' attacks on constitutions. Lastly, I engage with how L&E allows us to re-examine the old stereotype about populism as 'too much emotion' and ask whether populism is not a matter of 'the wrong emotions' instead.

Law and Emotions refers to a research trend which began in the late 1980s and early 1990s. The building blocks of this trend, at first scarce and isolated, soon became systematic and impossible to ignore due to their scale, the variety of topics, and the interdisciplinary tools they used. L&E started with inquiries into how emotions are written into legal institutions; the affective dynamics of judging and practising law; the influence of emotional biases on legal decisions; and more. L&E scholarship was fully fledged by the 2000s, when the exploration of different facets of emotions in law and legal theory covered so many topics that they can be systematised into institution, theory, actor and emotion foci.[5] Much of the discussion took place through symposia and conferences, such as the 2009 Nebraska symposium on motivation, which resulted in a book volume that attracted the biggest names of the movement.[6] The routes that scholars have taken since then have been diverse, but it can be safely said they have one thing in common: acknowledging the aspect of human nature that has long flown under the radar of legal scholarship.

2. THE AFFECTIVE IN THE LEGAL

Rather than suddenly introducing emotions to an emotionless field, L&E explicates the affective undertone which is already present in law, but which has been downplayed or ignored by dominating positivist or natural law theories. Many L&E scholars attempt to bring out this unspoken presence and show how it is embedded in the very nature of legal institutions, or even more: how law brims with affect. As Terry Maroney said, 'criminal proceedings work to channel anger, indignation, fear, and disgust; rehabilitative programs encourage hope'.[7] Not only do emotions shape

5 T. Maroney, 'Law and emotion: A proposed taxonomy of an emerging field' (2006) 30 *Law and Human Behavior* 2, 119.

6 B.H. Bornstein and R.L. Wiener (eds), *Emotion and the law: Psychological perspectives*, Springer, New York 2009.

7 T.A. Maroney, 'A Field Evolves: Introduction to the Special Section on Law and Emotion' (2015) 8 *Emotion Review* 1, 4.

law, but also legal regulations can work to evoke or inhibit an emotional reaction.[8] The movement took it upon itself to expose, understand and perhaps harness these emotional forces in creating and applying law. L&E argues that letting emotions go unaddressed creates problems for law and jurisprudence. By exploring those aspects, it is possible not only to create more effective and responsive law, but also to give voice to neglected but essential human experiences,[9] as well as to learn about more general structures that underpin law and its social functioning at a given moment in history.

Populism too is often characterised by its emotional underpinning. This has two dimensions: regarding populism as a form of irrationality or unreason, and exploring how collective emotions are created, channelled, controlled or expressed in distinctly populist actions. The approaches to the topic often stem from political science or from the sociology of emotions. However, one important – but less explored – aspect is populists' emotional engagement not only with other groups or nations, but with law itself. Indeed, some theorists point to legal resentment[10] as defining populists' attitude: it seems to encompass not only scepticism or critique, but also anger and even violence towards conceptions of the rule of law or particular constitutions of elements of legal systems.

L&E is uniquely equipped to explore this topic. As shown above, it is devoted to mapping out the network of affective engagements among legal institutions, legal actors and legal theories, as well as their relations with culture and society. This kind of investigation is possible thanks to the integration of perspectives: empirical verification of neurosciences; insights of psychology, ethics and epistemology; and social science. The innovation that L&E offers hinges, in no small part, on the bottom-up response it creates across a range of legal domains and among scholars of different traditions. The transdisciplinary character of this enterprise contributes to unique insights and a more holistic understanding of the connections between the social and the natural world. L&E, uniquely rooted in legal and psychological realism, has managed to create a platform

---

8 A. Acorn, *Compulsory compassion: A critique of restorative justice*, University of British Columbia Press, Vancouver 2004.

9 See e.g. S. Cowan, V.E. Munro and H. Baillot, 'Second-hand emotion? Exploring the contagion and impact of trauma and distress in the asylum law context' (2013) 40 *Journal of Law and Society* 4, 509–540; M.K. Miller and B.H. Bornstein, *Stress, Trauma, and Wellbeing in the Legal System*, Oxford University Press, Oxford 2013.

10 P. Blokker, 'Populism as a constitutional project' (2019), 17 *International Journal of Constitutional Law* 2, 536–553.

for the particularities of the human experience, which legal literature used to gloss over. The realist aspect of this scholarship is entangled with social engagement: this manifests in the attention that L&E gives legal actors as well as those who come before courts.

As Nicolas Demertzis has pointed out, 'nearly all interpretations of populism, include the affective factor only in a disguised or implicit way (...) few are those who approached it in a systematic way, the others depending on its "commonsensical", allusive and elusive presence.'[11] This systematic approach Demertzis talks about could be offered by L&E's sociological strand of scholarship, which could offer a deeper insight on how law 'combines subjective action with social structures'.[12] The interdisciplinarity and realism of L&E is both a result and a cause of entanglements with humanist sciences, resulting in attempts to write a holistic, empirically grounded history of interactions between affect and law. Emotions function not in a vacuum, but in a given society in a historical moment; theorists of emotion like that of Ute Frevert have studied affective codes in a historical manner.[13] Many L&E scholars have taken note of that and undertaken an exploration of social and historical factors surrounding emotions in law. Often, this is done with reference to the paradigmatic theories of social science. Roger Cotterell, following in Max Weber's footsteps, has proposed a theory of affective community, held together by a common legal system.[14] There have been also many investigations showing that the relationship between emotions and the law runs deep in history: among the most interesting examples are historical works on the perception and norms connected to emotions, bodies and social roles in medieval criminal trials.[15] By grounding law and emotions' relations in social structures and history, knowledge can be carried over to the study of populism: specifically, a knowledge of how emotions are channelled in social institutions like court proceedings and punishments; how legal policies mould to emotional postulates or how they result in displays of

---

[11] N. Demertzis, 'Emotions and populism' in S. Clarke, P. Hogett and S. Thompson (eds), *Emotion, politics and society*, Palgrave Macmillan, London 2006, pp. 103–22.

[12] *Ibid.*

[13] U. Frevert, *Emotions in History ? Lost and Found,* Central European University Press, Budapest 2011.

[14] R. Cotterell, 'Law, Emotion and Affective Community' Queen Mary University of London, School of Law Legal Studies Research Paper No. 282/2018.

[15] L. Kounine, 'Emotions, mind, and body on trial: a cross-cultural perspective' (2017) 51 *Journal of Social History* 2, 219–230, see also M.L. Bailey, 'Most Hevynesse and Sorowe The Presence of Emotions in the Late Medieval and Early Modern Court of Chancery' (2019) 37 *Law and History Review* 1, 1–28.

emotions; and how legal and affective frameworks overlap in the conception of humanity.

Noting that 'populist emotions' have a connection to law should not be neglected. I propose introducing a tool that is uniquely equipped to deal with this. In fact, this perspective offers the most promise in the study of one of the most discerning factors proposed by Paul Blokker, the afore-mentioned 'legal resentment' – which hinges not only on rational engagement with law, legal institutions and policies, but also a critical attitude that voices an emotional viewpoint. To study how people feel or how they try to incite others to feel about the law, one needs more than a lens of one science. What is needed is the integration of several assumptions about law, society, emotions and politics – which L&E explores.

3. THE MYTH OF IRRATIONALITY

L&E's engagement entails not only the unmasking of the presence and importance of emotions in the legal discourse, but its aim is also to help revise and change outdated convictions about the nature of emotions and reason and the relation between them, sometimes referred to as emotional myths. One such myth is the conviction that reason and emotion are mutually exclusive. Such a conviction can be found in many accounts of populism: in fact, 'populist irrationality' seems to have become a staple in discussions of populism which traces its origins to the masses' lack of competence, bigotry, but most of all, the inability to use reason and being utterly overpowered by emotion.[16] In fact, among most anti-populist pundits a conviction seems to prevail that the masses not only do not know what is best for them, but are also 'easily swayed by the manipulation of its irrational emotions by the simplistic arguments of populist politicians'.[17] Critics have begun to point out this stereotype: 'Hofstadter's "The Age of Reform" was criticized precisely because focusing on populist irrationality: he wrote of a soft-headed populism correlating with a feminized irrationality, contrasting it with manly rationality.'[18] John Abromeit, York Norman, Gary Marotta and Bridget Maria Chesterton underline that it has

---

16 C. De La Torre, 'Populism Revived: Donald Trump and the Latin American Leftist Populists' (2018), 75 *The Americas* 4, 733–753.

17 F. Furedi, *Populism and the European culture wars: the conflict of values between Hungary and the EU*, Routledge, London 2017, p. 135.

18 J. Abromeit, Y. Norman, G. Marotta and B.M. Chesterton, 'Introduction' in J. Abromeit, Y. Norman, G. Marotta and B.M. Chesterton (eds), *Transformations*

become almost a reflex to pin down populism as irrational and paranoid. Therefore, the components of being liable to emotions or overly emotional, and being irrational, seem to be connected inevitably and feeding from one another in the typical accounts of populism. For this, the blame is assigned not merely to the masses, but to the modern media, which created the conditions in which a charismatic individual may seduce the people into following them.[19]

This emotional myth has an important dimension: populist emotionality, or the 'people's' emotionality, is often juxtaposed with legal rationality. Many critics argue against 'the tendency to represent tradition as irrational and the rational-legal as its opposite'.[20] It is a tendency to show law as rational and rationality as legitimate, contrasting law with ill-conceived emotions and contrasting law-abiding, civic-educated citizens with uneducated mobs:

> ... contrary to citizens who reason their political preferences and vote on behalf of political platform, the mob supposedly follows their emotions. Plebiscitary democracy based on the manipulation of emotions by demagogues is the antagonist, it is argued, to a democracy based on reason. This notion of the people as irrational mob was very influential in the development of the concept of populism in Latin America and Europe.[21]

Such an approach is not only factually wrong – contradicting new, empirically supported visions of emotions as complex, intentional phenomena rather than primal impulses – it is also harmful because 'it dismisses populism as irrationality *en masse*, downplaying grievances and concerns of populist voters as irrelevant or wrongly placed.'[22] Thus, by labelling emotional reactions of people as irrational, and labelling irrationality as essentially illegitimate, the anti-populism movement might inadvertently contribute to exclusion and discrimination.

What is debated as much as the nature of emotions, is the rationality of law itself. The statement that law is a rational enterprise would provoke little objection from the majority of legal theorists. The roots of such a

---

of Populism in Europe and the Americas: History and recent tendencies, Bloomsbury Publishing, London 2015.

19 *Ibid.*

20 Furedi, above n. 17, p. 135.

21 C. De la Torre (ed.), *The promise and perils of populism: Global perspectives*, University Press of Kentucky, Lexington 2014, p. 12.

22 D. Bonansinga, 'Who Thinks, Feels. The Relationship Between Emotions, Politics and Populism' (2020) 13 *Partecipazione e conflitto* 1, 83.

conviction reach deeper than the 19th- and 20th-century legal positivism: to quote Cicero, 'law is the highest reason, embedded in the nature of the world, requiring what must be done and prohibiting what must not be done.'[23] And yet, the creatures under the jurisdiction of law – those who apply and create it – are all emotional beings.

Law and emotions scholarship breaks this paradigm of legal rationality by integrating psychological findings which suggest the cognitive nature of emotions to criticise assumptions written into legal institutions – for example, crimes of passion. This is a demonstration of how social science may include the new conception of emotions in its analysis. This has not only wide-reaching implications for law and legal discourse, but also for populism: in typical accounts, law's rationality is said to depend on the legal system being 'clear, consistent, detailed and technical',[24] and populism is something that often proposes hindering this ideal by distorting it with violent passions and drastic solutions. In the eyes of L&E, however, this ties the law with humanity. This entanglement may be dangerous, as popular panic or bloodlust can lead to excessive or cruel legal solutions. But it can be equally humanising, allowing, for example, to more strongly connect this law to social life, as opposed to the abstract elevation it allegedly enjoys. But studies of L&E show how law is neither fully rational nor emotionless, and that reason and emotion are in fact inseparable and miscible in law and other social institutions. If we strip law of the assumption of coldness and indifference, populism would have less to attack. Demonstrating how constitutions are already imbued with emotions and sentiments from the past will render them less vulnerable to populist attacks.

L&E breaks new ground by showing that law is not purely rational and abstract, which in turn addresses many concerns populists have about law. If populists think law is cold and emotionless, L&E scholars are showing that it is not. The main takeaway is that it is important to resist the temptation to depict populism as irrational and law as rational: law is also emotional, and emotions themselves have a cognitive component. Some emotions are already codified within law – even the form of law conceived of by populists as the most universalist, abstract and removed, that is, constitutions.

---

23 M.N. Sellers, 'Law, Reason, and Emotion' in M.N. Sellers (ed.), *Law, Reason and Emotion*, Cambridge University Press, Cambridge 2017.

24 C. Rega, *Ecological Rationality in Spatial Planning*. Springer Nature Publishing, New York 2020, p. 32.

4. ARE CONSTITUTIONS DEVOID OF EMOTIONS?

The constitution itself is the most frequent target of populist attack. In fact, populism is often defined by its relationship to constitutions: either trampling them to achieve political goals, or promising the restoration or drafting of a new, fairer and more just constitution. As Paul Blokker notes, 'the populist constitutional attitude can be understood as the result of populism's overall negative evaluation of liberal constitutionalism, and it manifests itself in the downplaying of the constitution's status as a rigid, higher law'.[25] This inflexibility and detachment from social life is what populists often attack. The angle of this attack often includes playing up current social inequalities as the constitutions' fault; accusing the latter of not reflecting the values held by most of the society; and promises of amendments aimed at introducing a better constitution, which supposedly reflects the populous agenda. The vertical rank of an act in the legal hierarchy is correlated with the intensity with which it is negated: not only constitutional, or quasi-constitutional, but also international law regulations are ignored or attacked.[26] The erosion of constitutionalism rarely takes the form of direct derogation: what occurs instead is what Wojciech Sadurski called 'constitutional backsliding':[27] best exemplified by the Polish case of the paralysing of the Constitutional Tribunal.

Although perhaps less prominent than in cases of criminal or family law, constitutional law is not devoid of emotions – an issue which L&E explores. The engagement of L&E with this topic uncovered another layer of interpretation: the affective roots of modern constitutionalism. The main trend has been the works that expose the significance of emotions for constitutions and constitutional theory. Here, the work of Andras Sajó is of prominence: he engages with the assumption that constitutions are a result of purely rational processes, an emanation of collective reason and a containment of emotion. He explores how 'constitutions are created through emotionally driven processes and reflect the public sentiments of the day as well as – at least to some extent – basic moral emotions.'[28] This depicts constitutions in a new light: as a codification of social sentiments

---

25 Blokker, 'Populism as a constitutional project', above n. 10, p. 545.

26 G. Boggero, '"Kicking the Can Down the Road" Deferring Fiscal Adjustment as a Premise for Italian Budgetary Populism' in Delledonne, Martinico, Monti and Pacini, above n. 3, p. 153.

27 W. Sadurski, 'How Democracy Dies (in Poland): A Case Study of Anti-Constitutional Populist Backsliding' (2018) No. 18/01 Sydney Law School Research Paper.

28 A. Sajó, 'Emotions in constitutional institutions' (2016) 8 *Emotion Review* 1, 44.

of the particular time and place, rather than as a detached and timeless legal framework. Sajó coins the term 'constitutional sentiments' to describe the affective processes that underlie the bills of rights. He also notes that this situation is not fixed and draws attention to the role of emotions in future constitutional developments: the two-way relationship between constitutions and emotions will continue to evolve. This knowledge makes it possible to try to assess, model and predict possible changes to constitutional law dictated by a shift in public sentiments, as well as the emotional implications of proposed legislative changes. This insight is especially relevant in the modern constitutionalism troubled by populist political movements: the engagement of the latter with the former is often modelled by emotion.

In his other work, 'Emotions in Constitutional Designs', Sajó puts more emphasis on how constitutions influence public emotions, rather than on how public emotions influence constitutions. This creates grounds for an inquiry into how public moods and emotions are awoken by constitutional law and the manner in which constitutional law is applied. The anti-constitutional populism that has been observed in some countries, relying on vehement protesting, wilful ignorance or straight-up disdain of constitutions, must also be mediated emotionally. Just as 'sentiments have an important role in setting up constitutional designs and interpretation'[29] and 'law is both trying to script emotions (in order to prevent challenges to the status quo) and accommodates prevailing (or preferred) emotions',[30] constitutional law and legal frameworks of constitutional democracy are no exception: populist claims that constitutions are cold and indifferent no longer hold water. While populism tries to condemn the rule of law because it is cold and removed,[31] L&E shows how it is not, by explaining how various legal acts and institutions are entangled with a lively, emotional human experience. What is more, this experience is organic rather than artificial, firmly grounded in historical conditions and ways of thinking about rights and the state. Showing that emotions have always underlain constitutions and pointing out mechanisms codified in constitutions due to emotional knowledge[32] disarm the arguments of populism: if there were no

---

29 A. Sajó, 'Emotions in constitutional design' (2010) 8 *International Journal of Constitutional Law* 3, 354.

30 *Ibid.*

31 Blokker, 'Populism as a constitutional project', above n. 10, p. 536.

32 D. Gewirtzman, 'Our founding feelings: emotion, commitment, and imagination in constitutional culture' (2008) 43 *University of Richmond Law Review* 623, 323–339.

underlying public sentiments, constitutions would not take their current shape. Moreover, constitutional judges and tribunals are not devoid of affect, either, as suggested by research into the US Supreme Court's emotional expressions and the affective dynamics of groups.[33] L&E provides a description of the emotion behind and around constitutions, and as such can help decode affective mechanisms employed in populist attacks on constitutions.[34] Addressing the sentiments which are underlying foundational acts allows us not only to understand the ways in which populists misrepresent constitutions, but also arms us with the anticipatory knowledge about new sentiments that are likely to modify constitutions and the methods of enacting them during our lifetime.

5. TOO MUCH EMOTION, OR NOT THE RIGHT EMOTION?

In 'Constitutional Sentiments', Sajó states: 'the enemy of reason is not passion; it is fanaticism. This message of Voltaire is to be remembered in our age of new fanaticism'.[35] Fanaticism, or the excess of emotions and overwhelming expression, is often used to characterise populism. But does populism really consist of 'too much emotion', or is it instead case of 'not the right emotion'? Susanne Karstedt, in her account of populism, points out that the emotions that populism feeds on are 'resentment, alienation, anger and fear, that are transmitted into an anti-government and more broadly anti-political impulse'.[36] The findings of law and emotions about the penal populism and from evolutionary psychology are of use here to explain connection of such emotions, reflected in populist policies, with deep psychological structures of hostility towards the out-group and a drive for retribution.

Populism, especially right-wing populism as exemplified by recent cases in Central Europe, is characterised by anti-internationalism,

---

[33] L.K. Ray, 'Judicial personality: Rhetoric and emotion in Supreme Court opinions' (2002) 59 *Washington & Lee Law Review* 193.

[34] Blokker, 'Populism as a constitutional project', above n. 10, p. 536.

[35] A. Sajó, 'Constitutional sentiments' (2006) 47 *Acta Juridica Hungarica* 1, 1–13.

[36] S. Karstedt, I. Loader and H. Strang, *Emotions, Crime and Justice* (Onati International Series in Law and Society), Bloomsbury Publishing, London 2011, s. 15.

anti-globalism and even manifestations of xenophobia. This channels tribalistic feelings of belonging, fear and anger that solidify in-group social bonds and disgust and hatred directed towards an out-group. A new way of studying populist attitudes could be based on the postulates of Patrick Carlton, who proposed using evolutionary psychology in the study of law and emotions.[37] Popular rule, becoming a metaphysical and unified construct, could be explained by referring to the distinction between exclusionary and inclusionary emotions, as described by evolutionary psychologists, who explain how such emotions interact with law and how this can be salvaged. Evolutionary psychologists propose using knowledge about primal psychological mechanisms in the analysis of complex cultural phenomena, among them social institutions such as the law, offering yet another emotion-conscious way of looking at the problem.

L&E offers not only a description of the mechanisms at work in populism, but it also allows to develop a solution to counteract these emotions. As populist politics may be tempted to use public discourse in such a way that emphasises the feelings of fear and anger and intensifies the exclusionary sentiments, the remedy may be to cultivate feelings of inclusion and to broaden the circle of empathy towards the out-group instead, so as to evoke curiosity and empathy for diverse peoples with various interests. An alternative way is to reanimate people's feelings towards the constitution itself. I argue that the affective removal of the constitution in traditional discourse may actually be part of the problem and may make populism easier: emotions are connected with assigning judgments of significance, and for what one does care, one usually feels strongly. Constitutions should be considered not a matter of cold, removed reason, but, in Sajó's vein, an outcome of collective emotions and sentiments; perhaps by returning to their affective roots, it is possible to counter the populist narratives. To put it in Roger Cotterell's terms, the broadening of the affective community through extending the legal community could be attempted. This concept is important here because populism addresses such a community, but seeks to remove the role of law in shaping it as an obstacle, rather than a cohesive force. This could be turned around by promoting and highlighting the affective, cohesive and communal dimensions of law.

---

[37] C.J. Patrick, 'A new synthesis for law and emotions: insights from the behavioral sciences' (2015) 47 *Arizona State Law Journal* 47, 1239.

6. CONCLUSION

L&E may offer a remedy to what is perceived by some scholars to be a true ailment of contemporary constitutionalism, not invented as much as uncovered by populists' ambitions. Paul Blokker aptly pointed out the factors that make the law vulnerable to attack by populism:

> ... (...) abstract, universalist, and internationalist legal narratives (...); the ultimately unconvincing or at least fragile narrative of the neutrality and apolitical nature of the rule of law; the widespread lack of possibilities for meaningful civic engagement; and the incapacity of liberal democratic regimes to convincingly and consistently promote the common good.[38]

Several of these problems manifest nowhere else but at the level of a community's shared feelings and values. What L&E proposes is, *inter alia*, re-contextualising law and imbuing it with life. It proposes to do so by promoting opportunities for channelling collective sentiments in law; acknowledging law's and lawyers' emotional natures rather than pretending to be neutral; and fine-tuning the legal discourse to the social problems of the times. In these deeply uncertain times, although creating space for emotion may seem like a dangerous thing to do, it might be just the integration of L&E's perspectives that studies of populism need. It may turn out that we do not need to abolish emotions from law after all: we just need to nurture a different kind.

---

38 Blokker, 'Populism as a constitutional project', above n. 10, p. 552.

PART V

CHALLENGES TO CONSTITUTIONAL DEMOCRACY IN TIMES OF COVID-19 CONSTITUTIONALISM AND BEYOND

THE ROLE OF FEAR POLITICS IN GLOBAL CONSTITUTIONAL 'ERNSTFALL'

Images of Fear under COVID-19 Health Paternalism

Martin Belov

1. INTRODUCTION[1]

'Your body is a battleground' says an inspiring poster of the artist Barbara Kruger published in 1989. Privacy, self-determination, personal autonomy and the general right to liberty[2] have traditionally served as reliable barriers against excessive state health paternalism. This does not seem to be the case

1 I am grateful to prof. Mauro Zamboni and prof. Antoni Abat i Ninet for their useful comments and suggestions on this chapter.

2 See R. Alexy, *Theorie der Grundrechte*, Suhrkamp, Frankfurt am Main 1994, pp. 309–57.

any longer. The COVID-19 pandemic has been used by governments all over the world as an excuse to impose massive and largely disproportionate restrictions on freedom. Thus, COVID-19 has triggered the birth of an omnipotent and largely uncontrollable 'health Leviathan' creating visible threats to human rights, liberty and the pillars of the liberal constitutional order promoted during the second 'Belle Époque' that stretched through the post-Cold War period. This health Leviathan is especially dangerous when combined with the incredible technological advancement which has not been paralleled by corresponding demo-technocratic public culture and reliable constitutional and legal frameworks capable of coping with the achievements of the information technology (IT) revolution. The emergent health Leviathan has been defined in even harsher terms by Hans Michael Heinig and by Jürgensen and Orlowski as a fascist-hysterical hygiene state.[3]

COVID-19 has produced tremendous pressure on constitutionalism. It is not only the virus itself that has so profoundly shaken the well-ordered constitutional orders of the states, so carefully arranged according to the political imperatives of post-Cold War period and the socio-legal imperatives of neo-liberal globalisation. What was so frightening is that a pandemic of moderate intensity – produced by a dangerous flu, but still not by Ebola or plague – was able to trigger radical and devastating effects on constitutional order. Governments were introducing states of siege and states of emergency, enabling them to suspend fundamental rights and infringe cornerstone principles of constitutionalism which had remained unchallenged and sacred for decades. Discriminatory nationalism, populism and authoritarianism blossomed. The risk of this new type of 'health authoritarianism' became visible.[4] Disproportionate limitations of liberty were mushrooming. People were eagerly denouncing their fundamental rights in the name of their physical survival of the 'invisible

---

3 See H.M. Heinig, 'Gottesdienstverbot auf Grundlage des Infektionsschutzgesetzes Verfassungsrechtliche Rechtfertigung und Grenzen' <https://verfassungsblog.de/gottesdienstverbot-auf-grundlage-des-infektionsschutzgesetzes/> last accessed 15.07.2020 and S. Jürgensen and F. Orlowski, 'Critique and Crisis: The German Struggle with Pandemic Control Measures and the State of Emergency <https://verfassungsblog.de/critique-and-crisis-the-german-struggle-with-pandemic-control-measures-and-the-state-of-emergency/> last accessed 15.07.2020.

4 For the concept of 'health authoritarianism', see K. Lachmayer, 'Austria: Rule of Law Lacking in Times of Crisis' <https://verfassungsblog.de/rule-of-law-lacking-in-times-of-crisis/> last accessed 15.07.2020, as well as S. Platon, 'From One State of Emergency to Another – Emergency Powers in France' <https://verfassungsblog.de/from-one-state-of-emergency-to-another-emergency-powers-in-france/> last accessed 15.07.2020.

enemy' (a term that was used by many politicians): the SARS-CoV-2 virus. Many key politicians declared war on the virus. A new 'health crusade' against the virus was launched. Humanism, liberalism and freedom were halted in the global emergency. Global pandemics produced 'global de-globalisation'. Global trends of pandemic-induced illiberal politics were visible. They were reversing in months the trends of neoliberal globalisation that had been achieved with so much hardship for decades.[5] In 2020, the world has been close to a 'global civil war'.[6]

This chapter does not aim to explore the whole range of issues produced by the COVID-19 pandemic on constitutionalism. Its target is not to analyse the different constitutional and legislative provisions for declaring states of siege or states of emergency. It will not engage with the impact of the pandemic on inter-institutional relations, especially those between the parliament and the government in times of pandemic crisis. It will not tackle the role of people and the courts as potential constitutional checks on government. Needless to say, the chapter cannot enter into the scientific discussion on the biological nature of the virus and the biological and medical threats it exposes to humans. It will also refrain from engaging in the discussion about the geopolitical impact of the virus and the crisis it triggered on international law and international relations. These are actually acute problems with immense importance for our societies.

The goal of this chapter is different and very specific. It only aims to explore the fear politics[7] and the images of fear that emerged in the context

---

5 In the words of Kriszta Kovács 'on 23 March 1933, an act was adopted in Nazi Germany in response to the "crisis" of the Reichstag fire to enable Hitler to issue decrees independently of the Reichstag and the presidency. Article 48 of the constitution of the Weimar Republic made this act possible. Eighty-seven years later, on 23 March 2020, the so-called "Enabling Act" was put before the Hungarian Parliament. This was drafted under emergency constitutional provisions in Articles 48–54.' See K. Kovács, 'Hungary's Orbánistan: A Complete Arsenal of Emergency Powers', <https://verfassungsblog.de/hungarys-orbanistan-a-complete-arsenal-of-emergency-powers/> last accessed 15.07.2020.

6 See G. Agamben, *Stasis. Civil War as a Political Paradigm*, Stanford University Press, Stanford 2015, pp. 1–96, S. Civitarese Matteucci, 'The Italian Response to Coronavirus and Constitutional Disagreement' <https://ukconstitutionallaw.org/2020/04/30/stefano-civitarese-matteucci-the-italian-response-to-coronavirus-and-constitutional-disagreement/?fbclid=IwAR1XiPp-IRpNgbPh1ZXLHZVe0O_BSL0ZfhY0KKy6k3P2hHmTmnZuDW1Eql4> last accessed 15.07.2020.

7 For more about fear politics and the culture of fear, see B. Glassner, *The Culture of Fear: Why Americans Are Afraid of the Wrong Things: Crime, Drugs, Minorities, Teen Moms, Killer Kids, Mutant Microbes, Plane Crashes, Road Rage, & So Much More*, Basic Books, New York 2010.

of the COVID-19 global pandemic. The analysis will be focused on the role of fear politics in global constitutional 'Ernstfall'.[8] The chapter will explore the devastating effects of constitutional paternalism on liberalism and humanism as key normative ideologies of modern constitutionalism. The focus on the images of fear will allow the analysis to be performed from the viewpoint of symbolic-imaginary constitutionalism. The images of fear and the fear politics will be explored against the background of a broader theoretical concept of COVID-19 constitutionalism. The chapter will explore the impact of COVID-19 on constitutionalism, constitutional principles and human rights. It will especially outline how fear and fear politics in constitutional law are leading to a reformulation of normalcy, thus making stigmatisation and war rhetoric part of the new normal.

2. THE CONCEPT AND FEATURES OF COVID-19 CONSTITUTIONALISM

The COVID-19 pandemic has produced unprecedented reactions of governments to a health crisis, in a context where COVID-19 has been compared to medieval plague epidemics and to the post-World War I Spanish flu. But in none of the previous cases have we witnessed such sudden and exponential growth of 'big government'. The immediate emergence of the health Leviathan also produced unprecedented state intrusion in the private sphere and in civil society. Unfortunately, it has also opened the Pandora's box of various infringements of constitutional rights in both democratic and authoritarian orders.

In Europe, the achievements of the European Union (EU) integration, which seemed stable and almost sacred for decades, were deeply shuttered in just weeks and months. COVID-19 pandemic measures suspended the free movement of people and called into question the primacy of EU law. National protectionism – both overt and hidden – and disregard of well-established EU rules (e.g. related to non-discrimination, state aid and competition law) became almost the 'new normal' for months, with the perspective to remain for years. Key standards of human rights protection established in the European Charter of Human Rights, in EU law and in domestic constitutions were disregarded or at least limited

8 C. Schmitt, *Political Theology: Four Chapters on the Concept of Sovereignty*, University of Chicago Press, Chicago 2006, pp. 5–16.

in very disproportional ways. No proper balancing between the human rights and especially between the right to life and the rest of the human rights has been accomplished.[9] Proportionality and balance were at once forgotten.

In several countries, parliaments have been suspended, and the governments have started legislating by decree – in many cases, in unconstitutional manners.[10] In many countries, this has produced visible infringement of parliamentarism, democracy and separation of powers, also leading to rule-of-law violations. In most countries where it has been allowed, legislating by decree concentrated legislative activity in the government or the president.[11] In other states (e.g. in Bulgaria), a new, semi-institutionalised and rather unconstitutional legislative unit emerged. It was composed by the minister of health and an expert advisory and non-elected body – the National Operative Headquarter – which produced the bulk of the perplexing and controversial legislation[12] in the form of orders of the minister.

Such massive human rights' limitations – especially in Western societies and in the global North – have not been observed since the end of the Cold War. Thus, the COVID-19 crisis marks the end of the second

---

9 See J. Habermas and K. Günther, 'Kein Grundrecht gilt grenzenlos' <https://www.zeit.de/2020/20/grundrechte-lebensschutz-freiheit-juergen-habermas-klaus-guenther?fbclid=IwAR1sy4JcLGo5UNLYu4pDSxglvPCf4ce4Lbdg4lW5CC6amPCyGS2O27oADXM> last accessed 15.07.2020, G. Frankenberg, 'COVID-19 und der juristische Umgang mit Ungewissheit' <https://verfassungsblog.de/covid-19-und-der-juristische-umgang-mit-ungewissheit/?fbclid=IwAR124mNjX5XLFVp6v1pl4NAzl-PBa9O5eqR1UWkNHow5Blcrv-Dc6vBdzKQ> last accessed 15.07.2020 and the citation of the speech of the President of the German Bundestag, Wolfgang Scheuble published in SWR Aktuell 'Menschenleben versus Menschenwürde?' <https://www.swr.de/swraktuell/schaueble-wertediskussion-zu-corona-100.html?fbclid=IwAR1xfhaSvsTRSEhzrYQqZsbEDPdffmtoANvUhI8McuWyXASqiFQE_E5ge-o> last accessed 15.07.2020.
For a different approach see the statement of the Prime Minister Xavier Bettel of Luxembourg: 'the protection of health and life takes precedence over economic interests', cited in E. Stoppioni, 'The Protection of Health Must Take Precedence: Testing the Constitutional State of Crisis in Luxembourg' <https://verfassungsblog.de/the-protection-of-health-must-take-precedence-testing-the-constitutional-state-of-crisis-in-luxembourg/> last accessed 15.07.2020.

10 For example, the Romanian Constitutional Court abolished at the first possible moment the sanctions for the violation of quarantine measures imposed by the Romanian government, declaring them unconstitutional.

11 A clear example here is the general empowerment of the Hungarian government with Prime Minister Victor Orban to legislate by decrees until the end of pandemics.

12 For example, there have been orders of the Bulgarian health minister which prescribed in detail how to wash one's hands, or how to walk in parks.

'Belle Époque' which lasted for three decades after the fall of the Berlin wall. This was a period which was dominated by the flourishing of freedom and liberty as pillars of constitutional order. More precisely, two fundamental freedoms were the pillars of the second 'Belle Époque': the freedom of information and the freedom of movement.

In the context of the COVID-19 political regime, the freedom of movement has been suffocated by the reintroduction of a variety of travel bans impeding free movement even within state territories.[13] Check points within national territories have been mushrooming. Blockades and local lockdowns were widespread. Non-compliance with the new regime of 'territorial austerity' was paralleled by disproportional fines. This territorial austerity is based on this volcano of travel restrictions, which were suddenly imposed 'glocally' (i.e. being global and universal but imposed on multiple local places) after the unprecedented blossoming of free travel in recent decades.[14] Numerous implicit travel restrictions, such as quarantine periods, testing and suggested health passports, have additionally overburdened and impeded free travel. The free movement of people as one of the four fundamental liberties of the EU has been massively infringed upon. The free movement of people as a global phenomenon was instantly forgotten for months. The radical and immediate disavowing of free movement as a central value of our constitutional and political orders in less than two months comes as a surprise, especially against the background of the massive migratory flows experienced during the last decade.

The COVID-19 pandemic has also been paralleled by massive infodemia.[15] Indeed, the quantity of the circulation of information has

---

13 Another important characteristic of COVID constitutionalism is that it 'staged ratcheting up of border controls and executive powers to prevent and control the spread of COVID-19, and a 'hibernation' approach to the conduct of business and exercise of fundamental rights'. Indeed, this argument has been expressed for the case of Australia and the way the Australian government tried to manage the COVID-19 crisis, but it is valid worldwide. See T. Tulich, M. Rizzi and F. McGaughey, 'Cooperative Federalism, Soft Governance and Hard Laws in Australia's State of Emergency', <https://verfassungsblog.de/fighting-covid-19-legal-powers-and-risks-australia/> last accessed 15.07.2020.

14 Which have been rarely reconsidered. The annulment of sanctions for non-compliance with COVID-19 restriction measures – as e.g. in the Romanian Constitutional Court – have been rare so far.

15 See C.M. Pulido, B. Villarejo-Carballido, G. Redondo-Sama and A. Gómez, 'COVID-19 infodemic: More retweets for science-based information on coronavirus than for false information', (2020) 35 *International Sociology* 4, 377–92 <https://journals.sagepub.com/doi/full/10.1177/0268580920914755> last accessed 15.07.2020

dramatically increased due to the lockdown of people and their necessary recourse to Internet-based and distance communication. Distance learning and working from home flourished. Many online courses as well as webinars have been offered. COVID-19 has revived the political by fostering fierce debates on its origin, nature, impact and consequences on the state, society, economy, culture and human existence in all possible aspects. And this can be eventually regarded as a decisive push in the digital era even of social strata that resisted modernisation. Thus, the COVID-19 pandemic has been also used as a tool for forced modernisation via digitalisation.

However, fake news has also flourished, and massive manipulation in various forms stemming from all possible sources has been an eminent feature of the COVID-19 regime.[16] The infodemia has swirled most of the political players, but has hit predominantly democratic and open societies and – to a lesser extent – illiberal democracies. This is due to the fact that in authoritarian regimes, there has been already established censorship, so information has been initially biased and channelled by the government.

What is truly troublesome, however, has been the pandemic of fear triggered by COVID-19.[17] People in all parts of the world have been horrified by the existential threat to their lives. Such an existential threat has never been expected in the Western world, with the possible exception of the fear of nuclear war at the peaks of the Cold War (e.g. during the Cuban missile crisis). In parallel to the necessary warnings needed for due prevention of the disease, there has been a flood of fear-based messages, which have been systematically disseminated.

Unfortunately, the source of such messages of fear amounting to systematic fear politics have been the governments, the media and many other key political players. This period will be known for the widespread

---

and D. Orso, N. Federici, R. Copetti, L. Vetrugno and T. Bove, 'Infodemic and the spread of fake news in the COVID-19-era' (2020) *European journal of emergency medicine: official journal of the European Society for Emergency Medicine*, 10.1097/MEJ.0000000000000713. Advance online publication. <https://doi.org/10.1097/MEJ.0000000000000713> last accessed 15.07.2020.

16 See G. Agamben, 'The state of exception provoked by an unmotivated emergency' <http://positionswebsite.org/giorgio-agamben-the-state-of-exception-provoked-by-an-unmotivated-emergency/> last accessed 15.07.2020.

17 See K. Kelland, 'U.N. warns of global mental health crisis due to COVID-19 pandemic' <https://uk.reuters.com/article/us-health-coronavirus-mentalhealth/u-n-warns-of-global-mental-health-crisis-due-to-covid-19-pandemic-idUKKBN22Q0AO?fbclid=IwAR0OgvkLxWMzEqsN-cm0KM-N33zxfckE5gZe2RddR0oScKDQHe5kX1P-ri4> last accessed 15.07.2020.

panic attacks, some of which took curious and comic shapes, such as the 'toilet paper war' and 'pasta war' in supermarkets. It is interesting to note that fear politics has been based on a particular and rather perplexing and complex mixture of fear of disease and fear of liberty, and fear of a lack of authority combined with fear of hyper-authority.

It seems that individualism, consumerism and biologism (focusing on the biological instead of the social aspect of the human being) are prerequisites for the easy and fast establishment of COVID-19 constitutionalism.[18] As properly suggested by Lambaerts, the values exposed by the COVID-19 pandemic 'idolize the individual and vitalize in particular the biological aspect of life. This cultural emphasis on the biological becomes visible in our day-to-day activities'.[19]

Apart from the individual stress and the devastating effects on mental health, the rising domestic violence and increased depression, there have been other important negative side effects of the COVID-19 pandemic, with larger socio-political impacts. Violence against foreigners and migrants, as well as isolation of vulnerable groups and of potential bearers of the virus, have been on the rise. The most dangerous effect of the fear pandemic has been that it has legitimated authoritarian leaders to establish or to solidify their regimes using fear politics. The 'invisible enemy' – the virus – or the visible enemies, such as foreign countries, hidden or overt elites and even the World Health Organization (WHO) have been the perfect excuse for deepening authoritarian tendencies. Unfortunately, such a stable and increasing trend towards authoritarian features and limitations and violations of democracy, rule of law and human rights has been also visible in countries which were supposed to be democracies.

Indeed, states of emergency have always been available to governments to cope with crisis situations. And governments have frequently been tempted to use and misuse emergencies and to rely on human fear in order to achieve their goals and maximise their power. Moreover, fear politics has always been a key strategy going along with emergencies and power misuse.[20] Lord Acton famously says that 'power tends to corrupt, and absolute power corrupts absolutely. Great men are almost always bad men …'.[21] Government by decree was typical in the interwar period.

---

18 See J. Lambaerts, 'The Plague was Already Present (Critique in Times of Coronavirus)', <https://criticallegalthinking.com/2020/04/29/the-plague-was-already-present-critique-in-times-of-coronavirus/> last accessed 15.07.2020.

19 See Lambaerts, above n. 18.

20 See Glassner, above n. 7.

21 See <https://www.acton.org/research/lord-acton-quote-archive> last accessed 22.09.2020.

It was used not only by authoritarian and totalitarian governments of the time (e.g. in Germany,[22] Italy, Spain, the Balkan states, the USSR, etc.), but was also the new normal in democracies such as France.[23] The 'war on terror' declared by the United States President George W. Bush also marked an intense period of extraordinary measures taken for the sake of public security and to the detriment of human rights. France has been governed for several years in the context of a state of emergency – again due to combatting terrorism.[24]

However, the COVID-19 crisis has been a period of unprecedented infringement of constitutional rights, both in democracies and authoritarian orders comparable only with the two world wars. There are several specific features of the COVID-19 pandemic which differentiate it from the previous periods of emergency government and crisis constitutionalism.

First, the political regime which was established due to the COVID-19 pandemic consists of (hopefully temporal) infringement of key human rights and rule-of-law standards was truly global and universal, although it was performed predominantly on the national level. The political regime which was established due to the COVID-19 pandemic has spread in all continents and in all countries of the world, with few exceptions. The emergency regimes have been mushrooming in almost all constitutional orders, disrespecting the distinctions between democracy, illiberal democracy, non-established democracy, authoritarian regimes and dictatorships. Almost all constitutional regimes have offered more or less similar answers to the pandemic, irrespective of whether their constitutions contained provisions for the emergency; whether it has been introduced by an act or decision of the parliament; or whether constitutional rights have been limited without any form of emergency.

---

22 According to K.L. Scheppele, 'The emergencies that keep constitutionalists awake at night are the ones in which political leaders control both cause and effect. The Reichstag Fire. The self-generated terrorist attack. The sudden discovery of a trumped-up conspiracy to kill the leader that results in the convenient roundup of the political opposition. The state unleashes its fury on those who attacked it, but it turns out that those who plotted the attack are none other than those who benefit from the fury. These emergencies kill constitutions'. See K.L. Scheppele, 'Underreaction in a Time of Emergency: America as a Nearly Failed State', <https://verfassungsblog.de/underreaction-in-a-time-of-emergency-america-as-a-nearly-failed-state/> last accessed 15.07.2020.

23 See G. Agamben, *Homo Sacer II*, Kritika i humanisam, Sofia 2019, (in Bulgarian), p. 13 and the following.

24 See Platon, above n. 4.

Second, the human rights limitations have been very intense. They concerned not only the specific and limited sphere of human empowerment (e.g. political rights or free movement), but were massive and extremely intrusive. Their cumulative effect was tremendous in most of the countries, simultaneously limiting personal rights, political rights and social, economic and cultural rights. The harshest infringements have been on the freedom of personal life, the freedom of movement and the free choice of residence. However, freedom of assembly and freedom of expression as key political rights have been severely limited, although, to some extent paradoxically, there has been also massive civil disobedience, unrest and even revolts (e.g. in the US, Serbia and Bulgaria), triggered by different reasons frequently not directly related to COVID-19. The right to education and the right to work were significantly infringed upon, as well. And this constitutes merely a short list of constitutional rights which have been disproportionately, sometimes unconstitutionally, limited. The health Leviathan has prioritised life and health as seemingly supreme values and rights deserving absolute protection at the expense of all other constitutional rights – and even at the sacrifice of the free and democratic constitutional order. The overemphasis on COVID-19 has to an extent paradoxically also endangered the right to health of sick people, who were suffering from other illnesses and who had to postpone their health treatment due to the pandemic.[25]

Third, the COVID-19 pandemic has produced an unprecedented rise in paternalism.[26] Indeed, people have been forced to behave against their will many times in history. The clearest example is wars. Different variants of totalitarianism and authoritarianism are important examples as well. Nevertheless, the state has rarely – if ever – behaved as 'body and soul saving Leviathan' in the context of well-established democracies. Indeed, there have been natural disasters and epidemics in history when the state

---

25 According to the German magazine Spiegel citing DPA, 50,000 necessary surgeries of people sick from cancer have been postponed in Germany in the period from the beginning of the pandemic until mid-July 2020. One can suppose that in most cases, this meant lethal results for the patients from cancer, not from coronavirus. See <https://www.spiegel.de/wirtschaft/service/wegen-coronavirus-rund-50-000-krebs-operationen-in-deutschland-verschoben-a-d327e5ea-6552-4f9b-9adb-0b95b9001f36> last accessed 15.07.2020.

26 For the interrelation of paternalism and biosecurity, see the Australian Biosecurity (Human Biosecurity Emergency) (Human Coronavirus with Pandemic Potential) (Emergency Requirements for Remote Communities) Determination 2020 made under the Biosecurity Act 2015 (Cth), s 477(1). See Tulich, Rizzi and McGaughey above n. 13.

has had to intervene and offer authoritative guidance, frequently paralleled by compulsion and sanctions. The state has implemented protective health policy related to bans on dangerous substances, such as tobacco products and alcohol. There are mandatory vaccinations for dangerous contagious diseases in many countries. However, such intrusive and compulsory preventive biopolitics[27] on the global scale is unprecedented in human history. The COVID-19 pandemic enabled the state to intrude in the deepest corners of our privacy, breaching established red lines in conventional bioethics.

A flagrant example of one such previously unthinkable and heavily disproportional paternalistic attitude is the order of the Bulgarian minister of health adopted on 14 May 2020, just one day after the expiration of the state of emergency and in the context of rather low comparative levels of COVID-19 contamination in the Bulgarian population. It allowed compulsory medical treatment and compulsory medical detention. The state health authorities have been authorised to detain people older than 60 years of age, even with only very mild COVID-19 symptoms, as well as people with multiple health problems, and to take them to hospitals without their consent or the consent of their relatives for compulsory medical treatment. In fact, this is a form of officially permitted kidnapping which is definitively unconstitutional and in contravention of the international and EU human rights standards of personal autonomy. Compulsory tracking and controlling devices in the form of mobile phone applications, eye and face recognition systems and even robots have been used in some countries in Asia, and their introduction has been discussed in established democracies such as the United Kingdom, France and Australia.[28] The tracing of COVID-19-infected people by sniffer dogs has been cautiously advertised as a scientific and security policy achievement.[29]

---

27 For the concept of biopolitics, see M. Foucault, *The Birth of Biopolitics: Lectures at the Collège de France, 1978–1979: Lectures at the College De France, 1978–1979*, Palgrave Macmillan, London 2008, pp. 1–368.

28 See P. Howell O'Neill, T. Ryan-Mosley and B. Johnson, 'A flood of coronavirus apps are tracking us. Now it's time to keep track of them', MIT Technology Review, <https://www.technologyreview.com/2020/05/07/1000961/launching-mittr-covid-tracing-tracker/> last accessed 15.07.2020.

29 See M. Weisberger, 'Dogs are being trained to sniff out COVID-19 in humans' <https://www.livescience.com/dogs-smell-covid-19.html> last accessed 15.07.2020 and 'Dogs Could Assist in Mass COVID-19 Infection Screening by Sniffing Out Coronavirus', <https://www.hospimedica.com/covid-19/articles/294781948/dogs-could-assist-in-mass-covid-19-infection-screening-by-sniffing-out-coronavirus.html> last accessed 15.07.2020.

The 'pandemic health Leviathan' has sacrificed many human rights for the sake of health protection, in line with the official and globally coordinated politics of the states. Most of the suspended or limited human rights have been essential. The state behaved as an omnipotent health sovereign, possessing a monopoly on choice and knowledge which was cynically supposed to be inaccessible to the 'ordinary citizen'. Indeed, such powerful invasion of the state and the public power in the realm of privacy and human rights is a very demanding move, especially against the background of the pitiful reality in which US President Trump has officially advised people to use bleach as an antidote against the coronavirus, and Bulgarian Prime Minister Borisov has appointed an accountant as minister of health and a stomach surgeon as the chief of the National Operative Headquarter for combatting COVID-19.

This health Leviathan has been paralleled by a criminal Leviathan.[30] States used the emergency as an excuse to impose different types of administrative and even criminal sanctions. In Romania, these sanctions have been declared unconstitutional by the constitutional courts. According to Alexandra Mercescu:

> … paradoxically, in wanting to be a Hobbesian sovereign that protects citizens from each other (the Other being here the bearer of the virus), the Romanian state ended up instituting a war of all against all (patients vs. doctors, doctors vs. the state, doctors vs. doctors, first-order Romanian citizens vs. second-order Romanian citizens). Fighting nature, it brought back 'the state of nature.[31]

Thus, Mercescu is claiming that a new 'criminal Leviathan' has emerged in Romania.

Unfortunately, this phenomenon has not been limited to Romania, but is instead widespread. The president of the Bulgarian Pharmaceutical Association, Asena Stoimenova, was even detained in April 2020 for publicly saying that the pharmacies in Bulgaria may eventually run out of some preventive materials. However, this provision of the Bulgarian Criminal Code has not been consistently applied to Prime Minister

---

30 See A. Mercescu, 'The COVID-19 Crisis in Romania, or on How One Cannot Escape (Bad, Legal) Culture', <http://exceptions.eu/2020/05/11/the-covid-19-crisis-in-romania-or-on-how-one-cannot-escape-bad-legal-culture/?fbclid=IwAR3hTyciWC-Kiei2r9KFjHVN0KjGzx6aepFuZ9VYlnDz89Jr94dWUydAh_Y> last accessed 15.07.2020.

31 See Mercescu, above n. 30.

Borisov, who publicly declared that Bulgarians could expect mountains of dead bodies in just a few weeks and that the children's playgrounds would soon be transformed into morgues.[32] This is an excellent example of the politics of fear which has been widely used in order to frighten the population and make it more easy to accept the significant and detrimental infringements of their constitutional rights.

Nevertheless, the COVID-19 political regime has key similarities with previous crisis management political regimes, such as war-time regimes and the political regime related to the 'war on terror'. This is the structuring of the political reality into 'friend and enemy' – a bipolar, black-and-white logic clearly defined by Carl Schmitt.[33] War, civil war, the 'war on terror', the global pandemic as a war against a virus – all of these require an enemy by necessity. This can be an external enemy, an internal enemy or even an 'invisible enemy',[34] but still an enemy against which we must align. Such alignment presupposes fear. And fear can be created by fear politics. In addition, the emergency exposes society to existential choices. Hence, in times of permanent emergencies created by financial and migration crises, by the 'war on terror' and recently by the 'war on viruses and the global pandemic', the Schmittian 'Ernstfall' is transformed from exception into normalcy.[35]

Moreover, all crisis management regimes contribute to the conceptualisation of the state as a necessary Leviathan saving us not only

---

32 The Bulgarian Prime Minister Borisov said: 'When you start registering 100, 200, 300 dead Bulgarians then you will ask me this question … If the situation gets like in the other states – to use refrigerator trucks not for meat but for corpses or the children playgrounds where the children play to be morgues – then you will ask such questions'. See <https://www.plovdiv24.bg/novini/Bylgaria/Borisov-s-mrachni-misli-Zagovori-za-hladilni-kamioni-za-trupove-i-detski-ploshtadki-prevurnati-v-morgi-957258 and https://fakti.bg/mnenia/473537-blagotvoritelna-diktatura-na-straha-sreshtu-covid-19> last accessed 15.07.2020.

33 See C. Schmitt, *Der Begriff des Politischen*, Duncker & Humblot, Berlin 2015, pp. 1–119. See also R. Mehring, 'Carl Schmitt und die Pandemie. Teil I', <https://verfassungsblog.de/carl-schmitt-und-die-pandemie-teil-i/?fbclid=IwAR0oLewmdX13rFYCdOSDS7T1wSy7Usc6yF_unAW7m5WxMlDDyrbSwu8_32g> last accessed 15.07.2020.

34 The definition of the COVID-19 as an 'invisible enemy' has been provided by US President Donald Trump in his speeches. See J. Schafer, 'Behind Trump's Strange "Invisible Enemy" Rhetoric', <https://www.politico.com/news/magazine/2020/04/09/trump-coronavirus-invisible-enemy-177894> last accessed 15.07.2020.

35 According to Jürgensen and Orlowski, 'even if the Corona pandemic will not reveal the Schmittian sovereign, it sheds a light on the very different perceptions of the state, its boundaries and the role of a critical public sphere in times of crisis'. See Jürgensen and Orlowski, above n. 3.

from our enemies, but also from our own dangerous personal freedoms, which we may unreasonably and childishly use against ourselves. Thus, we must be pushed towards the conclusion of Hobbesian *pactum subjectionis* even if we have not entered into *pactum unionis*.[36] Hence, it seems that Schmitt and Hobbes were revived as 'the names of the day'.[37] In parallel, the Schmittian 'Ernstfall' and the Hobbesian 'Leviathan' became the terms which deeply mark the 2020 political situation – in stark contrast to proportionality, which has been deeply neglected in the 2020 emergency situation.[38]

Thus, the question arises as to what kind of phenomenon we had to endure in 2020. What is the most appropriate definition of the emergency regime that so brutally entered into our well established constitutional orders, some of which are traditionally rooted in liberalism, humanism and exposed to globalisation and open statehood? Can we define the phenomenon as crisis constitutionalism or crisis management constitutionalism? Or it is simply a process of de-constitutionalisation fostering 'global civil war', 'global emergency',[39] illiberal constitutionalism, neo-nationalism and emergency constitutional authoritarianism?[40] Are we experiencing the end of globalisation, open society and liberal democracy?

What is obvious is that independently of how we define the regime or whether we approve of or criticise it (e.g. on grounds of [dis-]proportionality), this regime has visible features of paternalism. And its paternalism is based on the politics of fear. Thus, we are experiencing a new trend in populism – 'health populism' – which strongly overemphasises threats to human life and health and produces multiple images of fear, which will be explored in this chapter.

A possible hypothesis is that the COVID-19 pandemic has advanced a form of crisis management constitutionalism. Crisis management

---

36 See T. Hobbes, *Leviathan*, CreateSpace Independent Publishing Platform, 2011, pp. 1–118.

37 See Mehring, above n. 33.

38 Paradoxically, in wanting to be a Hobbesian sovereign that protects citizens from each other (the other being here the bearer of the virus), the Romanian state ended up instituting a war of all against all (patients vs. doctors, doctors vs. the state, doctors vs. doctors, first-order Romanian citizens vs. second-order Romanian citizens). Fighting nature, it brought back 'the state of nature'; see Mercescu, above n. 30.

39 See Civitarese Matteuci, above n. 6.

40 See also 'crisis management constitution' Kovács, above n. 5.

constitutionalism usually functions on the basis of states of siege or states of emergency provisions which have constitutional and legislative bases. Sometimes, however, the constitutional foundations of crisis management constitutionalism are fragile or even non-existent. The difficulty of constructing constitutional foundations and of giving a legal framework or at least a resemblance of legality to emergencies has been well described in the intellectual debate, between authors attempting to legalise the state of emergency, such as Carl Schmitt, and authors who believe that the state of emergency is purely an extra-legal and entirely political phenomenon (such as Walter Benjamin and to a certain extent Giorgio Agamben). Hence, the COVID-19 political regime and its legal parameters can be defined as an emergency regime rooted in the legal order and obeying certain constitutional principles. Alternatively, it can be conceived of as a political regime based on health paternalism, justified by global pandemics and based on politics of fear. According to this second reasoning, the COVID-19 political regime, despite having legal repercussions and legal shapes, is in its nature an extra-legal state of exception which thus essentially belongs to the sphere of the political.

Indeed, COVID-19 crisis management constitutionalism is not the first and will probably not be the last crisis management constitutionalism. Other clear examples are the global 'war on terror' constitutionalism (which emerged after the 9/11 terror attacks in 2001); the financial crisis austerity constitutionalism (which emerged after the financial crisis in 2009); and the migration crisis constitutionalism (which emerged after the migration waves experienced in Europe since the Arab spring in 2011 and the subsequent civil wars in North Africa and the Middle East). Now, we have a new emergency and crisis management constitutionalism: COVID-19 constitutionalism.[41]

COVID-19 crisis management constitutionalism is the result of the political and the constitutional approaches to the COVID-19 pandemic. It is the reflection of a mixture of medical – as well as psychological, political, geopolitical and economic – concerns in constitutional politics. COVID-19 crisis management constitutionalism does not have an immediate reflection in the written constitution since, it has not yet triggered explicit constitutional amendments or durable shifts in the official, explicit and valid constitutional design. However, it has massively reshaped the balance between constitutional principles and within the system of human

[41] For more about the risks of such emergency or crisis management constitutionalism, see Frankenberg, above n. 9.

rights. It has destroyed the long-established but obviously fragile balance between state power and private autonomy and human rights.

Hence, the question arises as to whether we can define as constitutionalism a phenomenon such as the COVID-19 crisis management regime, which in fact led to massive and disproportionate human rights limitations and collided with key principles of constitutionalism. Perhaps such a phenomenon can be defined as an anti-constitutional regime instead of labelling it as crisis management constitutionalism. Due to space constraints, I will refrain from entering into this discussion since it also concerns the question of whether we can have authoritarian constitutionalism, illiberal constitutionalism and paternalistic constitutionalism, as well.[42]

However, it is clear that the COVID-19 regime, even if defined as crisis management constitutionalism, is deeply rooted in a paternalistic state. It is based on the politics of fear. It fosters the emergence of surveillance capitalism[43] and new health and pandemic paternalism.

Hence, defining the COVID-19 regime requires us to frame it within the realm of the overall legal regimes governing intrinsically political issues of general importance and including the relationship among the state, the society and the individual. Therefore, all forms of crisis management constitutionalism, including the COVID-19 regime, may be allocated in a scheme of constitutionalism in a wider sense. This formal constitutionalism more broadly includes not only the different manifestations of crisis management constitutionalism, but also authoritarian constitutional regimes (historic or present, monarchical or republican), and forms of constitutional dictatorship, authoritarian constitutionalism and illiberal democracies.

The main reason to work with such forms of quasi-constitutionalism, which are in fact a negation of the understanding of constitutionalism as a regime for the maximisation of liberty and the minimisation of oppression, is that they may have constitutional foundations in certain states and societies. But most importantly, such 'anti-constitutional constitutional regimes' are the perfect and true background against which we can appreciate the value of the liberal-democratic constitutionalism.

There are several features of COVID-19 crisis constitutionalism, which are deeply interrelated in multiple ways. Some of these interrelations have been produced by the pandemic crisis, but most of them seem to have

42 See Lachmayer, above n. 4.

43 See S. Zuboff, *The Age of Surveillance Capitalism. The Fight for a Human Future at the New Frontier of Power*, Public Affairs, New York 2019.

been co-existing and working 'under the surface' of the official liberal-democratic constitutionalism. Thus, COVID-19 constitutionalism may be a manifestation of a specific variant of the 'dual state',[44] where the official constitutional institutions are misused for unconstitutional purposes.

3. THE IMPACT OF COVID-19 ON CONSTITUTIONALISM, CONSTITUTIONAL PRINCIPLES AND HUMAN RIGHTS

The impact of COVID-19 on constitutional law and constitutionalism has been widely discussed in the field of constitutional theory. A significant number of publications emerged within weeks or even days after the declaration of the pandemic and the response of the governments to it. The scholarly interest has been devoted to multitude of problems created by the COVID-19 regime. Due to space constraints, I will not engage in detailed analysis. I will merely provide a brief summary and outline of the problem, which will allow me to expose the constitutional framework of the phenomenon of fear politics and subsequently to provide an analysis of the constitutionally relevant images of fear created in the context of the COVID-19 crisis.

There are several main issues discussed in the literature. The first group of issues are conceptual in nature. They are part of the discussion of the kind of legal and constitutional response that is needed in the case of pandemics. Some of the main questions belonging to this group can be summarised as follows: is there a constitutional regime that copes with crises such as the COVID-19 pandemic? What should the proper constitutional response to COVID-19 be? Is there a concept of 'emergency governance architecture'[45] enshrined in the constitutional orders or invented during COVID pandemic, and if so, what are its legal parameters? Is there 'health' or 'sanitary' emergency which is different from the ordinary emergency, since quasi-emergency sanitary and health regimes have been to a significant extent unconstitutionally established via ordinary legislation in Bulgaria, Romania and elsewhere? This also advances the need for reflection on whether an emergency must be declared, or whether COVID-19

---

44 See E. Fraenkel, *The Dual State*, Oxford University Press, Oxford 1941.

45 For the concept of 'emergency governance architecture', see Tulich, Rizzi and McGaughey, above n. 13.

could also be combatted without implementing states of emergency.[46] Can the COVID-19 pandemic be resolved through recourse to soft-law means, such as warnings and explanations of the peril to citizens, as well as 'nudging'[47] and 'soft governance', or emergency and 'hard laws' where required, necessary and proportional?[48]

It should be especially emphasised that the COVID-19 regime has endangered constitutional supremacy, the primacy of EU law and the primacy of parliamentary legislation over governmental policy-making, based on booming expansion of legislation by decrees. There has been a disproportionate and pandemic-induced rise of 'executive-made emergency regulations' and governance by decrees as in Hungary, Bulgaria, Romania, Austria, France, Hong Kong[49] and many other areas. This means that governing by decrees came into practice in both illiberal regimes and in traditional liberal democracies.

The second group of issues concerns the impact of the COVID-19 crisis on democracy, parliamentarism and the separation of powers. The questions that frame these issues can be formulated as follows: how does COVID-19 impact on governmental powers? Should it lead to a limitation of parliamentary powers, and if so, why, under which circumstances and to what extent should it do so? How does the COVID-19 crisis influence the vertical separation of powers in federations?[50]

Furthermore, an answer should be given to the more concrete questions which are making explicit the perils of the COVID-19 regime to democracy, parliamentarism and the separation of powers. Such questions include: what should be the involvement of parliaments in resolving pandemics and medical crises? Should parliaments always approve emergency measures? Should parliaments be in session during the pandemic?

---

46 For the three options – 'ordinary powers theory', 'extraordinary powers theory' and the political option, see J. Gaviria-Mira and E. Hoyos-Ceballos, 'Pandemic and Executive Powers in Colombia: A Problem and a Modest Proposal', <https://verfassungsblog.de/pandemic-and-executive-powers-in-colombia-a-problem-and-a-modest-proposal/> last accessed 15.07.2020.

47 G. Yeung, 'Fear of Unaccountability vs Fear of a Pandemic: COVID-19 in Hong Kong', <https://verfassungsblog.de/fear-of-unaccountability-vs-fear-of-a-pandemic-covid-19-in-hong-kong/> last accessed 15.07.2020.

48 See Tulich, Rizzi and McGaughey, above n. 13.

49 See Yeung, above n. 47.

50 See Tulich, Rizzi and McGaughey, above n. 13 and E. Peluso, N. Meyer and T. Bustamante, 'Authoritarianism Without Emergency Powers: Brazil Under COVID-19', <https://verfassungsblog.de/authoritarianism-without-emergency-powers-brazil-under-covid-19/> last accessed 15.07.2020.

Do we need intense parliamentary control in times of COVID emergency?[51] Some authors have remarked that we may be experiencing a 'lockdown of democracy'.[52]

The third group of issues concerns the preservation of rule of law in times of pandemic constitutionalism, witnessing the emergence of a health Leviathan manifested especially through the activities of the government. Here, one should ask the following questions: what should be the involvement of courts – especially of the constitutional courts and the administrative courts? How can we safeguard the observation of the principle of proportionality in limiting human rights, as well as the proper balancing of human rights – a concern raised even by President of the German Bundestag, Wolfgang Scheuble?[53] The issues of massive human rights infringements have proven to be particularly problematic with regard to the rule of law (they have already been discussed above).

There is also a fourth group of issues concerning institutional novelties. There has been a remarkable rise in the role of experts and technocratic bodies. Constitutional courts started using medical experts to resolve constitutional cases related to the control of the constitutionality of pandemic measures.[54] Emergency health councils were created as advisory bodies to the governments. However, they gradually have gained a *de facto* central role in coping with pandemics. Thus, they have actually impacted the separation of powers, shifting the decisive role in coping with pandemics from the political representatives of the nation to the experts. Nevertheless, such a power expansion of experts has been used as an excuse by governments to impose restrictions on human rights and to play with technocratically justified politics of fear. The range of institutional novelties has gone beyond technocratic advisory councils of experts. For example, in Australia, a new temporary decisive body – the National Cabinet[55] – has been established.

Hence, the COVID-19 crisis has promoted new heroes and new saints. These consist of the experts in general, and the doctors and medical

---

51 In the words of Sébastien Platon, 'As the name of the regime suggests, the state of health emergency mimics the "normal" state of emergency, especially from the procedural point of view … However, and for no clear or convincing reason, this involvement of the Parliament is, in certain respects, more limited than under the "normal" state of emergency.' See PLATON, above n. 4.

52 See KOVÁCS, above n. 5.

53 See the citation of the speech of SCHEUBLE, above n. 9.

54 See the Ruling of the Bulgarian Constitutional Court from 22.05.2020.

55 See TULICH, RIZZI and MCGAUGHEY, above n. 13.

personnel in particular. It seems also that the ratings of governmental officials, prime ministers and presidents have risen together with the predominantly positive attitude towards expert advisory bodies. This does not seem to be a durable tendency. It may well be reversed after the inevitable economic and political crisis that will follow the pandemic. But at least for a while, COVID-19 has stabilised the status of many autocratic leaders and has pushed experts to the forefront, to the detriment of national parliaments.

Lastly, a fifth group of problems is related to violations of EU law. Economic and health nationalism has been blossoming. Non-protectionism and free competition have been (hopefully temporarily) forgotten (these problems have already been analysed above).

4. FEAR AND FEAR POLITICS IN CONSTITUTIONAL LAW AND THE REFORMULATION OF NORMALCY

Crisis constitutionalism is supposed to serve only as a constitutional framework for governing societies during periods of crisis. States of emergency are supposed to be an exception, especially in democratic societies. However, politicians with ambitions of power are both tempted and thrilled at the prospect of using the crisis as a proxy for attempts to maximise their own power. Even in times of constitutional normality, politicians use the 'friend-enemy' logic, defined by C. Schmitt as the key code of the political,[56] as an excuse for unpopular measures.

The crisis situations, however, offer the perfect justification for power concentration. A good example is the official concentration of power in the hands of Hungarian Prime Minister Victor Orban, who was empowered to govern by decree for months.[57] Another comparable example is that of US President Donald Trump, who officially stated in a speech that he has the absolute power in the country and that this is normal and in accordance with the US Constitution. Unfortunately, elements of emergency constitutionalism have also been activated in many established

56 See C. Schmitt, *Der Begriff des Politischen*, Duncker & Humblot, Berlin 2015, p. 25.

57 See Z. Simon, 'Orban's Hungary Is No Longer a Democracy, Freedom House Says', <https://www.bloomberg.com/news/articles/2020-05-06/orban-s-hungary-is-no-longer-a-democracy-freedom-house-says> last accessed 15.07.2020.

democracies, and the temptation to use extraordinary measures during periods of normality has been visible even in traditionally democratic contexts.[58]

So it seems that the simulation of a crisis, the introduction of elements of crisis management constitutionalism and the misuse of crisis management so as to augment the power of elites and office-holders is a broader phenomenon in constitutional law, with an enduring history and long and traceable patterns. Crisis simulation and crisis staging can be defined as the covering up of an existing crisis with another crisis. This is actually crisis management based on the production and reproduction of another crisis, frequently paralleled by the populist masquerading of the previously existing crisis. The concealment, replacement and mimicry of crisis is, unfortunately, a vital strategy for political mobilisation, for instrumental misuse of the people and for a shift of the political responsibility for misfortunate governmental decisions and policies.[59]

In this regard, the COVID-19 pandemic has been the perfect excuse for the dramatic problems in healthcare systems; for the inevitable arrival of a drastic economic crisis of almost unprecedented level and design; for the suffocation of the problems triggered by economic asymmetries; for the destruction of the civic society; and for geopolitical misbalances and problems caused by the inability to resolve migration and financial crises.[60] Thus, it seems that the political exhaustion of the model and the enormous economic problems resulting from the crisis of neoliberal capitalism have been replaced in the focus of the public opinion with a pandemic.[61] The latent migration crisis, exemplified quite well by the dramatic situation on the Turkish–Greek border at the beginning of 2020, which had been resembling an undeclared war, has also been covered up with health problems, lockdowns and pandemic issues.[62]

---

58 See Lachmayer, above n. 4.

59 See Lambaerts, above n. 18.

60 See J. Fernandez, T. Fleury Graff and A. Marie, 'La crise sanitaire, prétexte à une fragilisation du droit d'asile' <https://www.leclubdesjuristes.com/blog-du-coronavirus/que-dit-le-droit/la-crise-sanitaire-pretexte-a-une-fragilisation-du-droit-dasile/?fbclid=IwAR34KHus0ggvFmkke9gowXIVneWbIP4X5uuKtbwG_IVbOMuYPXxz-VD6BNw> last accessed 15.07.2020.

61 See S. Ganty, 'Belgium and COVID-19: When a Health Crisis Replaces a Political Crisis', <https://verfassungsblog.de/belgium-and-covid-19-when-a-health-crisis-replaces-a-political-crisis/> last accessed 15.07.2020 and Yeung, above n. 47.

62 See S. Laulhé Shaelou and A. Manoli, 'A Tale of Two: The COVID-19 Pandemic and the Rule of Law in Cyprus', <https://verfassungsblog.de/a-tale-of-two-the-covid-19-pandemic-and-the-rule-of-law-in-cyprus/> last accessed 15.07.2020.

One of the prominent dangers is that states of emergency will remain the new normal.[63] Thus, it is vitally important to see how the constitutional orders will start domesticating emergency, most likely by making emergency 'the new normal' and somehow incorporating it into the constitutional design and political order, in the months and years after the COVID-19 crisis.[64] The fear of emergency situations governed by politics of fear and visible trends towards authoritarianism and paternalism functioning as the new normal have already existed even before COVID-19.

During the period of the COVID-19 pandemic, we have witnessed key politicians using what Kriszta Kovács defines as 'indefensible war rhetoric'.[65] Indeed, she has used this term to describe the political speeches of Victor Orban, but the term is applicable also to the speeches of Donald Trump, Emmanuel Macron, Boris Johnson and many other politicians. They all have spoken of war. President Macron has used the word 'war' multiple times in his 'opening speech' to the COVID-19 emergency regime in France. President Trump has even declared himself to be 'a war time president'. The political leaders use 'war' as a key term in structuring the political communication regarding the COVID-19 pandemic. According to Kriszta Kovács: 'the government felt inclined to "wage war" against the financial crisis, against the "illegal migrants", against the "terrorists" and most recently, against the "invisible and unknown enemy" called the novel coronavirus'.[66]

Similar rhetorical strategies have been used also elsewhere. For example, in Cyprus, according to Stéphanie Laulhé Shaelou and Andrea Manoli: 'the President addressing the public in early March referred to the current situation as "war"'.[67] The Bulgarian Prime Minister Boyko Borisov in a public speech transmitted on television and over the Internet warned that if no harsh measures were taken, the playgrounds would be loaded with sacks full with human corpses. In another interview weeks later, he wrongly pointed out that only on this very day, more than 30,000 people have died in Europe of COVID-19 and the number of victims is incomparably larger

---

63 More about the 'growing tendency to use the state of exception as a normal governing paradigm' see G. Agamben, 'The state of exception provoked by an unmotivated emergency', <http://positionswebsite.org/giorgio-agamben-the-state-of-exception-provoked-by-an-unmotivated-emergency/> last accessed 15.07.2020.

64 See Jürgensen and Orlowski, above n. 3 and Lachmayer, above n. 4.

65 See Kovács, above n. 5.

66 See Kovács, above n. 5.

67 See Laulhé Shaelou and Manoli, above n. 62.

than in the case of war. Of course, this statement has been a clear case of drastic misinformation. In addition, General Mutafchiysky, who was the chief of the Bulgarian National Operative Headquarters (the advisory body to the government managing the crisis), defined the Bulgarian people who are dissenting with the emergency measures and the limitations and infringements of their constitutional rights as 'armchair warriors' and an 'armchair army'. In Australia, the national cabinet has been 'described in the media as a "war cabinet," it also departs from the war cabinet formed during World War II which comprised government and opposition members of the Federal Parliament'.[68]

The evil, collective suffering and pain usually lead to long-lasting imprints in the collective memories of the socio-political communities. Wars, dictatorships, massacres, terrorist acts and other disasters are deeply entrenched in the collective memory. They have a durable impact on constitutional design, as well. The reflectivity and reactivity of constitutions are structured around creative reflection and reformulation of institutions; human rights; and constitutional aims, values and principles on the basis of negative social and political experiences. Constitutional taboos are deeply rooted in reflexive and reactive constitutions.

However, so far, our constitutional orders have not experienced constitutional reflection of epidemics and pandemics. Illness and disease have not been part of the arsenal of constitutional memories or of the imaginary of fear. None of the big epidemics and pandemics from the past have had a long-lasting impact on constitutions or constitutionalism. The Spanish flu, as well as the SARS and MERS epidemics, have not been conceived of as phenomena with real constitutional importance. There has been very weak remembrance of previous epidemics in Hong Kong and Canada.[69] Thus, it seems that COVID-19 is the first pandemic which has had such a profound impact on constitutionalism and constitutional law. Hence, it has provoked a scholarly interest in the study of the role of social memories of pandemics and of social codes during pandemics.

Fear seems to work as code of emergency constitutionalism in both democracies and in authoritarian states. In authoritarian and totalitarian regimes, fear is structural pillar of the state based on fear politics. Here,

68 See Tulich, Rizzi and McGaughey, above n. 13.

69 See Yeung, above n. 47, D. Dyzenhaus, 'Canada the Good?', <https://verfassungsblog.de/canada-the-good/> last accessed 15.07.2020.

fear politics is based mostly on fear from the external and internal enemy and fear from the state. In democracies, there is another type of fear which is of pivotal importance for fear politics in formally liberal-democratic regimes: the fear of death, which is equal to fear of individual and personal extinction. This very personal and intimate type of fear is engaged in more complex systematic types of fear politics related to terrorism, mass violence, migration waves, revolution and – recently – illnesses, epidemics and pandemics.

This type of fear and fear politics is well explained by the critical writings of Giorgio Agamben.[70] According to Lambaerts:

> Without its cultural and social dimension, only the biological life remains to be defended. We might be willing to give up our cultural or social life, but we are not ready to die. This fear of death is the second reason Agamben sees for our easy surrender to a totalitarian regime (or at least politics that display totalitarian traits). Only on fear, Agamben states, can tyranny be founded. Our best defence against the threat of a totalitarian regime is to make sure that we feel like we have more to lose than just our biological lives.[71]

Agamben's critique on coronavirus politics is well known. He is very critical of confinement, social distancing and the destruction of the socio-political community.[72] According to Agamben and his interpreter, Lambaerts:

> ... social distancing cuts the ties between people and radicalises our sense of individualism. And thus it feeds our concern for ourselves, our bodies, its health and its survival. In short, it strengthens our fears and our readiness to hand us over to totalitarian politics.[73]

This finding requires social scientists to explore what mechanisms are used to turn a crisis into a political opportunity and how the state of exception and state of emergency are being transformed into the new normal. In this regard, Vertovec believes that COVID-19 produces an

---

70 See AGAMBEN, above ns. 6, 16 and 23.

71 See LAMBAERTS, above n. 18.

72 See G. AGAMBEN, 'Distanziamento sociale', <https://www.quodlibet.it/giorgio-agamben-distanziamento-sociale> last accessed 15.07.2020 and LAMBAERTS, above n. 18.

73 See LAMBAERTS, above n. 18 and AGAMBEN, above n. 72.

'enduring stigma' for constitutionalism. According to him, stigma acts as a cause of health inequalities.[74] He claims that:

> COVID-19 potentially transforms pandemic prejudices and 'blame game' dynamics into stigma. Stigma entails labelling an entire group or category of people, and purporting them to have undesirable traits and behaviors such as laziness, immorality or lack of hygiene. Stigma results in low status, bias and discrimination affecting social relations, public images and institutional structures. Stigma subsequently acts as a cause of health inequalities as well as a magnifier of them.[75]

In the subsequent section, I explore how fear is encoded in pandemic politics and how it has produced a durable stigmatisation of people, places and artefacts. Thus, I will approach fear politics from a semiotic viewpoint, clarifying the production of socio-political imaginaries of pandemic fear with a significant negative impact on constitutionalism.

5. ENCODING FEAR IN CONTEMPORARY CONSTITUTIONALISM THROUGH FEAR POLITICS

5.1. PERSONALISATION OF FEAR AND THE SUBJECT OF FEAR POLITICS

The personalisation of fear has played a central role in fear politics. Indeed, many of the addressees of pandemic fear have been stigmatised as targets of fear in a way that presumably has objective grounds. They were launched in the official policy of the states and in the media as 'the natural bearers of the pest', being the segments of society expected to be specifically exposed to the disease and thus, to serving as its natural transmitters. However, fear politics has influenced in a tripartite way the shaping of these social roles, functioning as the personalisation of fear.

First, many of the social categories shaped within the imaginary of fear of disease have been put in the role of the 'dangerous other' even before the pandemic. This 'otherness' has played a political role as a criterion

74 S. Vertovec, 'Covid-19 and enduring stigma. The corona pandemic increases xenophobia and exclusion worldwide', <https://www.mpg.de/14741776/covid-19-and-enduring-stigma?fbclid=IwAR1tjr5Zqjjj3YZ0lDt39IKWm3KvoD_KiXcqrcMpSWvLiAYZlxzETw8Kk1I> last accessed 15.07.2020.

75 See Vertovec, above n. 74.

for distinction of 'health enemies' endangering 'our' communities with contamination. This is especially true for the migrants,[76] but also for foreigners, 'guest workers' and homeless people. Thus, xenophobia and radical neo-nationalism have been serving as the perfect background for COVID-19 stigmatisation by virtue of the politics of fear.[77]

Second, there have also been targeted state politics of fear directed against people who have been deliberately put into the role of 'the dangerous other'. The closure of borders and the introduction of strict confinement policies have been justified by the fear that there is a dangerous 'other' – clusters of people who are especially prone to spreading disease. The 'travel ban' policy of US President Trump for people from Europe, Asia and – later – also from South America (especially from Brazil) is a good example of such a combination of reasonable preventive sanitary policy with targeted politics of fear of foreigners as disease-bearers. Thus, confinement has also been used as a political pressure tool and implicitly as an instrument for economic protectionism and the achievement of economic concessions from targeted states and regions.

In actuality, the pandemic measures have been less of a radical novelty and in fact a continuation of previous trends of closures of society, expulsion of otherness and reintroduction of the confines of territoriality as neo-nationalist and populist policy. Thus, the 'health paternalism' has actually facilitated stateism, paternalism and illiberalism as broader tendencies of neo-Westphalian and populist policy-making. The COVID-19 pandemic has offered the perfect excuse for neo-nationalists and authoritarian and illiberal regimes to stigmatise groups of people who have already been targeted as enemies by them. Unfortunately, supposedly liberal-democratic regimes have not performed much better. Discrimination against EU citizens from other Member States has been observed even

---

76 See M. Ceccorulli, 'The EU and Covid-19: Overcoming the lockdown mindset on migration', <https://www.globus.uio.no/resources/global-justice-blog/covid-19-series/ceccorulli-corona-migration-may20.html?fbclid=IwAR0155fXWv01r-jxYIaM9zC3F9iDeeY5iE_B0pHJiLgMht7BehgHZ_shslU> last accessed 15.07.2020. According to Vertovec, 'stigmatic suspicions of migrants and refugees as potential disease-carriers might encourage new modes of ethnic profiling in regimes at borders (where new biometric measures would sort the presumed healthy from the health-risky), in practices of institutional discrimination, in patterns of geographical segregation and in everyday social interactions'. See Vertovec, above n. 74.

77 According to Vertovec: 'It is becoming rapidly clear that Covid-19 exacerbates xenophobia and racism worldwide'. See Vertovec, above n. 74.

in the EU where some border authorities denied access to 'undesirable' types of internal migrants on the grounds of public health protection.

Third, the overall fear politics – spreading messages of horror and despair – have also reflected the stigmatisation of social roles and statuses of vulnerable people, marginal people and at-risk individuals. Here, one should count not only the 'traditional suspects of disease spreading', such as migrants, foreigners and travellers, but also 'new dangerous groups', such as homeless people,[78] elderly people, infected individuals and even the disobedient. Disobedient individuals were actually the most dangerous type, since this category of people was demonstrating civic discontent with disproportional and obsolete governmental measures, such as the wearing of masks in parks, bans on sitting on benches and other anti-pandemic regulations. The infodemia and the fear politics used during the COVID-19 regime has built invisible but palpable walls within societies, dividing its social strata and alienating the people with disproportionate confinement policies and producing an implosion of the constitutional order and its liberal-democratic foundations.

Hence, several types of objects of fear have been created in the course of the deployment of COVID-19 fear politics. Such objects include migrants, foreigners, homeless people, the elderly, the infected and the disobedient. In addition, minorities have been also targeted as dangerous transmitters of disease. For example, in Bulgaria, the parts of the capital city of Sofia where the members of the Roma minority are concentrated have been isolated with established check points resembling practices known from apartheid regimes.

It should be noted, however, that stigmatisation as disease disseminators has not been limited to vulnerable and minority groups. It also targeted well-off and even privileged parts of the society. A typical example is the blaming of tourists (e.g. the skiers on holiday in Austria and Italy) for frivolous spreading the disease.

It is also interesting to note that there have been 'fear waves' directed towards different groups of people, such as, *inter alia*, the Chinese, Asians in general, the Italians and the Spanish. Thus, health related panic, fear and frustration have been percolating with national and regional hatred,

---

78 See O. Bowcott, 'Judge questions coronavirus case against "homeless" London man', <https://www.theguardian.com/uk-news/2020/may/12/judge-questions-coronavirus-case-against-homeless-london-man?CMP=Share_iOSApp_Other&fbclid=IwAR1lstN-4_vkj5INVeWXV5Kc5c_XBZV33kpWuI_dIU2KPClRe8cWe-bSPaA> last accessed 15.07.2020.

xenophobia and nationalism. Implicitly, these types of negative feelings have been paralleled by increasing apprehension of an economic and social crisis. Gradually, the attitude towards the health Leviathan has been one of mixed feelings: 'love-hate'; 'Stockholm syndrome'; and appreciation of the 'Big Brother' which has emerged from the pandemic.

5.2. MESSAGES OF FEAR: THE CONTENT OF FEAR POLITICS

Constitutional semiotics is a traditionally underestimated discourse in national, European and comparative constitutionalism. This is especially true for the semiotics of fear. Fear is rather under-researched as a phenomenon with strategic constitutional importance, in spite of the fact that fear is a traditional resource of politics and signs of fear are also encoded in constitutions and in constitutional and administrative law.

Crisis management constitutionalism abounds with signs and messages of fear. Altogether, they serve the promotion of fear politics. During the age of the 'war on terror', the symbols of Islamic culture were largely perceived as semiotic signs of fear in the global North and the global West. Now, with the COVID-19 pandemic, new messages of fear have been signified with new signs of fear and codes of fear politics. These codes of fear are visual and symbolic representations of what can be defined as 'emotional totalitarianism'.[79]

Emotional totalitarianism can be defined as a political strategy for manipulation of the people on the basis of negative and destructive emotions. Fear, hate and greed play a central role among such emotions. Thus, fear politics is an important aspect of emotional totalitarianism, together with hate politics and greed politics. Hate politics is usually intertwined with fear politics, because they are typically structured on the basis of 'friend–enemy' logic. Although emotional totalitarianism can exist in times of presumed normality, it blossoms in times of crisis, emergency and extraordinary situations, when power actors can speculate about internal and external enemies. Thus, COVID-19 has been the perfect context for the development of emotional totalitarianism. COVID-19 emotional totalitarianism is based on fear politics and structured around

---

[79] I am indebted to prof. Jorge Sampaio for the term 'emotional totalitarianism', which he used as a title of a picture on fear that he shared on Facebook on 19.05.2020.

a multitude of enemies, including the virus as 'the invisible enemy' and many other candidates for 'horsemen of the Apocalypse'.

Several symbols of fear have been widely promoted during the COVID-19 regime. They have served as signifiers of fear and, thus, as codes of emotional totalitarianism. These include the face mask and special protective clothing, the intubation machine, the coffins and the refrigerator trucks ready to transport corpses. For example, there has been a picture of the intubation machine circulating on the Internet and on Internet-based social networks (e.g. Facebook), captioned: 'Do you know what this is? If you do not want to know – stay home'. In such a context, the face mask has been frequently compared with the masks that the medieval and renaissance doctors were wearing during plague pandemics.

In many countries, public parks were closed. But in Bulgaria, when they re-opened, people were allowed to walk in circles only within permitted paths, while being controlled by guards and the police. All other paths and walkways, which were not allowed to be re-opened by the authorities, were marked with police signage, resembling a large and surreal crime scene. Fences, security lines and guards in parks with masks encircling confused families with children banned from approach prohibited playgrounds – a surreal picture indeed!

Another scary example comes from Slovakia. According to Kovac's report on the state surveillance and quarantine isolation practices promoted by some authorities in this country, 'those in compulsory home quarantine are obliged to post a sign from the authorities ("a red card") on their door to warn others that a potentially infected person inside is under disease control observation'.[80] Fortunately, again according to Kovac's report, the 'Slovak Prime Minister Igor Matovič has condemned the regulation requiring special signs on doors and compared the red card houses to the yellow star houses, that is, the designated compulsory places of residence for Budapest's Jews in the Second World War'.[81]

The horrible idea of dogs recognising and sniffing out COVID-infected people[82] has been lauded as a scientific and policy achievement in the media. None the less terrifying is the news of people-tracing apps and city guard robots which have actually been put into practice in Singapore and elsewhere, tracing, chasing and surveying potential disease disseminators.

80 See Kovács, above n. 5.
81 See Kovács, above n. 5.
82 J. Kossoff, 'Medical detection dogs able to sniff 750 people an hour could help identify coronavirus cases, researchers say', <https://www.businessinsider.com/sniffer-dogs-answer-to-the-covid-19-testing-crisis-mirror-2020-4> last accessed 15.07.2020.

Last but not least, there has been a visible trend for demonising hugging, kissing and hand shaking. There were even articles written by medical specialists stating that hand shaking has always been extremely dangerous, since hands are transmitters of multiple diseases. Therefore, according to them, we are almost lucky to have had the experience of the COVID-19 pandemic, as this will finally allow us to ban this dangerous habit from the 'barbarous' pre-coronavirus times.[83]

Thus, social distancing has been carefully supplemented with a series of strategies, tactics and codes which profoundly change our semiotic culture and may have deep and long-lasting effects on the ways we socialise and understand social life. In this context, one should never forget that socialising and extensive social life is of pivotal importance for the establishment of a vivid civil society capable of controlling the government and sustaining democratic constitutional order. Hence, the face mask and the hand shake are artefacts that bear strategic semiotic meaning and are phenomena with vast constitutional importance.

5.3. PLACES OF STIGMA: THE LOCUS OF FEAR POLITICS

The COVID-19 pandemic has drawn a new 'map of fear politics', giving the 'invisible enemy' its physical locus and thus concretising the physical and territorial shapes of fear. Confinement politics have never been practised on such a global scale. The temporally nearest experiment with territorial closure what that which was implemented in communist regimes. But even then, mobility within the states was not been limited to such an extent. Indeed, the reintroduction of free movement limitations due to migration crises by several EU member states, as well as by France on the grounds of terrorism-related states of emergency, served as the first signs that emergency and crisis management constitutionalism based on the politics of fear can be used for the re-introduction of 'imposed territoriality' and 'territorial austerity' as impediments of free movement in its capacity as a key pillar of the second 'Belle Époque'. But the COVID-19 regime has raised 'territorial austerity' and the limitations on free movement to an extreme level.

---

[83] See J. Scipioni, 'White House advisor Dr. Fauci says handshaking needs to stop even when pandemic ends – other experts agree', <https://www.cnbc.com/2020/04/09/dr-anthony-fauci-handshaking-needs-to-stop-even-after-pandemic.html> last accessed 15.07.2020.

The territories of the states have been redrawn into zones (e.g. the red and other 'colour zones' in Italy). Check points have been established where the police and even the military have been guarding, imposing sanctions and demonstrating authority. These zones and check points, as well as quarantined regions, cities, neighbourhoods and homes became places of territorial stigmatisation.

In fact, the COVID-19 regime of territorial politics has produced several types of 'cursed spaces'. These include not only the cities and parts of cities under quarantine,[84] but also migration and refugee camps, dedicated COVID-19 hospitals and isolation camps and even cruise ships held in confinement and isolation. The cruise ship, for example, has been transformed from a symbol of liberty, luxury and entertainment into a symbol of confinement and fear. The ordinary hospitals and retreat centres for elderly people have undergone a similar transformation. The frightening scenes of the large hospital built in the city of Wuhan in China and the scary pictures from the New York field hospitals and hospital extensions, with the refrigerated trucks waiting to collect corpses, have been disseminated globally, creating 'glocal' territorial stigmatisation and traumas. The term 'glocal' can be used here, because local 'cursed spaces' have been presented as symbols of horror and fear, which are globally recognisable. Thus, they have started to serve as semiotic codes of global (anti-)constitutional fear politics.

In the media and in public opinion, the spread of COVID-19 has usually been associated with hubs of free mobility which served as loopholes for the import of the virus. Thus, although local, these hubs were serving the purpose of demonising free movement. Such a territorial stigmatisation has been imposed on certain free movement hubs of the pre-coronavirus world, irrespective of whether they were promoting and serving the free movement of tourists belonging to the middle or the upper social classes (like the cities of Ischgl, Austria; Bergamo, Italy; and Bansko, Bulgaria) or free movement related to global business, politics and science (such as New York and Milan).

Protected corridors – for deliveries, truck drivers, sick people, administrators and politicians – have even increased the feeling of 'territorial austerity'. 'Sanitary corridors', 'holiday maker corridors' and

---

84 Konrad Lachmayer reports: 'the small village of Ischgl in the Tyrolean mountains, where an après-ski bar seems to have been a main hotspot for spreading the virus across Europe, has since become the symbol for the Austrian chapter of the pandemic'. See LACHMAYER, above n. 4.

'migratory corridors' served as exceptions to the exception. They were forms of conditionally free territoriality imposed and allowed from above by the national governments. They served as 'worm holes' for free movement in the context of territorial austerity imposed during a state of emergency. These corridors, as exceptional exits from confinement, in fact increased the feeling of territorial stigmatisation.

Territoriality experienced a crisis that was visible until the end of 2019. Territory seemed to be of less and less relevance for power. A-territorial, trans-territorial and post-territorial forms of power have been blossoming.[85] But with the COVID-19 crisis management regime, the burden of territoriality started to be felt with power which has been unprecedented for many decades. Two types of regimes of spatiality and allocation of power have emerged: the 'territorial austerity regime' with all its prohibited zones, check points, 'cursed cities' and special territorial corridors has been paralleled by an extreme form of post-territoriality based on the Internet. Internet-based platforms are blossoming, producing spaces of post-territoriality paralleling the territorial austerity of the official territorial confinement policies. Thus, the COVID-19 regime has produced a massive swirl of territoriality as a basis for socio-political co-existence. Whether the territorial stigmatisation and the reintroduction of the burden of territoriality will have an enduring impact on our constitutional and political orders remains to be seen.

6. THE NEW PATERNALISTIC STATE: THE HEALTH LEVIATHAN

The restrictive measures associated with the COVID-19 pandemic, in the case that they are temporary, may be conceived of as another state of emergency in the line of historic manifestations of emergency constitutionalism. Indeed, they will still raise concerns of disproportionality and imbalance. Constitutional law, EU law and international law infringements will endure as bad memories of a perplexed time, managed by misfortunate and to a great extent incompetent political elites. They may even have a mobilising effect, raising human right awareness and providing immunity for civil society and serving as a vaccine against authoritarianism.

---

85 See M. Belov, 'Rule of Law in Space of Flows' in M. Belov (ed.), *Rule of Law at the Beginning of the Twenty-First Century*, Eleven, The Hague 2018, pp. 97–141.

However, the health Leviathan may remain with us for a much longer period than we initially expected. It may stay even after the COVID-19 pandemic, which served as its justification, fades away. The fears of a fascist-hysterical hygiene-state,[86] of a 'state governed as a "pest hospital"'[87] and of health authoritarianism[88] may prove to be well grounded. Paternalism, technocratic tutelage of the people by power-hungry elites and the proliferation of restrictions on liberty and human rights for the sake of imposed security may be the key features of the new normal triggered by the COVID-19 regime.

Thus, if we do not return immediately or at least soon after this pandemic to the 'traditional normality' of the pre-coronavirus times, we may have to live in a much more de-globalised, illiberal and paternalistic world, dominated by the health Leviathan. According to Günter Frankenberg, 'we can hope that now it has become clear that a sovereign will be the one that do not declare the state of emergency. And the one that normalises the situation not under the flag of protection against infections'.[89] In other words, the real sovereignty, aiming at the restoration of freedom and self-determination, will belong to those states which return to the normalcy of the liberal-democratic constitutionalism and reject the temptations to perpetuate the existence of the state of health emergency. Otherwise, we might be doomed to sink in the swamp of health paternalism, maintained on the basis of politics of fear, for a long time. And this may mark a new era of post-human and illiberal constitutionalism paralleled by surveillance capitalism and a dangerous combination of a 'double state' combining technocracy and populism.

Thus, constitutionalists must try to imagine what the 'emergency governance architecture'[90] of the near future will look like. What will the consequences of the COVID-19 emergency be for constitutionalism and the democratic political order based on the rule of law? Will we be put under pressure to make compromises or to even drastically change out liberal-democratic constitutional design? Are we going to witness the rise and cementing of authoritarianism, illiberalism and populism? Will there be a rise of nationalism or a new impetus for regional and global

---

86 See Heinig, above n. 3 and Jürgensen and Orlowski, above n. 3.

87 See Frankenberg, above n. 9.

88 See Lachmayer, above n. 4 as well as Platon, above n. 4.

89 See Frankenberg, above n. 9.

90 For the concept of 'emergency governance architecture', see Tulich, Rizzi and McGaughey, above n. 13.

cooperation? Will there be a rise of paternalism or a new stimulus for individual self-assertion, and will a re-establishment of democracy and rule of law emerge? Are we at the eve of a new 'pandemic constitutionalism' which will last longer than the temporary and presumably exceptional COVID-19 constitutionalism? Why are some governments preparing for a long period of COVID-19 constitutional emergency (e.g. in Hungary), and even adopting a special regime of 'health emergency', as in France, Romania and Bulgaria? These are just few of the questions to which answers will be provided in the not-so-distant future.

DEMOCRACY AND HUMAN RIGHTS IN ILLIBERAL CONSTITUTIONALISM

Tímea Drinóczi and Agnieszka Bień-Kacała*

* The research in this chapter is supported by the National Science Centre, Poland, 2018/29/B/HS5/00232, 'Illiberal constitutionalism in Poland and Hungary'.

1. INTRODUCTION

The term 'illiberal constitutionalism' describes the Hungarian and Polish governmental systems since 2010 and 2015, respectively.[1] In these states, every element of liberal constitutionalism, such as the rule of law, democracy and human rights, is observable; none is missing, but no element prevails in its entirety. Hungary and Poland have been slowly sliding from their previous status as constitutional democracies toward authoritarianism. In this chapter, we argue that up until the COVID-19 crisis, no reform, steps, actions, decisions or attitudes had come together to make Hungary and Poland authoritarian regimes within the EU. Nonetheless, there is no doubt that the weak but tacitly existing constitutional constraint on public power has been gradually reducing even during the COVID-19 emergency, but, at this moment, it cannot be said that it has reached a turning point.[2]

Against this background, we claim, first, that the historical trajectories, value orientation and emotional profiles of both countries have facilitated the creation and consolidation of illiberal constitutionalism. Its elements – illiberal legality,[3] illiberal democracy (Section 3) and the reduced protection of human rights (Section 4) – are intrinsically connected, but even if we consider them together, we could conclude that up until spring 2020 they had not constituted an authoritarian regime. That is our second claim. Our third claim is that the COVID-19 crisis could be seen as the factor that has accelerated the process of reaching an authoritarian turn – a final assessment, however, can only be made after the pandemic ultimately, both *de facto* and *de jure*, is over (Section 5).[4] Exploring these areas demands the examination of what 'illiberal democracy' means in an illiberal constitutional

---

[1] T. Drinóczi and A. Bień-Kacała, 'Illiberal Constitutionalism: The Case of Hungary and Poland' (2019) 20 *German Law Journal* 8, 1140–66.

[2] As the submission date was 31.05.2020, the information provided here is up to date as of the end of May 2020.

[3] We have already discussed this in Drinóczi and Bień-Kacała, above n. 1 and T. Drinóczi and A. Bień-Kacała (eds), *Rule of Law, Common Values and Illiberal Constitutionalism. Poland and Hungary within the European Union*, Routledge 2020, forthcoming.

[4] When we submitted this chapter (31.05.2020), neither the Hungarian constitutional nor the Polish statutory emergency was over. Bills intending to terminate the Hungarian emergency were submitted to the Parliament at the end of May. The constitutional emergency was terminated in mid-June, and a new statute-based emergency was introduced until the end of the year. The new state-based emergency raises similar concerns as the Coronavirus Act 2020. In Poland, the assessment is still dependent on how the PiS-dominated Sejm will continue its work together with the re-elected President Duda. For a discussion on how emergency powers have been used, misused

setting; how, or to what extent, the attitude toward human rights has changed; and how all of this has been affected by the COVID-19 crisis.

2. ILLIBERAL VALUES AND COLLECTIVE NARCISSISM

Hungarian and Polish populist leaders, starting from 2010,[5] have, with increased intensity, exploited the emotional needs of their compatriots and used different techniques to gain political support for remodelling constitutional settings. This support seems to be stable because it originates from a historically shaped value orientation, which is connected to the group identification so widely shared by Hungarians and Poles.[6]

2.1. HISTORICAL TRAJECTORY, VALUE ORIENTATION AND COLLECTIVE NARCISSISM

Social science research[7] shows that neither the Hungarian nor the Polish historical trajectory provides favourable grounds on which to build an emotionally stable identity.[8] Hungarians experience a feeling of collective

---

and not used in these countries, see T. Drinóczi and A. Bień-Kacała, 'COVID-19 in Hungary and Poland: extraordinary situation and illiberal constitutionalism', in *Theory and Practice of Legislation* (2020) https://www.tandfonline.com/doi/full/10.1080/20508840.2020.1782109, last accessed 31.05.2020; on how the Polish judicial independence has further deteriorated during spring 2020, amidst the pandemic, see A. Bień-Kacała, 'Polexit is Coming or is it Already Here? Comments on the Judicial Independence Decisions of the Polish Constitutional Tribunal', *International Journal of Constitutional Law Blog*, 28.04.2020, at: http://www.iconnectblog.com/2020/04/polexit-is-coming-or-is-it-already-here-comments-on-the-judicial-independence-decisions-of-the-polish-constitutional-tribunal, last accessed 31.05.2020.

5 2010 was the year when the Fidesz Party won the parliamentary election and started to develop an illiberal Hungary, and when the tragic plane crash happened in Smoleńsk. This event is a continual point of emotional reference for the PiS Party.

6 A. Cichocka and A. Cislak, 'Nationalism as collective narcissism' (2020) *ScienceDirect Current Opinion in Behavioral Sciences* 34, 69–74.

7 See e.g. É. Fülöp et al., 'Emotional Elaboration of Collective Traumas in Historical Narratives' (2014), http://real.mtak.hu/20201/3/emotional_elaboration_of_collective_traumas.pdf, last accessed 31.05.2020; A. Tarnowska, 'The Sovereignty Issue in the Public Discussion in the Era of the Polish 3rd May Constitution (1788–1792)' in U. Müßig (ed.), *Reconsidering Constitutional Formation I National Sovereignty*, Springer Open, 2016, p. 215; W. Wrzesiński, *Charakter narodowy Polaków. Z rozważań historyka [National character of Poles. From the historian's reflections]*, Wrocław 2004.

8 Fülöp et al., above n. 7, 11.

victimhood, primarily because of the Trianon Peace Treaty (1918),[9] as well as a feeling of being abandoned, to their disappointment, by all regimes throughout Hungarian history.[10] Poles are also traumatised because of the loss of statehood and independence.[11] Both nations feel disappointed with democracy[12] and share distrust in public institutions.[13] It seems that traumatisation and low trust in institutions, as well as reliance on the state's support, provide fertile ground for sacrifices in freedom. This is supported by research on value orientation. The results show that the value profile common in Eastern European countries, which lacks commitment to values of egalitarianism and autonomy, is ill-suited for the development of democracy.[14] Research on value orientations during communism in our region ascertained that people can indeed gradually acclimate their values to changed circumstances, upgrade the importance of values that become attainable and downgrade the importance of those whose pursuit is no longer achievable.[15] The question is how long this acclimation takes and whether

---

9 https://www.britannica.com/event/Treaty-of-Trianon, last accessed 31.05.2020.

10 G.Y. Spiró, *Két középkelet-európai mentalitás az államiság szempontjából*, 2000 Irodalmi és Társadalmi havi lap 6 (2007); A. Schmidt, 'Challenges of the illiberal democracy in Hungary. Some aspects to the 2018 elections', (2018) 6 *Polski Przegląd Politologiczny* 2, 88.

11 T. Drinóczi and A. Bień-Kacała, 'Extra-legal particularities and illiberal constitutionalism. The case of Hungary and Poland' (2018) *Hungarian Journal of Legal Studies* 4, 346–47.

12 For Hungarians, democracy seems to be associated more with economic well-being than with democratic freedoms (of speech, assembly and association). Only 49% of Hungarians see democracy as a better system than others. However, they still believe that the type of the form of government that guides their lives does not make much difference to them; see: A. Bíró-Nagy, 'Illiberal democracy in Hungary: the social background and practical steps of building an illiberal state', Barcelona Centre for International Affairs, 2017, https://www.cidob.org/en/articulos/monografias/illiberals/illiberal_democracy_in_hungary_the_social_background_and_practical_steps_of_building_an_illiberal_state, p. 35, last accessed 31.05.2020. Economic support by the state is very important for Poles, and it has been one of the most important issues during electoral campaigns.

13 Around 40–50% of the Polish population/voters/those who participated in a study do not trust in political institutions, such as the government or parliament, https://www.cbos.pl/SPISKOM.POL/2018/K_035_18.PDF, p. 9, last accessed 31.05.2020.

14 S.H. Schwartz and A. Bardi, 'Influences of adaptation to communist rule on value priorities in Eastern Europe' (1997) *Political Psychology* 2, 407–08. Similarly, G. Skąpska, 'Law and society in a natural laboratory: the case of Poland in the broader context of East-Central Europe' in M. Kaase, V. Sparschuh and A. Wenninger (eds), *Three social science disciplines in Central and Eastern Europe: handbook on economics, political science and sociology (1989–2001)*, Informationszentrum Sozialwissenschaften; GESIS Servicestelle Osteuropa; Collegium Budapest, Institute for Advanced Study, Berlin 2002, p. 597.

15 Schwartz and Bardi, above n. 14, 394.

it can happen at all to the extent that it could have transformative force in society. It is intriguing, especially in the Eastern part of Europe, that scholars have identified distinctively Western European values.[16] They found that – when comparing the values with those more commonly shared in Eastern Europe – the following stand out in Western Europe: low importance is given to mastery values; the most importance is given to affective autonomy values; the least importance is given to conservative values; more appreciation is accorded to initiative and achievement; and more tolerance is shown to outgroups and post-material values, such as freedom and social responsibility. In contrast to the West, it was found that in our region, mastery values are even less important, while conservativism and hierarchy are more important.[17]

It thus seems that the emotional attitudes of the people are behind illiberal transformations. Regardless of the 20 or 25 years of liberal constitutionalism in Hungary and Poland (1990–2010/2015), what we seem to have is as follows: a lack of respect for others; compromised self-confidence; the feeling of being a victim, with the attached sense of inferiority; the need for a strong leader; prioritisation of values of conservativism and hierarchy; and a reluctance – or controversial attitudes – towards the values of liberal constitutional democracy or open society. All of these identity-related phenomena, which had apparently already been internalised, have eventually combined to form a national and constitutional identity.[18] This illiberal mentality extends to the area of law, either 'consciously' (through direct actions such as constitutional amendment or constitutional court decisions)[19] or 'subconsciously', through elections,[20] and due to the lack of effective social resistance and

16 From a different perspective, see M. Weber, *The Protestant Ethic and the Spirit of Capitalism*, Routledge 1930; Wrzesiński, above n. 7.

17 Schwartz and Bardi, above n. 14, p. 406.

18 For constitutional identity, see M. Rosenfeld, 'Constitutional Identity' in M. Rosenfeld and A. Sajó (eds), *The Oxford Handbook of Comparative Constitutional Law*, Oxford University Press, Oxford 2012, pp. 756–76; G. Jacobsohn, *Constitutional identity*, Harvard University Press, Cambridge MA 2010. For a European perspective, see T. Drinóczi, 'Constitutional Identity in Europe: The Identity of the Constitution. A Regional Approach' (2020) 21 *German Law Journal* 2, 105–30. On Hungary and Poland, see Drinóczi and Bień-Kacała, above n. 11, 338–54.

19 See the Hungarian amendment to the Fundamental Law (FL) on constitutional identity, the decision of the Constitutional Court (CC) on the constitutional identity from 2016 and the Polish Constitutional Tribunal (CT) on the sovereignty of Poland that shall be defended against EU law and enforceable CJEU decisions from April 2020, Drinóczi, above n. 18; Bień-Kacała, above n. 4.

20 See all the Hungarian elections from 2010 and the Polish elections since 2015 – with some setback (Hungarian local elections in 2019 and the election to the Polish Senate 2019); both Fidesz and PiS claimed victory.

automatic submission to unquestionable authority.[21] Societies thus create their own illiberal constitutions, which can either be enacted (Poland 1935, Hungary 2010) or remain invisible (Poland 2015). In the latter case, the constitution consists of illiberal practices and unconstitutional rules instead of legitimate legal provisions in the codified constitution. The societal illiberal value orientation also has an impact on notions of democracy, sovereignty and attitudes towards human rights protection.

These specific value orientations and attitudes overlap with collective narcissism.[22] Collective narcissism is defined as:

> ... a belief that one's own group (the ingroup) is exceptional and entitled to privileged treatment, but others do not sufficiently recognize it. Thus, central to collective narcissism is resentment that the ingroup's exceptionality is not sufficiently externally appreciated.[23]

As such, collective narcissism is a core source of political choices that undermine liberal democracy. In particular, it is linked to intergroup hostility and aggression, voting behaviour, political conservatism and conspiratorial thinking. It is related to the biased perception of intergroup reality, in which events are selectively seen and remembered in the service of the in-group's image and linked to a divisive social identity.[24] Hungarians and Poles share such a belief and raise political demands on it.[25]

2.2. POSSIBLE ROOT CAUSES OF HUNGARIAN AND POLISH ILLIBERALISM

In Hungary, the paradigm for conspiratorial thinking is evident in the hate campaign against György Soros, non-governmental organisations (NGOs) and those supporting and promoting human rights. In Poland, it is clearly

21 Similarly, see A. Sajó, 'The Constitution of Illiberal Democracy as a Theory About Society' (2018) *Polish sociological review* 4, 405–10.

22 A. Golec de Zavala, K. Dyduch-Hazar and D. Lantos, 'Collective Narcissism: Political Consequences of Investing Self-Worth in the Ingroup's Image' (2019) 40 *Advances in Political Psychology* 1, 46; A. Cichocka and A. Cislak, 'Nationalism as collective narcissism' (2020) *ScienceDirect – Current Opinion in Behavioral Sciences* 34, 69–74. J.P. Forgas and D. Lantos, 'Understanding Populism: Collective Narcissism and the Collapse of Democracy in Hungary', http://www.sydneysymposium.unsw.edu.au/2019/chapters/ForgasSSSP2019%20.pdf, p. 28, last accessed 31.05.2020.

23 Golec de Zavala, Dyduch-Hazar and Lantos, above n. 22, 37.

24 Golec de Zavala, Dyduch-Hazar and Lantos, above n. 22, 44.

25 Forgas and Lantos, above n. 22, 6–7.

visible in relation to the Smoleńsk plane crash in 2010.[26] Conspiratorial thinking is associated with the fictional aggression of outgroups, which leads to physical aggression against members of the out-group (e.g. attacks on people of colour, including physical attacks or spitting on them) because they speak and look differently or are associated with political opposition.

The continual references to the achievements of Hungarians who became famous after leaving the country, and the historical role of Hungary in the defence of Europe against the Ottoman Empire, which appears in the Fundamental Law (FL) and political speeches, indicate a pride that is not recognised by others to a sufficient extent. Poles share similar feelings of pride and refer to the defence of Christian Europe against Ottoman (Muslim) culture. Poles were able to preserve national and Catholic values to a greater extent than Western countries. Western states abandoned Hungary and Poland after the Second World War and contributed to their becoming 'occupied' by the Soviet Union. There is a demand in political communications for respect to be shown to Hungarians and Poles.

The biased perception of intergroup reality could be connected in both states to the ways in which they dealt with their past in between the two world wars and during the Second World War when collaborating with Nazi Germany and playing their part in the Holocaust, even if we take into consideration that Poland never institutionally collaborated with Nazi Germany.[27]

As far as voting behaviour is concerned, collective narcissism is associated with the support of populists worldwide and in Poland and Hungary.[28] Another phenomenon is the divisive social identity: especially in political communications, we can see that there is a division between the 'true' members of the in-group and those who are 'less worthy', which could increase the bond between the true members and secure a feeling of belonging.

Hungarian and Polish collective narcissism also claims for itself exceptional national moral characteristics, such as honesty, decency, fairness, kindness and hospitality. Such a constructed 'perfect' picture of a nation is then exploited by state propaganda. The notion of the 'nation' is exaggerated, abused and based on the specific importance of nationalism

---

26 Twenty-four conspiratorial theories have been collected and are shown at https://oko.press/katastrofa-smolenska-24-teorie-spiskowe/, last accessed 31.05.2020.

27 See, e.g. in Poland, the Law on the Institute of National Remembrance 26 January 2018 (Dz.U. 2018 poz. 369), in which a crime of 'defamation of the Polish Nation' was introduced, but after sharp international reaction it was repealed on 27.06.2018; and in Hungary, the revival of nostalgia towards the Horthy regime and the refusal to face this element of the past.

28 Golec de Zavala, Dyduch-Hazar and Lantos, above n. 22, 55.

that is bound to freedom.[29] In both states, the fight for personal freedom in the mid-19th century was connected with a claim for a sovereign state.

Moreover, Polish – and, we may add, Hungarian – collective narcissism is linked to religious fundamentalism,[30] misogyny[31] and homophobia.[32] Being Polish, stereotypically, means being a male, heterosexual, Catholic person.[33] By the same token, being a Hungarian, stereotypically, means being a male, heterosexual Christian individual.

Consequently, the assumed victimised past that has remained unresolved, and the intense feelings of exceptionality have created an environment that is friendly towards illiberal remodelling, including the transformation of the components of constitutionalism to illiberal legality, illiberal democracy and the misuse and lowering of human rights protection.

3. ILLIBERAL DEMOCRACY

Neither Poland nor Hungary has reached a state of authoritarianism as systemic mechanisms do not feature among those of authoritarianism. Discussing the differences between liberal constitutional democracy and competitive authoritarianism, Ginsburg and Huq describe pure authoritarian regimes as countries in which there is a complete absence of effective political competition and where power cannot be lost in elections. At the same time, however, there is a written constitution, courts and other rule-of-law accoutrements.[34] Gábor Attila Tóth lists five defining elements of authoritarianism (ruler, façade-constitution, hegemonic voting practices, shortfalls in institutional checks and restricted individual and collective rights),[35] which partly coincide with the description by Arch Puddington.

---

29 I. Krastev and S. Holmes, 'Explaining Eastern Europe: Imitation and Its Discontents' (2018) 29 *Journal of Democracy* 3, 120.

30 Golec de Zavala, Dyduch-Hazar and Lantos, above n. 22, 7, 44.

31 See, e.g. the underrepresentation of women in the public sphere, especially in Hungary. Speeches of MPs in the Hungarian Parliament have proclaimed that the women's place is in the kitchen and the role of the women in society is to give birth; a Polish PiS MP during the 2019 electoral campaign used similar rhetoric to the effect that if a woman gave the first birth at the age of 30, how many children can be born? These are the consequences of telling women that they do not have to do what God has called them to do.

32 See the polish LGBT case, below n. 90.

33 Golec de Zavala, Dyduch-Hazar and Lantos, above n. 22, p. 44.

34 T. Ginsburg and A.Z. Huq, *How to save constitutional democracy?* The University of Chicago Press, Chicago 2018, pp. 22–23.

35 G.A. Tóth, 'Authoritarianism', *Max Planck Encyclopedia of Comparative Constitutional Law*, February 2017.

Puddington defines modern authoritarianism as the more enlightened, 21st-century version of the authoritarianism of the previous century, in terms of its pretension to be something else, especially being less authoritarian. He also admits that the modern authoritarian systems sometimes revert to the methods applied by their former counterparts. There is, for instance, economic openness and, to a certain extent, pluralist media, political competition, civil society and the rule of law. There is also, however, retained or direct control of the economy or media outlets, co-opted political opposition, the legal harassment of politicians and the employment of instruments for keeping civil society closely watched as an (almost) daily practice.[36]

Our claim here is, thus, that neither Hungary nor Poland can be called (modern) authoritarian, as compared to Russia, Turkey and Singapore (that is, labelled authoritarian constitutionalism due to the tangible commitment to restraint on public power).[37] The reasons for this are that the political opposition is free; free establishment of political parties are ensured; and there is political competition and power can be lost in elections, at least in local elections and elections to the Polish Senate. However, there are some defective practices as well, which we can call authoritarian tendencies, and which we discuss below. Thus, the issue of degree is a matter of kind here, too, just in the case of the rule of law deterioration.[38]

3.1. THE TERM: ILLIBERAL AND DEMOCRACY COMBINED

We view the concept of illiberal democracy differently than did Fareed Zakaria (1990s) or Viktor Orbán (2014).[39] Zakaria perceived democracy

---

36 A. Puddington, 'Breaking down democracy: global strategies, and methods of modern authoritarians', June 2017, https://freedomhouse.org/sites/default/files/June2017_FH_Report_Breaking_Down_Democracy.pdf, last accessed 31.05.2020.

37 M. Tushnet, 'Authoritarian Constitutionalism' (2015) 100 *Cornell Law Review* 391, 438. On the difference among authoritarian systems, authoritarian constitutionalism and illiberal constitutionalism, mainly from the perspective of the constraint on public power and the rule of law, see Drinóczi and Bień-Kacała, above n. 1, 1148, and T. Drinóczi and A. Bień-Kacała, 'Illiberal Constitutionalism and the European Rule of Law', in Drinóczi and Bień-Kacała, above n. 3.

38 This is precisely what allows us to argue that Hungary and Poland have created illiberal constitutionalism. See Drinóczi and Bień-Kacała, above n. 1, 1150.

39 'New state that we are constructing in Hungary is an illiberal state, a non-liberal state. It does not reject the fundamental principles of liberalism such as freedom, and I could list a few more, but it does not make this ideology the central element of state organisation, but instead includes a different, special, national approach', Speech

and liberalism as two separate ideals that are independent of one another but which have developed close to each other.[40] Therefore, states that previously became liberal could easily become democratic, while states that absorbed democracy first could disregard liberal rights and turn to being illiberal and democratic at the same time. Our point is, however, that both states, as a result of the democratic transition of 1989/1990, created fully fledged constitutional democracies. These then became downgraded to something else in the 2010s – which we call 'illiberal constitutionalism'. Our views thus relate to different directions of change. As for Orbán's concept, we simply regard it as a political slogan, which we borrow and try to conceptualise from a constitutional law perspective. For us, the term expresses the main idea of how Orbán's and Kaczyński's democracy works.

As opposed to what evolved after the transition to constitutional democracy, illiberal democracy is conceptualised as a formal, manipulated, profoundly majoritarian and non-inclusive democracy in which constitutional institutions (such as elections and connected electoral rights and principles, representation and accountability and the central tenets of democratic law-making) are, to a certain extent,[41] misused, abused or neglected. It seems that this conceptualisation is supported by the value preferences of the population for hierarchical structures and autocratic leadership. Opposing views and considerations are not welcome, as the will of majority, which represents the 'sovereign' state and the 'sovereign people' – which covers only 'good Poles/Hungarians' – should prevail. Therefore, the departure from the previous liberal constitutionalism is visible, as the vector of change is turned towards authoritarianism.[42] However, the remodelling had not reached this point by the beginning

on 26.07.2014; https://www.kormany.hu/en/the-prime-minister/the-prime-minister-s-speeches/prime-minister-viktor-orban-s-speech-at-the-25th-balvanyos-summer-free-university-and-student-camp, last accessed 31.05.2020. The new label (Christian democracy) instead of illiberal democracy does not alter the content. Orbán's full speech at Tusványos: political philosophy, upcoming crisis and projects for the next 15 years, 29.07.2019, https://visegradpost.com/en/2019/07/29/orbans-full-speech-at-tusvanyos-political-philosophy-upcoming-crisis-and-projects-for-the-next-15-years/, last accessed 31.05.2020.

40 F. Zakaria, 'The Rise of Illiberal Democracy' (1997) *Foreign Affaires* 76, 22; see more: F. Zakaria, *The Future of Freedom: Illiberal Democracy at Home and Abroad*, W.W. Norton and Company, New York 2007.

41 This 'extent', i.e. the degree of backsliding does not reach the level of that of authoritarian regimes in different indices. See below in n. 46, 50 and 53.

42 Drinóczi and Bień-Kacała, above n. 37.

of 2020, as political pluralism and the possibility of changing the ruling majority were still present.[43] Even if elections did show some degree of being flawed, as in Hungary, which sunk from being a semi-consolidated democracy to a transitional or hybrid regime,[44] or some elements of political influence, as in Poland,[45] which is now labelled a semi-consolidated democracy, political pluralism and political competitiveness were still in place.[46] Nevertheless, at the beginning of 2020, almost half of the Hungarian voters surveyed reportedly did not trust that the government could be removed in a democratic way.[47] Moreover, the management of the COVID-19 pandemic resulted in changes that show a serious backsliding in democracy, which we discuss below, and which fits into the trend of steady deterioration since 2010 (Hungary) and 2015 (Poland).[48]

3.2. ILLIBERAL DEMOCRACY AT WORK

3.2.1. Electoral Democracy: Illiberalisation

In both the Hungarian and the Polish constitutions, the formal condition of the minimalist version of democracy associated with electoral rights and procedures[49] is provided for, and it is still about 'rule by the people'. Against this background, the electoral concept and practice were illiberalised up to 2020. Nevertheless, even if Freedom House considers Hungary

---

43 See the 2019 general election in Poland in which PiS lost the Senat, and the results of the local election in both states.

44 A. Bozóki and D. Hegedűs who labelled Hungary as a hybrid regime as early as 2018 in A. Bozóki and D. Hegedűs, 'An externally constrained hybrid regime: Hungary in the European Union' (2018) 7 *Democratization* 1173–1189.

45 The National Electoral Commission (NEC) or the SC – the newly and unlawfully created chamber instead of the SC as a whole – has the ability to validate the election.

46 According to Freedom House, both countries deteriorated in 2020. Hungary scored 49, Poland 65, while Russia reached 7, https://freedomhouse.org/countries/nations-transit/scores, last accessed 31.05.2020.

47 A. Bíró-Nagy and G. Laki, *Orbán 10. Az elmúlt évtized a Magyar társadalom szemével*, Budapest 2020, https://www.policysolutions.hu/userfiles/Orban10_final.pdf, p. 78, last accessed 31.05.2020.

48 Z.S. Csaky, *Nations in transition. Dropping the democratic façade*, Freedom House 2020, https://freedomhouse.org/report/nations-transit/2020/dropping-democratic-facade#Facade, p. 25, last accessed 31.05.2020.

49 J. Schumpeter, *Capitalism, Socialism and Democracy*, 2nd ed., Allen & Unwin, London and New York 1947, Chapters 21–23.

to be a hybrid regime, the electoral process is assessed relatively highly (9 out of 12), while Poland scored 11 out of 12 in 2019 and 2020.[50]

In Hungary, electoral illiberalisation features gerrymandering, diversification of the methods of casting votes, packing electoral bodies and a non-inclusive legislative process on electoral rules.[51] These are then supported by the biased media.[52] There is a factual inequality regarding the ways voters who are abroad on the day of the election can cast their votes. Hungarians who do not have a national address (Hungarians who are the nationals of neighbouring countries and who received citizenship based on rules that do not require a national address) can cast their votes by post. However, those who have a national address (e.g. they are only working or studying abroad – voters who have already voted with their feet) have to go to the Hungarian embassy.[53] In Poland, there are only two outstanding problems: the increased political control over electoral administration and the state-controlled propaganda during electoral campaigns. The organs responsible for the electoral process (such as the National Electoral Commission (NEC)) and validating of the elections (the newly created chamber of the Supreme Court (SC)) have been refashioned, and they are now more political than judicial bodies. As regards any other aspects of electoral rights, procedures and institutional guarantees were in place in Poland – until the electoral reform of 2020 to the presidential election.

Campaigning in democracies should be free and fair. Media coverage should be unbiased – which presupposes independent media. In an illiberal democracy, this is only partially true. The electoral campaigns in both states instead featured state-controlled propaganda, media bias due to the monopolisation of the media, smear campaigns and intimidating rhetoric. On the other hand, the private media tend to be neutral or slightly in favour of the either opposition or the government, depending on the profile of their target audience. The Internet is free, but similar trends regarding political influence can be seen as in print media.

---

50 For a comparison, in 2019, Russia scored 0 and Turkey scored 5. https://freedomhouse.org/countries/freedom-world/scores, last accessed 31.05.2020.

51 These irregularities have been noted by the OSCE ODIHR (2018), https://www.osce.org/odihr/elections/hungary/385959?download=tru, last accessed 31.05.2020, the Freedom House (2019) and by other scholars; Schmidt, above n. 10, p. 82, T. Drinóczi, 'Dialogic interaction and legislation on parliamentary election in Hungary 2010-2014' (2016) *Osteuropa Recht* 4, 452–467.

52 Reporters Without Borders, 'Things do not improve', https://rsf.org/en/hungary, last accessed 31.05.2020.

53 Not surprisingly, the CC did not find this mechanism unconstitutional.

Hungarian illiberalisation is more advanced in this respect.[54] The electoral campaign in 2018 and 2019 did not provide fully informed possibilities of the choices available to voters.[55] Signs of deterioration, however, had also appeared as early as 2014, when political competition was more balanced, even though political institutions already worked in favour of the ruling party.[56] Such deficiencies appeared in the electoral campaign in Poland in 2019. The public television and radio stations were biased,[57] and, just like in Hungary, they reported more often on the activities of the ruling party connected to the campaign than those of the opposition.[58] When the public media broadcast information on the opposition, they portrayed them in a negative light. Nevertheless, studies show that Law and Justice (Prawo i Sprawiedliwość (PiS)) voters were aware of the media bias.[59] It was a general feature of the private media in both Hungary and Poland that they displayed a mostly balanced attitude. The private media assessed the opposition in a positive way and did not report only negatively about the ruling party.[60]

One common failing in both countries is that the discussions on electoral reforms have been non-inclusive. The illiberalisation here may be linked to the need to control – and to the collective feeling of belonging and the exclusion of 'others', including political opponents and those who are independent and not subordinated to the political leader – both of which legitimise inequality. The Hungarian political majority also considers itself to be entitled to decide who can 'better' and 'more easily' belong to the

---

54 In the Freedom House survey concerning media freedom as one of the civil liberties (i.e. not narrowed down to electoral campaign coverage), in 2019, Hungary scored 2 and Poland achieved 3 out of 4. In contrast, media freedom does not exist in Russia (it scored zero) and had almost vanished in Turkey (it scored 1). No changes were detected in Hungary and Turkey in 2020. When writing this chapter, the reports on Poland and Russia are not available (https://freedomhouse.org/countries/freedom-world/scores). On Hungary, see, e.g. the Conclusions of the Joint International Press Freedom Mission to Hungary from 03.12.2019, https://rsf.org/en/news/level-media-control-hungary-unprecedented-eu-member-state, last accessed 31.05.2020.

55 https://freedomhouse.org/country/hungary, last accessed 31.05.2020.

56 Schmidt, above n. 10, p. 78.

57 Report of Journalist's Society, http://towarzystwodziennikarskie.pl/wp-content/uploads/2019/10/2019RaportTDParFin5.pdf p. 1-2, last accessed 31.05.2020.

58 The situation has not changed during the presidential campaign of 2020. See the Human Rights Commissioner's rapport https://www.rpo.gov.pl/pl/content/koronawirus-i-kampania-wyborcza-w-mediach, last accessed 31.05.2020.

59 P. Sadura and S. Sierakowski, 'Political cynicism: The Case of Poland', http://politicalcritique.org/cee/poland/2019/poles-political-cynicism-research-report/, pp. 15–16, last accessed 31.05.2020.

60 Report of Journalist's Society, above n. 57, pp. 2–3.

nation of Hungary: that is, most certainly, those with whom they share common values and emotional links towards the Hungarian nation and state.

3.2.2. Procedure in Parliaments: Illiberal Practices

In liberal constitutionalism, parliaments are both the endpoint and the starting point of popular sovereignty. They are the representative body of the people, and they are created to adopt binding rules for everyone, including the people. It follows that not only should the electoral process be inclusive, fair and democratic, but the decision-making process, as well. In illiberal democracy, formalism and the rule of the majority prevail, and thus the legislative quality is defective.[61] There is also an extensive use of accelerated, symbolic,[62] personalised and omnibus legislation.

The application of a mere majority rule can be seen in the constitution-making process in Hungary[63] and in the legislative processes in both states.[64] In the parliamentary procedure, both the Polish and Hungarian oppositions have to face exclusion, that is, they are either outvoted or suppressed.[65] While the former can obviously happen in a parliamentary democracy, the latter must be viewed as a somewhat foreign concept therein. In illiberal decision-making, formal requirements meet the demands of legislative quality: there are laws on consultation, impact assessment and ex-post evaluation of laws, *inter alia*. The expression of conflicting views is thus ensured in both the drafting and the parliamentary processes. Consultations and the participation of NGOs are, however, defective; in spite of the freedom of information laws and

61 T. Drinóczi, 'Concept of quality in legislation – revisited: matter of perspective and a general overview', (2015) *Statute Law Review* 3, 211–27.

62 B. van Klink, 'Symbolic Legislation: An Essentially Political Concept' in B. van Klink, B. van Beers and L. Poort (eds), *Symbolic Legislation Theory and Developments in Biolaw*, Springer International Publishing, Switzerland 2016, pp. 22–23.

63 T. Drinóczi, 'Constitutional politics in contemporary Hungary' (2016) *Vienna Journal or International Constitutional Law* 1, 63–98.

64 T. Drinóczi, 'Legislation in Hungary', in H. Xanthaki and U. Karpen (eds), *Legislation in Europe-A Country to Country Guide*, Hart Publishing, Oxford forthcoming; V. Kazai, 'The Illiberal Challenge to the Rule of Law Principle: The Neglected Procedural Aspect (With Special Focus on Hungary)' 2019 ESIL Annual Research Forum, Göttingen (4–5 April 2019), available at https://ssrn.com/abstract=3513204, last accessed 31.05.2020.

65 Poland: Only 30 seconds are allowed for expressing opinions during the legislative process; amendments to bills proposed by the opposition are voted not individually but jointly as decided by parliamentary commission and Marshal of the Sejm.

the transparency principle, drafts are not provided on time, and reports sometimes do not exist at all. Thus, the substantial quality of laws is usually below standard. This is mostly explicable by the fact that the legislative process, even in 'normal times', is sometimes hectic and extremely speedy, and accelerated procedures are abused.[66] Given the lack of trust and cooperation, parliamentary deadlines for submission are not always met. Thus, parliamentary deliberation cannot truly develop into a discussion, and a discussion cannot result in a deliberated decision.[67] Formalism is present here, as well: the minimum condition to be met by a parliament is that all parties or members of parliament (MPs) must be given the floor. Other expressions of opinion of MPs (billboards, etc.), however, are not allowed, and MPs could even be fined by the leader of the plenary session – which has already been found to be contrary to the European Convention on Human Rights (ECHR).[68]

Personalised legislation is a tool that helps the leading political power to secure key positions for loyal friends. This practice could range from stacking previous judicial-type bodies with political nominees (NEC – Poland), to lifting certain preconditions for an elected position or appointment (mayor and judges – Hungary), to supporting particular foreign investments (via tax laws). This type of legislation usually pretends to have general applicability, when it has in fact been customised for a particular situation.

When the legislator uses symbolic legislation, it merely seeks to confirm or revitalise a particular value system.[69] We need only think of the Polish Demotion Act and the Hungarian Act on National Cohesion for remembrance of the Trianon Peace Treaty. The former Act also caused Poles to recall the martial law introduced by Jaruzelski, and it was intended to symbolically purify the armed forces – some 37 years *ex post facto* or even *post mortem* (in the case of Jaruzelski). The Defamation of the Polish Nation Act[70] could also demonstrate the power, that is, the ability,

---

66 Drinóczi, above n. 61.

67 A. Bień-Kacała, A. Tarnowska and W. Włoch, 'Representative Democracy in the Times of Populism: The Case of the Polish Parliament as a Delegated Power', within this volume.

68 *Karácsony and Others v. Hungary*, Judgment 17.05.2016 (app nrs 42461/13 and 44357/13). They protested in the session by holding up a banner stating 'Fidesz. You steal, you cheat, and you lie'.

69 A. Bień-Kacała, 'Illiberal democracy in action: Polish kind of symbolic legislation' (2019) *European Studies. The Review of European Law, Economics and Politics* 6, 268–78.

70 The Act of 26.01.2018 amending the Act on the Institute of National Remembrance – Commission for the Prosecution of Crimes against the Polish Nation (Dz. U. 2018 poz. 369). Act of 27 June 2018 (Dz.U. 2018 poz. 1277) repealed the controversial provision.

to respond to or resolve a conflict between two or more social groups or political parties – which could also have been resolved without legislative intervention.

The reason for the issues described above may be that the majority feel themselves to be the sole, real representatives of the 'the will of the people'. They use this, however, in a populist manner, through the exclusion of those who do not share their particular worldview or values. Consequently, and also following from their value orientation, people (have started to/continue to) believe in the omnipotence of political leaders and feel subordinate to them and their political partners. Therefore, they are reluctant to hold MPs politically accountable. They are not bothered by the lack of quality of legislation because, first, they are unaware of the need for this quality and its components, such as regulatory impact assessment and consultation and *ex post* evaluation of law, *inter alia*. They also believe that the increase in the volume of legislation and the increasingly fast processes are characteristics of a strong and capable state. The value orientation of society is enlarged and exploited by legislative and other political actions, and therefore the people either applaud the laws or simply do not care. This attitude supports the illiberal legislative trends.

4. RELATIVISATION OF HUMAN RIGHTS

4.1. STEPS TOWARDS ILLIBERALISATION AND COMMON CHALLENGES

Human rights regimes provide for a kind of constraint on public power. Illiberalisation in this field is a much slower process than the remodelling of the rule of law and democracy, and it has three stages. The first phase is when the positive obligation of the state to provide an adequate legislative and institutional framework for human rights protection has been considerably weakened. The second phase consists of the accompaniment of the first phase by a decrease in the importance of human rights. The regular, reluctant direct application of international and supranational human rights obligations by ordinary judges contributes to this process.[71]

[71] Z.S. Szabó, 'Többpólusú alapjogvédelmi rendszer a gyakorlatban – a kormánytisztviselők indokolás nélküli felmentésének tükrében [Multilevel protection of human rights in practice – in the light of dismissal of government officials without

Furthermore, in both Hungary and Poland, the inappropriate and 'decorative' use of the case law of the European Court of Human Rights (ECtHR),[72] the lack of human rights-related thinking during the judicial decision-making process and the failure of judges to perceive themselves as judges of human rights pose further challenges.[73] Nevertheless, just as happened in Western Europe, it needs to be noted that regular reliance on the case law of the ECtHR by ordinary judges does not happen overnight, but could take decades.[74] As for the Charter of Fundamental Rights of the EU,[75] scholars find that the common challenges Member States face relate to awareness, inadequate legislative responses, more restricted application and missed opportunities of reference.[76] Beyond these, European states commonly share other challenges, such as the most common violations of the ECHR[77] and the human rights challenges that have emerged in the past decades.[78] Concerns relating to external and internal threats have not

justification]', (2015) *Pro Futuro* 1, 138 (Hungarian judges do not invoke ECtHR case law, but apply domestic law).

72 P. Bárd and K. Bárd, 'The European Convention on Human Rights and the Hungarian Legal System', http://real.mtak.hu/65944/1/Bard_Bard_Comparative_study_on_the_implementation_of_the_ECHR_at_the_national_level_ENG_149_168_u.pdf, 152, last accessed 31.05.2020; E. Csatlós, 'The Application of International Law as an Instrument of Interpretation in Hungary – the Practice of the Constitutional Court and Ordinary Courts in a Comparative Approach', http://publicatio.bibl.u-szeged.hu/7049/8/2961433.pdf, p. 137, last accessed 31.05.2020.

73 A. Kúria, 'Az Alaptörvény követelményeinek érvényesülése a bírósági ítélkezésben' Joggyakorlat-elemző Csoportja2016.El.II.JGY.K.1., p. 194, https://kuria-birosag.hu/sites/default/files/joggyak/alaptorveny_osszefoglalo_velemeny.pdf, last accessed 31.05.2020; Szabó, above n. 71, p. 140.

74 Bárd and Bárd, above n. 72, p. 165.

75 O. Hamilak, M. Sulyok and L.N. Kiss, 'Measuring the "EU"-clidean distance between EU law and the Hungarian Constitutional Court – focusing on the position of the EU Charter of Fundamental Rights', (2019) *Czech Yearbook of Public & Private International Law* 10, 145–48; A. Kastelik-Smaza, https://karolinum.cz/data/clanek/6410/Iurid_64_4_0101.pdf 101, p. 112, last accessed 31.05.2020.

76 See, e.g. A. Kastelik-Smaza, https://karolinum.cz/data/clanek/6410/Iurid_64_4_0101.pdf, pp. 101, 112, last accessed 31.05.2020; M. Klamert, https://karolinum.cz/data/clanek/6409/Iurid_64_4_0089.pdf, pp. 89, 99, last accessed 31.05.2020; A. Kustra-Rogaska and O. Hamulak, 'Keeping distance: chapters from randomized (non)application of the European Court of Human Rights before the Polish Constitutional Tribunal' (2019) 9 *Baltic Journal of European Studies* 4, 90; R. Arnold and L. Cerny, https://karolinum.cz/data/clanek/6407/Iurid_64_4_0065.pdf, pp. 65, 77, last accessed 31.05.2020.

77 The length of the proceedings has been the main, or second-biggest, cause of concern in most of the more advanced signatory states to the ECHR: https://www.echr.coe.int/Documents/Stats_violation_1959_2018_ENG.pdf, last accessed 31.05.2020.

78 E.g. cases before the ECtHR concerning the UK and its regulatory responses to internal and external terrorism in the 1970–1980s and after 2000 may be recalled.

only not been diminished, but have been worsened in Europe by populist anti-immigration, anti-refugee and anti-Muslim agendas.[79]

Against this political and legal background, sensitivity to human rights violations and tolerance towards 'otherness' decreases in society, as well. After 'sensitising' society to the above-mentioned illiberal values and attitudes, or, rather, triggering these emotions in the population, the third phase is the emergence of a new 'theory' of human rights. It might have already set seed in Hungary, and, at the present time, it manifests itself in the concept that state organs can invoke their fundamental rights in the proceedings of the Constitutional Court (CC). It changes the main tenet of the theory of human rights, which holds that human rights are attributed to human beings, who need to be protected against powerholders, the most prominent among which is the state. Right now, in the midst of the COVID-19 crisis, however, the emergence of the new 'theory' of human rights does not seem to have much importance.

4.2. ILLIBERALISATION PROCESS

After the weakening of the legal infrastructure (phase one of the process), the illiberalisation of human rights attacks politically and economically sensitive rights. Here, a matter of degree again becomes a matter of kind.

Populist politicians not only want to seize political power, but – more characteristically in Hungary – intend to create their own oligarchs. These oligarchs are expected to be politically loyal and to financially support the political endeavours of their populist masters.[80] Illiberal populism invades the intellectual arena of society as well, because it hopes for more support from the people who do not question authority, but instead, obey it. Thus, beyond the obviously disrespected rights, such as the right to assembly, freedom of political speech (including media and civil society, too) and privacy rights vis-à-vis the police and secret service forces,[81]

---

79 See, e.g. Human Rights Watch World Report 2019 Events of 2018, https://www.hrw.org/world-report/2019, last accessed 31.05.2020, Fundamental Rights Report 2019, https://fra.europa.eu/en/publication/2019/fundamental-rights-report-2019, last accessed 31.05.2020.

80 B. Magyar, *Post-Communist Mafia State – The Case of Hungary*, CEU Press and Noran Libro, Budapest 2016.

81 See e.g. W. Sadurski, *Poland's Constitutional Breakdown*, Oxford University Press, Oxford 2019, pp. 150–59 and Ginsburg and Huq, above n. 34, pp. 68–72.

the illiberalisation of human rights also includes higher education, the freedom of academic research and certain economic freedoms, as well as the rights of minority groups and groups of vulnerable people, such as people of colour and women.

For instance, Hungary, along with some other states,[82] have not ratified the Istanbul Convention,[83] while Poland intends to withdraw from it.

Nevertheless, what has not been experienced in either Hungary or Poland, despite the undisputed backsliding in human rights protection, is the extent and gravity of human rights violations seen in Russia, Turkey and Singapore, according to Freedom House.[84] Anti-government demonstrations have not been banned and dispersed, the politics of the government can be criticised and ideologies which are usually disliked by illiberal regimes can be supported. The regime, which controls the public media, has not blocked online sites or banned messaging sites; journalist and editors have not been killed or imprisoned; and propaganda and political repression have not yet reached a level that would have a palpable chilling effect on the expression of opinions on political or even sensitive topics. Efforts to achieve such an effect are, however, all too clear and are related to the work of media outlets critical to the government, NGOs and political speech and academic freedom (e.g. the discrediting of academics[85] and the cases of Professor Sadurski,[86] the Central European University (CEU) and the Hungarian Academy of Sciences).[87] They also extend to opinions on historical events (Holocaust law) or jurisprudential matters, especially in Poland, where criminal proceedings against scholars

---

82 Bulgaria, Latvia, Lithuania and Ireland.

83 Istanbul Convention on preventing and combating violence against women and domestic violence.

84 In the category of 'global freedom', Russia, Turkey and Singapore scored 20 (not free), 32 (not free), 50 (partly free) out of 100 in 2019, respectively, while Hungary achieved 70 (the same as the previous year; partly free), and Poland 84 (free): https://freedomhouse.org/countries/freedom-world/scores, https://freedomhouse.org/country/hungary/freedom-world/2020, last accessed 31.05.2020.

85 K. Łakomiec, 'Academic freedom(s) in the drift towards authoritarianism (4/4) – Poland', 15.11.2019, https://ds.hypotheses.org/6391, last accessed 31.05.2020.

86 G. de Búrca, J. Morijn and M. Steinbeis, *Stand with Wojciech Sadurski: his freedom of expression is (y)ours, VerfBlog*, 18.11.2019, https://verfassungsblog.de/stand-with-wojciech-sadurski-his-freedom-of-expression-is-yours/, last accessed 31.05.2020.

87 https://www.france24.com/en/20190212-hungarian-researchers-rally-against-government-attack-science, last accessed 31.05.2020.

have been considered, but abandoned due to popular discontent. Beyond the aforementioned issues, Poland[88] has also experienced controversies about abortion,[89] LGBTIQ rights[90] and the right to a fair trial.[91]

4.3. NOT UNCOMMON STRUGGLES WITH INTERNATIONAL AND SUPRANATIONAL OBLIGATIONS

The Polish and Hungarian legal systems do not allow their constitutional courts or other judicial bodies to decide on the non-execution of the judgments of the ECtHR, which has been legally possible and applied practice in Russia since 2015.[92] As the Polish and Hungarian constitutions and statutes require the implementation and invocation of the ECHR and the case law of the ECtHR, there is no real intention to challenge the ECtHR as openly as the Russian legislative power and the Constitutional Court did. Nonetheless, Kosar and Petrov mention the possibility of challenging the ECtHR in the near future – stating that 'especially if the ECtHR increases the number of highly divisive judgments against these countries that would resonate with the ruling political forces and the public at large' – which, according to them, is already happening.[93] The Hungarian example is life imprisonment without the possibility of

---

88 See e.g. Sadurski, above n. 81, pp. 150–59, Łakomiec, above n. 85.

89 While Ireland has just adopted the constitutional amendment on abortion; Thirty-sixth *Amendment* of the Constitution of Ireland.

90 In Poland, during the electoral campaign of 2019, strong language was used against LGBT people; and the CT judgment of 26 June 2019 (K 16/17) allows discriminatory market actions against people who belong to the LGBT community. For Hungary, see L. Arato, 'Homophobia is on the rise in Hungary', 30.10.2019, https://www.europeandatajournalism.eu/eng/News/Data-news/Homophobia-is-on-the-rise-in-Hungary, last accessed 31.05.2020; https://index.hu/kulfold/eurologus/2019/09/24/egyre_tobb_magyart_zavarnak_a_melegek/, last accessed 31.05.2020.

91 See the reports in above n. 79, Helsinki Foundation for Human Rights Report – Poland threatening human rights protection, https://www.liberties.eu/en/news/hfhr-report-poland-threatening-human-rights-protections/18206, last accessed 31.05.2020; Sadurski, above n. 81, pp. 150–59.

92 See, e.g. Final Opinion on the Amendments to the Federal Constitutional Law on the Constitutional Court adopted by the Venice Commission at its 107th Plenary Session' (Venice, 10-11 June 2016), available at www.venice.coe.int/webforms/documents/?pdf=CDL-AD(2016)016-e, para 144, last accessed 31.05.2020.

93 D. Kosar and J. Petrov, 'The Architecture of the Strasbourg System of Human Rights: The Crucial Role of the Domestic Level and the Constitutional Courts in Particular' (2017) *ZaöRV* 77, 617, https://www.zaoerv.de/77_2017/77_2017_3_a_585_621.pdf, last accessed 31.05.2020.

parole, which found its way to the FL, just to prevent a constitutional review.[94] In another case (i.e. public use of the red star and its criminalisation), however, the state neither disregarded nor bypassed ECtHR decisions, even if there was an intention to do so.[95]

When it comes to the application of the EU Charter, both the Constitutional Tribunal (CT) and the CC, and ordinary courts[96] as well, for different reasons, are reserved and minimalist in their approach towards it. Their detachment considerably influences the willingness to invoke the Charter and the frequency of its invocation: the Hungarian CC developed the constitutional identity model in order to preserve the identity of Hungary and promote popular sovereignty.[97] In Poland, the Charter is perceived as a mere international law instrument,[98] which by itself calls for restraint in the courts. On the other hand, the Polish judiciary, including the CT[99] (save for its decision in April 2020), is aware of its role as a European court, which is demonstrated by its use of the preliminary reference procedure and willingness to start a dialogue with the Court of Justice of the European Union (CJEU), as can be seen in a case on judicial independence and retirement that affected Charter rights.[100] Nevertheless, in April 2020, the CT seemed to follow the footprints of the CC in its detachment exercise: it emphasised the sovereignty of Poland, which has to be defended against EU law and enforceable CJEU decisions.[101]

The CC engages in 'dialogue' differently.[102] It has never initiated any preliminary procedures, but now, in connection with the Lex CEU[103]

---

94 App nr 73593/10, judgment of 20.05.2014. For a more detailed summary, see Bárd and Bárd, n. 72, pp. 155–57.

95 See the Hungarian parliamentary resolution of 2012 on the disagreement on the judgment of the ECtHR in the *Fratonoló* case, app nr 29459, judgment of 03.11.2011. Csatlós, above n. 72; Bárd and Bárd, above n. 72, p. 163.

96 Ordinary courts have been using preliminary ruling procedures, but here, we focus more on their attitude towards the direct application of the charter and its method.

97 Drinóczi, above n. 18.

98 Kustra-Rogaska and Hamulak, above n. 76, p. 99.

99 The CJEU Judgment of 07.03.2017, C-390/15, ECLI:EU:C:2017:174. In this case, the issue did not relate to charter rights, but was the only preliminary ruling decision at the request of the CT.

100 Joined cases C-585/18, C-624/18 & C-625/18; cases C-558/18 and C-563/18. However, the decisions of the CT of 20 and 21 April 2020 (U 2/20 and Kpt 1/20) changed the attitude of the CT towards EU law.

101 Bień-Kacała, above n. 4.

102 E. Várnay, 'Az Alkotmánybíróság és az Európai Bíróság. Együttműködő alkotmánybíráskodás?' (2019) *Állam és Jogtudomány* 2, 66–70.

103 Case C-66/18 *Commission v. Hungary*. Advocate General says Hungary must treat foreign and national higher education institutions equally. https://curia.europa.eu/jcms/upload/docs/application/pdf/2020-03/cp200025en.pdf, last accessed 31.05.2020.

and the Act on foreign-funded NGOs,[104] it has suspended its procedure. It has argued that it needs to wait for the ruling of the CJEU on the already ongoing infringement procedures. However, it is simply disregarded the ongoing CJEU proceedings in the cases concerning the retirement of judges (2012)[105] and the quota case in 2016.[106] On the other hand, referring to the difference in the procedural stage of the ongoing infringement case as compared to the cases of CEU and foreign-funded NGOs, the CC did not suspend its proceedings, but upheld the constitutionality of the Stop Soros law.[107] Thus, at this stage, it is uncertain what actually motivated the CC to start this practice of suspension.

5. COVID-19

Without a doubt, extraordinary times require extraordinary measures. Unlike 'typical' pandemics and natural catastrophes, any fight against COVID-19 demands unusually fast, controlled, coordinated and expertise-driven governmental actions (with a broad range of necessary expertise) over the entire territory of a state. It is also unquestionable that the 'normal order' must be reinstated after the end of the emergency. More constitutional bedrock can be assumed to assist a smoother, quicker and constitutionally more relaxed return to normal once the crisis is over. This might be different in illiberal constitutionalism, due to its very nature of continuous deterioration from substantial constitutional democracy. The European Rule of Law can slow down this process and keep Hungary and Poland within the group of states embracing 'constitutionalism',[108] but in this crisis, the rule of law, democracy and human rights are as much endangered as human life and health. Nevertheless, since the crisis started in Europe, Hungary continues using and abusing its FL, while Poland keeps disregarding its binding 1997 Constitution and, at the same time, creating

---

104 Case C-78/18 *European Commission v. Hungary*. P. Bárd, 'The Hungarian "Lex NGO" before the CJEU: Calling an Abuse of State Power by its Name', *VerfBlog*, 27.01.2020, https://verfassungsblog.de/the-hungarian-lex-ngo-before-the-cjeu-calling-an-abuse-of-state-power-by-its-name/, last accessed 31.05.2020.

105 33/2012. (VII. 17.), C-286/12.

106 22/2016 (XII. 5.), C-643/15 and C-647.

107 The law criminalises activities in support of asylum applications and further restricts the right to request asylum.

108 Drinóczi and Bień-Kacała, above n. 37.

a new, invisible, illiberal constitution. The European Parliament (EP) is rightly of the view that the actions of the Hungarian and Polish governments are 'totally incompatible with European values'.[109]

5.1. VALUES DURING THE PANDEMIC

The newest insight delivered by Freedom House clearly shows the trajectory of value orientation and deterioration of values.[110] Both states moved away from their 2019 positions. The drop-off is associated more with the attitude towards the judiciary and local governments than with the pandemic; nevertheless, value research may lead to the assumption that the fear of losing one's health or life, caused by COVID-19, has supported political decision-makers,[111] at least at the beginning of the crisis. It seems that Orbán has taken advantage of this emotional response when playing the role of the sole saviour of the nation, as has Kaczyński when kept pushing for the presidential election to be held as soon as possible.

The pandemic is also a useful time to push the illiberal value system in the face of an EU that is reported to abandon states in their time of need. Therefore, almost no one in Poland protested against decisions of the CT that may push Poland away from the European community.[112] At the same time, the effort, which began to emerge in April 2020, to build the CEE identity based on an alternative vision of European values (i.e. opposed to what is being done by the liberal elite in the EU) has

---

109 The European Parliament resolution on EU coordinated action to combat the COVID-19 pandemic and its consequences, On protecting democracy, rule of law and fundamental rights, https://www.europarl.europa.eu/doceo/document/RC-9-2020-0143_EN.html, [36] last accessed 31.05.2020. Moreover, the EPP wants to kick out Fidesz, and the EP urges the Council to put back on its agenda the discussions and procedures related to the ongoing Article 7 procedures. *Ibid.*, in this note, [37]. https://www.politico.eu/article/jourova-brussels-concerned-by-polish-hungarian-coronavirus-measures/, last accessed 31.05.2020.

110 Csaky, above n. 48.

111 M. Babińska, J. Matera and M. Bilewicz, Zaraza ponad podziałami. Związki poglądów politycznych z postawami wobec epidemii SARS-CoV-2, Warszawa March 2020, http://cbu.psychologia.pl/uploads/f_bulska/Polityka_COVID.pdf?fbclid=IwAR1vVyh-DBQwhQYBMUDER-0H1wGRTW7pC_hTOI5q6qCXpd9thlTzVflX0OQ, last accessed 31.05.2020.

112 Bień-Kacała, above n. 4. 'Protests come from abroad rather than Poland', https://ruleoflaw.pl/call-to-jourova-and-reynders-act-to-save-democracy-in-poland/, last accessed 31.05.2020.

remained almost unnoticed.[113] In Poland, attitudes towards the EU are not very optimistic,[114] while in Hungary, the population is told that the EU does not provide financial help during the crisis. Again, collective narcissism creates a demand to appreciate particular values against common ones. In this context, if we consider the European law as a constraint within illiberal constitutionalism, we can see this departure from European values as diminishing democracy and human rights protection even faster during the emergency.

The illiberal agenda has a tendency to push both countries towards authoritarianism. In Poland, the most worrying issue has been the presidential election, while in Hungary, almost everything that is connected to the pandemic is suspicious. A few examples that are related to illiberal legality and illiberal democracy include: the questionable legitimacy of the declaration of emergency; and the unlimited authorisation of the Coronavirus Act, which did not and – given the supermajority of the government in Parliament – could not render effective parliamentary oversight. In both states, the nature of COVID-19 legislation provokes serious questions, as well as direct and deep violations of some constitutional rights.[115]

5.2. ILLIBERAL DEMOCRACY AND COVID-19

The illiberalisation of democracy, along with the appearance of illiberal legality, in its electoral component is palpable if we consider the Polish presidential election. The ruling majority in Poland seemed to be determined to organise the election for political gain. That is why they did not declare a constitutional emergency, but a statute-based one. From the beginning, the epidemic seemed to favour President Duda,[116] who could still move around in his capacity as president, while other candidates were

---

113 https://rmx.news/article/v4/poland-hungary-czechia-and-slovakia-need-a-joint-treaty-that-presents-alternative-vision-of-european-values?fbclid=IwAR1A7AhiboVppMkFMPZcGButa1gk6onRM61suynHwotGxj6t5y8MKBVqjgc, last accessed 31.05.2020.

114 https://oko.press/konsensus-polakow-w-sprawach-europejskich-sie-skonczyl-nowe-badania/, last accessed 31.05.2020.

115 More about Hungary, see T. Drinóczi, 'Hungarian Abuse of Constitutional Emergency Regimes – Also in the Light of the COVID-19 Crisis', *MTA WLP* 2020/13.

116 https://wyborcza.pl/7,75398,25820060,dlaczego-pis-prze-do-wyborow-podczas-epidemii-zamowilismy.html#a=190&c=8000, last accessed 31.05.2020.

more restricted. Moreover, Kaczyński announced that successful crisis management could not be undertaken without winning this election.[117] Therefore, first, one of the COVID-19 Acts introduced remote voting (by post) for those in quarantine and aged above 60.[118] This could be seen as a more democratic move. Later, the constitutional amendment to increase the mandate of the current president for two years was put forward by the Deputy Prime Minister (PM) Gowin, which contradicts democratic rule.[119] This plan, however, seems not to be realistic, as the ruling alliance has no constitutional majority. Another controversial bill[120] on the presidential election[121] was also submitted and passed on 7 May, three days before the assigned election day, which contradicts European and international standards.[122] That Act contains rules for all-postal voting, without adequate guarantees. Its provisions on the right to vote of those living abroad are vague, as they can easily be excluded from voting. Additionally, there are serious concerns about the secrecy of voting. The most worrying issue, however, is that on 10 May, the vote was not held. On 6 May, the ruling camp decided not to proceed with the election without a formal legal ground. This move was a result of political agreement by Kaczyński and his ally Gowin. All of these irregularities and manipulations could have extended the boundaries of illiberal democracy to the stage where a change to the ruling majority would have been impossible. However, there seems to be a need to legalise and legitimise decisions on this election, that is, comply with illiberal legality, instead of using tools from the toolbox of authoritarianism. Therefore, returning to the normal illiberal practice, the ruling alliance seems to have created an invisible constitutional rule that allows for the moving of the election day to summer. Unsurprisingly, the CT, the NEC and newly captured SC[123] are ready to serve this purpose.

---

117 https://www.rmf24.pl/tylko-w-rmf24/rozmowa/news-jaroslaw-kaczynski-w-rmf-fm-wybory-10-maja-powinny-sie-odbyc,nId,4393207, last accessed 31.05.2020.

118 The COVID-19 Amendment Act of 31.03.2020.

119 https://www.sejm.gov.pl/Sejm9.nsf/PrzebiegProc.xsp?id=DED36818BF3F27E0C125854B0031EFCD, last accessed 31.05.2020.

120 E.g. http://www.hfhr.pl/en/position-of-the-helsinki-foundation-for-human-rights/, last accessed 31.05.2020.

121 https://ruleoflaw.pl/pis-pushing-elections-during-epidemic-special-law-on-postal-vote-debated-in-sejm/, last accessed 31.05.2020.

122 Opinion Nr ELE-POL/373/2020 OSCE ODIHR, https://www.osce.org/odihr/elections/poland/450856?download=true, last accessed 31.05.2020.

123 The term of office of the first president of the Supreme Court expired on 30 April, and the new person was appointed by the Polish President on 25 May.

In Hungary, in the first days of the outbreak, the government declared a constitutional emergency, called a 'state of danger', and started to issue emergency decrees affecting shops, borders, courts, schools and universities.[124] It asked for and received an unconstitutional unlimited authorisation in the Coronavirus Act 2020,[125] based on which it started to govern by emergency decrees without any meaningful parliamentary oversight by a completely functioning parliament. All of these actions fit into the logic of illiberal constitutionalism,[126] the role model for which is the Coronavirus Act. The Act satisfies the government's understanding of the Rule of Law (i.e. illiberal legality): it partially implements the partisan constitution, but does not comply with the rule on temporal parliamentary supervision of governmental emergency measures. Observing this rule would have just involved the pretence of oversight, as the government has a supermajority in parliament, but would have shown its willingness to cooperate with the opposition, which does not fit in with the idea of an autocratic populist leader. The elimination of oversight has made democratic control impossible during this crisis, which is another example of how an illiberal democracy is conceptualised in Hungary.[127]

The Hungarian Parliament, however, still delivered regular legislative acts, as the emergency 'legislation' was done through governmental decree. As the government has a supermajority in parliament, ordinary legislation – mainly omnibus laws – and regular decrees were used to further concentrate power (the Coronavirus Act), pursue conservative policies (e.g. the refusal of legal recognition of transgender people; rejection of the Istanbul Convention in a political declaration), please oligarchs (e.g. providing real estate free of charge to foundations run by persons loyal to the government, 'outsourcing' higher education) and reform entire sectors (e.g. withdrawing the status of civil servants from individuals who are employed in the cultural sector).[128] Furthermore, the content of emergency decrees were transformed into statutes.[129] Thus, there seemed

---

124 Drinóczi, above n. 115.

125 https://hungarianspectrum.org/2020/03/21/translation-of-draft-law-on-protecting-against-the-coronavirus/, last accessed 31.05.2020.

126 https://verfassungsblog.de/illiberal-constitutionalism-at-work/, last accessed 31.05.2020.

127 Drinóczi, above n. 115.

128 The bills on these issues have been submitted to Parliament. The Coronavirus Act has already been adopted.

129 See some economy-related measures; bills submitted on 21 and 28 April: https://www.parlament.hu/irom41/10527/10527.pdf, https://www.parlament.hu/irom41/10314/10314.pdf, https://www.parlament.hu/irom41/10217/10217.pdf, https://www.parlament.hu/irom41/10315/10315.pdf, last accessed 31.05.2020.

to be no need to use the state of emergency to grab more power and further hollow out the notion of democracy relating to parliamentary processes.

Legislative quality and practice have remained the same in both countries.[130] There is no substantial consultation – no actual involvement – but there is significant omnibus legislation. The Polish legal response to the pandemic is driven by massive and chaotic legislation. There are many COVID-19 Acts, some of which have amended more than 50 other statutes. What is distinctive is the substantive discussion at the Senat stage of the legislative procedure. This could be seen as a factor pushing Poland away from an authoritarian regime, a little bit up the imaginary slide towards liberal constitutionalism. However, this is a misleading assumption, as the Senate can be, and in fact is, outvoted by the PiS-led Sejm.

5.3. HUMAN RIGHTS DURING THE PANDEMIC

The legislation passed during the pandemic gives rise to many concerns about respect for human rights. Some of these measures could turn out to be just mere consequential effects of the pandemic, as many other countries have been struggling with similar issues, such as the use of surveillance apps. In Poland, this is mandatory for those in quarantine,[131] but the issue here is, most probably due to the accelerated and hasty legislation, that both criminal and administrative sanctions may be applied to the same misconduct. The legal background might be better but no less concerning in Hungary. A decree issued in May 2020 requires the consent of the patient for the use of such an app, and such consent may be gained by pressuring the data subject: in the event of no consent, more intensive physical monitoring by the police is expected, and breaching the quarantine rules would be punishable with a bigger fine. While the use of such an app could be necessary, the 'necessity' to exert pressure to gain consent is questionable, especially in the light of another emergency decree on the suspension of the rights of the data subject and making access to public information impossible in a timely manner.[132] As a result, patients

---

130 For more on this, see: Drinóczi and A. Bień-Kacała, above n. 4.

131 https://www.politico.eu/article/poland-coronavirus-app-offers-playbook-for-other-governments/, last accessed 31.05.2020.

132 T. Drinóczi, 'Hungarian Democratic Backsliding in light of the recent emergency coronavirus legislation' Public Jurist, Hong Kong University Political Science Magazine, June 2020, http://www.hkuglc.org/government-and-laws-committee-hku-public-jurist; https://drive.google.com/file/d/1ybMnONflLzu_Zw2AT9nacy4ryNwlLz9d/view, last accessed 31.05.2020.

may be pressurised to give consent to the processing of their data while in quarantine, but they are given no right to follow up on that data, until the pandemic is over.

Changed circumstances caused by the pandemic and social distancing have also needed to be legalised: Hungary has used emergency decrees (issued during the constitutional emergency) and Poland has continued applying its ordinary measures. The rules require, for instance, that schools and universities undertake digital teaching, and that deadlines do not expire. In Hungary, after a break, courts started to work remotely, while in Poland, court proceedings are delayed.[133] In Hungary, no personal presence was required in court proceedings; in criminal cases, it could be requested. Ministerial letters demand the emptying of Hungarian hospital beds for future COVID-19 patients. Some of these measures may suffer from substantial unconstitutionality – regardless of the intention to provide an adequate legal background in the changed circumstances. They may raise doubts concerning the appropriateness of the legal source, proportionality, the right to due process, the rights of the child (e.g. the right to education) and the right to health.[134]

The most worrying issue in Poland, which exemplifies the opportunistic misuse of law, is the limitation on the right to assembly by governmental regulations. According to the Polish Constitution, the right to assembly cannot be limited, even during a constitutional 'state of natural disaster', beyond ordinary necessity and proportionality. This means that general rules should apply and no limitation can infringe the core of this right, even in a constitutional emergency, not to mention the statute-based emergency that applies in Poland. However, the Polish authorities have banned any kind of assembly. This unconstitutionally violates the essence of this right, which is an even more serious human right violation at this moment, as this ban has been imposed during an electoral campaign.

---

133 https://www.hfhr.pl/wp-content/uploads/2020/04/Access-to-court-in-times-of-a-pandemic.pdf, last accessed 31.05.2020.

134 Another issue is that the Hungarian Coronavirus Act amended the Criminal Code by creating a new crime of spreading 'false information' during an emergency. This ambiguously formulated rule, reportedly, was enacted against 'fake news', but it could have a chilling effect on journalism and academia. If the latter happens, this act and its practice will also exemplify the relativisation of human rights.

6. CONCLUSION

In this chapter, we have shown how historical trajectories, value orientation and emotional profiles facilitated the creation and consolidation of illiberal constitutionalism. We have also made a case for how illiberal democracy and human rights relativisation can be conceptualised in illiberal constitutionalism. We have presented some examples which, as it has turned out, have *led* Hungary and Poland closer to the antechamber of authoritarianism, but which did not *push* them there. We have concluded that the forces that emotionally impel Hungary and Poland increasingly in the direction of authoritarianism – through the continuous illiberal remodelling exercise – were, until and during 2020, counterbalanced by the weak and tacitly existing powers of containment of the very same illiberal constitutionalism. This constraint, however, seems to be reducing even faster during the pandemic-induced emergency, or simply by the passing of time. The value orientation and the people's fear of the present disease do not seem to demand any legal constraint.

PART VI

THE SPREAD OF POPULISM AND ILLIBERAL DEMOCRACY IN EUROPE

LAW, REVOLUTION AND POPULISM IN ITALY

The Path from Constitutional Resentment to Constitutional Renaissance

Monica BONINI*

1. IN SEARCH OF THE ROOTS OF ITALIAN POPULISM

Where does Italian populism come from?[1] In Europe, populism is marked by a variety of forms.[2] For Italian constitutional scholars, too, it represents

---

* The author wishes to thank professor Maria Paola Viviani Schlein for helpful remarks concerning the thesis of the present chapter, and professor Dario Scarpa for the review of the work.

1 On the rise and the transformation of the concept of populism, I. DIAMANTI, 'Alla periferia della crisi. Il populismo e il disagio della democrazia rappresentativa' (2018) 1 *Stato e mercato* 117–25, 117–119.

2 Literature on the issue is abundant: see J.W. MÜLLER, *Che cos'è il populismo?* Università Bocconi Ed., Milano 2017; M. TUSHNET, 'Varieties of Populism' (2019) 20 *German Law Journal*, 382–89; P. BLOKKER, B. BUGARIC and G. HALMAI, 'Introduction: Populist Constitutionalism: Varieties, Complexities, and Contradictions' (2019) 20 *German Law Journal*, 291–95; P. BLOKKER, 'Varieties of Populist Constitutionalism: The Transnational Dimension' (2019) 20 *German Law Journal* 332–50.

a significant challenge.[3] This challenge is grounded on one theoretical question: can domestic populism develop into an anti-constitutional phenomenon? The answer may be simple if legal scholars limit their analysis to countries under Article 7 of the European Union Treaty's procedure.[4] The answer is difficult if Italian scholars address it through the perspective of domestic constitutional law and history.

In Italy, existing populism's forms may be defined by adopting Cesare Pinelli's words. These forms of populism all embody 'an ideology claiming that "the political class" has lost contact with the "real will of the people", and promising to give it voice through new leaders, movements, or parties'.[5] Furthermore, Italian populism seems to be double-faced. Michela Manetti, recalling Benjamin Arditi's position, explains that the phenomenon is slippery. Depending on the context, it may express democracy's malaise or threat. In the first case, democracy may react by finding again its original calling. In the second case, democracy risks being defeated.[6] This chapter tries to explain that in Italy, populism was born as democracy's malaise,[7] and today risks developing into a threat.

Italy's experience shows that the adoption of a democratic constitution does not necessarily protect from authoritarian temptations.[8] Even a constitutional order based on human dignity, the protection of

---

3 Y. Mény, *Populismo e democrazia*, Il Mulino, Bologna 2004.

4 *Ex multis*, J.W. Müller, 'Should the EU Protect Democracy and the Rule of Law inside Member States?' (2015) 21(2) *European Law Journal* 141–60; R.D. Kelemen, 'Europe's Other Democratic Deficit: National Authoritarianism in Europe's Democratic Union' (2017) 52 *Government and Opposition* 2, 211–38.

5 C. Pinelli, 'The Populist Challenge to Constitutional Democracy' (2011) 7 *European Constitutional Law Review* 5–16, 5: even if the author does not analyse Italian populism, his definition mirrors the domestic experience.

6 M. Manetti, 'Costituzione, partecipazione democratica, populismo' (2018) 3 *Rivista AIC* <https://www.rivistaaic.it/it/rivista/ultimi-contributi-pubblicati/michela-manetti/costituzione-partecipazione-democratica-populismo> last accessed 02.04.2020, 376–401, 382. See then, as quoted by M. Manetti and B. Arditi, *Politics on the Edges of Liberalism*, Edinburgh University Press Ltd., Edinburgh 2007, p. 62.

7 Based on a serious drift: party failings changed into popular antipolitical culture (infra, subsection 2.1).

8 The paper delves not into judicial events involving extreme far-right Italian movements such as 'Ordine Nuovo' (1973) 'Avanguardia nazionale' (1976) and 'Fronte nazionale' (1999/2000): regarding these same events see B. Pezzini, 'Attualità della Resistenza: la matrice antifascista della Costituzione repubblicana' in B. Pezzini and S. Rossi (eds), *I giuristi e la Resistenza. Una biografia intellettuale del Paese*, Franco Angeli, Milano 2016, pp. 230–31, fn. 32.

fundamental rights and the rule of law[9] may suffer from a dangerous illness. The Constituent Assembly clearly designed the idea of democracy on which the Italian Constitution (ItC) is grounded. Democracy is anchored in a representative system, limiting not only every branch of government, but also the people.[10] As things are, this idea seems to be forgotten. Why?

Today, Italian populism is marked by several aspects. In short, populist rhetoric appeals to direct democracy and the personalisation of politics. It is anchored to the belief of the existence of one people, to be protected from all outsiders – that is, 'enemies' not belonging to its conceptual and territorial boundaries. In Italy, at least two parties can be defined as populist: 'Lega-Salvini Premier' and 'Movimento 5 Stelle-M5S'. Others are more difficult to categorise. 'Forza Italia' adopted at the time of its foundation a populist communication pattern[11] (infra, section 2.1). 'Fratelli d'Italia' is a far-right party rooted in the former neo-fascist party. Nonetheless, it claims to be 'on the people's side'. In this strict sense, it may be called 'populist'.[12]

These political actors are characterised by differences and commonalities (the chapter delves later into peculiar aspects marking 'Forza Italia'). In brief, 'Lega Nord-Salvini Premier' and 'Fratelli d'Italia' are grounded in a strong individual leadership,[13] 'M5S' is based in a democracy that is increasingly going virtual.[14] Despite their differences, all three parties developed anti-European Union (EU) and anti-establishment

9 On fundamental constitutional principles, see C. Mortati et al., 'Principi fondamentali, artt. 1-12', in G. Branca and A. Pizzorusso (eds), *Commentario della Costituzione*, N. Zanichelli-Soc. Ed. del Foro italiano, Bologna-Roma 1975.

10 S.V. Regasto, *La forma di governo parlamentare fra innovazione e tradizione*, Giuffré, Milano 2008; Manetti, above n. 6, 397.

11 Diamanti, above n. 1, p. 122.

12 *Ibid.*, p. 118 for Marine Le Pen's identical position.

13 Both allied with other European populist and extremist movements: S. Fabbrini, 'Quella santa alleanza fra populismo e nazionalismo' (2017) 22 January, *Il Sole 24 Ore* <https://www.ilsole24ore.com/art/quella-santa-alleanza-populismo-e-nazionalismo-AEBsNCF?refresh_ce=1> last accessed 08.05.2020. On Salvini's personalisation of the former party 'Lega Nord' see G. Di Cosimo, 'Personale e digitale: le metamorfosi del partito' (2019) *Forum di Quaderni costituzionali* <http://www.forumcostituzionale.it/wordpress/?p=11849> last accessed 08.05.2020. On the 'television-based political process' 'focused on political leaders at the expense of political parties', S. Fabbrini, 'When Media and Politics Overlap: Interferences from the Italian Case' (2011) 46 *Government and Opposition* 3, 345–64, 346–50.

14 *Ex multis*, Di Cosimo, above n. 13; see then F. Pallante, *Contro la democrazia diretta*, Einaudi, Torino 2020, p. 53, where the author observes that, in the end, such sort of democracy deeply limits voters.

rhetoric. When compared to other populist models, these parties exemplify opposing characteristics. As the left-oriented models, they claim the right to protect citizens, domestic workers and entrepreneurs from global or EU markets. On the other hand, the right-oriented models (more 'Lega-Salvini Premier' than 'M5S') claim to protect national and religious/Catholic values from immigrants and foreigners.[15] Even if their rhetoric seems to respect constitutional rules, it essentially targets fundamental constitutional principles and values (infra, sections 3 and 4).[16] Furthermore, the roots and the evolution of their original calling (infra, section 2.1) may today put the democratic state at risk.[17]

A brief historical reconstruction helps understanding the origins of the existing tension between Italian populists and constitutional democracy.[18] Before delving into this analysis, two preliminary remarks are necessary. First, the chapter is grounded on Cesare Pinelli's definition of populism (supra) – the Italian experience perfectly mirrors it. Second, the work does not take a neutral stand. This chapter does not analyse the wide concept of populism, but focuses on one premise. Italian constitutional democracy is anchored in social cohesion and solidarity.[19] Moreover, this same design is based on a carefully balanced architecture of people's and institution's limits, as well as EU membership. With the aim of understanding whether today's domestic populists may put at risk such fundamental political choices, this chapter reflects on these same parties' political roots. Their roots, more so than their actual claims, clearly explain why they may erode constitutional democracy from within. The following section delves into the events which influenced this view.

---

15 Here, the paper partially differs from the position expressed by Manetti, above n. 6, 376.

16 T. Fournier, 'From Rhetoric to Action – a Constitutional Analysis of Populism' (2018) 08 *EUI Working Papers*, 1–18, pp. 2–4.

17 Manetti, above n. 6, 382, analyses this aim, referring to it in general to populist movements.

18 For one of the most interesting reconstructions of Italy's political life until the 1990s, see N. Bobbio, *Ideological Profile of Twentieth-Century Italy*, Princeton University Press, Princeton 2014.

19 F. Giuffré, *La solidarietà nell'ordinamento costituzionale*, Giuffré, Milano 2002; A. Schillaci, 'Dalla crisi economica alla crisi democratica: la sfida populista alla solidarietà e l'identità europea' (2020) 4 May 2020, *Federalismi.it* 15–39, 37, https://www.federalismi.it/nv14/articolo-documento.cfm?Artid=42232&content=Dalla%2Bcrisi%2Beconomica%2Balla%2Bcrisi%2Bdemocratica%3A%2Bla%2Bsfida%2Bpopulista%2Balla%2Bsolidariet%C3%A0%2Be%2Bl%E2%80%99identit%C3%A0%2Beuropea&content_author=%3Cb%3EAngelo%2BSchillaci%3C%2Fb%3E, last accessed 05.05.2020.

2. AFTER WORLD WAR II: THE SOWING OF A DANGEROUS SEED

'If populism aims only to reconcile people and political leaders, movements, and parties', why should it represent 'a threat for Italian constitutional democracy?'[20] As this chapter suggests, Italian populism fails to live up its own democratic argument by confusing law – that is, constitutional order – and revolution (i.e. the destruction of that same constitutional order). From this perspective, two historic periods and one specific instrument marked its path to success.

In 1946, a neo-fascist party was founded, in whose ideology the existing far-right party 'Fratelli d'Italia' has its roots. In the 1990s, the defeat of the mainstream parties[21] had severe consequences for the relationship between people and representatives. In those years, the former 'Lega Nord' rose in northern Italy. Since then, the increasing role of communication media also had a significant impact on such a relationship. Both television – at the time of the foundation of 'Forza Italia'[22] (Silvio Berlusconi's party)[23] – and social media, today, helped to develop a peculiar ostracism targeting constitutional democracy.[24]

2.1. FROM POST-WAR FASCISM TO THE DEFEAT OF MAINSTREAM PARTIES: THE PATH OF ITALIAN POPULISM

On the country, fascist ideology survived World War II. Still today, ItC's XII transitional and final provision[25] only forbids the organising,

---

20 The question has been put by Pinelli, above n. 5, p. 5. See also A. Floridia, 'Il 'caso' italiano: il circuito perverso del populismo' (2013) 78 *Ábaco*, 67–72.

21 Due to an anticorruption judicial investigation, infra, subsection 2.1.

22 On the sad polemic regarding the 'partito persona' see N. Ajello, Norberto Bobbio e il Partito persona' 09.04.2008 *La Repubblica* <https://ricerca.repubblica.it/repubblica/archivio/repubblica/2008/04/09/norberto-bobbio-il-partito-persona.html> last accessed 09.05.2020.

23 Manetti, above n. 6, 377 defines the recalled attitude as a communication style. Furthermore, G. Di Cosimo explains that the Berlusconi model has been also adopted by former left-oriented politicians such as Matteo Renzi: Di Cosimo, above n. 13, p. 1.

24 On the clash with the ItC of decisions taken by leaders who claim a direct relationship with people, see F. Pizzolato, *I sentieri costituzionali della democrazia*, Carocci editore, Roma 2019, pp. 18–26, esp. p. 22.

25 The Italian Constitution counts 139 articles and 13 transitional and final dispositions: for an in-depth study of this issue see A. Pizzorusso et al., 'Disposizioni

under any form whatsoever, of the dissolved Fascist Party.[26] Therefore, a post-war, far-right party became part of the Italian political scene.[27] Even if rooted in the same beliefs of the dissolved Fascist Party,[28] it was at least formally different from the latter. Therefore, it was not strictly unconstitutional. A political belief marked such a development. Including post-war fascists in the political and parliamentary dialogue would oblige them to act in full sight and according to the new constitutional rules. Excluding them could have potentially disruptive consequences.[29] After all the events the domestic political system went through, it seems that this choice has had unpredictable implications.

Until the crisis of the 1990s, Italian politics was marked by the so-called 'conventio ad excludendum'.[30] Far-left or far-right parties were kept out of government.[31] It was only after the judicial anti-corruption investigation of the early 1990s that the 'conventio ad excludendum' changed into a different phenomenon: after Duncan McDonnell, the 'coercitio ad includendum'.[32] 'As part of a systemic change', almost 'all parties gained coalition potential and most have held governmental relevance'.[33] Why? The answer is rooted in ancient times.

---

transitorie e finali, 1-18. Leggi costituzionali e di revisione costituzionale (1948–1993)', in G. Branca and A. Pizzorusso (eds), *Commentario della Costituzione*, N. Zanichelli-Soc. Ed. del Foro italiano, Bologna-Roma 1995, and S. Vinciguerra, 'Fascismo (sanzioni)' *Enciclopedia del Diritto*, Giuffrè, Milano 1967, ad vocem.

26 G.E. Vigevani, 'Origine e attualità del dibattito sulla XII disposizione finale della Costituzione: i limiti della tutela della democrazia' (2019) 1 *Media Laws* <http://www.medialaws.eu/rivista/origine-e-attualita-del-dibattito-sulla-xii-disposizione-finale-della-costituzione-i-limiti-della-tutela-della-democrazia/> 1-18 last accessed 08.05.2020.

27 Even if, as G.E. Vigevani explains, the XII disposition aimed exactly to exclude the Fascist party from 'the concept of Italian people': Vigevani, above n. 26, pp. 18–26, p. 29.

28 N. Bobbio, 'The ideology of Fascism' in Bobbio , above n. 18, pp. 122–132.

29 F. Ferraresi, *Threats to Democracy. The Radical Right in Italy after the War*, Princeton University Press, Princeton 2012.

30 This thesis has been developed by the legal scholar and politician Leopoldo Elia: see L. Elia, 'La peculiarietà e l'evoluzione del sistema italiano riguardo ai partiti politici', in Idem, *Costituzione, partiti, istituzioni*, Il Mulino, Bologna 2009, pp. 257–74.

31 D. Albertazzi, D. McDonnell and J.L. Newell, 'Di lotta e di governo: The Lega Nord and Rifondazione Comunista in Office' (2011) 17(4) *Party Politics* 471–87, 472.

32 See, as quoted by Albertazzi et al., above n. 31, p. 472: D. McDonnell, 'Eviction Canceled: The 2006 Local Elections', in J.L. Briquet and A. Mastropaolo (eds), *Italian Politics: the Centre-left Poisoned Victory*, Berghahn, New York 2007, pp. 81–98, 88.

33 Albertazzi et al., above n. 31, p. 472, rely on Sartori's position: G. Sartori, *Parties and Party System: A Framework Analysis*, ECPR Press, Colchester 2005.

The 'Movimento Sociale Italiano' (MSI) was founded in 1946. As James L. Newell observes, it has been 'a vehicle for perpetuating the Fascist political tradition', oscillating 'between attempts to overcome its isolation by de-emphasising its antisystem ambitions and phases of re-radicalisation'.[34] Anna Cento Bull explains that 'groups to the right of the party' did want to revitalise 'the anti-democratic fascist tradition'.[35] Worst, some of them have been implicated in the neo-fascist 'Strategy of Tension'. In Italy, 'since the late 1960s political violence escalated. It included bomb attacks against civilians, starting with a massacre in Milan, on 12 December 1969, and culminating with another one in Bologna, on 2 August 1980'. The aim of such a brutal 'strategy' was to 'create an atmosphere of subversion and fear' in the country 'to promote a turn to an authoritarian type of government'.[36]

In brief, the history of the party is a story of slow integration in the political system. Other anti-establishment movements have been spawned by 'MSI' or judicially banned.[37] In the 1990s, 'MSI' succeeded in acquiring 'the status of acceptable coalition partner'.[38] As a matter of fact, its new leader[39] dimmed the founding neo-fascist ideology of the party. He transformed the neo-fascist ideology into an (apparently) European right-oriented one. This evolution was the result of Italy's 1992 crisis, which changed 'the terms of political competition'.[40] Ultimately, this change worked in favour of a centre-right-oriented coalition including former 'MSI' (known, since 1992, as 'Alleanza nazionale').

In the 1990s, a severe scandal made citizens loose trust in traditional parties. A nationwide judicial investigation uncovered a corruption system involving politicians and industry leaders.[41] As a consequence, many of

---

34 On events related to the Fascist party 'Fiamma Tricolore' see J.L. Newell, 'Italy: The Extreme Right Comes in from the Cold' (2000) 53 *Parliamentary Affairs*, 469–85, p. 469. See also above, n. 8.

35 A. Cento Dull, *Italian Neofascism The Strategy of Tension and the Politics of Nonreconciliation*, Berghahn Books, New York and Oxford 2012, p. 13 and pp. 20–43.

36 *Ibid.*, p. 19 for all quotations. See again above, n. 8.

37 Pezzini, above n. 8, pp. 230–31 (esp. footnote 32).

38 Newell, above n. 34, pp. 469 and 470.

39 By the time, Gianfranco Fini.

40 Newell, above n. 34, pp. 469–470.

41 In the 1990s, a renowned judicial investigation into political corruption led to the demise of the so-called 'First Republic': for related constitutional and political aspects, see G. Silvestri, 'La Commissione di inchiesta su Tangentopoli. Considerazioni ingenue di un costituzionalista' (2000) 1 *Quaderni costituzionali*, 121–122, and G. Pasquino, 'La transizione politica italiana. Da Tangentopoli ad oggi' (2015) 20 *Journal of Modern Italian Studies* 1, 155–57.

the existing parties disappeared from the political scene.[42] Disappointed by mainstream parties, citizens trusted public prosecutors more than their representatives. This experience indirectly damaged an important equilibrium and sowed a dangerous seed. From that time onwards, citizens confused party failings[43] and anti-political culture.[44] In the space of a few years, anti-political culture affected the equilibrium of popular choice, political representation and the essence of contemporary democracy – in Italy, of constitutional democracy.

Without any formal constitutional change, the 1990s events deeply influenced the political and social system rooted in anti-fascism. The so-called 'Second Republic' gave 'anti-Fascism a less central place'.[45] As obvious as it may sound, corruption affecting the representative system does not mean that the system itself is wrong – only that politicians misbehaved. Moreover, combating corruption never aimed to crush fundamental choices – as anti-fascism or parliamentary forms of government are.[46] Nonetheless, in the 1990s, a common feeling emerged. People believed that the Italian representative system was not simply corrupt. Giving only 'indirectly a chance of popular intervention in public affairs',[47] it seemed inadequate 'for ensuring a genuine democracy'.[48] Therefore, 'representation was incompatible with liberty', since it delegated 'the political will of the people, to the prejudice of genuine self-government and autonomy'.[49] This feeling gave rise to at least three consequences.

---

42 Even if former parties disappeared, a considerable part of its MPs entered new ones.

43 For this issue, see Pizzolato, above n. 24, pp. 18–26 and 35.

44 Schillaci, above n. 19, pp. 15-39, esp. p. 23, and Mény, above n. 3.

45 Newell, above n. 34, p. 478.

46 Regarding the studies on the form of government by Leopoldo Elia, see M. Olivetti, 'Partiti e regime parlamentare in Italia nella riflessione di Leopoldo Elia' in G. D'Andrea, F. Marini, S. Mattarella, M. Olivetti, F. Pizzetti, P. Ridola and A. Silvestrini (eds), *Leopoldo Elia. Costituzionalista e uomo politico rigoroso e innovatore*, Diabasis, Reggio Emilia 2009, pp. 27–40. On the Italian form of government, whose pillars are parliamentarism and rule of law, *ex multis*, P. Pasquino, 'Dalla democrazia della paura alla democrazia dell'alternanza' (2015) 3 *Quaderni costituzionali*, 731–34, p. 732.

47 Pinelli, above n. 5, p. 9.

48 *Ibid.*

49 *Ibid.*

First, after the April 1993 referendum, a new electoral system[50] was created. It had several consequences for voters and parties.[51] As James L. Newell observes, the expectation of the referendum's promoters was to 'move towards a predominantly single-member, single-plurality system'. Such a system would create 'two strong coalitions, one of the left the other of the right, each capable of governing alone'. Most importantly, only such an alternative policy[52] would 'reduce clientelism and corruption in the political system'.[53] Unfortunately, the ultimate result was different. Barely one year later, the tycoon Silvio Berlusconi rode this wave to power.[54] Sergio Fabbrini explains that Berlusconi 'entered politics through the media in order to save and expand his economic business interests and power'.[55] As Mauro Calise recalls, for the first time in Italian politics a party leader adopted populist rhetoric.[56] Furthermore, Berlusconi allied his party, 'Forza Italia', with 'Alleanza nazionale' and 'Lega Lombarda' – but only to gain votes in southern and northern Italy, respectively.

Ultimately, the consequences of his political actions were disruptive for the whole system. His political communication undermined 'the traditional class- or culture-based identities of sections of society' and personalised Italian politics'.[57] Moreover, by allying his party with 'Alleanza nazionale', Berlusconi started the process which resulted in the 'coercitio ad includendum'. Therefore, the first result of the so-called 'Second Republic' consisted of giving anti-fascism a less central place in politics.[58]

---

50 For a critical analysis of the creation of that electoral law, see G.U. Rescigno, *Corso di diritto pubblico*, Zanichelli, Bologna 1994, p. 265, and M.J. Bull and J.L. Newell, 'Still the Anomalous Democracy? Politics and Institutions in Italy' (2009) 44 *Government and Opposition* 1, 42–67, esp. fn. 5.

51 G. Pasquino, 'Der unerwartete Machtwechsel. Die italienischen Wahlen vom März 1994 und ihre Folgen' (1994) 35 *Politische Vierteljahresschrift* 3, 383–401.

52 On the tie between fundamental rights and majoritarian decision, Pizzolato, above n. 24, p. 20.

53 Newell, above n. 34, pp. 476–77.

54 Fabbrini, above n. 13, pp. 361–62.

55 *Ibid.*, p. 362.

56 M. Calise, *La democrazia del leader*, Laterza, Roma-Bari 2016.

57 Fabbrini, above n. 13, p. 352.

58 Infra, section 2.1. See also P. Pasquino, 'Le Gouvernement Berlusconi: une année après' (2002) 103 *Pouvoirs* 4, 13–28.

Second, the 'Lega Lombarda' party was born as a federalist movement against territorial unity,[59] corruption and fiscal overreach of the central government. Founded in 1991, it emerged in the 1992 political elections. It only recently changed its ideology. After Umberto Bossi, the new leader Matteo Salvini wanted to make the 'Lega' more appealing on a national level, as well.[60] He modified the party's name and allied it with anti-Euro and xenophobic movements. This path transformed the 'Lega' into the third party on a national scale in the 2018 elections.[61]

Third, another step was critical for the rise in the political system of these three parties. In 1997, the creation of Parliament's Bicameral Commission for constitutional reforms[62] included all three parties ('Lega' did not participate in the parliamentary work only for a brief period). Even if the Commission failed, parties participating in its work gained political legitimacy. Moreover, in 1997, for the first time in Italian republican history, a secessionist and a former neo-fascist party became part of the national government.[63] In short, the latter was composed of 'Forza Italia', managed by a tycoon to protect his private interests, 'Alleanza nazionale', rooted in 1946's fascist-nostalgic party, and 'Lega', born as a secessionist movement. From that time onwards,[64] their rhetoric slowly eroded from within the cohesion of a country build on solidarity, republican and anti-fascist values.[65]

The following years did not deeply change this political landscape, with one significant exception – the foundation of 'Movimento Cinque Stelle -M5S'. In 2008, 'Forza Italia' developed into 'Popolo della libertà',

---

59 On the clash between the ItC and the secessionist ideology, see L. Elia, *La Costituzione aggredita: forma di governo e devolution ai tempi della destra*, Il Mulino, Bologna 2005.

60 Diamanti, above n. 1, p. 124.

61 A. Stille, 'How Matteo Salvini pulled Italy to the Far Right' (2018) *The Guardian* https://www.theguardian.com/news/2018/aug/09/how-matteo-salvini-pulled-italy-to-the-far-right, last accessed 02.05.2020.

62 In 1997, Massimo D'Alema (a leading figure of left-oriented party) chaired the Bicameral Commission. Once Silvio Berlusconi stopped cooperating with the Commission, it was the end of its functioning: S. Panunzio (ed.), *I costituzionalisti e le riforme: una discussione sul progetto della Commissione bicamerale per le riforme costituzionali*, Giuffrè, Milano 1998; G. Pasquino and C.M. O'Neill, 'A Postmortem of The Bicamerale' (1998) 14 *Italian Politics*, 101–20.

63 M.S. Piretti, *Le elezioni politiche in Italia dal 1848 ad oggi*, Laterza, Roma-Bari 1996.

64 For an in-depth study of such an evolution, see Elia, above n. 30, pp. 257–74.

65 Newell, above n. 34, pp. 476–77, 482: to become an ally of Berlusconi, who had several judicial problems to solve, 'Alleanza nazionale' took distance from the 1990's investigation – even if supporting it would create the image of a conservative party 'capable of attracting votes on 'law-and-order' and similar issues'.

including 'Alleanza nazionale'.[66] 'Lega' only recently became a national party. After several internal events involving 'Alleanza nazionale' and 'Forza Italia', since 2012 the new party 'Fratelli d'Italia', led by Giorgia Meloni, embodies the Italian extreme far-right. All three took part in the coalition which represented the second winner of the 2018 national elections. All three, as this chapter argues, try to transform 'electoral personalisation' into 'personal power at governmental level'[67] (or at the parliamentary level).

'M5S' was founded in 2009 by Beppe Grillo (a renowned comedian) and Gianroberto Casaleggio (a web strategist). One year after, Grillo proclaimed himself as 'capo politico' (i.e. political head) of the movement. For the first time in republican history, a political leader marked his position publicly using Benito Mussolini's words. Furthermore, Grillo often referred to 'M5S' as a populist movement. The movement's name refers to its five keystone issues: fundamental right to Internet access; environmentalism; sustainable development; sustainable transport; and public water. Today, its ideology is rooted in a strong belief in e-democracy; on other issues, its members seem to be less united.

Currently, only 'Lega-Salvini premier' and 'M5S' strictly embody populism.

3. PEOPLE AND DEMOCRACY IN THE ITALIAN CONSTITUTION

The evolution recalled in section 2 above is two-faced. Politically, more than 80% of the voters approved the April 1993 referendum. It was a victory of the people. Constitutionally, the new electoral system was the result of a referendum manipulating the existing electoral law. It was the defeat of representative democracy and constitutional architecture.[68] The combination of these two 'factors' (political result and constitutional

66 Fabbrini, above n. 13, pp. 353–55 for the evolution of Berlusconi's party.

67 For the description of the parliamentary consequences of the rivalry between Berlusconi and Fini, see Fabbrini, above n. 13, p. 354 (the author relates the quoted sentence only to Berlusconi). On the influence on the party system of such a personalisation, see Di Cosimo, above n. 13, §1.

68 Pallante, above n. 14, 49 also discusses the role played at that time by the Italian Constitutional Court.

violation)[69] had severe consequences. Moving towards a predominantly single-member, single-plurality system was not negative *per se*. The concrete problem emerged because of a peculiarity.[70]

The combination of the new electoral system and the media's role contributed to the personalisation of party leaders. Since the 1990s, at the heart of electoral campaigns were not (only) political programs, but also the leader's personality.[71] Furthermore, the new leaders' rhetoric was no longer grounded on anti-fascism and on other constitutional values. In short, personalisation consisted of 'aggregating a society' that became 'increasingly individualistic'.[72] Worse still, it was focused on an individualistic society, removed from constitutional values.[73] Actually this (and, of course, the 2010 financial crisis) was the heart of Italian populism. Only after its electoral explosion and alliance with other European populist (or extreme far-right parties), was it possible to clearly recognise its real nature.

The Constituent Assembly openly took a position against fascism. The XII transitional and final provision (supra, section 2.1) simply represents one side of this choice. The other consists of accurately designing citizens' rights and duties and public powers. This architecture has been built to prevent the return of fascist ideology – even if disguised.[74] Furthermore, the ItC praises the human being as the centre of the social and political organisation,[75] not as the key opening the door to an individualistic society. The mainstream parties which produced the constitution were Catholics, Socialists and Communists. As different as they were, they succeeded in finding a compromise embodied in the actual constitutional text. Social justice, substantial equality and labour are fundamental values.[76] Even the

---

69 Pallante, above n. 14, 49: under Art. 75 ItC, the referendum should only abrogate laws or decree laws (in the whole or in part). It is not meant as an instrument to manipulate such acts by modifying parts of them.

70 For an in-depth reflection on these issues, see G. Pasquino, *1945–1996: profilo della politica in Italia*, Laterza, Roma 1996.

71 Di Cosimo, above n. 13, §1; Pallante, above n. 14, 51.

72 Fabbrini, above n. 13, 352; Manetti, above n. 6; Calise, above n. 56.

73 Pizzolato above n. 24, pp. 18–26, and p. 66.

74 V. Onida, 'Le Costituzioni. I principi fondamentali della Costituzione italiana' in G. Amato and A. Barbera (eds), *Manuale di diritto pubblico. I. Diritto pubblico generale*, 5th ed., Il Mulino, Bologna 1984, pp. 77–116, 88. For the Constituent Assembly's works see *La Costituzione della Repubblica nei lavori preparatori della Assemblea costituente*, (I), Camera dei Deputati – Segretariato Generale, Roma 1970.

75 Onida, above n. 74, 89.

76 Onida, above n. 74, 89–90.

tax system ought to be progressive, in order to let every person contribute to public expenditure according to his or her capability.[77] Briefly, solidarity (not only with nationals) is a principle permeating the constitutional order. This net (constitutional rights and duties, social justice, solidarity, etc.) left no space for an individualistic society gravitating towards personalised political leadership.[78] Moreover, this same net was a response to the former fascist one-man leadership of Benito Mussolini.[79] There is an even more important aspect, however. The Constituent Assembly did not fear only the imposition of a dictatorial leadership from above.

According to Article 1 ItC, sovereignty belongs to the people, but it is exercised by it in the forms of and within the limits of the Constitution. This prescription is based on two pillars: on the one hand, the abstract ownership of sovereignty (i.e. the people); and on the other hand, the practical exercise of that same sovereignty (i.e. the institutions). Briefly, sovereignty fully belongs to the people. Practically, people may exercise that same sovereignty only respecting the constitutional boundaries. Therefore, even if 'popular sovereignty represents a prius with respect to the state',[80] and even if the state and institutions 'are an expression, in a democratic system, of popular sovereignty',[81] the latter is not limitless. Under the ItC, people may elect representatives, exercise fundamental liberties and even introduce legislation. In any case, the most significant part of sovereign power is exercised by public institutions (directly or indirectly representing the popular will).[82] In short, the Constituent Assembly also feared the return of authoritarian attitudes under a popular guise. The representative system was chosen as a 'defence to the people against their own temporary

---

77 C. Buzzacchi, *La solidarietà tributaria. Funzione fiscale e principi costituzionali*, Giuffré, Milano 2011, pp. 2–24.

78 On this kind of political leadership see again Pallante, above n. 14, 48 ff.

79 This same constitutional net, of course, represents also a response to the legal order characterising Italy before Mussolini's dictatorship, roughly from 1861 to 1924.

80 A. Algostino, 'Participatory Democracy and its Dark Sides' (2020) 12 *Federalismi* https://www.federalismi.it/nv14/articolodocumento.cfm?Artid=42222&content=Fascicolo%2Bn%2E%2B12%2F2020&content_author=%3Cb%3EFederalismi%3C%2Fb%3E, last accessed 22.04.2020.

81 *Ibid.*, §1.

82 On this point, the paper mirrors E. Cheli, 'La sovranità, la funzione di governo, l'indirizzo politico' in G. Amato and A. Barbera (eds), *Manuale di diritto pubblico. II. L'organizzazione costituzionale*, 5th ed., Il Mulino, Bologna 1984, pp. 7–27, pp. 11–12. In Italian literature, a fundamental work on Art. 1 ItC is Mortati, above n. 9.

errors and delusions'.[83] In other words, as a system able to prevent people's tyranny, too.[84]

Therefore, the repeal referendum also has strict constitutional rules. Originally, members of the Constituent Assembly worried that such an instrument could not fit with the parliamentary form of government,[85] and moreover, that it could be used in order to stop or to complicate parliamentary reforms.[86] Ultimately (even if this choice has been denied by later domestic history),[87] the repeal referendum was designed as a marginal instrument.[88]

A final characteristic belongs to the Italian constitutional conception of democracy:[89] the prohibition of the binding mandate of the members of parliament (MPs).[90] Cesare Pinelli explains the significance acquired by this principle in 'democratic mass party' states, including Italy. It consists of

> the function of preventing parties from repealing MPs countering their own decisions or guidelines. [...] Without the rule prohibiting the MP's imperative mandate, electors would be free of changing their representatives whenever they wish, but, at the same time, they would renounce the opportunity of evaluating how representatives converted their interpretation of the common interest into certain policies.[91]

Like many others, the Italian political system is also based on two pillars. National politics is at the same time the result of parliamentary and

83 Analysing James Madison's speech to the people of the State of New York, C. Pinelli stresses only his idea of the representative system, not the one suggested in this essay: PINELLI, above n. 5, p. 9. See only MORTATI, above n. 9; C. MORTATI, *Istituzioni di Diritto pubblico*, IXth ed., Cedam, Padova 1975–1976, p. 148 and ff. On that same issue PIZZOLATO, above n. 24, p. 24.

84 Regarding Art. 1 ItC, see again MORTATI, above n. 9, and MORTATI, (1975–1976), above n. 83, p. 148 and ff.

85 P. BERRETTA, 'I poteri di democrazia diretta' in G. AMATO and A. BARBERA (eds), *Manuale di diritto pubblico. II. L'organizzazione costituzionale*, 5th ed., Il Mulino, Bologna 1984, pp. 29–66, p. 31.

86 Marxists were against the adoption of the weimarian referendum's model: BERRETTA, above n. 85, p. 31.

87 Regarding the complexity of the latter, see A. BARBERA and A. MORRONE, *La Repubblica dei referendum*, Il Mulino, Bologna 2003.

88 For an in-depth study of the repeal referendum, see M. LUCIANI, 'Il referendum abrogativo. Commento dell'art. 75' in G. BRANCA and A. PIZZORUSSO (eds), *Commentario della Costituzione*, N. Zanichelli-Soc. Ed. del Foro italiano, Bologna-Roma 2005.

89 I.e. to the Italian parliamentary form of government.

90 A. MANZELLA et al., 'Artt. 64-69. Le Camere' in G. BRANCA and A. PIZZORUSSO (eds), *Commentario della Costituzione*, N. Zanichelli-Soc. Ed. del Foro italiano, Bologna-Roma 1986.

91 PINELLI, above n. 5, p. 11.

party decisions.[92] The democratic link between the two is represented by the 'electoral tie' – that is, by MPs.[93] Given that Parliament has a central position in the whole system, the Constituent Assembly also disciplined the parliamentary mandate.[94] According to Art. 67 ItC, 'each member of parliament represents the nation and carries out his duties without a binding mandate'. Nonetheless, Italian parties did not always respect the threshold separating party organisation and parliamentary representation. The latter aims to realise the national interest,[95] and the former aims to realise only the party's interest, which is why it may impose rigid inner-party rules on MPs.[96] Even this development is rooted in a misunderstanding.

The Constituent Assembly refused to adopt strict rules regarding the inner-party organisation because it did not want to disrupt their freedom.[97] Today, however, Italy is facing a different threat. 'M5S', claiming a new, virtual democracy (supra, section 1), and promising a direct link with its constituencies, has a severe influence on its MPs. The latter face a serious choice when and if they want to defend the national interest.[98] They may lose their party's support. As a matter of fact, MPs' independence assures – at least theoretically – that the interest of the people, of the whole community, prevails over the 'egoistic' interests of parties.[99]

In this light, populists do not simply want to reconcile people and political leaders, movements and parties. They aim to strengthen direct democracy in a way that the ItC rejected. Moreover, the demand for an increase of direct democracy goes hand-in-hand with a further distinctive mark of Italian political experience. Considered together, these aspects seem to threaten constitutional democracy.

---

92 A. Manzella, 'Il Parlamento' in G. Amato and A. Barbera (eds), *Manuale di diritto pubblico. II. L'organizzazione costituzionale*, 5th ed., Il Mulino, Bologna 1984, pp. 103–68, p. 112.

93 *Ibid.*

94 *Ibid.*, p. 111.

95 As the personal experience of L. Elia clearly shows: *Ibid.*, p. 394.

96 Manzella, above n. 92, p. 112. On the binding mandate, see G. Azzariti, 'Passato e presente. Cittadini, partiti e gruppi parlamentari: esiste ancora il divieto di mandato imperativo?' (2009) III/IV *Democrazia e Diritto* 311–64.

97 Manetti, above n. 6, 395.

98 For an in-depth reflection on this matter see again Pallante, above n. 14, 57–64.

99 See P. Calamandrei, 'Appunti sul professionismo parlamentare' in P. Calamandrei, (N. Bobbio ed), *Scritti e discorsi politici*, Vol. II, La Nuova Italia, Firenze 1966, pp. 607–614, as quoted by E. Bindi, 'Calamandrei e la questione sociale' in (2012) 3 *Gruppo di Pisa. La Rivista* <https://www.gruppodipisa.it/8-rivista/262-elena-bindi-calamandrei-e-la-questione-sociale> last accessed 01.04.2020, p. 19 footnote 61.

4. ITALIAN POPULISM: A THREAT TO CONSTITUTIONAL DEMOCRACY?

In the Italian legal order, only constitutional rules can frame the reconciliation between people and parties.[100] According to Art. 49 ItC, 'every citizen has the right to freely establish parties to contribute to determining national politics through democratic processes'.[101] This discipline partially mirrors Maurice Duverger's theory on the functions of contemporary parties.[102] Under Duverger's theory, parties frame citizens' ideologies; then, they select candidates participating in the electoral competition; and finally, in the periods between elections, parties link voters and representatives.[103] However, the constitutional discipline also means something different.[104]

Art. 49 ItC is intertwined with other constitutional prescriptions: Art. 1, stating that sovereignty is exercised by the people in the forms and within the limits of the ItC; Art. 2, which guarantees fundamental rights belonging to individuals and 'social groups where human personality is expressed'; Art. 18, which recognises the citizens' right to form associations freely and without authorisation';[105] and Art. 3, para 2, according to which the Republic must remove all those obstacles preventing the full participation of all workers in the political, economic and social organisation of the country. This interlacement has a clear constitutional meaning. As Filippo Pizzolato recently recalled,[106] under the ItC, democracy does not just consist of the act of voting. It is a constant process involving people's participation at any level in the country – being in the social, economic or political level.[107] Unfortunately, in Italy, the 'complexity of political

---

100 On the concept of representative democracy, see Pizzolato, above n. 24, pp. 18–26, 36–41.

101 Regarding the original debate on Art. 49 ItC see, *ex multis*, P. Pombeni, 'I partiti. La 'costituzione' che c'è e quella che verrà' in D. Verdini (ed.), *Popolo e leader. Il tempo dei partiti nuovi*, Fondazione Magna Carta, Roma 2008, pp. 79–98.

102 M. Duverger, *Les parties politiques*, Colin, Paris 1954.

103 Chimenti sums up the theory of the French scholar in C. Chimenti, 'I partiti politici' in G. Amato and A. Barbera (eds), *Manuale di diritto pubblico. II. L'organizzazione costituzionale*, 5th ed., Il Mulino, Bologna 1984, pp. 51–66, p. 53.

104 C. Mortati, 'Sulla posizione del partito nello Stato' in C. Mortati (ed.), *Problemi di politica costituzionale*, Vol. 4, Giuffré, Milano 1972, pp. 495–515.

105 If they do not pursue ends forbidden by criminal law. Moreover, 'secret associations and associations that, even indirectly, pursue political aims by means of organisation having a military character shall be forbidden'.

106 Pizzolato, above n. 24, p. 26.

107 *Ibid.*, pp. 18–26, 47.

phenomena has been replaced by the personal abilities or shortcomings of a leader' (supra, section 2.1).[108] Since the moment of that shift, something deeply changed.

Democracy was no longer a complex process grounded on the involvement of politically far-sighted citizens. As Sergio Fabbrini explained, in former years, 'the leader, not the party' became 'the message'.[109] Moreover, 'the logic of television communication [led] to an interpretative typology of politics based on the friend/foe dichotomy' (supra, section 2.1). In Sergio Fabbrini's words, 'television' 'resurrected Carl Schmitt'.[110]

This primarily cultural decline produced two connected results. First, the relationship between leader and people was no longer based on a rational evaluation of a party's political program.[111] Since the 1990s, people have voted for certain parties for different reasons. As consequence, there occurred an identification process with the leader's lifelong success (Silvio Berlusconi and 'Forza Italia'), and/or an opposition to corrupted national parties (Umberto Bossi and 'Lega Nord'). Later, identification became rooted in a social conflict (people vs. the establishment and élites: Beppe Grillo and 'M5S'). Only recently has the search for a scapegoat responsible for every domestic difficulty become more important than ever (immigrants and the EU: Matteo Salvini and 'Lega-Salvini Premier'; Giorgia Meloni and 'Fratelli d'Italia').[112] Second, as part of this same process, people no longer evaluate the leader's concrete governmental results. As Michela Manetti observes, citizens simply trust leaders giving voice to their resentment – even when these same leaders do not offer any concrete solutions facing social or economic issues.[113]

This evolution jars with the constitutional concept of popular sovereignty. According to the ItC, this notion 'is accompanied by a broad concept of participation'.[114] As Alessandra Algostino affirms, this concept reflects several aspects marking substantial democracy.[115] In this light,

---

108 Fabbrini, above n. 13, 349.

109 *Ibid.*

110 *Ibid.*

111 For an in-depth analysis of the issue, see Manetti, above n. 6, p. 385 and ff.

112 See, as quoted by Schillaci, above n. 19, p. 38, fn. 108, N. Urbinati, *Me the People. How Populism Transforms Democracy*, Harvard University Press, Cambridge MA 2019, pp. 113–18.

113 This position has also been expressed by Manetti, above n. 6, pp. 377–78.

114 Algostino, above n. 80, §1 p. 3.

115 That is why, e.g. Art. 3, para. 2 ItC adopts the formula 'political, economic and social organisation': Algostino, *ibid.*

democratic participation plays a fundamental role in the democratic process as a whole – not only when citizens vote. Participatory democracy, surveillance activity,[116] democracy from below: all these phenomena contribute to designing the interlacement between participation and democratic process.[117] Furthermore, this explains why Art. 3, para 2 ItC reads: 'It is the duty of the Republic to remove those obstacles of an economic or social nature which constrain the freedom and equality of citizens, thereby impeding the full development of the human person and the effective participation of all workers in the political, economic and social organisation of the country'.

Ousting the participatory side of contemporary democracy risks intensifying the direct relationship between leader and people. As part of such a process, this tie may develop into a sort of symbolic representation[118] – a dangerous memory of the past, not a mark of contemporary democracies. In short, given such conditions, representative democracy is concretely at risk.[119] As Sergio Fabbrini explains recalling Bernard Manin, in such an audience democracy, the 'electoral decision has become personalised, (the electorate votes for a person rather than a party); the representatives enjoy an almost complete autonomy from those they represent (because the voters respond to the proposals of the elected and no longer the other way round); and the cleavages in the electorate are virtual rather than real (to the extent that they are created from above by the politicians instead of being the result of processes occurring in the society'.[120]

As said, in the Italian experience, audience democracy is grounded in a specific development: people transformed their resentment towards corrupt politicians into an anti-political attitude (section 2.1). After a few years, with the tragic complicity of the 2010 financial crisis, that same attitude again overwhelmed people's trust in institutions. Populist parties could rise in this fertile soil. It was not difficult for them to aim for generically called 'strong powers'; eventually, to link the latter to elected and non-elected national institutions; and ultimately, to target existing

---

116 See also, as quoted several times by Algostino, above n. 80, P. Rosanvallon, *La légitimité démocratique. Impartialité, reflexivité, proximité*, Éditions du Seuil, Paris 2008, p. 323.

117 Rosanvallon, above n. 116, p. 323.

118 But only regarding Berlusconi: Manetti, above n. 6, p. 378.

119 Manetti, above n. 6, p. 382 does not refer to Italy. See also Pallante, above n. 14, 48–55 on the leader personalisation, and pp. 57–63 on 'M5S'.

120 Fabbrini, above n. 13, pp. 350–51.

democracy (institutions and procedures) making people believe that only a new, direct democracy (going virtual or based on a strong leader, voice of the people) would solve any problem.

5. BACK TO PIERO CALAMANDREI: THE TIME HAS COME FOR THE 'PROMISED REVOLUTION'

Italian populist rhetoric appeals to direct democracy and is grounded in the personalisation of politics. Moreover, it believes in the existence of one people, to be protected from 'enemies' who do not belong to its conceptual and territorial boundaries. As said, such an ideology clashes with the Italian constitutional project, which is grounded in solidarity and pluralism. Furthermore, this same rhetoric gave new life to a party inheriting the neo-fascist ideology. From this perspective, one question urgently needs an answer. Echoing Filippo Pizzolato's work, does the Italian Constitution design a path to confront such phenomenon?[121]

Recently, Ilvo Diamanti pointed the way to developing an understanding of the actual face of populism, noting that: 'the social basis of populism is different among different populisms'.[122] Nonetheless, various types of populism have something in common. They are all grounded on 'the perception of being "periphery", and express the growing discomfort of the peripheries'.[123] The analysis of the 2018 Italian national elections proves this assumption to be correct.[124] Citizens who voted for the centre-left parties more often belonged to the heart of big cities, and 'M5S' mostly gained votes in the peripheries of these same cities and in South Italy. 'Lega-Salvini Premier' succeeded in harnessing all citizens who were feeling excluded[125] – by Italian and European institutions and markets, and by the favourable treatment of immigrants in need, *inter alia*. The case of 'Fratelli d'Italia' and 'Forza Italia' is slightly different. Even if the former party rides the populist wave, too, it remains the last heir presumptive to the post-war neo-fascists. The latter party, given the less important political weight of its founder, seems to be a ghost of the original party. As things stood, all four parties did win at the 2018 elections.

---

121 For the formulation of that same question see the title of Pizzolato, above n. 24: the author faces a wider range of problems, not only populism's origins and consequences.

122 Diamanti, above n. 1, pp. 119, 122.

123 *Ibid.*, p. 125.

124 *Ibid.*, p. 123.

125 *Ibid.*, p. 124.

Neo-fascism is – and always will be – a brutal reality in Europe (and elsewhere). It still appeals to people – and not only because of the feeling of exclusion described by Ilvo Diamanti. For example, recently, during the first few weeks of the Coronavirus crisis,[126] opinion polls revealed that a considerable number of citizens rated Giorgia Meloni (leader of the far-right party 'Fratelli d'Italia') more highly than Matteo Salvini (leader of the 'Lega-Salvini Premier'). This chapter does not analyse the reasons for such a phenomenon; that is the work of political scholars, historians and philosophers.[127] By contrast, in 2018, Italian populist parties succeeded in gaining the votes of the former centre-left- and centre-right-oriented electors, who were disappointed by the related movements and leaders. Therefore, populism in Italy may be politically defeated by recreating believable left and right parties. However, if the latter want to protect constitutional democracy, they all must be aware of one demand: the only demand which may be resolved in the name of the constitution.

Years ago, one of the most enlightened Italian intellectuals, Piero Calamandrei,[128] never forgot that democracy can only exist hand-in-hand with social rights.[129] In his perspective, social justice represented the first condition for the concrete fulfilment of freedom.[130] He spoke of the ItC, of its social and civic contents, as a 'promised revolution': a revolution whose only weapon was social dignity; a dignity capable of fully developing any individual's participation in the political, economic and social organisation of the country.[131] Today, social justice still seems to be the tool to confront

---

126 Regarding the clash between the regulatory governmental choices and the ItC see F. Rescigno, 'La gestione del coronavirus e l'impianto costituzionale' (2020) 3 *Osservatorio AIC* <https://www.osservatorioaic.it/it/osservatorio/ultimi-contributi-pubblicati/francesca-rescigno/la-gestione-del-coronavirus-e-l-impianto-costituzionale-il-fine-non-giustifica-ogni-mezzo> last accessed 19.05.2020. For the author's reflections on the absolute respect of fundamental rights even in a peculiar situation like the pandemic, and on the role of social fear in the coronavirus crisis, see pp. 6–7, and p. 18.

127 *Ex multis* U. Eco, *Il fascismo eterno*, La nave di Teseo, Milano 2017, esp. p. 45 for the tie between 'Ur-fascism' and 'qualitative populism'.

128 P. Calamandrei, 'La Costituzione e le leggi per attuarla' in P. Calamandrei (ed.), *Opere giuridiche*, Morano, Napoli 1965.

129 *Ex multis* A. Pace, 'Diritti di libertà e diritti sociali nel pensiero di Calamandrei' in P. Barile (ed.), *Piero Calamandrei*, Giuffré, Milano 1990, p. 328.

130 The paper is here based on the brilliant work of Bindi, above n. 99, spec. §§2 and 3.

131 For the position adopted by Calamandrei before, during and after the Constituent Assembly's works, see Bindi, above n. 99, p. 9 ff. (also for his position recalled in the text).

the perception of being on the periphery. But two further conditions must be accomplished.

First, in order to make people understand that democracy is a constant process, parties should revalue territorial autonomy. Democracy from below brings new life to several facets of democracy: the representative, the participative, and the decisional one.[132] In other words, reborn territorial involvement may defeat the periphery complex. Second, to make people consistently participate in the democratic process, it is necessary to promote the conditions rendering the right to work effective. Only the sum of these two actions can provide the material and spiritual progress of a democratic society – that is, of Italian constitutional democracy.

Nonetheless, Camilla Buzzacchi[133] recently observed that today, the constitutional right to work is itself in danger. The latest developments[134] threaten the ItC's model of social democracy.[135] Under Art. 1 and 4 ItC, work is a keystone of Italian social-constitutional democracy. As a social right, it requires peculiar public intervention; by contrast, from the markets' perspective, work is just one brick in a larger construct. It aims to realise the purpose of efficiency and employment rate.[136] In this light, the 21st century's social and political question needs an answer more than ever. In Italy, rediscovering the constitutional tie between human dignity, territorial autonomy and work[137] would have a double meaning. On the one hand, it would erode from within the periphery complex which gives life to populist claims. On the other, it would finally fulfil the Italian constitutional democracy which is rooted in that same tie between human dignity, territorial autonomy and work.[138] Today, as in the time of renowned poet James Oppenheim, only 'bread and roses'[139] can peacefully feed constitutional solidarity and pluralism.

---

132 More in Pizzolato, above n. 24, pp. 71–82 (regarding territorial autonomy) and pp. 83–91 (on democracy from below).

133 C. Buzzacchi, *Il lavoro da diritto a bene*, Franco Angeli, Milano 2019, pp. 33–51.

134 For the judgments of the European Court of Justice influencing the Italian model anchored on the work as a right, see Buzzacchi, above n. 133, p. 33.

135 *Ibid.*, pp. 15 and esp. pp. 24–28.

136 *Ibid.*, pp. 55–59.

137 *Ibid.*, pp. 108–109.

138 Bindi, above n. 99, at fn. 49 of p. 15 recalls two works of Calamandrei: regarding the failed full realisation process of the ItC, see Calamandrei, above n. 128, p. 533 and ff.; on the Constitution as 'promised revolution' instead of a 'realised revolution', see P. Calamandrei, 'Cenni introduttivi sulla Costituente e i suoi lavori' in P. Calamandrei (N. Bobbio ed), (1966) Vol. II, p. 421.

139 The slogan 'bread and roses' was used for the first time by the activist Helen Todd. Then, in 1912, it was adopted during the famous textile strike in Massachusetts.

POLISH CONSTITUTIONALISM UNDER POPULIST RULE

A Revolution without a Revolution

Przemyslaw Tacik

1. INTRODUCTION

Not all revolutions succeed: some fail on their way to a better future, and some are doomed from the beginning. Perhaps, with a hint of Žižekean melancholic sobriety,[1] it should be argued that failure is inherent in the very notion of the revolution: as its repressed undertone, hovering possibility and the final calculus of gains and losses. Failed revolutions are much more common than the handbook history seems to suggest. Apart from the great epochal failures whose despairingly disappointing consequences are measured against the background of their initial promises – as in the case of the October revolution – there are revolutions of smaller scope and ambition. Some of them do not even take the name of the revolution, and this name may be nothing but a subsequent academic label. These pose the

1 S. Žižek, 'Introduction: Remembering, Repeating and Working Through' in S. Žižek (ed.), *Lenin. The Day after the Revolution*, Verso, London and New York 2018, pp. vii–xxxii.

greatest problems in identification: without reflexive self-imposition of a category, a revolution would be typically experienced passively, without a clear goal or a coherent agenda. Only an *après coup* identification could reveal the properly revolutionary momentum which was concealed under chaos and provisionality that was not properly linked to the symbolic level.

Such a revolution produces unpredictable side-effects and distortions of its objectives which even originally were muddled. Even though it does not have to necessarily be a failure in itself – it might bring about some beneficial socio-political changes – it remains problematic due to its alienating and obfuscating character. Measures which are undertaken are often haphazard – tactical rather than strategic and deprived of a clear-cut social support. Moreover, 'a revolution without a revolution' opens up a problematic ideological battlefield dominated initially by a strong need to define what actually happened. Only after marking the goalposts and building the first footholds for a future hegemony does the revolution begin to be represented symbolically, even if at the price of deep ideological deformations that sometimes consist of denying that a revolution took a place at all.

Such a 'revolution without a revolution', failed not only in the final juxtaposition of goals and effects, but even in the possibility of building a coherent framework of such an assessment, is a concept that allows us to grasp the current socio-political developments in Central and Eastern European (CEE) countries afflicted by 'populism' (unfortunate,[2] elusive[3] and replaceable[4] as this term is). Fierce ideological battles coupled with a fundamental uncertainty about what these changes 'really' are – and what future they augur – point to the fact that the scope of the ongoing transformations is incommensurable with its symbolic representations.

---

2 Z. Oklopcic, 'Imagined ideologies: Populist figures, liberalist projections, and the horizons of constitutionalism' (2019) 20 *German Law Journal*, 201–06.

3 J.-W. Müller, *What Is Populism?* University of Pennsylvania Press, Philadelphia 2016; C. Mudde and C. Rovira Kaltvasser, *Populism: A Very Short Introduction*, Oxford University Press, Oxford 2017; B. De Cleen, J. Glynos and A. Mondon, 'Critical Research on Populism: Nine Rules of Engagement' (2018) 25 *Organization*, 649–61; B. De Cleen and Y. Stavrakakis, 'Distinctions and Articulations: A Discourse Theoretical Framework for the Study of Populism and Nationalism' (2017) 24 *Javnost-The Public*, 301–19; P. Aslanidis, 'Is Populism an Ideology? A Refutation and a New Perspective' (2016) 64 *Political Studies* (1S), 88–104.

4 G.A. Tóth, 'Constitutional Markers of Authoritarianism' (2019) 11 *Hague Journal on the Rule of Law*, 41–42.

Concurrently, contemporary right-wing populism, while gradually turning into yet another fashionable object of study in legal scholarship, is disconcertingly shrouded by a thick level of academic clichés and political naiveté. Apart from breakthrough insights[5] or just thought-provoking contributions,[6] academia seems to suffer from an unfortunate bifurcation. On the one hand, there is an abundance of technical analyses of the measures that populists in power undertake.[7] On the other, liberal democracy is sometimes defended as something which is taken for granted or essentially unproblematic, just as if populism were not a phenomenon born in its midst as a response to unresolved conflicts simmering under the lid of optimist democratism.[8]

Both approaches are often imbued with a post-colonial/post-dependence undertone which strives to identify rhetorically problematic populism only with non-Western countries. Yet even if their 'illiberal' or undemocratic tendencies are most conspicuous, it is not because they relapse into their alleged essential 'barbarism' – only passingly covered with varnish of liberalism – but because they belong to semi-peripheries of the West, where economic and political tensions are more acute. Naturally, the burden of their legal cultures, influenced by long-term experience of authoritarian rule, might make it easier to return to illiberal legal means or sometimes even repeat historical patterns. The introduction of some elements of authoritarianism, however, is not the ultimate *datum*. It should be understood rather as a local answer to a simmering socio-political conflict which is the proper phenomenon that calls for an explanation.

---

5 C. Cercel, 'The Destruction of Legal Reason: Lessons from the Past' (2019) 89 *Folia Iuridica*, 15–30.

6 P. Blokker, 'Populism as a Constitutional Project' (2019) 17 *International Journal of Constitutional Law*, 536–53; O. Doyle, 'Populist constitutionalism and constituent power' (2019) 20 *German Law Journal*, 161–80; Oklopcic, above n. 2; G. Hálmai, 'Is there Such Thing as 'Populist Constitutionalism'? The Case of Hungary' (2018) 11 *Fudan Journal of the Humanities and Social Sciences*, 7–8; D. Landau, 'Abusive Constitutionalism' (2013) 47 *UC Davis Law Review*, 189–260.

7 See for example A. Pin, 'The transnational drivers of populist backlash in Europe: The role of courts' (2019) 20 *German Law Journal*, 225–44; A. Śledzińska-Simon, 'The Rise and Fall of Judicial Self-Government in Poland: On Judicial Reform Reversing Democratic Transition' (2018) 19 *German Law Journal*, 1839–69.

8 L. Pech and K.L. Scheppele, 'Illiberalism Within: Rule of Law Backsliding in the EU' (2017) 19 *Cambridge Yearbook of European Legal Studies*, 4; G. Hálmai, 'A Coup Against Constitutional Democracy. The Case of Hungary' in M.A. Graber, S. Levinson and M. Tushnet (eds), *Constitutional Democracy in Crisis?* Oxford University Press, Oxford 2018, pp. 243–56.

Therefore, populism may be viewed through the perspective of a 'revolution without a revolution' not only in the countries where populists actually came to power, but also in those where they are strong enough to rearrange the political scene, impose their agenda and thus make clear the need of unblocking the political status quo. In this light, the 'really existing populism' in its many versions (for example, the Hungarian overt authoritarianism or the Polish crypto-authoritarianism that suspends the very applicability of the law) may be interpreted more fruitfully than in the perspective of a barbaric onslaught on the trenches of liberal democracy. The practice of populism in power is a magnifying glass for processes that take place in countries where populists do not (yet) govern – not necessarily because they prepare a repertoire of measures and tactics that Western populists may adopt once they gain power (although that is also probable), but because they reveal more openly the fundamental dilemmas of contemporary democracy.[9] A revolution without a revolution may be the conceptual corollary of liberal consensus: a token of a profound need for change of the system that circumscribes the possibility of change with a wall of circumspection and deferral.

In this chapter, the Polish case will be analysed in all its specificity, but with a view of giving a general account of the populist mechanism of the 'revolution without a revolution'. The post-2015 situation in Poland is unique due to the development of authoritarianism by suspension of liberal legality and effective dismantlement of the applicability of some norms. Contrary to the Hungarian case where 'illiberal' democracy was built by the Fidesz party disposing of constitutional majority and adopting a new Basic Law, Polish populist authoritarianism arose under the formal validity of the liberal constitution which was *de facto* suspended with sub-constitutional laws that violated it, but were applied instead of its norms. Whereas Hungary attempted to proclaim a new beginning and give it a constitutional expression – flawed and paradoxical as it might be[10] – Poland underwent

9 On the general process of – variously described – 'democratic decay' see: T.G. Daly, 'Democratic Decay: Conceptualising an Emerging Research Field' (2019) 11 *Hague Journal on the Rule of Law*, 10–26.

10 G.A. Tóth (ed.), *Constitution for a Disunited Nation: On Hungary's 2011 Fundamental Law*, CEU Press, Budapest 2012; B. Bugarič, 'Protecting Democracy and the Rule of Law in the European Union: The Hungarian Challenge' (2014) 79 *LSE 'Europe in Question' Discussion Paper Series*, 7–14; K.L. Scheppele, 'Understanding Hungary's Constitutional Revolution' in A. von Bogdandy and P. Sonervend (eds), *Constitutional Crisis in the European Constitutional Area. Theory, Law and Politics in Hungary and Romania*, Beck, Hart & Nomos, München 2014, pp. 111–24; Sólyom, 'The Rise and Decline of Constitutional Culture in Hungary' in von Bogdandy and Sonervend *ibid.*, pp. 5–31.

a change without its proper symbolic and constitutional representation. Perhaps then the Polish case is the most clear-cut example of how contemporary populism undertakes a revolution without a revolution. If properly understood, it might shed light on some crucial dilemmas of today: (1) why is there be a need for a revolution in our times? (2) what can a revolution look like today? (3) why are populist 'revolutions' undertaken in a concealed way that deliberately muddles the relationship among acts, goals and their symbolic grounding?

The chapter will be structured in the following manner. First, I will take a longer detour in order to propose a basic theoretical framework of understanding 'a revolution without a revolution' as a concept that might serve for understanding the populist revolts. Then I will present the Polish case, focusing on populists' initial projects of constitutional reforms as contrasted with their subsequent actions that lead to an effective suspension of some norms of the Polish constitution. Finally, I will offer some tentative answers concerning the link between contemporary populism as a revolution without a revolution and a structural blockade of today's democracy.

2. WHAT IS A REVOLUTION WITHOUT A REVOLUTION?

'A revolution without a revolution' connotes a political process – sometimes compressed into one or a few key events, sometimes dragged out for a longer period – in which the dimension of effective socio-political changes is *underrepresented* at the symbolic level. One can safely claim that the two levels never square with each other, both in failed and successful revolutions: there is always an element of symbolic misrepresentation and ideological warping that separates them. But in a revolution without the revolution, this misrepresentation comes to the fore as diminishing the historical significance of the changes that take place. 'Misrepresentation' is a term flexible enough to encompass both situations of deliberate deceit, undertaken by the government in order to make changes happen without the need of obtaining explicit social support for it, and cases when the government itself ventures a sea-change whose scope and consequences it does not envisage.

Apart from the element of symbolic underrepresentation, a revolution without a revolution still connotes a transformation radical enough to reach the level of 'revolutionarity'. It needs to be construed broadly enough to encompass situations more subtle and inconspicuous than mass revolts. For the purposes of this chapter, I will understand a revolution as a significant *disturbance in relations between constituent and constituted powers*.[11] It could be easily objected that constituent power appears otherwise than just a legal fiction only when a revolution takes place, making this understanding circular. Yet whether we approach this event from the point of view of the revolution itself or from the point of view of relations between the two powers, the event remains the same: that is, *a disturbance* which is precisely the revolution. And if the boundaries between constituent and constituted powers are notoriously blurred and fictitious, this disturbance may remain the only detectable event in their assumed relationship.

In order to approach the conceptual boundaries of a revolution without a revolution, it is instructive to look back at one of the earliest theoretical accounts of relations between a constitution, constituent power and constituted power.[12] Emmanuel Joseph Sieyès' seminal work *Qu'est-ce que le Tiers-État?* introduces a broad understanding of the constitution – not

---

11 For other conceptual frameworks for revolutions from the point of view of constitutional law, see: A. Arato, 'Revolutions and constitution making' in D. Landau and H. Ferner, *Comparative Constitutional Making*, Edward Elgar, Cheltenham, Northampton, MA 2019, pp. 27–46; H. Kelsen, *General Theory of Law and the State*, Harvard University Press, Cambridge MA 1945, p. 117. Notably, both Kelsen and Arato prefer the term 'break' (or 'replacement') which, however, do not sufficiently grasp the revolutionarity which can be veiled by symbolic underrepresentation. Moreover, a 'break' assumes a clear-cut possibility of identifying a radical discontinuity, whereas a revolution may as well be a crawling process without easily discernible boundaries. Gary Jacobsohn uses a term close to 'disturbance' – 'displacement' – but not in the context of a revolution without a revolution; see G. Jacobsohn, 'Anchoring and sailing: contrasting imperatives of constitutional revolution' in G. Jacobsohn and M. Schor, *Comparative Constitutional Theory*, Edward Elgar, Cheltenham, Northampton, MA 2018, p. 334.

12 A concise exposition of this conceptual opposition can be found in C. Klein, *Théorie et pratique du pouvoir constituant*, Presses Universitaires de France, Paris 1996. See also J. Colón-Ríos, 'Five Conceptions of Constituent Power' (2014) 13 *Law Quarterly Review* 2, 306; M. Loughlin, 'The Concept of Constituent Power' (2014) 13 *European Journal of Political Theory* 2, 218; Y. Roznai, *Unconstitutional Constitutional Amendments. The Limits of Amendment Powers*, Oxford University Press, Oxford 2017, pp. 105–10; M. Tushnet, *Advanced Introduction to Comparative Constitutional Law*, Edward Elgar, Cheltenham, Northampton, MA 2014, pp. 13–18; Y. Roznai, '"We the people", "oui, the people" and the collective body: perceptions of constituent power' in Jacobsohn and Schor, above n. 11, 295–315.

as a written legal text, but a general organisational framework of the body politic:

> It is impossible to create a body for an end without giving it the organization, forms, and laws it needs in order to fulfil the functions for which it has been established. This is what is meant by the constitution of that body. It is obvious that it could not exist without one. It is equally obvious that any delegated government must have its constitution and that what is true of government in general is also true of each of its component parts. Thus the body of representatives entrusted with the legislative power, or the exercise of the common will, exists only by way of the mode of being which the nation decided to give it. It is nothing without its constituent forms; it acts, proceeds, or commands only by way of those forms.[13]

The pivotal function of the constitution is therefore to give an organisational form to the polity and 'to subject a government to fixed forms … in order to guarantee its ability to meet the ends for which it was established and to make it incapable of diverging from these ends'.[14] In light of the Agambenian concept of the state of exception as the fundamental mode of the law's (in)applicability,[15] it might seem utopian to believe that a government might be *structurally* bound to pursue constitutionally imposed ends. But in Sieyès' account, it is precisely this vague concept of an end – coupled with organisational and institutional provisions – that links constituent and constituted power in their mutual pact. The former is nation itself – allegedly pre-legal (at least in the sense of positive law) – an eternal entity from which all state power is deduced,[16] whereas the latter is established through a legal act:

> The nation exists prior to everything; it is the origin of everything. Its will is always legal. It is the law itself. Prior to the nation and above the nation there is only natural law. To have a proper idea of the sequence of *positive* laws, all emanating solely from the nation's will, the first in order of precedence will be the *constitutional* laws, which will be divided into two parts. Some will

13 E.J. Sieyès, 'What is the Third Estate?' in *Political Writings*, tr. M. Sonenscher, Hackett, Indianapolis & Cambridge 2003, p. 135.

14 *Ibid.*, p. 136.

15 G. Agamben, *State of Exception (Homo sacer II, 1)*, tr. K. Attell, The University of Chicago Press, Chicago and London 2005, p. 40.

16 For this reason, Mark Tushnet rightly notices that in Sieyès' account it is rather a justification of the assembly's power than a real representation of constituencies. Tushnet, above n. 12, 24.

> regulate the organization and functions of the *legislative* body; others will fix the organization and functions of the various *active* bodies. These laws are said to be *fundamental*, not in the sense that they can be independent of the national will, but because bodies that can exist and can act only by way of these laws cannot touch them. In each of its parts a constitution is not the work of a constituted power but a constituent power. No type of delegated power can modify the conditions of its delegation. It is in this sense, and in no other, that constitutional laws are *fundamental*.[17]

This classic liberal vision takes both powers as circumscribed entities that maintain relations sealed by the constitution. The establishment or re-establishment of these relations is a revolution. But this old-age liberal myth hangs upon a few presumptions: (1) there are pre-legal methods of a nation's self-expression;[18] (2) constitutional laws provide an immutable framework that is not affected by derivative laws; and (3) abuse of the delegation by the constituted power does not undermine the constitution in its structure, but is tantamount to its breach.

The division between the constituent and the constituted powers does not have to be put into such a rigid framework, however. Carl Schmitt, who was well aware of practical paradoxes that this division implies, decided to preserve it nonetheless as a distinction capable of explaining modern tensions among state power, the law and exception.[19] Schmitt's well known distinction between commissarial and sovereign dictatorship is based on their relations to constituent and constituted powers. Sovereign dictatorship is exercised in the name of constituent power:

> From the perspective of sovereign dictatorship, the entire existing order is a situation that dictatorship will resolve through its own actions. Dictatorship does not *suspend* an existing constitution through a law based on the constitution – a constitutional law; rather it seeks to create conditions in which a constitution – a constitution that it regards as the true one – is made possible. Therefore dictatorship does not appeal to an existing constitution, but to one that is still to come. One should think that such an enterprise evades all legal considerations, because the state can be conceived of in legal terms only in its constitution, and the total negation of the existing constitution should

---

17 Sieyès, above n. 13, p. 136.

18 On the problem of representability of constituent power see: Roznai, above n. 12, 301–04; M. Tushnet, 'Amendment theory and constituent power' in Jacobsohn and Schor, above n. 12, pp. 329–30.

19 See also C. Schmitt, *Constitutional Theory*, tr. J. Seitzer, Duke University Press, Durham 2008, pp. 61–77.

> normally relinquish any legal justification – since, by definition, a constitution that is to come does not yet exist. Consequently we would be dealing with sheer power. But this is not the case if the power assumed is one that, without being itself constitutionally established, nevertheless is associated with any existing constitution in such a way that it appears to be foundational to it – even if it is never itself subsumed by the constitution, so that it can never be negated either (insofar as the existing constitution negates it). This is the meaning of *pouvoir constituant*.[20]

Commissarial dictatorship, on the other hand, is exercised at the level of constituted power within the boundaries of constitutional commission and only to pursue a legally defined aim: 'The commissary dictator is the unconditional commissar of action of a *pouvoir constitué*, and sovereign dictatorship is the unconditional commission of action of a *pouvoir constituant*'.[21]

The difference between both types of dictatorships may boil down to the existence or absence of *constitutional fetishism*. Commissarial dictatorship believes it defends a suspended constitutional order, so all its actions are motivated in relation to an increasingly vague goal of self-preservation. The more or less imaginary constitutional commission is a fetishist shield that does not allow it to recognise the proper value and meaning of its actions. Its perception is narrowed to an image of what is necessary. By contrast, sovereign dictatorship renounces constitutional fetishism and seeks a new legal framework, thus effectively acting in the position of constituent power.

In both types of dictatorship, the Sieyèsian concept of an 'end' is still a foundation of constitutionalism, even though it is much reworked in comparison with its original understanding. In Sieyès, ends – defined in the constitution – were part of the legal framework that aimed at circumscribing acts of the constituted power. This link is preserved to some extent in Schmitt's commissarial dictatorship, but here the end – preservation of the constitution – is more vague, non-material (it does not define any particular policy, but the overall goal of all policies) and flexible, as it allows for more discretion on the part of constituted power. The concept is so vague that its maintenance, juxtaposed with great arbitrariness given

20 C. Schmitt, *Dictatorship. From the origin of the modern concept of sovereignty to proletarian class struggle*, tr. M. Hoelzl and G. Ward, Polity Press, Cambridge and Molden, MA 2014, p. 119.

21 *Ibid.*, p. 127.

to the dictatorship, makes it effectively fetishist. In sovereign dictatorship, however, the end is preserved as the general non-legal utopian direction of the new power.

Nonetheless, both the concept of an end and detailed institutional regulations of constituent power in Sieyès and Schmitt assume a general structure of relations between both powers as based on unilateral determination. The very opposition of constituent/constituted powers presupposes that the former gives a mandate and determines a particular institutional field that the latter exercises.[22] In other words, the constituent power is envisaged as sovereignly determining constituted power. As a result, actions of the constituted power are seen in advance through a restricted perspective of respecting or disrespecting its constitutional mandate. Neither path is supposed to change the scope of the mandate or transform its relation with constituent power. The stiffness of Schmitt's distinction epitomises this: if a given constituted power seeks reconstitution of its relation to the constituent power, it changes its essence, becomes a sovereign dictatorship and effectively turns into constituent power.

Closer scrutiny, however, reveals the entanglement of constituent and constituted power which is much more intricate than the rigidity of their separation by a legal fiction would suggest. In the everyday exercise of power, the constitution is being permanently concretised and developed. Every act of its application enriches it: either with new a detailed understanding, if it presents a legal case that demands resolution, or at least with a routine of following a typical interpretation if a case does not seem to present any legal dilemma. To both cases the rigid distinction between the two powers would have a simplifying answer: either the process of development remains within the mandate and thus is nothing but exercise of constituted power, or it violates the mandate, being nothing but illegal usurpation of the position of constituent power. But the distinction of the two powers in this account may be upheld only if the mandate is understood as a stiff legal instrument that always permits to separate legal and illegal exercise of power. It might be, as Nico Krisch noticed,[23] helplessly mired in its modern Enlightenment context, but precisely in this respect it may demonstrate how postmodern practice of power is incongruent with its still modern underpinning.

---

22 See Roznai, above n. 12, 297.

23 N. Krisch, '*Pouvoir constituant* and *pouvoir irritant* in the postnational order' (2016) 14 *I•CON*, 657.

Therefore it is much more accurate to assume that the gradual process of development and expansion of constitutional norms – undertaken not only by the executive or the legislative, but also (or sometimes even principally) as a result of judicial activism – blurs the distinction between constituent and constituted powers. It is no accident that the division recurs in moments of constitutional crises: if taken seriously, it proves impractical in the everyday exercise of power in which the boundaries between constituent and constituted power are shifting sands. In this position, constituent power is a legal fiction[24] (or 'myth'[25]) used in order to criticise ongoing constitutional transformations by recalling 'the original constitutional mandate' (by originalists, for example).

But even in moments of crises, the distinction is not rigid. The state of exception which Schmitt hails as the device aiming for the preservation of the constitutional mandate[26] and, consequently, the clarity of difference between constituent and constituted power, is in fact nothing but acting in the name of the mandate in suspension of the mandate. The interpretation of how far the constituted power may go in the state of exception is practically carried out by this power itself. The constituent power, assumed as always to be retaining the power to 're-constitute the constitution on its own terms',[27] does not have, however, its proper 'speaker'.[28] Normally, it may be claimed that constitutional courts (or their equivalents in other judiciaries) speak in its name, but despite their borderline position, they still belong to constituted power. 'The people' may speak as constituent power, but its channels of expression – as well as the very problematic construction of what a people is and how it organises itself – are notoriously vague. Finally, legal jurisprudence may speak in the name of constituent power, but only as an *après coup* reconstruction of how a particular mandate was transformed in the state of exception. To sum up, the constituent power, precisely for its normative universalism, has no 'proper' channel of communication with the constituted power that would not be effectively organised and dominated by the latter.

---

24 Tushnet, above n. 12, 14.

25 Loughlin, above n. 12, 222.

26 C. Schmitt, *Political Theology. Four Chapters on the Concept of Sovereignty*, tr. G. Schwab, MIT Press, Cambridge MA and London 1985, pp. 5–15.

27 Tushnet, above n. 12, 15.

28 On this age-old problem with the concept of constituent power, see Loughlin, above n. 12, 220–21; Krisch, above n. 23, 660–61.

These observations necessarily affect the notion of the revolution. In the logic of strict distinction between the two powers, the revolution should be understood as a situation in which the constituent power breaks with the previous mandate given to the constituted power. The constitution is not amended, but either abrogated or replaced. The necessary discontinuity in the exercise of constituted power in such situations is supplemented by the evocation of constituent power. The organs of constituted power may be elevated – through new forms of political organisation (referenda, plebiscites, participation of the masses) or by sheer usurpation – to the rank of 'speakers' of constituent power. But the problematic aspect of this perspective is that it assumes a sufficient level of symbolic representation of the revolution. If constituent power is evoked in the suspension or abrogation of the constitution, the actors of this transformation must not only be aware of it, but must also give it a proper form. Consequently, the rigid distinction of the two powers – which assumes that the shift in relations between them transforms organs of constituted power into 'speakers' of constituent power – is less suitable for understanding revolutions which take place without a proper symbolic representation.

If, however, we assume a flexible map of relations between constituent and constituted powers, encompassing conceptually small shifts that amend the constitution without a 'proper' symbolic act of abrogation or replacement, we can understand much better that not all revolutions are based on the unidirectional command of constituent power over constituted power. A revolution might instead consist of a disturbance between the two, not necessarily initiated or carried out by constituent power. *Pouvoir constitué* may overstep its constitutional mandate and transform the very way that *pouvoir constituant* is supposed to 'express itself'. Additionally, it may simply blur this mandate – by an activist interpretation of constitutional norms – thereby effectively disturbing the relations between the two powers without a proper constitutional amendment or a revolutionary symbolic act.

This more subtle and detailed relation between the two powers makes the concept of a revolution without a revolution satisfyingly explicable. Otherwise, we are too dependent on the notion of violation of a norm (in this case, a norm of constitutional rank, determining the mandate of the constituted power) to account for conundrums that contemporary European populist regimes have created: situations of persisting structural violations of the constitution which last long enough to effectively create a different regime, even if formally liberal norms are still in force.

Naturally, 'violation' is an indispensable term, but as long as it is construed as if its denotation did not effectively transform the norm which is violated, it blocks understanding of how these regimes practically function. In contrast, a revolution without a revolution is a term that goes beyond the mere acknowledgement that some norms have been violated to encompass situations where the constituted power shifts the goalposts of its mandate to effectively modify the relations with constituent power. Schmitt's intuition that by doing so *pouvoir constitué* is elevated to the rank of *pouvoir constituant* is not fully adequate, because such an elevation is done tacitly and is discernible only in doctrinal retrospection. A revolution without a revolution consists precisely of actions of *pouvoir constitué* that does not want to take the position and responsibility of *pouvoir constituant*, but exercises it in practice.

This usurpation, shrouded with ideological displacements and repressions, has a dynamic of its own. This dynamic might entail at least two types of processes: legal and socio-political. Legally speaking, a revolution without a revolution undermines the very sense of constitutional law and borders on legal anarchy. The persuasive and commanding roles of legal norms are hampered. The legal system becomes blurred and lacks legal certainty.[29] On the socio-political level, a revolution without a revolution might entail passivation of the population which no longer feels capable of exercising constituent power. Transformations undertaken without an adequate symbolic representation may lack social support and, consequently, legitimacy.

These consequences make a revolution without a revolution a particularly problematic social transformation. As I will attempt to demonstrate with the example of Polish populism, its intricacies and long-lasting side effects may be as complex as in the case of a proper revolution.

3. A REVOLUTIONARY PROJECT BEFORE THE REVOLUTION: THE 2010 CONSTITUTIONAL DRAFT

Law and Justice, the right-wing party which has been building a populist regime in Poland since 2015, was first in power between 2005 and 2007.

---

29 On historical examples of a vague exercise of *pouvoir constituent*, see: J. Blount, 'Participation in constitutional design' in T. Ginsburg and R. Dixon (eds), *Comparative Constitutional Law*, Edward Elgar, Cheltenham, Northampton, MA 2011, pp. 44–45.

At that time, it already displayed some features that were later developed into daily strategies of populist rule, such as extreme polarisation, scapegoating, usage of the prosecution apparatus for political goals, attacks against the judiciary and questioning the authority of state institutions they did not control (such as the Constitutional Court). Nonetheless, as its rule was wobbly – dependent on two other coalition parties and facing a strong opposition – it did not last long and naturally could not involve an overhaul of the liberal regime established by the 1997 constitution. Despite this weakness and notwithstanding its swift tactical manoeuvres, the party referred to a vision of the state it wanted to build. Vague as it was, it had a few clear ideological footholds: a 'strong state' with a presidential regime, nationalism, a privileged position of the Catholic religion and primacy of the national community over liberal individualism.

In the spirit of what now seems old-fashioned constitutionalism, the Law and Justice party twice attempted to propose a draft of the new constitution that would correspond to their vision of the so-called 'Fourth Republic' (as opposed to the Third Republic that succeeded the socialist state in 1989). The first draft, published in 2005, had no chance of being seriously considered as a bill because the party lacked even a simple majority in Parliament. The then-rhetoric put stress on building elements of the new regime within the boundaries of the liberal constitution, although tensions between its norms and the ambitions of the party were manifest.

In 2010, when Poland was ruled by a centre-right coalition, the Law and Justice party updated its draft constitution.[30] Its meaning remained purely symbolic, but it pointed not only to the fact that the party intended to replace the liberal regime with a more authoritarian and community-oriented state, but also that it sought to undertake this transformation with legal means. Nonetheless, the constitutional ambitions were soon replaced with a day-to-day tactics focused on reaching rhetorical hegemony and gaining power. This shift was complete when the 2010 draft constitution was quickly removed from the website of the party as it prepared for the 2011 election.[31]

---

30 *Projekt Prawa i Sprawiedliwości. Konstytucja Rzeczypospolitej Polskiej*, January 2010, available at: http://niezniknelo.com/konstytucjaPiS2010.pdf, last accessed 02.03.2020.

31 P. Wroński, 'PiS chce zmienić konstytucję. Będzie odwołanie do Boga i likwidacja autonomii państwa i Kościoła?', *Gazeta Wyborcza*, 04.05.2017, available at: http://wyborcza.pl/7,75398,21761057,pis-chce-zmienic-konstytucje-bedzie-odwolanie-do-boga-i-likwidacja.html, last accessed: 02.03.2020.

Such a change was a crucial step in the transformation of Polish right-wing populism from a movement with 'ordinarily' revolutionary ambitions to the one that undertook a proper revolution without a revolution. In order to grasp this change, it is essential to put the 2010 draft under closer scrutiny.

The constitutional draft of Law and Justice from 2010 differed from the 1997 liberal constitution in many respects. Already the preamble accentuated a non-liberal approach to the relations between the state, the nation and their symbolic mediation. The draft began with an *invocatio dei*; the godhead was referred to as an omnipotent entity, to whom the constitution was addressed and who was responsible – as 'Providence' – 'for the gift of independence'. The independence was not an attribute of the state, but of the 'Polish Nation' (notably spelled with capital letters, against the rules of Polish orthography). In clear contrast to the 1997 constitution, the draft did not specify that the nation was to be understood as all the citizens of Poland. It was understood rather as an *ethnos* – guided by Christianity for over a thousand years, liberated from the yoke of 'foreign violence and communism', spiritually linked to past and future generations and, finally, demanding a republic which would be 'strong by its truth, honesty and justice'.[32]

In its ideological representation, the preamble of the draft shifted the source of power in the state from the body politic as composed of citizens, whose individual worldviews are necessarily multifarious, to the nationalist vision of a godhead-supported nation that endures throughout centuries and only contingently assumes the garb of a given state form. Simultaneously, it posited an ideological overlap between the nation and the state: the former, by 'gaining independence', was assumed to be the direct sovereign of the state; there was no assumed tension between the two.

Furthermore, the differences with the 1997 liberal constitution were expressed through a complex web of re-hierarchisations and omissions. This strategy proved that the state intended to be built on the basis of the draft was closer to an authoritarian variation on liberal democracy than a self-sufficient constitutional project. Whereas the 1997 constitution[33] – drawing from a tradition of post-socialist transition – established the Polish Republic as a democratic state ruled by law (Art. 2), the draft declared also in Art. 2 that sovereignty, independence and territorial integrity are key

32 *Projekt Prawa i Sprawiedliwości. Konstytucja Rzeczypospolitej Polskiej*, p. 4.
33 Konstytucja Rzeczypospolitej Polskiej, Dz.U. 1997, no. 78, at 483.

values of the state. Moreover, sovereignty was referred to as 'the condition of preserving the heritage of all the generations of Poles and development of a person in the national community' (Art. 2 par. 1), thereby sealing the unholy equivalence between the sovereign state, 'the national community' and the 'development of a person'. Some crucial omissions concerned the legal status of women (whose equality with men, declared in Art. 33 of the 1997 constitution, was dropped in favour of declaring the state's protection of marriage understood as a relationship of a man and a woman in Art. 4, par. 3, p. 3 of the draft) and freedom of the press, which was no longer mentioned in the draft.

The whole text was permeated with subdued allusions corresponding to the image that the Law and Justice party intentionally adopted, presenting itself as targeting criminals and defending victim-focused laws which are tough, but just. A good example is Art. 17, par. 2 of the draft, which copied almost verbatim the provision of the 1997 constitution on the conditions of limiting human rights and freedoms (limitations must be declared by law, must be necessary and legitimate and cannot infringe on the essence of a given right), with one telling modification. The last condition – non-infringement on the essence of a right – was supplemented with the following condition: 'unless a given limitation consists in administering by the court a just penalty or a measure which is necessary to prevent commission of crimes'. Consequently, 'a just penalty' could entirely infringe on the essence of a given right – which concerned, *inter alia*, the possibility of the right to life being annihilated by death penalty. It is noteworthy, however, that this provision used the condition of 'justness' of a penalty which legitimised an infringement on the essence of rights. Apart from its vagueness, arbitrariness and material character, it also contains a characteristic insinuation addressed at courts: the law itself assumes that punishments might be 'just' or 'unjust'. This innuendo went hand-in-hand with a few other provisions which questioned *pro futuro* – in a mockingly reversed presumption of innocence – the qualities of persons occupying public posts. Accordingly, the president of the republic was to be granted the power to dismiss judges 'whose previous behaviour displays inability or lack of will to hold the office in an honest way' (Art. 145, par. 2). The president could also refuse to swear in a minister 'if there is a legitimate ground to believe that this person will not obey the law' (Art. 122, par. 1).

Finally, the 2010 draft intended to change the regime of the state to an unambiguously presidential system. Instead of the balance of powers inscribed in the 1997 constitution, the draft gave to the president of the republic broad competences to dissolve Parliament, almost entirely at the president's will (Art. 94), significantly influence nominations in the executive and the judiciary (including one-third of judges of the Constitutional Court) and use elements of direct democracy (referenda) against decisions of the legislative.

This brief overview of the 2010 draft demonstrates that what later developed into one of the strongest populist movements of Europe began as a project of a constitutional revolution. Mild as it might have been against the background of CEE history, it implicated a profound transformation of a state towards a combination of conservatism, nationalism and community-centred republicanism. Apart from a new institutional setting, the draft aimed to reshape relations between constituent and constituted power. The ideological locus of the former was to be shifted from a civic nation to the *ethnos*. At the same time, the constitutional bulwarks against frequent amendments of the constitution were to be lifted: whereas the 1997 constitution required a referendum for confirming amendments pertaining to its key provisions (determining foundations of the state as well as human and civic rights), the 2010 draft – otherwise so open to direct democracy – did not demand popular endorsement of constitutional amendments. Consequently, the draft assumed a clearly more decisive role of constituted power vis-à-vis the channels of 'self-expression' of constituent power.

In its construction, the new constitutional project was dependent on the liberal democracy that it attempted to overhaul. It is precisely for this reason that it implicitly targeted symbols of liberal democracy: rule of law, national inclusiveness and gender equality, as well as the position of the legislative and the judiciary. These negative points of reference haunt the text, displaying the movement's reliance on a dynamic, anti-liberal agenda which cannot allow the draft to be stabilised on solid, positively determined provisions. When the draft was abandoned and the movement concentrated on flexible and vague anti-liberalism, the symbolic dimension of the revolution was therefore easily discarded for the sake of revolutionary practice.

4. EFFECTIVE SUSPENSION OF THE CONSTITUTION

After 2010, Law and Justice took a swerve towards a more postmodern form of populism. Instead of the old-fashioned politics pegged on a huge ideological project topped with a constitutional draft, it gave preference to a permanent spectacle rooted in the cultural war between the 'national-conservative' and 'liberal' camps as demarcated by floating signifiers. The clearly exposed strategy of transforming the state was discarded in favour of swift tactical moves covered up with profuse rhetoric. The ideological fight was expanded to encompass even the hitherto neutral institutions of the state and legal devices. This overt 'turn to postmodern politics' was accompanied by dismantlement of the symbolic framework that would allow for remarking of the revolutionarity of the planned transformations. As the party's popularity was on the rise and it prepared itself to get hold of state apparatus (2014–15), it became clear that the link between the true significance of measures it intended to adopt and their symbolic recognition was engulfed by politics focused on spectacle and tactics.[34]

Accordingly, the symbolic dimension of the revolution was obliterated. This tendency was reinforced by the path to power of Law and Justice: the coalition led by the party won both presidential and parliamentary elections in 2015, but did not gain constitutional majority. Adoption of a new constitution would thus require a compromise with the opposition. Confronted with a structural blockade of its plans to rebuild the state, the new coalition could not follow their Hungarian partners. Instead of amending the constitution, it decided to effectively modify it via adoption of unconstitutional laws.

Therefore, in recent Polish history, the year 2015 marks a sea change in the approach to the rule of law, democratic values and, consequently, to relations between constituent and constituted powers. The constitutional mandate was effectively modified without any proper amendment of its written form. Some norms of the constitution were rendered inoperative by the adoption of sub-constitutional laws which are incompliant with it, whereas the institution that could declare their unconstitutionality (the Constitutional Court) was paralysed.[35]

---

34 See G. Debord, *The Society of the Spectacle*, tr. D. Nicholson-Smith, Zone Books, New York 1994.

35 A good overview of the key developments in the crisis can be found in: W. Sadurski, *Poland's Constitutional Breakdown*, Oxford University Press, Oxford 2019, pp. 62–65; S. Jankovic, 'Polish Democracy Under Threat? An Issue of Mere Politics or a Real Danger?' (2016) 9 *Baltic Journal of Law & Politics*, 49–68; T.T. Koncewicz, 'The Capture of the Polish Constitutional Tribunal and Beyond: Of institution(s), Fidelities and the Rule of Law in Flux', (2018) 43 *Review of Central and East European Law*, 116ff; W. Sadurski, 'Polish Constitutional Tribunal Under PiS: From an Activist Court, to a Paralysed Tribunal, to a Governmental Enabler' (2019) 11 *Hague Journal on the Rule of Law*, 63–84.

As a result, the key safeguard of maintaining the proper balance between constituent and constituted power was defused. Both links between the two powers enshrined in the constitutional mandate – the institutional and procedural framework, as well as setting objectives for constituted power – began to erode, as any sub-constitutional law adopted by constituted power effectively could freely amend it. Soon after the CC was intercepted, the ruling coalition targeted another branch of the state apparatus that could defend the constitutional mandate – the judiciary.

Since 2016, the populist coalition adopted a number of far-fetched unconstitutional measures curbing the independence of the judiciary: (1) strengthening disciplinary procedures against judges and establishing a new Disciplinary Chamber of the Supreme Court,[36] which the other chambers – applying the CJEU's answer to a preliminary question on this matter[37] – found to be established in breach of EU law and therefore illegitimate;[38] (2) introducing an extraordinary legal remedy against all final judgments delivered after the entry into force of the 1997 Constitution;[39] (3) appointing lay judges of the Supreme Court, whose duties encompass adjudicating on these extraordinary remedies and who are appointed by the Senate;[40] (4) changing the composition of the National Council of the Judiciary – a constitutional organ in charge of nominating candidates for judges – whose members representing the judiciary are no longer elected by judges themselves, but by the lower chamber of the Parliament;[41] (5) establishing direct control of the Minister of Justice – Prosecutor General over presidents of common courts who can effectively discipline and block judges who are loyal to the constitution and European law;

36 Ustawa o Sądzie Najwyższym *[The Supreme Court Law]*, 8.12.2017, Dz. U. 2018, at 5, Art. 27, 72–76.

37 Case C-585/18, C-624/18 and C-625/18, *A. K. and Others v. Sąd Najwyższy*, ECLI:EU:C:2019:982. See also order of the Grand Chamber in case C-791/19 R, *Commission v. Poland*, ECLI:EU:C:2020:277.

38 Case BSA I-4110-1/20, RESOLUTION of the formation of the combined Civil Chamber, Criminal Chamber, and Labour Law and Social Security Chamber, 23 January 2020. English version available at: http://www.sn.pl/aktualnosci/SiteAssets/Lists/Wydarzenia/AllItems/BSA%20I-4110-1_20_English.pdf; last accessed 26.04.2020.

39 Ustawa o Sądzie Najwyższym, Art. 115 §1, 89 §1.

40 Ustawa o Sądzie Najwyższym, Art. 61 §2.

41 Ustawa o zmianie ustawy o Krajowej Radzie Sądownictwa oraz niektórych innych ustaw, 8.12.2017, Dz. U. 2018, at 3, Art. 1 (1). See also P. Filipek, 'The New National Council of the Judiciary and Its Impact on the Supreme Court in the Light of the Principle of Judicial Independence' (2018) XVI *Problemy Współczesnego Prawa Międzynarodowego, Europejskiego i Porównawczego* 177–96.

(6) adopting the so-called 'muzzle law' which punishes judges who – in application of EU law and the Polish Constitution – cast doubt on the legality of appointment of judges nominated by the 'new' National Council of the Judiciary;[42] and (7) appointing – with a violation of the constitutional procedure – the new First President of the Supreme Court, who is a former vice-minister in a Law and Justice government.

These revolutionary measures were concealed by a patchy ideological smokescreen that did not correspond to the measures' real significance. The aforementioned unconstitutional measures, which aimed to undermine the division of powers and the state of law, should be viewed in the context of the anti-liberal rhetoric in which they are heavily imbued. Using a distinctively populist gesture of identifying with the whole nation and attacking illegitimate 'elites',[43] especially judges,[44] the ruling coalition presented undermining of the independence of the judiciary as performed in the interest of the nation. Judges as a professional group were systematically defiled; and incidental misdemeanours perpetrated by some of them were decried as symptoms of their generalised corruption. The Constitutional Court, previously hailed by the liberal doctrine as a stronghold of impartiality, independence and loyalty to the Constitution,[45] was now denounced – in a vulgar version of critical approach to law – as elitist, post-communist and politicised, but of course only until it was fully intercepted.

As a result, the most significant determinant of Polish constitutionalism after 2015 is the effective unconstitutional suspension of certain constitutional norms. Simultaneously, in discourses produced by the ruling majority,

---

42 Ustawa z dnia 20 grudnia 2019 r. o zmianie ustawy – Prawo o ustroju sądów powszechnych, ustawy o Sądzie Najwyższym oraz niektórych innych ustaw, Dz. U. 2020, at 190.

43 Cf. B. Bugarič and A. Kuhelj, 'Varieties of Populism in Europe: Is the Rule of Law in Danger?' (2018) 10 *Hague Journal of the Rule of Law*, 22.

44 In 2017, a Polish government-funded organisation, the Polish National Foundation, prepared a billboard smear campaign targeted at Polish courts and judges. It was meant to justify the reforms adopted by the right-wing government, such as lowering the retirement age for the Supreme Court judges (in order to appoint new ones in their place) and gaining political control over the National Council of the Judiciary which plays a pivotal role in the process of appointing judges. See M. Orłowski, 'PiS kontratakuje ws. sądów. Rządowe billboardy zawisną w całej Polsce', *Gazeta Wyborcza*, 07.09.2017, available at: http://wyborcza.pl/7,75398,22335331,pis-kontratakuje-ws-sadow-rzadowe-billboardy-zawisna-w-calej.html; last accessed 26.04.2020.

45 T. Warczok and H. Dębska, 'Sacred Law and Profane Politics: The Symbolic Construction of the Constitutional Tribunal' (2014) 188 *Polish Sociological Review*, 462.

the constitution became an object of repression. The Polish constitutional language became ravaged with taboos and ceased to describe the political community. While unable to *describe* the community, it still *expresses* it in a paradoxical way – as a split body politic unable to define itself or to refer to itself in a self-reflexive manner.

Thus, Polish constitutionalism lost one of the features that is usually associated with constitutions in liberal jurisprudence: the orientating and unifying factor. Currently, it is split into at least four different levels: (1) the level of unconstitutional laws which effectively modify the regime of the state in order to subordinate independent institutions to the ruling coalition; (2) the level of official rhetoric produced by the ruling majority (notably nationalist, populist and anti-elitist, praising the Polish nation understood as the *ethnos*, unified by Catholicism and homogenous culture);[46] (3) the level of constitutional narrative produced by judicial institutions, torn between loyalty towards constitutional and European values and loyalty to the ruling majority (especially in the case of the CC); and (4) the Constitution as a point of reference in the political struggle between the ruling party and the opposition.

All four levels are separate to a significant degree and communicate occasionally. As a result, the constitution is not only the source of political polarisation, but its suspension and repression lead to profound fragmentation of Polish constitutionalism. The ruling coalition, by pushing forward with its unconstitutional agenda, managed to gain more power that the constitution allowed for;[47] nonetheless, it effectively deprived itself of the constitutional language, thus losing the means to express the revolutionarity of its actions. The praxis of power lost its ideological grounding in the constitution, which turned into a fragile subject of repression in the discourse of the ruling majority and becomes a 'semantic constitution' only.[48] This absence is supplemented with excessive reliance on extra-constitutional populist platitudes, such as equivocation of the

46 M. Kotwas and J. Kubik, 'Symbolic Thickening of Public Culture and the Rise of Right-Wing Populism in Poland' (2019) 33 *East European Politics and Societies and Cultures*, 435–71; M. Bucholc, 'Commemorative Lawmaking: Memory Frames of the Democratic Backsliding in Poland After 2015' (2019) 11 *Hague Journal on the Rule of Law*, 86–105.

47 It is in this sense that András Sajó claims that contemporary populisms 'cheat on democracy'; A. Sajó, 'The Rule of Law as Legal Despotism: Concerned Remarks on the Use of "*Rule of Law*" in Illiberal Democracies' (2019) 11 *Hague Journal on the Rule of Law*, 376.

48 Tóth, above n. 4, 52–53.

nation with the ruling majority and witch-hunting against more or less imaginary 'elites'.

It is therefore of little surprise that the rupture in the symbolic underpinning of the state caused by evisceration of constitutionalism was covered with profuse nationalist (and often religious)[49] rhetoric. In the classic populist short circuit of identifying the nation with the populist movement, the current ruling majority sometimes fashions itself as speaking directly in the name of the sovereign, thereby arrogating the position of constituent power.[50] This manoeuvre was a ritual counter-argument to objections to violations of the constitution. Nonetheless, it retained in its essence the accusation that the 1997 constitution, adopted in a referendum by a small margin of votes (53% with 43% turnout)[51] was illegitimate.

It might seem that in this, the populist revolution without a revolution was most opposed to the idea of constitutional mandate, which precludes – at least in normal times – taking the role of constituent power by constituted power. Yet perhaps the greatest contradiction exists in the fact that whereas constitutional mandate is supported by a vision of symbolic stability, in which roles are assigned in advance, the malleable and flexible populist rhetoric swiftly recombines and dissolves the division of powers for its tactical purposes. *Pouvoir constituant* may be a liberal avatar, but if it is removed from the position of the legal fiction, it returns at the level of ideological smokescreen that covers abuse of the constitutional mandate.

5. A REVOLUTION WITHOUT A REVOLUTION: POPULIST DISCONNECTION

The example of Polish populism epitomises the fundamental contradiction on which 'a revolution without a revolution' is founded: transformations which are of revolutionary character – given that they reshape the

49 See R. Markowski, 'Creating Authoritarian Clientelism: Poland After 2015' (2019) 11 *Hague Journal on the Rule of Law*, 130–31.

50 This is a fundamental threat inscribed from the beginning into the concept of constituent power – see D. Landau and H. Ferner, 'Introduction to *Comparative Constitution Making*: The state of the field' in Landau and Ferner, above n. 11, 6.

51 *Obwieszczenie Państwowej Komisji Wyborczej z dnia 26 maja 1997 r. o wynikach głosowania i wyniku referendum konstytucyjnego przeprowadzonego w dniu 25 maja 1997 r.*, O. J. 1997, no. 54, at 353.

relationship between constituent and constituted power – are shrouded by a set of linguistic practices that obfuscate their true character.

These practices may be divided into two groups. The first encompasses all forms of short-term tactical rhetoric that bear affinity with the 'salami technique' (to use Mátyás Rákosi's infamous term). What they perform is a narrowing of the horizon of political imagination in order to present each adopted measure as a local and short-distance remedy to a particular problem (for example, the refusal of the Polish president to swear in three legally elected judges of the CC was originally presented only as a 'neutral' rejection of an allegedly illegal act of the previously ruling coalition). Only retrospectively do their measures add up to a perhaps incoherent, but unidirectional trend towards interception of independent state institutions by the ruling majority against the constitutional mandate. The second group of rhetorical practices represents an elusive representation of the significance of the ongoing transformations, distorted through its inherent vagueness. The term used by the Polish populists is 'a good change' (*dobra zmiana*), which is the ultimate floating signifier: it could be used by a mostly moderate party to describe its practices, yet it was adopted by *de facto* revolutionaries. In an inventive travesty of strategies used by liberal 'catch-all' parties, this signifier carries no more meaning than just a call for support of the undertaken measures which are reportedly 'good'. The contrast between the overt radicalism of the 2010 constitutional draft and the deceiving mildness of 'a good change' epitomises how far the process of symbolic underrepresentation went.

Simultaneously, both sets of techniques may be effective only within a specifically transformed society of spectacle. Populist governmentality reduces the public opinion to a field of struggle between two camps of cultural war whose quarrel is managed through a chain of local skirmishes pegged on vaguely marked ideological floating signifiers. This war also blurs the boundaries of constitutionalism, disfiguring the dividing line between constituent and constituted powers as defined by the written mandate of the former for the latter. Naturally, the mandate can still be reconstructed by the doctrine or independent state institutions (and, consequently, the erosion of constitutionalism can be denounced), but it loses the function of providing a stable channel of 'expression' for constituent power. The state's regime is thus set adrift: the general public is witnessing a mystified process of transformation whose scope and goal it can no longer easily recognise.

Moreover, a populist revolution without a revolution warps the teleological element of each constitutional mandate and reveals its partly utopian character. Schmitt, in his concept of dictatorships, already pointed to the illusiveness of making goals binding legal provisions: goals may be disjointed from their legal embedding and therefore are prone to being fetishised. Populist legality proves that apart from this drift, the teleological device within contemporary liberal constitutionalism may be paralysed by a combination of two strategies: (1) interception of mechanisms of judicial review that remain the only practical goal checkers within the system; and (2) substitution of general teleology, based on an overt account of pursued objectives as compared with concrete measures, with a set of unholy motives concealed behind official rationalisations. In this sense, contemporary populism in power acts parasitically on what Agamben identified as a crucial abyss in law-application:[52] it disjoins constitutional norms from their realisation and colonises this hiatus with an agenda imposed by the executive.[53] For this reason, a populist revolution without a revolution is a state of exception in the Agambenian sense (regardless of whether the legal device of the same name is practically used).

A revolution without a revolution may be interpreted as one step further in the decline of liberal constitutionalism caused by a combination of factors: proliferation of the society of spectacle; expansion of purportedly non-political concepts of governance; transformation of the public sphere due to new communication technologies;[54] and the short-term framework of thinking, but also a decline of what since Lyotard has been fashionably dubbed 'great narratives' (or 'master-narratives' in Lyotard's own parlance).[55] Liberal constitutionalism, especially that which relies on a rigid distinction between constituent and constituted power, corresponds to a top-down relation between a symbolic recognition of an act and its execution. Against this background, the liberal capitalist technocracy already gave priority to executive acts against a teleological framework that supposedly was meant to control them. Populist legality extrapolates this strategy by disjointing the symbolic anchoring of the legal system from its constitutional setting.

Both contemporary liberal governmentality and its official opponent, 'illiberal' populist governmentality, are in a complex relationship to the

---

52 G. Agamben, *Creation and Anarchy. The Work of Art and the Religion of Capitalism*, tr. A. Kotsko, Stanford University Press, Stanford CA 2019, pp. 50–51; *Opus Dei. Archeologia dell'ufficio (Homo sacer II, 5)*, Bollati Bolinghieri, Torino, pp. 140–43.

53 Priority of the executive is a characteristic feature of contemporary European populisms; see Tóth, above n. 4, 53, 57.

54 See J. Muis and T. Immerzeel, 'Causes and consequences of the rise of populist radical right parties and movements in Europe' (2017) 65 *Current Sociology Review* 6, 914.

55 J.-F. Lyotard, *The Postmodern Condition*, Manchester University Press, Manchester 1984, pp. xi–xii.

status quo. The decade 2010–2020, in which their clash was sanctioned as the main political expression of the social antagonism, was a period of swift social change in which development of new technologies with the accompanying forms of surveillance were just a token. Challenges of the climate and refugee crises epitomised the pressure of 'external' impulses on liberal democracies. Simultaneously, political life in democracies framed in liberal constitutional models has proven surprisingly resistant to transformation. It may be argued that illiberal populism was born in response to the structural blockade of the *status quo*: growing inequalities, misrepresentation of social antagonisms in political divisions and complexity of liberal state apparatus – all shrouded by various versions of the TINA doctrine. But in its concreteness and focus on rhetoric, it lacks the ability to offer a coherent and positive programme – at all symbolic levels, including the constitutional – that would be able to rebuild contemporary democracy.

As a result, contemporary right-wing populism is mired in 'a revolution without a revolution' approach. It promises a change that will not be symbolically represented as a real transformation. Without a proper re-constitution, it does not allow the people to choose the basic framework of the state.[56] It remains ironic as to its measures, because it disavows their significance in advance. Not a negligible number of malaises of the 20th century stemmed from overambitious programmes of social change, clashing against the inertia of reality; but it seems that the time of top-bottom revolutions is over at this moment. A revolution without a revolution, in its bottom-top approach that leads to blurring of the constitutional mandate and drifting of the regime in unknown directions, is the revolution for our times. It seems that until we get the grip of symbolic representability of socio-political change, it will be a permanent blockade for democratic trends for self-repair.

6. CONCLUSIONS

The demise of Polish constitutionalism in the 2015–20 period is a showcase of a populist revolution without a revolution: a profound disturbance of relations between constituent and constituted power that not only remains underrepresented on the symbolic level, but involves structural blurring

---

56 See H. Klug, 'Constitution making and social transformation' in Landau and Ferner, above n. 11, 52; Roznai, above n. 12, 298.

of boundaries between the two powers. This revolution has never been framed symbolically in a proper manner and, consequently, has never been a subject of popular approval. In this mystified state, it may be a renewed form of fascist revolutions from the interwar period.[57]

This process was due not only to its direct cause – the lack of constitutional majority – but also to the populist strategy of dropping the top-down perspective of constitutionalism and substituting it with a set of swift local tactical manoeuvres, held together with a spectacle of a permanent struggle along the lines of a deliberately rekindled cultural war. The price for this strategy is high: the ruling coalition lost the possibility to stabilise its hegemony through constitutional self-definition. The constitutional language became ravaged with taboos and stumbling blocks. As a consequence, in some areas the legal order degenerated into a bare tool of political power without any intra-legal ideological grounding – although it is still haunted by the cumbersome spectre of the 1997 constitution. Moreover, the constitutional language lost its inherent tension between the constituent power and the norms it imposes on constituted power: they were effectively conflated. In the rhetoric of the ruling party, the nation is the supreme order-giver and the only addressee of its own orders. In this process, law – constitutional law in particular – is nothing but a cumbersome block.

The Polish case is symptomatic of contemporary populist legality. A revolution without a revolution is, self-evidently, an obvious accusation of populist exercise of power. But it also poses crucial dilemmas concerning feasibility of liberal constitutionalism in times of an advanced society of spectacle. The rule of law is neither an answer nor an explanation, but just part of the riddle.

57 Cercel, above n. 5, 21–25.

REPRESENTATIVE DEMOCRACY IN THE TIMES OF POPULISM

The Case of the Polish Parliament as a Delegated Power

Agnieszka Bień-Kacała, Anna Tarnowska and Wojciech Włoch*

1. INTRODUCTION

In this chapter, by referring to theoretical concepts, we try to answer the question of whether the Polish Parliament is still a representative body. In responding to this question, we would like to contribute to a better understanding of how the concept of delegation in representative democracy may be misused and, consequently, may lead to the impairment of the role of the Parliament.

We take into account the formal and substantive conditions of representativeness. In our opinion, the formal condition is the existence of an appropriate electoral law, while the substantive conditions refer to

* The research on 'Law-making delegation in representative democracy' is supported by the National Centre of Science, contest Opus 11, registration no. 2016/21/B/HS5/00197.

deliberation and discussion within the legislative process. These issues are analysed with reference to constitutional events[1] throughout Polish history.

Thus, we discuss how the 'chain of delegation' is constructed (section 2). Then, we describe the significance of deliberations and discussions for the representativeness of the Sejm (section 3) in order to indicate the issues raised by populism for that representativeness (section 4). Subsequently, we indicate how the chain of delegation can be disrupted in legal solutions and parliamentary practice (section 5). Finally, we offer a brief conclusion to our research (section 6).

2. CONSTRUCTING THE 'CHAIN OF DELEGATION'

Our in-depth analysis is based on the concept described by K. Strøm, W.C. Müller and T. Bergman. According to their findings, a delegation within democratic politics is understood as a process of delegating. The process within a representative democracy creates a specific 'chain of delegation', beginning with the delegation of powers from voters to their representatives.[2] In the model approach, the nation (all citizens) delegates its legislative competence to representatives, who constitute the normative framework for the functioning of other authorities. In other words, democratic legislation takes the form of a special representative body – the Parliament. The nation is the first element of the chain of delegation, and the Parliament is the second. Thus, the existence of the Parliament as a representative body is necessary for the proper functioning of the chain of delegation.

Initially, we would like to detail the model of the Parliament as a representative body. The model is needed to properly answer the question of whether the Sejm – the lower house of the Polish Parliament – is still

---

1 We take into account the fully developed constitutions of 1921 (Constitution of the Republic of Poland of 17th March 1921, Journal of Law No. 44 item 267), 1935 (Constitutional Law of 23rd April 1935, Journal of Laws No. 30, item 227) and 1997 (Constitution of the Republic of Poland of 2nd April 1997, Journal of Laws No. 78 item 483) as creations of a sovereign constitutional legislator. We disregard the constitution of 1952 as an un-democratic act.

2 See K. Strøm, W.C. Müller and T. Bergman, 'Parliamentary Democracy: Promise and Problems' in K Strøm, W.C. Müller and T. Bergman (eds), *Delegation and Accountability in Parliamentary Democracies*, Oxford University Press, Oxford and New York 2006, pp. 3–32.

a representative body. According to E.-J. Sieyès, the Parliament is a body that represents the nation (demos) conceived as constitutive power. 'Government by proxy' (*gouvernement exercé par procuration*)[3] is a product of social development and the growth of society, which makes it impossible for direct democracy to form.[4] Representative institutions must be set up when it is not possible to directly establish the 'common will'. The institutions are based on three principles:

> Firstly, the community does not divest itself of the right to will. This right is its inalienable property. All it can do is to entrust the exercise of that right to someone else. [...] Secondly, the body of those delegated [*Le corps des délégués*] to exercise that trust cannot even enjoy the full exercise of the community's power. The community can entrust only that portion of its total power that will be needed to maintain good order. In this kind of delegation, nothing more than what is necessary is surrendered. Thirdly, it is not up to the body of delegates to alter the limits of the power with which it has been entrusted. It is easy to see that it would be self-contradictory to grant it this kind of faculty.[5]

In this way, the 'common will' transforms into the 'representative common will' (*volonté commune représentative*):

> Firstly, that will, as expressed by the body of representatives, is neither complete nor unlimited; it is no more than a portion of the great common national will. Secondly, those delegated to exercise that will do not do so as a right that is their own, but as a right exercised on others' behalf. The common will is exercised as a delegation or trust.[6]

---

3 E. J. Sieyès, 'What Is the Third Estate?', in E.J. Sieyès (ed.), *Political Writings. Including the Debate between Sieyès and Tom Paine in 1791*, tr. M. Sonenscher, Hackett Publishing Company Inc., Indianapolis and Cambridge 2003, p. 134.

4 Sieyès, above n. 3, p. 147 fn 33, where Sieyès points to the fact that direct democracy is not possible in a 'numerous nation'. Like Kant and the Federalists, he juxtaposed direct democracy in opposition to the representative system (*The Federalist No. 10*), see A. Hamilton, J. Madison and J. Jay, *The Federalist with The Letters of 'Brutus'*, ed. T. Ball, Cambridge University Press, Cambridge 2003, p. 44; I. Kant, 'Toward Perpetual Peace: A Philosophical Sketch' in I. Kant (ed.), *Toward Perpetual Peace and Other Writings on Politics, Peace, and History*, tr. D.L. Colclasure, Yale University Press, New Haven and London 2006, pp. 76–78. Until the end of the 19th century, the term 'democracy' was bound up with the concept of 'direct democracy', see M. Saward, *Democracy*, Polity Press, Cambridge 2003, Chapter 3.

5 Sieyès, above n. 3, pp. 134–35.

6 Sieyès, above n. 3, p. 135.

According to this approach, the Parliament ('the body of the delegated') is the forum in which the current understanding of what can be described as 'the common interest'[7] is formed. H. Kelsen specifies the concept of parliamentarianism in such a way that it means 'creation of the will of the state … by a collegial organ democratically elected by the People based on universal, equal suffrage and the principle of the majority'.[8]

'Creation of the will of the state' means the creation of a universally binding system of norms[9] by the 'body of the delegated', to which the creation of the will of the state is entrusted by the nation. It is assumed that there is a certain bond between the representatives and the represented, and that all delegates can participate in the elaboration of a 'representative common will'.

The role of the Parliament is evident when we consider the way and circumstances in which the 'will of the state' or the 'representative common will' (legislation) is created. The context in which legislative decisions are made is the diversity of positions and interests that causes the 'nation' – the first link in the representation chain – not to be a homogeneous entity.[10] The diversity of attitudes and preferences is reflected at the level of the Parliament as a representative body. However, beyond these differences, citizens – as part of the constitutive (supreme) power – are equal in a specific sense, as expressed by the universal suffrage. It should be understood as a situation where:

> The citizen, endowed with one vote, is seen as a pure individual, symmetrical with all other individuals and stripped of all specific characteristics. […] In exercising the right to vote, each individual is divested of his defining characteristics and associations. Abstraction is thus the quality that constitutes him socially and drives the development of the idea of political equality. That is why this form of equality is so radical and exemplary. It emancipates the individual from all the distinctions by which men are usually ordered and classified.[11]

---

7 Sieyès, above n. 3, p. 155.

8 H. Kelsen, 'Das Problem der Parlamentarismus' in H.R. Klecatsky, R. Marcic and H. Schambeck (eds), *Die Wiener rechtstheoretische Schule*, Franz Steiner Verlag, Wien 2010, p. 1361; H. Kelsen, *The Essence and Value of Democracy*, tr. B. Graf, Rowman and Littlefield Publishers, Lanham and New York 2013, p. 48.

9 Kelsen, above n. 8, pp. 52–53.

10 See R. Dahl, *Democracy and its Critics*, Yale University Press, New Haven 1989, Chapter 15; A. Przeworski, *Democracy and the Limits of Self-Government*, Cambridge University Press, New York 2010, pp. 31–32.

11 P. Rosanvallon, *The Society of Equals*, tr. A. Goldhammer, Harvard University Press, Cambridge and London 2013, p. 35.

Universal suffrage is not linked to any unique characteristics of the individual, and, from this point of view, all citizens are equal (without distinctive features): 'Universal suffrage opens up a new horizon for the collective imaginary: a horizon of radical, immaterial equivalence among men. It is a "constituent" right. It produces society itself: it is the equivalence among individuals that constitutes society'.[12]

Universal suffrage thus constitutes a democratic society of equal citizens and a people as a subject of political power. Voters acquire political significance and identity with the act of establishing political representation. Belonging to a political nation is based on a sense of participation in a collective action (something that is shared): a single voting act takes on importance only as part of a collective action.[13] Co-citizens constitute unity as participants in an electoral act, but as voters for particular candidates or parties, they are differentiated according to the options chosen in the voting.

The possibility to participate and express support constitutes a civic subjectivity, the importance of which is based on its collective character and the possibility to express different political identities. This subjectivity, of course, does not mean a one-sided citizen-representative relationship, since representation is, as E. Laclau claims, a two-way process: it is only through representation that citizens can perceive themselves as a causal political entity.[14] The fact that there is a certain connection – even a small one – between the voter and the representing entity gives citizens subjectivity, because they are no longer just the subject of sovereign decisions, but, most importantly, they can identify themselves with the positions expressed in the parliamentary forum. Thus, they can perceive themselves as having a minimal impact on the creation of a 'representative common will' (they are part of a community supporting certain groups or a political programme). In this sense, their political identity is publicly confirmed, and their right to express it is recognised.[15] This does not mean that electoral law creates a 'strong' sense of civic identity, but instead,

12 Rosanvallon, above n. 11, p. 36.

13 See Rosanvallon, above n. 11, p. 41.

14 E. Laclau, *On Populist Reason*, Verso, London and New York 2005, Chapter 6.

15 Mutual recognition creates a platform for the peaceful conduct of disputes between the different parties. See A. Honneth, *The Struggle for Recognition. The Moral Grammar of Social Conflicts*, tr. J. Anderson, The MIT Press, Cambridge 1995. If A does not consider B to be a fully-fledged entity, then B will not consider A to be such, and therefore, A will not be able to consider itself to be a fully-fledged entity, either. Mutual recognition determines both 'my own' subjectivity and that of the 'other'. Recognition is essentially relational and mutual. The obligation to recognise the other and to be recognised creates a non-violent bond between the various entities.

that it makes it possible at all to establish 'some' identities as a citizen in both unifying (on the part of the people) and differentiating (the part that supports different political options) dimensions. Through universal suffrage, citizens can perceive themselves as equal and equally entitled to political representation. In other words, a nation only becomes politically significant when its individual parts are represented in a chain of delegation (in the Parliament).

This general model of the Parliament as a representative body is reflected in legal regulation. This regulation can have different levels: constitutional and statutory. In the Polish constitutions of 1921 and 1997, universal suffrage for the Sejm was introduced using the principle of equality, with objective qualifications of age and citizenship.[16] At the same

---

16 Art. 12 of the Constitution of 1921:
The right to vote is granted to any Polish citizen, regardless of sex, who on the day of announcing the election is at least 21 years old, fully enjoys their civil rights and has been living in a constituency at least since the day before the announcement of the election in the Journal of Laws. The right to vote can only be exercised in person. Military officers in active service do not have the right to vote.

Art.13:
Every citizen who has the right to take part in the Sejm elections has the right to be elected, not excluding the military in active service, regardless of their place of residence, provided that they are over 25 years of age.

Art. 32 of the Constitution of 1935:
1. The Sejm is composed of members elected by universal suffrage, secret ballot, equal and direct voting.
2. The term of office of the Sejm is five years, counting from the day it is convened.

Art. 33:
1. The right to vote shall be vested in every citizen, without distinction of sex, who, before the date on which the election is ordered, is at least 24 years of age and enjoys their full rights as a citizen.
2. The right to be elected shall be vested in every citizen who has the right to vote if they reach the age of 30.
3. The Electoral Law to the Sejm shall determine the division of the State into constituencies, shall determine the number of deputies, regulate electoral proceedings or designate categories of persons deprived of the right to vote and to be elected for lack of sufficient moral or mental qualities.

Art. 62 of the 1997 Constitution:
1. If, no later than on the day of voting, he has attained 18 years of age, a Polish citizen shall have the right to participate in a referendum and the right to vote for the President of the Republic of Poland as well as representatives to the Sejm and Senate and organs of local government.

time, the electoral system is currently based on the principles of equality and universality.[17] In this way, the formal condition of representativeness at the level of electoral law is fulfilled.

At the same time, however, there may be some restrictive solutions that affect the equality of the electoral law. These can already be adopted at the level of constitutional regulation.[18] Another way is through statutory regulation (examples include the 1935 electoral laws regarding the Sejm[19] and the Senate;[20] and the provisions of the applicable election code that introduce election thresholds for elections to the Sejm).[21] Such solutions mean that a certain number of voters will not be represented in the Parliament at the stage of electing representatives.

3. FROM REPRESENTATION TO DISCUSSION

We have indicated that the chain of delegation is of great importance for the creation of 'the will of the state'/'representative common will'

17 Art. 96 of the 1997 Constitution:
2. Elections to the Sejm shall be universal, equal, direct and proportional and shall be conducted by secret ballot.

18 This is how Art. 7 of the Constitution of 1935, which found its development in the electoral laws of 1935, is to be interpreted:
Article 7 1. The citizen's entitlement to influence public affairs shall be measured by the value of his/her effort and contribution to the common good.

19 The Act of 8th July 1935 (the Electoral Law to the Sejm, Journal of Laws No 47, item 319) provided some limitations; e.g. the district assemblies determined the lists of candidates for deputies – 'single-list system' (Art. 31, 32). Cf. also A. Ajnenkiel, *Historia Sejmu Polskiego*, Vol. II, part II: II Rzeczpospolita, Państwowe Wydawnictwo Naukowe, Warszawa 1989, p. 192–93.

20 Art. 2 of the Act of 8th July 1935 (the Electoral Law to the Senate, Journal of Laws No 47, item 320) limits the electoral constituency to the Senate by merit (bachelors of orders), education and trust (e.g. persons holding elected office in local government or economic government). Cf. Ajnenkiel, above n. 19, pp. 193–94. One-third of the senators were directly nominated by the President of the Republic of Poland (Art. 1 (2)).

21 Act of 5th January 2011, electoral law (Journal of Laws, 2018 items 754, 1000, 1349), Art. 196.§1. Only the lists of candidates for those deputies of election committees whose lists received at least 5% of the validly cast votes at the national level are taken into account in the distribution of seats in electoral districts. §2. The lists of candidates for members of coalition election committees shall be taken into account in the distribution of seats in electoral districts if their lists received at least 8% of the validly cast votes country-wide.

in the form of legislation. For the legislative process, it is therefore not only the presence of representatives that is important. There must also be guaranteed deliberation in the representative body.

Taking into account civil equality (resulting from the universality of electoral law) and political diversity (reflecting different attitudes and preferences), the parliamentary way of creating the law must ensure conditions for expressing various views, opinions or demands. Then there is a properly functioning 'chain of delegation'. J. St. Mill sees the essence of parliamentarianism in deliberation. The final stage of the deliberation process is the legislation established in the Parliament. As a result, we can say that the Parliament is as much a forum for law-making in accordance with the majority principle as it is for expressing opinions, positions and demands. What J. St. Mill claimed is therefore clear: 'What can be done better by a body than by any individual, is deliberation. When it is necessary, or important, to secure hearing and consideration to many conflicting opinions, a deliberative body is indispensable'.[22] The Parliament then remains both a legislative and deliberative body. It is:

> ... an arena in which not only the general opinion of the nation, but that of every section of it, and as far as possible of every eminent individual whom it contains, can produce itself in full light and challenge discussion; where every person in the country may count upon finding somebody who speaks his mind, as well or better than he could speak it himself not to friends and partisans exclusively, but in the face of opponents, to be tested by adverse controversy; where those whose opinion is overruled, feel satisfied that it is heard.[23]

Political subjectivity of the represented citizens is reflected not in equal influence on the democratic decision-making process, but in the possibility to 'speak'[24] through a representative – that is, a person or a political party. Therefore, even though the participation of minorities in legislative decision-making may not be important for the intentions of the majority, the very possibility of expressing the position of minorities is important for ensuring the political subjectivity of their voters. The Parliament is a real 'body of delegates' when, in addition to executing the legislative function, there is a forum for deliberation.

---

22 J. St. Mill, 'Considerations of Representative Government' in J. St. Mill, *Essays on Politics and Society*, J.M. Robson (ed.), University of Toronto Press, Toronto 1977, p. 424.

23 Mill, above n. 22, p. 432.

24 'Speaking' is used above in a metaphorical sense – it means that one can identify with at least one of the positions expressed in the parliament.

The minimum condition for deliberation is the equal right to participate in the debate by all representative entities. It is also a prerequisite for legislation to be democratically legitimised. According to J. Habermas, democratic shaping of the will owes its legitimising power to: (a) communicative assumptions that allow better arguments to prevail in various forms of deliberation; and (b) procedures that ensure fair conditions of the deliberation process.[25] Democratic legislation should respect the equality of all entities and enable the right to participate equally in political deliberation. Thus, the Parliament as a 'delegation body' is by its very nature 'deliberative' in the form of an investigation into a legislative decision, which is already made in accordance with the majority principle. The majority dominates as a 'determining factor', but not as a 'participant in the debate'. In other words, the deliberative body should be open and inclusive. As Rawls points out:

> If the public forum is to be free and open to all, and in continuous session, everyone should be able to make use of it. All citizens should have the means to be informed about political issues. They should be in a position to assess how proposals affect their well-being and which policies advance their conception of the public good. Moreover, they should have a fair chance to add alternative proposals to the agenda for political discussion.[26]

The possibility of expressing 'alternative proposals' not only ensures the political subjectivity of the minority, but also ensures greater decision-making rationality by the majority, since they have to at least listen to other proposals. And even if they are not taken into account, they have a chance to appear in the public sphere through a special medium, which is the 'body of the delegated'. The minority thus obtains political confirmation of its identity and the right to participate in the democratic shaping of the 'will of the state'.

Deliberation is associated with a kind of 'visibility' of opposing views, that is, their expression in the Parliament. However, the legislative process seems to be more valuable when it is a consequence of a discussion (after B. Manin).[27] 'Discussion' here means: 'a type of communication in which

---

25 J. Habermas, 'Three Normative Models of Democracy' in S. Benhabib (ed.), *Democracy and Difference. Contesting the Boundaries of the Political*, Princeton University Press, Princeton 1996, p. 24.

26 J. Rawls, *A Theory of Justice*, The Belknap Press of Harvard University Press, Cambridge 1999, pp. 197–98.

27 Manin points to four constitutive elements for parliamentarianism: the election of representatives, partial autonomy of representatives, freedom of public opinion and

at least one of the parties (a) seeks to bring about a change in the other party's position, and (b) does so using propositions that are impersonal or relate to the long-term future'.[28]

In the course of the discussion, the opposing parties are seeking to change the position of the opponents, and so it is more than a deliberation. Importantly, persuasion takes place through argumentation.[29]

4. FROM DISCUSSION TO POPULISM

The categories of deliberation and discussion constitute a certain determinant for the three ideal types of representation, which are distinguished by B. Manin. We assume that, in a sense, they represent the development of parliamentarianism. In this sense, the personal bond between the represented and the representatives turns into a bond between the audience and the political leader.

The first type can be described as classic parliamentarianism, based on the personal bond between the represented and the representative,

---

the making of decisions after trial by discussion; see B. Manin, *The Principles of Representative Government*, Cambridge University Press, Cambridge and New York 1997. In the context of our deliberations, it is the latter element that is the most important.

28 Manin, above n. 27, p. 198.

29 C. Schmitt also points to this discussion: 'All specifically parliamentary arrangements and norms receive their meaning first through discussion and openness', C. Schmitt, *The Crisis of Parliamentary Democracy*, tr. E. Kennedy, MIT Press, Cambridge and London 2000, p. 3: 'To discussion belong shared convictions as premises, the willingness to be persuaded, independence of party ties, freedom from selfish interests. Most people today would regard such disinterestedness as scarcely possible. But even this scepticism belongs to the crisis of parliamentarianism. [...] By contrast conduct that is not concerned with discovering what is rationally correct, but with calculating particular interests and the chances of winning and with carrying these through according to one's own interests is also directed by all sorts of speeches and declarations', Schmitt, 2000, pp. 5–6. Schmitt also points to the tension between homogeneous democracy and the parliament as an institution based on difference. Democracy based on homogeneity cannot be reconciled with the existence of an institution in which discussions by independent representatives are held – the tension between democracy (homogeneity of the nation) and parliamentarianism (equality of people) is inevitable. In response, one can say that democracy does not presuppose homogeneity, but the equality of political rights to participate in a political dispute, see Ch. Mouffe, *The Democratic Paradox*, Verso, London and New York 2000, Chapter 2; see also A. Bień-Kacała, A. Tarnowska and W. Włoch, 'The nation, delegation, and constitutional change in Poland' (2018) 59 *Hungarian Journal of Legal Studies* 4, 355–77.

broad autonomy of the representative and freedom of expression – but relatively narrow suffrage.[30] Within such a framework, 'parliament can be a deliberating body in the fullest sense – that is to say, a place where individuals form their wills through discussion and where the consent of a majority is reached through the exchange of arguments'.[31]

Such a type of representation cannot be found in the Polish history of modern constitutionalism. When this kind of constitutionalism was formed in the 19th century, the Polish state did not exist as a sovereign entity. The Polish community could only be represented in foreign parliaments – those of the partitioning states.

In the second ideal type, that is, party democracy, personal ties between the representative and the represented are broken – one votes for the party and not for the person. The division into parties in the Parliament corresponds to the divisions existing in the society. The act of voting for a particular party becomes an act that expresses the identity of the voter. The way in which the representatives themselves vote is linked to party affiliation; similarly, the content of the expressed opinions depends on which party is represented.[32] In such a type:

> … plenary sessions of Parliament are no longer a forum of deliberative discussion. Strict voting discipline reigns within each camp. Moreover, representatives cannot change their minds as a result of the exchange of parliamentary debate, once the position of the party has been decided. Finally, voting alignments within parliament are virtually identical on all questions.[33]

The vote of the representatives is not influenced by the arguments put forward in the discussion, but by the party's position: the members of the ruling party usually support the government's proposals, and the opposition is against whatever arguments are put forward in the discussion.[34] It can be said that in a party democracy, the essence of parliamentary debate is

30 The deliberations contained in Hamilton, Madison and Jay, above n. 4, may be used as a theoretical example of this type.

31 Manin, above n. 27, pp. 205–06.

32 The deliberations contained in Kelsen 2013 may be used as a theoretical example of this type.

33 Manin, above n. 27, p. 216.

34 On the role of political parties for the functioning of a representative democracy, see N.W. Barber, 'Populist leaders and political parties' (2019) *German Law Journal* 20, 134–36.

not to convince and persuade the opponents, but it is the very possibility of expressing a view other than that of the majority.[35]

This type of representation can be identified in the current systemic arrangements. The Constitution of the Republic of Poland of 1997 gives a significant role in the formation of the parliamentary majority to political parties,[36] taking into account proportional voting for party lists with the indication of preferences only for specific representatives.[37] During the work of the Parliament, however, the existence of voting discipline is provided for, and the Constitutional Tribunal found such a solution to be compatible with the Constitution.[38] The Tribunal assumed that the existence of party discipline (in particular, voting discipline) is a necessary precondition for the Parliament's ability to act.

At the same time, we observe a steady increase in the importance of the party leader. The political discourse has focused at least since the 2005 parliamentary election on two key figures: Donald Tusk and Jarosław Kaczyński. These figures play (or played) the role of strong leaders – heads of political camps based on their parties' leadership structure. The constitutionality of such a form of activity of political parties (parties with strong leaders) has been confirmed in the jurisprudence of the Constitutional Tribunal.[39] We can, therefore, point to this fact as creating the conditions for the transition to a third type of parliamentarianism.

---

35 However, Manin points out that although parliamentary discussions do not change the party's position, the parties themselves develop their proposals through discussions: 'The party leadership and Members in Parliament debate among themselves what collective position should be adopted. And in that debate, the participants are able to change their minds as a result of the exchange of arguments', MANIN, above n. 27, p. 217.

36 Article 11:

1. The Republic of Poland shall ensure freedom for the creation and functioning of political parties. Political parties shall be founded on the principle of voluntariness and upon the equality of Polish citizens, and their purpose shall be to influence the formulation of the policy of the State by democratic means.

Article 100:

1. Candidates for Deputies and Senators may be nominated by political parties or voters.

37 Election Code: Article 2 32.§1. The District Election Commissions shall divide the seats between the eligible lists of candidates. And also Article 233.§1. The candidates receive the mandates that are attributable to a given list in the order of the number of received votes.

38 Judgement of Polish Constitutional Tribunal of 24 November 2010 (sign. Pp 1/08).

39 Judgement of Polish Constitutional Tribunal of 8 March 2000 (sign. Pp 1/99).

The third ideal type, audience democracy, is characterised by yet another increase in the importance of the personal dimension of the bond between the representative and the represented, but it refers primarily to the leader of the political party. The process of personalising power takes place – elections focus on the leader and his/her personality, whereas parties become a tool in the hands of leaders. The leadership of executive power, rather than being an MP, becomes the highest form of representation.[40] In the electoral process, however, voters do not so much express their identity as react to current issues in the public sphere:[41] 'Thus, the electorate appears, above all, as an audience which responds to the terms that have been presented on the political stage. Hence, this form of representative government is called here "audience democracy"'.[42]

As far as audience democracy is concerned:

> ... parliament is not the forum of public discussion. Each party is grouped around a leading figure, and each parliamentary party votes in a disciplined manner in support of its leader. Individually, however, representatives meet and consult with interest groups and citizens' associations. In such meetings, positions are not rigidly fixed, and thus some deliberative discussion takes place.[43]

An extreme audience democracy could be detected if the leader of the dominant party usurped the representation of 'the whole nation', and thus denied the opposition the right to participate in 'democratic' deliberation.[44] T. Ginsburg and A.Z. Huq identify charismatic populism with the emphasis on an individual leader as the systemic dysfunction that results in democratic erosion,[45] whereas J.-W. Muller observes the worldwide wave of populism

---

40 Manin, above n. 27, p. 219.

41 According to M. Gdula: 'In the past it was a discourse that was important, today it is an event that is important. In the past it was the structures that won, today it is the leader that wins. In the past, the dividing lines used to be determined by the mainstream, but today the audience is made up of all sorts of niches. All that creates completely new conditions for doing politics. [...] The media and politicians stand in one line, desperate for social attention', M. Gdula, *Nowy autorytaryzm*, [The New Authoritarianism], Wydawnictwo Krytyki Politycznej, Warsaw 2018, pp. 28–29.

42 Manin, above n. 27, p. 223.

43 Manin, above n. 27, p. 231.

44 N.W. Barber, 'Populist leaders and political parties' (2019) *German Law Journal* 20, 129–34.

45 T. Ginsburg and A.Z. Huq, *How to Save a Constitutional Democracy*, The University of Chicago Press, Chicago and London 2018, p. 78.

and argues that populism is a permanent shadow of representative politics.[46] According to populists, only they themselves are legitimate representatives of society. At the same time, populists are anti-pluralist. Referring to J.-W. Muller's thesis, the populists claim that they alone represent the people, perceived as a moral and homogeneous entity. Other political options and competitors (opposition or government, depending on election results, even international or supranational organisations and their officials, or people who do not share the populist political ideas) are illegitimate, immoral and beyond the margins of society (they are not an appropriate category of citizens). Therefore, the will of the people, to which the populists constantly refer, is not built on a genuine process of will-formation, because the non-inclusive rhetoric of the populists by definition cannot affect increasing participation in politics. Various different opinions are clearly discarded and refused. In practice, the populist morality leads to the point that the state becomes a place only for 'real people', clearly excluding a plurality. Furthermore, the populists intend to appropriate all state organs with the misuse of legal means (in this respect, the hasty and bogus legislative process is the most visible). Such a situation may currently be observed in Poland. The social and political discourses have been dominated by the 'exclusion' category.

As a result of the populist correction of the audience democracy model, the Parliament may become a representation of an imaginary (constructed by a political narrative) 'whole nation', at the same time excluding a real political minority. This would be a violation of the equal right to deliberation and, as a consequence, would limit the scope of what we can perceive as the first link in the representative chain – a political nation (equal citizens). The more homogeneously the community is perceived, the less need for deliberation and uniformity follows. The same axiological message dominates.

5. DYSFUNCTION OF THE 'CHAIN OF DELEGATION'

We pointed out that the representativeness of the Parliament is made up of several factors. The first condition for representativeness is the existence of

---

46 See J.-W. Müller, *What Is Populism?*, University of Pennsylvania Press, Philadelphia 2016, Chapter 1.

a properly equal and neutral electoral standard. However, this is, in a sense, a formal condition. We believe that ensuring this element alone does not yet determine the representativeness of the Parliament. The Parliament will be a representative body when it encompasses deliberation and discussion. Therefore, in a sense, the substantive conditions of representativeness will be met. In addition to guaranteeing the presence of representatives, deliberation also requires the possibility to articulate divergent views. Finally, we assume that citizens feel most represented when legislation is the result of discussion, that is, when decisions are taken on the basis of convincing arguments from the whole political spectrum, not just the majority.

In our opinion, the formal condition necessary to perceive the Sejm as a representative body has not been violated, although undoubtedly high electoral thresholds (5% for a political party and 8% for an electoral coalition) mean that part of the electorate will not be represented in the Sejm at the election stage. Undoubtedly, the electoral law affecting the Sejm was not the subject of legislative changes inspired and carried out by the current ruling majority.

Nevertheless, we believe that substantive conditions that relate to the quality of the legislative process are more important in the context of evaluating the political practice of the current term of the Polish Sejm. It is here that we can identify certain violations of the chain of delegation understood in an ideal manner. They provoke us to ask the question embedded in the title: 'is the Sejm still a representative body?'

Referring to the Polish situation, we believe that the scenario known from the history of the interwar period, in which the position of the Parliament was formally weakened by the establishment of a competitive legislator in the form of executive power,[47] is not possible. This is a reference to the events following the *coup d'etat* by Marshall Józef Piłsudski in 1926. At that time, the President of the Republic of Poland elected by Parliament was given the authority to issue regulations with the force of law (under the so-called August Novelization, Art. 5,[48] and then the April Constitution, Art. 49 (1)b, Art. 55-57). The executive also acquired other powers

47 We identified some similarities with Hungarian 'pandemic decrees', introduced to legal system by Victor Orban`s government. See also the chapter by T. Drinóczi and A. Bień-Kacała in this volume.

48 Act of 2 August 1926 amending and supplementing the Constitution of the Republic of Poland of 17 March 1921 (Journal of Laws No 78 item 442).

vis-à-vis the Parliament, such as the right to dissolve the Parliament (Art. 4 of the Amendment) and to adopt the budget even though it had not been adopted by the Parliament in due time (Art. 3 of the Amendment). The President made instrumental use of, among other things, the right to open and close sessions.[49] As a result, the Parliament was truly neutralised as a legislative body, and its crucial representative role was deliberately minimized. From the historical and legal perspective, it seems that it is not possible to deprive the representative body of its legislative powers today.

However, we observe a practice that undermines the substantive conditions of representation to a significant degree. The existing parliamentary model seems to be situated at the borderline of the discussed ideal models: party democracy and audience democracy. Party affiliation and the party's way of making legislative decisions are still important. The role of party leaders is also growing (even those who do not perform an official function, as in the case of the president of the Law and Justice party, who remains a 'regular deputy').[50] Genuine audience democracy, however, cannot exist due to populist anti-pluralist tendencies that homogenise and exclude political opponents. Populist tendencies are already visible at the stage of political narration, where opposition parties are refused the right to represent the 'Polish nation' and 'Polish interests',[51] *inter alia*. However, it seems particularly important that the delegation chain is violated through the exclusion of some representatives from fully participating in political deliberation. An example of this is undoubtedly the practice of limiting the speaking time of Members of Parliament (MPs) to, for example, 30 seconds during a parliamentary debate, especially in politically sensitive cases. We can also observe, departing from previous customs, a practice of taking the floor away from members of the opposition or rejecting amendments to bills proposed by the opposition *en bloc* without due consideration in the Parliament. Furthermore, the legislative procedure has been radically

---

49 Ajnenkiel, above n. 19, pp. 125–26. In October 1929 an attempt took place to open a parliamentary session in the presence of a group of armed officers. The speaker of the Sejm (Marshal of the Sejm) refused to open the session despite Piłsudski's pressure. *Ibid.*, pp. 146–147.

50 A. Bień-Kacała and A. Tarnowska, 'Power of Authority. A few words on the Chief of State one hundred years ago and the present' (2019) 46 *Przegląd Prawa Konstytucyjnego*, 6, 124–35.

51 As Jacek Sasin, Minister of State Assets, said, 'the opposition is ready to put itself ahead of the interest of Poland and Poles' by trying to adjourn the presidential election, planned for 10 May 2020; 'Senate mischievous in holding the legislation': https://www.pap.pl/aktualnosci/news%2C629317%2Csasin-wybory-prezydenckie-10-maja-musza-sie-odbyc.html, last accessed 24.04.2020.

shortened (one or two days from initiation to promulgation).[52] In such conditions, no genuine discussion exists. There is also the issue of physical exclusion from making decisions, as was the case with the events of 16 December 2016, when the budget was being adopted, on which occasion the MPs of the ruling party moved the proceedings from the Session Room to the Column Hall in the Sejm and effectively prevented opposition MPs from taking part in the debate and voting. In such a situation, the deliberation necessary in a representative legislative process does not take place. It is in this element that we see a real threat to the perception of the Sejm as a representative body.

Hopes for the recovery of good parliamentary practices were initially bound up with the results of 2019 parliamentary elections. The ruling party achieved a majority in the lower chamber, but in the upper chamber, based on single-deputy districts ('first-past-the-post'), held only 49 seats out of 100. The opposition was thus able to elect the speaker of the chamber and to shape the Senate's work. Contrary to the Sejm, the Senate became a chamber of lengthier and deeper deliberation (with visible attendance of non-governmental organisation members and external experts).[53] Still, this practice is being depreciated by the Sejm's rejection of amendments

---

52 Cf. among others: 'XI Komunikat Obywatelskiego Forum Legislacji o jakości procesu legislacyjnego na podstawie obserwacji prowadzonej w okresie od 16 listopada 2017 do 15 maja 2018 roku', p. 4, named 18 such cases (22.5% of all government legislative drafts), in the following six months, 16 cases (17%). Cf. 'XII Komunikat Obywatelskiego Forum Legislacji o jakości procesu legislacyjnego na podstawie obserwacji prowadzonej w okresie od 16 maja do 15 listopada 2018 roku oraz podsumowujący aktywność legislacyjną rządu i parlamentu w trzecim roku ich działalności', p. 20; available at: http://obserwatoriumdemokracji.pl/temat/proces-stanowienia-prawa/ last accessed 27.05.2020; 'Ustawa w 2 godziny 20 minut. XIII Komunikat Obywatelskiego Forum Legislacji podsumowujący aktywność legislacyjną rządów Zjednoczonej Prawicy, Sejmu VIII kadencji i Senatu IX kadencji (2015–2019)', available at: https://www.batory.org.pl/upload/files/Programy%20operacyjne/Forum%20Idei/Komunikat_2019-1.pdf, last accessed 27.05.2020. See in English: W. Sadurski, 'How Democracy Dies (in Poland): A Case Study of Anti-Constitutional Populist Backsliding' (17.01.2018), Sydney Law School Research Paper No. 18/01. Available at SSRN: https://ssrn.com/abstract=3103491 or http://dx.doi.org/10.2139/ssrn.3103491, last accessed 27.05.2020.

53 As an example we can invoke the proceedings on the new electoral law, which establishing voting by correspondence in 2020. The Senate has the opinions of, among others, the Legistative Bureau of the Senate, the Bureau for Analysis of the Senate, legal experts, Towarzystwo Epidemiologów [Epidemiologists' Society], Rzecznik Praw Obywatelskich [Polish Ombudsman], legal councils, the Helsińska Fundancja Praw Człowieka, związek zawodowy Poczty Polskiej [trade association of Polish Post], Generalny Inspektor Sanitarny [General Health Inspector] and UODO [Personal Data Protection Office] at its disposal.

proposed by the Senate in block voting without any discussion (even when some of the amendments are used by ruling party in their later drafts, as happened with some Senate ideas concerning the 'anti-crisis shield'[54] during the pandemic). The undermining of any Senate efforts might lead to rising social mistrust and may eventually polarise society.

6. CONCLUSION

In concluding our findings, we would like to reflect on the answer to the question: is the Parliament still a representative body?

In our opinion, in the formal sense (electoral law), we are dealing with such representativeness. Nevertheless, this answer is not complete. We have to take into account substantive factors in the form of deliberations and parliamentary discussion. In this context, we note that parliamentary deliberation does not turn into a discussion, nor does a discussion develop into a decision. This applies particularly to politically sensitive cases. The minimum condition to be met by a representative parliament is that all parties or MPs must be given the floor. If a Parliament as a deliberative body is restricted, the right to equal participation in the debate is also thus restricted. Therefore, neither representatives nor voters are equal. In a situation where the majority considers that itself, as a party or its leader, represents the whole nation and this declaration is followed by restrictions on minorities within the Parliament, in fact, the Parliament not only ceases to be a deliberative body, but a representative body, as well.

Therefore, the existing dysfunction of the process of deliberation and discussion reduces the representativeness of the Parliament; nevertheless, we believe that such dysfunction has not yet reached a critical mass that would disrupt the delegation chain. In other words, although the Parliament remains a representative body, this position is under fundamental threat.

---

54 There are many COVID-19 acts that are jointly referred to as the 'anti-crisis shield', which consists of several statutes in force and acts to be enacted concerning five pillars: employee safety, financing of enterprises, health, strengthening the financial system and public investment. See https://www.gov.pl/web/tarczaantykryzysowa, last accessed 26.04.2020.

THE ROOTS AND GUISES OF LEGAL POPULISM IN RUSSIA

The *Narodniki*, Statism and Legalism of Soviet Law and the Political Theology of Ivan Ilyin

Wojciech ENGELKING

1. INTRODUCTION

Despite the recent triumphs of populism in the Western world, its analysis is not very popular among theorists of public law, who usually pass it on to political scientists. It is not difficult to understand the reasons for such an omission.

The first such reason is the fact that the study of populist law as a separate phenomenon is impossible because, like populism itself, populist law is a heterogeneous trend. Populist leaders of the world include figures with such different views and backgrounds as Donald Trump, Silvio Berlusconi and Andrej Babiš – who have their roots in big business; TV personalities such as Beppe Grillo and Volodymyr Zelensky; professional politicians like Jeremy Corbyn and Boris Johnson; and former oppositionists in Central European countries, like Jarosław Kaczyński and Viktor Orbán. Whoever wants to equate their styles of exercising power falls into the trap of reducing populism to its one incarnation: '[one] element, often one of a rightist kind ... Generalizing views tend not to capture all populisms'.[1]

However, populism is not a completely elusive trend for a theoretician, and defining it is not impossible. Although numerous attempts have been made to do so, each of them highlights only one aspect of populism. For example, Chris Berlet and Matthew Lyons argue that populism is generally characterised by 'attacks on socially oppressed groups with grassroots mass mobilization and distorted forms of antielitism';[2] Jan-Werner Müller raises the problem of the populist claim to politically represent 'the people as a whole';[3] Ben Stanley points out that populism is a nihilistic trend, which does not have any 'core values';[4] Christopher Lash writes about Manichaean nature;[5] Cas Mudde talks about the populists' appeal to the most vulgar emotions of voters;[6] and Margaret Canovan posits that populists postulate the renewal of democracy which is presented by them as corrupt.[7] Definitions can be multiplied. For this chapter, the definitions offered by Berlet and Lyons as well as Stanley will be of key importance, along with another conceptualisation of populism, which highlights the second reason for lawyers' reluctance to deal with this political trend.

Paul Blokker writes that when it comes to the organising principles of public law, populism is the opposite of normativism. Having come to power, populists 'frequently engage in intense reform (and abuse) of the existing constitutional arrangements'.[8] They do so because, as Nadia Urbinati adds, they are 'impatient with procedures and institutions, and loath of intermediary bodies, as they prefer unmediated relations between the populist ruler and the people'.[9] However, they make use of the experience of experts neither by violating the law, nor by writing it again, instead

---

1 M. Molyneux and T. Osborne, 'Populism: a deflationary view' (2014) 46 *Economy and Society* 1, 3.

2 C. Berlet and M. Lyons, *Right-wing Populism in America,* Guilford Press, New York 2014, p. 1.

3 J.-W. Müller, 'The People Must be Extracted from Within the People: Reflections on Populism', (2014) 21 *Constellations* 4, 483.

4 B. Stanley, 'The Thin Ideology of Populism', (2008) 13 *Journal of Political Ideologies* 1, 95.

5 C. Lash, *The Revolt of the élites and the Betrayal of Democracy*, W.W. Norton, New York 1995, p. 12.

6 C. Mudde, 'The Populist Zeitgeist' (2004) 39 *Government and Opposition* 4, 550.

7 M. Canovan, 'Trust the People! Populism and the Two Faces of Democracy' (1999) 47 *Political Studies* 1, 2.

8 P. Blokker, 'Populist Constitutionalism', in C. de la Torre (ed.), *Routledge Handbook of Global Populism*, Routledge, New York 2018, p. 3.

9 N. Urbinati, 'Democracy and populism', (1998) 5 *Constellations* 1, 111.

relying on 'an elusive appeal to the fundamental values'.[10] For this reason, populist law is often seen as impossible to exist. Cesare Pinelli argues that legal culture (based on discussion and rational deliberation on laws) is a direct contradiction to populist culture and that the former cannot be born under the conditions of the latter.[11] Lucia Corso concludes: 'To many, the idea of a populist constitutional law appears to be an oxymoron. The most common view holds that constitutional law is designed … to prevent or limit the spread of populism'.[12]

All these arguments on how normative acts created in political systems managed by populists are not worth considering can be outweighed by a single argument: even if populists use the law in order to serve their particular political interests, they do indeed use the law.[13] And if the law is, as Nikolai Timasheff wrote long ago, 'a mirror of culture … its content reflects the value system of the corresponding society',[14] the examination of laws passed by populists (both on the material level, i.e. the axiological content that is the subject of the law, and the formal level, i.e. the way it is passed and the way specific norms are structured) should be a means of understanding their political success.

However, if one were to conduct such a study of populist law, it would not be an independent task. Rather, it would have to serve as an auxiliary activity in the field of classical political sciences. This is because the strategy would be aimed at dissecting normative acts in search of elements that would form a map of populist ideology. Of course, such a map cannot really exist because populism does not follow any conceptual trends of classical political science, operating merely under the guise of an ideology rather than any actual ideology, as we know from Stanley.

In this chapter, I would like to propose the opposite method. What interests me is finding both political and legal ideas that serve as building blocks for the façade of the ideology which supposedly legitimises a normative act. I have chosen one such act to treat as an example of populist law: the Russian federal law for the Purpose of Protecting

---

10 M. Hunter-Henin, 'The Legal Face of Populism: From the Classroom to the Courtroom', Jean Monnet Working Paper 9/17, p. 5.

11 C. Pinelli, 'L'Europa democratica nella strettoia fra populismo e tecnocrazia', (2013) *Meridiana* 77, 101.

12 L. Corso, 'What does Populism have to do with Constitutional Law? Discussing Populist Constitutionalism and its Assumptions', *Rivista di filosofia del diritto*, III, 2/2014, p. 444.

13 Blokker, 'Populist Constitutionalism', p. 14.

14 N.S. Timasheff, 'Soviet Law', (1952) 38 *Virginia Law Review* 7, 871.

Children from Information Advocating for a Denial of Traditional Family Values (in popular discourse, referred to as the 'anti-gay law'). It is a bill which, according to Berlet and Lyons' definition, serves to sanction state violence against 'socially inconvenient' groups. I choose the Russian case because, as Kathryn Stoner writes, Vladimir Putin's state populism is distinctly different from European and American populism, with the guise of ideology constructed extremely carefully.[15] Both the material and formal legitimisation of the bill discussed here draw heavily from Russian history.

John Hazard wrote in the 1930s about Soviet Union law: 'today's laws are but the outgrowth of yesterday's – not alone of recent years but from the very dawn of organized society'.[16] Similarly, it is in political and legal thought from centuries ago that one should seek the sources of ideological guise which serve as the material and formal legitimisation of the anti-gay law: 'to understand how Putinism works today, we must consider the past'.[17]

Still, contrary to Alexander Kondyakov's proposal, I do not intend to search for these sources in the times of Ivan the Terrible, but in the writings of political and legal thinkers closer to our times.[18] As such, I will first consider thinkers from the 19th-century Russian circle of the *Narodniki*; second, I will refer to Soviet philosophers of law (Andrei Vyshinsky in particular); and third, I will discuss the philosophy of Ivan Ilyin, the political theologian whose thought has recently been experiencing a renaissance. Before I discuss these three issues, I present the general premises of the bill. Then, I move on to identifying the source of the ideological guise for the bill's legitimacy in each of the mentioned philosophical trends.

2. RUSSIAN POPULISM, THE GUISE OF IDEOLOGY AND THE ANTI-GAY LAW

If we were to indicate another key feature that distinguishes Russian populism from the European or American sort, apart from its meticulous

---

15 K. Stoner, 'Russia in Retrospect and in Prospect' (2018) 50 *Comparative Politics* 3, 302.

16 J.N. Hazard, 'Soviet Law: An Introduction' (1936) 36 *Columbia Law Review* 8, 1236.

17 K.C. Langdon and V. Tismaneanu, *Putin's Totalitarian Democracy. Ideology, Myth, and Violence in the Twenty-First Century*, Palgrave Macmilllan, New York 2019, p. 90.

18 A. Kondyakov, 'Resisting the silence: The use of tolerance and equality arguments by gay and lesbian activist groups in Russia', (2013) *Canadian Journal of Law and Society*, 403.

construction, we would point to its systemic character. As Philipp Casula argues, Putinism covers all spheres of Russian public life and is a permanent way of managing the state.[19] Due to this, Russian populism is not ideological in any way – if we understand ideology as proposed by Cheng Chen (who defines it as a 'coherent and consistent system of ideas advanced officially by state elites to define and promote a regime identity and mission').[20] Putinism, according to Michel Eltchaninoff, is neither left-wing nor right-wing, and 'never confined by the parameters of a specific ideology'.[21] Instead of ideology, Putin offers Russians the appearance of ideology, which is important in the context of the 2013 bill. To reiterate, the guise of ideology lies in the fact that the laws proposed by the state do not serve to introduce broader ideological goals. Rather, purported ideological goals serve as a tool for legitimising the laws whose actual purpose is to sanction the state's oppression of certain social groups.

In the title of 2013 bill, the word 'values' necessarily goes together with the adjective 'traditional'. Although the concept of 'traditional Russian values' had been in development for some time by 2013, it was proposed by the authors of the act themselves. Vladimir Putin had been using the rhetoric of traditional values since 2006, when he stated that they should be a response to the demographic crisis consuming Russia. However, as Cai Wilkinson writes, it was only during the 2012 elections that the president directly 'linked the rebirth of Russian society's "spiritual bonds" to the preservation of Russia's collective identity. As a result, maintaining "traditional values" was now a politicised imperative for the survival of the Russian nation'.[22] Before this, there had been an intense discussion in Russia since the mid-1990s about how the country should adopt the Western way of life – and whether it should do so at all. This dispute, according to Andrei and Pavel Tsygankov, can be compared to the 19th-century discussion between Slavophiles and Occidentalists. It rendered Russia of that time a country 'with [a] Western Slavophile duality'.[23] The rhetoric applied by

---

19 P. Casula, 'Sovereign Democracy, Populism, and Depoliticization in Russia. Power and Discourse During Putin's First Presidency', (2013) 60 *Problems of Post-Communism* 3, 8.

20 C. Chen, *The Return of Ideology: The Search for Regime Identities in Postcommunist Russia and China*, Ann Arbor, University of Michigan Press 2016, s. 24.

21 M. Eltchaninoff, *Inside the Mind of Vladimir Putin*, C. Hurst and Co. Publishers Ltd., London 2018, p. 5.

22 C. Wilkinson, 'Putting "Traditional Values" Into Practice: The Rise and Contestation of Anti-Homopropaganda Laws in Russia', (2014) 13 *Journal of Human Rights* 3, 367.

23 A. Tsyganov and P. Tsygankov, 'Pluralism or isolation of Civilisations? Russia's foreign policy discourse and the reception of Huntington's paradigm of the post-cold war world', (1999) 4 *Geopolitics* 3, 51.

Putin in 2012 and the passing of the 2013 law, in which traditional values are already mentioned in the title, suggest that the contemporary version of the 19th-century clash has been won by modern Slavophiles (it should be noted that this is not necessarily apparent if we understand Occidentalism as a opposition to populism). Thanks to this victory, Russia transformed into a country in which 'conservative, traditionalist guardian forces become key political actors enjoying the support and patronage of the government, with their messages becoming the message of the government', as Valery Sozayev says.[24]

The verdict of their victory in 2013 is reinforced by the observation that legislation directly targeting the LGBT community had already been attempted in Russia at the federal level when this debate was circulating in the public sphere. In 2002 (three years after homosexuality was removed from the official list of mental disorders), a marginal conservative party proposed a law in the Duma (lower house of the Federal Assembly of Russia) that made sodomy a crime anew, but it was not passed.[25] Four years later, the Duma of the Ryazan Oblast passed a law that charged 'propaganda of homosexuality (sodomy and lesbianism) amongst minors' with penalties of up to 2000 roubles (without defining what propaganda is).[26] Local Dumas in the Arkhangelsk and Kostroma Oblast followed the Ryazan path in 2011, until finally a law was passed in St. Petersburg in March 2012 prohibiting '[p]ublic acts aimed at the propaganda of sodomy, lesbianism, bisexualism and transgenderism amongst minors'.[27] At the federal level, the law was passed a year and a half later.

As Isabelle Chopin and Catharina Germaine write about Turkey, in legal acts in populist-controlled countries, there is no explicit discrimination against ethnic or sexual minorities. This is also the case with the Russian law discussed here. Article 1 of the 2013 bill only deems unsuitable for children materials which are 'aimed at causing minors to form non-traditional sexual predispositions, notions of attractiveness of non-traditional sexual relationships, distorted ideas about the equal social value of traditional and non-traditional sexual relationships'. Article 2 requires the government

24 V. Sozayev, *Russia in the 21st century: A culture war caused by traditionalist revanchism*, in: *The Situation Of Lesbian, Gay, Bisexual And Transgender People In The Russian Federation (Last Three Months 2011 – First Half 2012)*, Moscow Helsinki Group, Moscow 2013, p. 2.

25 D. Healey, 'Untraditional Sex and the Simple Russian' in T. Lahusen (ed.), *What is Soviet Now?: Identities, Legacies, Memories*, Lit Verlag, Berlin 2008, p. 175.

26 P. Johnson, *Homosexuality and the European Court of Human Rights*, Routledge, New York 2013, p. 166.

27 Wilkinson, above n. 22, 366.

to protect children from such materials, and Article 3 indicates possible penalties for breaking the law. These penalties are divided into financial penalties (up to 50,000 roubles for public persons, and 1 million for organisations) and others, including arrest and deportation (in the case of foreigners).[28]

As it aroused outrage around the world (including a condemnation by the Venice Commission and the Council of Europe), the law was interpreted as state consent to the growing violence against LGBT communities in Russia. The theory of ideology that I proposed above – that is, the guise of ideology in systemically populist states – would make this interpretation appropriate. However, it is more important for legal populism how the law and its material and formal aspects were justified by Vladimir Putin for internal use. The Russian president responded to Western criticism simply by pointing out that the bill was aimed at the state's promotion of heterosexual relationships and an increase in population. At the same time, he stated in his September 2013 speech that Western countries today reject their Christian roots by introducing laws equating large families with same-sex relationships, faith in God with that in Satan and promoting paedophilia; in short, that they have lost the understanding of what Putin called traditional values. In this way, he presented Western countries as a threat to Russia, with homosexuality as a *pars pro toto* of this threat. In his vision, Russia was a country without sin, which was thanks not to the Westernised elites (who, like the West, had purportedly lost touch with traditional values), but their opposite: the common man.[29] As Andrew Foxall writes, it is on the alleged bond with the common man that Vladimir Putin's public image is based.[30] However, the 'commonness' of the man is merely a work in progress – just like the ideology is in fact only a pretence. Rather than finding legitimacy in any actual Russian traditions, the 2013 act was meant to create traditions – to define the common man's commonness as anti-Western and anti-homosexual. According to Cai Wilkinson, 'The development of "traditional values" as a concept broadly parallels the rise of the anti-homopropaganda laws'.[31]

---

28 I. Chopin and C. Germaine, A *comparative analysis of non-discrimination law in Europe 2017,* European Commission, Brussels 2017, p. 11.

29 R. Service, *Kremlin Winter: Russia and the Second Coming of Putin*, Picador, New York 2019, p. 156.

30 A. Foxall, 'Photographing Vladimir Putin: Masculinity, Nationalism and Visuality in Russian Political Culture', (2013) 18 *Geopolitics*, 132.

31 Wilkinson, above n. 22, 367.

Let us summarise this part of our considerations. Russian populism is anti-ideological because it excludes the coherence of ideas and values contained in legal acts that lead to its realisation. Therefore, it uses a guise of political ideology, which is built on the concept of 'traditional values' – found *in statu nascendi*, and only reverse-engineered on the basis of legal acts that supposedly serve to defend them. However, the real purpose of these acts is to enable the oppression of selected social groups as promoted by the state. These groups are depicted as hostile to the common Russian man and tainted by sin in the Christian understanding (hence Putin's emphasis on the West's alleged equation of faith in God with faith in Satan). Nevertheless, the law that makes this possible is masked as having a completely different purpose, with its formal properties adapted to it. In what follows, I will discuss the historical components of this façade: material components; formal components; and then both material and formal components.

3. THE MATERIAL ASPECT: THE CULT OF THE *MUZHIK*

Writing about how particular ideas swept through Russia throughout successive political movements and centuries, Stefano Bianchini highlights the special importance of *Narodnichestvo* as the trend from which the original Russian political, legal and social thought originated.[32] As Michael Kazin points out, its birth in Russia was also the birth of modern Russian populism.[33]

According to Kazin, populism was supposed to be the answer to the *Narodniki's* main question: whether Russia can bypass the capitalist stage of development of the economy (and the *Narodniki* saw capitalism as 'an alien, unwanted force, which threatened to press Russian life into a lethal strait jacket'[34]) and land in socialism right away. The *Narodniki's* method was to awaken revolutionary consciousness in representatives of peasantry, whom they idealised by practising the cult of the *muzhik*, the common

---

32 S. Bianchini, *Eastern Europe and the Challenges of Modernity, 1800–2000*, New York, Routledge 2009, p. 19.

33 M. Kazin, *The populist persuasion: An American history*, Cornell University Press, Ithaca 1998, p. 20.

34 T. Laue, 'The Fate of Capitalism in Russia: The Narodnik Version' (1954) 13 *The American Slavic and East European Review* 1, 17.

man as a living contradiction of the Europeanised urban intellectuals from which the *Narodniki* originated ('they are for the people but never completely of the people').[35] In the 1870s, they migrated to the countryside in order to prepare the peasants to be the forces of the political movement, which the *Narodniki* were to lead. The revolution was to come thanks to the organisation *Narodnaya Volya*, which succeeded in the murder of Alexander II in 1881. However, this did not increase the support among peasants; they were terrified of what happened in St. Petersburg – and the revolution did not come.

To suggest that *Narodnichestvo* was a fully modern movement, as Kazin did, may seem like an exaggeration. However, supporters of such a diagnosis argue that no matter how different the circumstances of the 19th century and today are, 'the conditions provoking populist response as well as the arguments and rhetoric employed by the populist movements then and today bear a striking resemblance'.[36] On the other hand, we can find the same idealisation of the common man in the *Narodniki's* thought and in Putin's populism. In the latter case, like all of Putin's ideology, it is merely a pretence. Looking for the source of this ideological guise as legitimisation of the 2013 law, we must therefore answer one question. Was the *Narodniki's* idealisation of the *muzhik* sincere (as a movement 'particularly aware of its artificial position')[37] and only insincerely exploited by populists today? In other words: had the Narodniki themselves *not* been populists, and was their thought only transformed into populism today? Answering this question in the affirmative would run contrary to the English translation of the word *Narodnik*, which 'is usually translated as "populist", both for etymological reasons and to highlight the extraordinary efforts that Russian students made to go directly to the people that they wanted to enlighten'.[38] However, if the *Narodnichestvo* was a sincere movement, we could consider references to its ideas as a populist component of Putinism. As such, it could lend credibility to the ideological guise that legitimises Putin's anti-gay law. On the other hand, if the *Narodniki's* idealisation of the *muzhik* was in itself intended to deceive, it could not be considered

---

35 B. Yack, 'Of Scribes and Tribes: Progressive Politics and the Populist Challenge' (2019) 1 *Critical Review* 14, 6.

36 H.-G. Betz, 'A Distant Mirror: Nineteenth-Century Populism, Nativism, and Contemporary Right-Wing Radical Politics' (2013) 9 *Democracy and Security* 3, 201.

37 'To define populism', discussion among I. Berlin, R. Hofstadter, D. MacRae, L. Schapiro, H. Seton-Watson, A. Touraine, F. Venturi, A. Walicki and P. Worsley, (1968) 3 *Government and Opposition* 2, 141.

38 *Ibid.*, p. 11.

as source for populism because, as Enrique Peruzzotti writes, populism never comes from another populism, but is the degeneration of classical political currents.[39]

Still, one can doubt the sincerity of the *Narodniki* – which is common outside Russia, because, as Theodore Laue writes, 'their almost mystical confidence in the *muzhik* [may seem] incomprehensible to many Western observers'.[40] At the level of political practice, their turn towards the *muzhik* was dictated by the awareness that there is no other group in society that would support them. The choice of peasants as their alleged supporters was inspired by Alexander Herzen, whose experience of the 'failure of the revolutionary wave of 1848-49, which was principally democratic, working class and urban, encouraged him to look more closely at the rural world'.[41]

On the other hand, the *Narodniki*'s activities were aimed at achieving ideological goals rather than gaining control over the social group for later use. The *Narodniki* were 'elitist in methods, but not in aim', and this is what distinguishes them from contemporary populists who 'are all aiming at an elitist hierarchical society'.[42] As Andrzej Walicki writes, their conviction that the peasants would support their ideals was not based on their disregard or willingness to use them for their particular purposes, but was an 'explosion of romantic faith'.[43] As part of this faith, not only did they consider the Russian peasant to be a political *tabula rasa*, ready to be filled with their views, but they also tried to learn from the peasants; for example, as Ann Pedler points out, the peasants' physical work was seen by the *Narodniki* as an introduction to the Community of People.[44]

For the purposes of their own political project, the *Narodniki* created a kind of conservative utopia (as Bianchini calls it), seeing the typical place of residence of the Russian peasant, the rural community (*obshchina*), as a place which, with a proper modernisation of the worldview of

---

39 E. Peruzzotti, 'Populism as Democratization's Nemesis: The Politics of Regime Hybridization' (2017) 2 *Chinese Political Science Review*, 320.

40 Laue, above n. 34, 27.

41 Bianchini, above n. 32, p. 44.

42 'To define populism', discussion among I. Berlin, R. Hofstadter, D. MacRae, L. Schapiro, H. Seton-Watson, A. Touraine, F. Venturi, A. Walicki and P. Worsley, (1968) 3 *Government and Opposition* 2, 170.

43 A. Walicki, *The controversy over capitalism: studies in the social philosophy of the Russian populists*, Clarendon Press, New York 1968, p. 81.

44 A. Pedler, 'Going to the People. The Russian Narodniki in 1874-5', (1927) 6 *The Slavonic Review* 16, 137.

its inhabitants, can become a space for a leap into socialist society that would transform it into an 'organization of work, collective ownership, and solidarity between the nuclear family and the village'.[45] According to the *Narodniki*, this was possible because the peasant inhabitants were not infected with the capitalist (Western, liberal, Darwinian) way of thinking and arranging the means of production. At the same time, the *Narodniki* adopted an attitude which was deeply ethical towards peasants (the idealisation of the peasant resulted from the *Narodniki's* willingness to repay their debts as representatives of the landowning class to those whose work they had exploited for centuries) and conservative (the idealisation of the *muzhik* as someone in whom the original Russianness is contained). This enabled them to maintain the conservative character of their entire movement, although conservatism was incompatible with such views, which later resulted in the murder of the tsar.

According to Eric Hobsbawm, this is what distinguished them from their successors, the Bolsheviks,[46] who criticised the inhabitants of the countryside for being stuck in the 'idiocy of rural life'.[47] The idealisation of the *muzhik* adopted by the *Narodniki* must therefore be considered sincere, which makes it impossible to see them as modern populists. At the same time, it also makes them a source of Putinian populism, which distorted their thought in order to produce the appearance of an ideology.

Let us now try to point out which elements of the *Narodniki's* thought are most evident in the 2013 law, and how it was presented for Russian internal use. It must of course be an idealisation of the common man as uncontaminated by Western ideas (for the *Narodniki*, it was capitalism, and in the 2013 law, it was homosexuality as a *pars pro toto* of Western ideas in general) and as a carrier of traditional values. Since these traditional values are only just being defined by the very same legislation, one could suspect that Putin, like the *Narodniki*, treats the *muzhik* as a *tabula rasa* waiting for revolutionary content to be written down on him. What distinguishes Putin from the *Narodniki* is that his treatment of the common man is instrumental, and thus it can only create the guise of an ideology, not the ideology itself.

---

45 Bianchini, above n. 32, p. 48.

46 'Lenin's Bolsheviks owe more than they have sometimes admitted to the experience and methods of work of the Buonarrotist-Narodnik tradition'. E. Hobsbawm, *Primitive Rebels*, University of Manchester Press, Manchester 1959, p. 173.

47 G. Soares and J. Collins, 'The Idiocy of Rural Life' (1982) 32 *Civilisations* 1, 31.

4. THE FORMAL ASPECT: STATISM AND LEGALISM OF SOVIET LAW

At the time when the *Narodniki* travelled to the *muzhik*, the metropolitan *intelligentsia* they came from underwent another change that is significant for today's legal populism: it awakened legal awareness as legalistic awareness. Earlier, according to Eugene Huskey, urban intellectuals displayed a nihilistic perception of the law and in their 'disdain for the law ... surpassed Russian officialdom'.[48] It seems that legalism was similarly rejected in favour of nihilism by another trend that I consider important for Russian populism and the 2013 anti-gay law: Bolshevism and its implementation in the form of the Soviet philosophy of law.

The popular opinion on legal science in the Soviet Union is that Russian 'publications of that time are poor',[49] and 'legal education went to decline'.[50] According to the critics of Soviet legal science, its crisis was caused by the very nature of Soviet law, which was created by those whom Nikolai Timasheff described as 'men who, in principle, denied the value of legal norms'.[51] Some researchers were slightly cooler in their approach, like Eugene Huskey, who claimed that according to the prevailing understanding of the law in the Soviet Union, 'law and socialism are incompatible. Law, like the state is a pillar of domination that rises from the economic foundation of capitalism'.[52] The person who laid the foundations for such a conceptualisation of the law was Lenin, who believed that the law is part of politics and contains tools to maintain the rule of a certain social class. He saw its instruments, such as courts, as class tools, 'an implement used by the state machine to further the interests of the ruling groups'.[53] For this reason, he treated the law instrumentally, as a protection of the new ruling class – whose goal would ultimately be to create a classless society. In 1936, John Hazard concluded: 'Law is again laid bare as a class weapon although different from all other law in that it is the class weapon of the proletariat'.[54]

---

48 E. Huskey, 'A Framework for the Analysis of Soviet Law' (1991) 50 *The Russian Review* 1, 68–69.

49 Timasheff, above n. 14, 872.

50 E. Huskey, 'Vyshinski, Krylenko, and the Shaping of the Soviet Legal Order' (1987) 46 *Slavic Review* 3/4, 416.

51 Timasheff, above n. 14, 871.

52 Huskey, above n. 50, 55.

53 Hazard, above n. 16, 1242.

54 *Ibid.*, 1265–66.

Must Soviet law thus be synonymous with legal nihilism? Apparently, yes. After all, we are dealing not only with the law of a totalitarian system (i.e. to use Ernst Fraenkel's concept, double law, functioning on the one hand as a set of regulations and on the other hand as an expression of the political will of the leader), but also with law deprived of tradition, which 'recognizes no innate rights, or established conventions. Everything is being adapted to current needs and, therefore, is easily and constantly changed, to conform with the Soviet policy of a given period'.[55] Therefore, it has traditionally been approached as an instrument of power that legitimised the current leader with its very existence. Such an approach, however, would make it impossible to recognise Soviet law as a source of Vladimir Putin's legal populism and a building block of the formal façade for the anti-gay law discussed here. This is because – as I wrote above – populism does not give birth to populism; it is instead a degeneration of classical political and legal trends.

I would then like to concentrate on two other approaches to Soviet law, rather than seeing it as nihilistic: a statist approach and legalistic approach. As Huskey wrote, 'Whether during Stalin's terror or Gorbachev's *pravovoe gosudarstwo* or law-based state, all three traditions have been at work in Soviet law, albeit with various degrees of influence'.[56] Of course, legal nihilism was indeed an important factor in the functioning of the Union of Soviet Socialist Republics (USSR) law, and its traditions should not be underestimated. As Eugene Kamenka and Alice Erh-Soon Tay write, the struggle among these three paradigms in the history of Soviet law was 'a half-conscious confrontation between three great paradigms of social ideology, social organization, and law and administration'.[57] However, it seems to me that while looking for the sources of the 2013 law and the formal aspect of its guise, the two other approaches indicated by Huskey are more applicable here.

Let us start with the statist approach, represented in the USSR by such legal theorists as Andrei Vyshinsky. Like Lenin, he considered law to be part of politics: 'Law is nothing unless connected with a definite policy … I don't accept the contention that policy ends where law begins. Law is an instrument of politics'.[58] However, he did not consider

---

55 G. Guins, 'Soviet Law-Terra Incognita', (1950) 9 *The Russian Review* 1, 17.

56 Huskey, above n. 50, 55.

57 E. Kamenka and A. Erh-Soon Tay, 'Social Traditions, Legal Traditions' in E. Kamenka (ed.), *Law and Social Control*, St. Martin's Press, New York 1980, p. 3.

58 Guins, above n. 55, 18.

his approach nihilistic, and he did not see socialism as an obstacle that prevented the implementation of the law. On the contrary, he argued that it is only under socialist conditions that law can be fully implemented because it is only under these conditions that it does not function as an instrument of class oppression. Instead, it can serve citizens because their interests as its subjects are aligned with the interests of the state as the one that creates and implements the law. Vyshinsky believed that in order to fulfil such a function, the law must be certain and stable, because the citizen must know what norms apply to him. However, the fact that citizens need such knowledge does not make it necessary to simplify it (as another theorist, Nikolai Krylenko, argued at the time); on the contrary, Vyshinsky advocated the professionalisation of legal professions.[59] It was the professionals who were supposed to demystify the law for the needs of the Soviet man and thus educate him, convincing him that his interests are those expressed by the law – in a way making him aware of these needs. Vyshinsky defined the law as 'rules of behaviour expressing the will of the ruling class',[60] while believing that this will is formed and the law is a tool to shape it.

Let us move on to legalism. In Vyshinsky's approach, we will find more than a few of its traces. Still, this trend did not really flourish in the Soviet Union until the time of Mikhail Gorbachev (with a little foretaste during the times of New Economic Policy (NEP)).[61] Legalists agreed with the statist approach which linked the interests of the state as the creator and implementer of the law to the citizens as its subject. In an attempt to reform Soviet law at the time, they pointed to the need to organise the hierarchy of norms. Until their time, the most important documents regulating the operation of administrative bodies, the *podzakonnye akty* (substatutory norms), were generally not published (especially not in rural areas) – condemning the subjects of the law to remain under the domination of the privileged. The publication of these acts was intended by legalists to 'shift power from the ministries, the authors of substatutory norms, to the Soviet organs responsible for the drafting and adoption of statutes'.[62]

---

59 Huskey, above n. 50, 412.

60 V. Tolstykh, 'The Nature of Russian Discourses on International Law' in P. Morris (ed.), *Russian Discourses on International Law: Sociological and Philosophical*, Routledge, New York 2019, p. 98.

61 S. Newton, *Law and the Making of the Soviet World: The Red Demiurge*, Routledge, New York 2015, p. 112.

62 Huskey, above n. 50, 63.

In short, the legalists proposed to remove the procedural element of the state prerogative, while maintaining a system in which socialist ideals determine the vector of the law: 'Under legalism law ceases to be a mere instrument of rule. To borrow an image appropriated by the KGB, it becomes both a sword for the state and a shield for the citizen'.[63]

Let us now look at how the statist and legalist trends in Soviet law manifest themselves in the anti-gay law and the legal guise from which it stems. In order to create this guise, the populists took from statists the perception of the law as an instrument for educating the citizen; not as a political tool that serves to oppress him, but as a positive proposal that makes him believe that his interests and the interests of the state are aligned. At the same time, without discriminating against any social group explicitly, the anti-gay law does not indicate clearly who is *not* this type of citizen (thus legally removing the element of prerogative). However, since it serves the purpose of discrimination and its legitimacy, its formal statism and legalism are only appearances which allow the state to oppress certain social groups – just like the contents of the act sanction the reference to the *muzhik*, like the one practised by the *Narodniki*.

5. THE MATERIAL AND FORMAL ASPECT: THE POLITICAL THEOLOGY OF IVAN ILYIN

It is difficult to find a thinker who has gained as much interest in recent years as Ivan Ilyin; the only one would be Carl Schmitt, to whom Ilyin is often compared. Despite all the similarities between the German and the Russian scholars, what makes them different is the openness with which their thought is received. Schmitt's writings are perceived in a distorted manner, and comparisons of contemporary political actions to his works serve to discredit whoever undertakes them.[64] Meanwhile, Putin boasts openly that Ilyin's works are the axiological basis for his proceedings. Not only has the Russian president quoted the author of *Our Tasks* several times in his speeches, he also brought Ilyin's ashes to Russia from Switzerland,

63 *Ibid.*, 64.

64 For example, S. Earle, 'The terrifying rehabilitation of Nazi scholar Carl Schmitt', *New Statesman*, 10.04.2019, https://www.newstatesman.com/2019/04/terrifying-rehabilitation-nazi-scholar-carl-schmitt, last accessed 05.05.2020.

and in 2013 he sent gift sets of books to governors of Russian provinces, which included a work by Ilyin.[65]

However, contrary to what Walter Laquer believes, one should not be under any illusion that Ilyin is supposedly Vladimir Putin's favourite philosopher, in whose thought the key to understanding Russian politics can be found.[66] Rather, Anton Barbashin is right in saying that 'to call Putin a politician who is pursuing any sort of ideological or philosophical concept in practice is total nonsense'.[67] Ilyin is important because the creators of the Russian ideological façade draw on his political theology. According to Schmitt's extended definition, political theology is the perception of the institution of politics and law as a secular extrapolation of religious institutions.[68] Thus, Ilyin's political theology elevates the Putinian guise of ideology to a higher level by taking away its secular character.

Who was Ilyin? Timothy Snyder writes that he was 'born to a noble family in 1883 … typical of his generation as a young man'.[69] In the early 20th century, he studied law in Moscow and then travelled around Europe. At that time, in terms of legal beliefs, he was a legalist and a Positivist, and politically, he was a liberal. Everything was changed by the Bolshevik Revolution, after which Ilyin began looking for a political movement that would defeat Communism – and found it in Christian counter-revolutionary fascism. Banished from Russia in 1922, he lived in Berlin, where he lectured at the Russian Scientific Institute; he also published the magazine *Russkiy Kolokol*. After the Nazis came to power, he was persecuted, and due to financial problems, it was only in 1938 when he managed to escape Hitler's country. He left for Switzerland, where he died in 1954.[70]

When looking for sources of the ideological guise which legitimises the Russian anti-gay law of 2013 in Ilyin's political theology, three of its

---

65 M. Laruelle, 'In Search of Putin's Philosopher', *Intersection Project* 03.03.2017, http://intersectionproject.eu/article/politics/search-putins-philosopher (last accessed 05.05.2020).

66 W. Laquer, *Putinism. Russia and Its Future With the West*, St Martin's Press, New York 2015, p. 50.

67 A. Barbashin, 'Ivan Ilyin: A Fashionable Fascist', https://www.ridl.io/en/ivan-ilyin-a-fashionable-fascist/ (last accessed 05.05.2020).

68 C. Schmitt, *Political Theology. Four Chapters on the Concept of Sovereignty*, tr. G. Schwab, foreword by T. B. Strong, The University of Chicago Press, Chicago 2005, p. 5.

69 T. Snyder, *The Road to Unfreedom. Russia-Europe-America*, Alfred A. Knopf, New York 2017, p. 88.

70 L. Chamberlain, *Lenin's Private War: The Voyage of the Philosophy Steamer and the Exile of the Intelligentsia*, St Martin's Press, New York 2015, p. 23.

elements should be pointed out: first, the belief in Russia's 'sinlessness' and the West as the root of all evil; second, the praise of masculinity and a strong man as a political leader; and finally, the idea of legal awareness.

The concept of sinlessness was created by Ilyin in the lectures he gave in his Swiss days. This was at the beginning of the Cold War, when the West feared the nuclear arsenal of the USSR. Ilyin tried to convince his German-speaking listeners that seeing Russia as a threat was a mistake, because it meant identifying the country with its Communist regime. Meanwhile, Ilyin argued, the world should in fact look to Russia as the future agent of Christian salvation, because it was in Russia that the spiritual struggle was taking place in the form of the fight against Communism. Ilyin believed that Communism was not born in Russia, but imposed on it by the decadent West. He added that there is nothing strange or new about it: in the historical cycles which Russia experienced as a country that remained part of the divine plan (unlike the West, which had been deserted by God), it had consistently been subjected to and struggled against threats, and the threats had always come from the outside.[71] Snyder concludes that:

> According to Ilyin, every single battle ever fought by Russians was defensive. Russia was always the victim of a 'continental blockade' by Europe. As Ilyin saw matters, 'the Russian nation, since its full conversion to Christianity, can count nearly one thousand years of historical suffering'. Russia does no wrong; wrong can only be done to Russia. Facts do not matter and responsibility vanishes.[72]

In Ilyin's political theology, Russia's sinlessness is literal. He saw this country as an immaculate, virgin body, and argued that it is a living organism, created in the Garden of Eden by nature and spirituality. For this reason, in Ilyin's political theology, the body must also have someone who defends Russia: a leader. Similar to the Schmittian figure of the *katechon* (because it fulfils the assumption of a person or institution that stops the pressure of evil and leads to the rebirth of the political organism),[73] the leader in Ilyin's theology was someone who comes from outside.[74] However, he

71 See: F. Hill and C.G. Gaddy, *Mr. Putin: Operative in the Kremlin*, Brookings Institution Press, Washington D.C. 2015, p. 147.

72 Snyder, above n. 69, p. 90.

73 A. Wielomski, *W poszukiwaniu katechona. Teologia polityczna Carla Schmitta*, von borowiecky, Warszawa 2018, p. 343.

74 P. Robinson, 'On Resistance to Evil by Force: Ivan Il'in and the Necessity of War' (2003) 2 *Journal of Military Ethics* 2,150.

did not mean the geographical exterior, but the outside of history (both the Western, linear one, and the Eastern, cyclical one). It was from the outside that a new leader was to come, and Russians would recognise him because they were Russians. If recognised, the leader would have the task of channelling 'the evil nature of the sensual' into a grand unity. The leader will be 'sufficiently manly', like Mussolini. He 'hardens himself in just and manly service … He stands alone and goes alone because he sees the future of politics'. Russians will kneel before 'the living organ of Russia, the instrument of self-redemption'.[75]

The question of recognising a *katechonical* leader leads us to legal awareness. At first glance, Ilyin seems to have derived his idea from Leon Petrażycki, and only when combined with Petrażycki's political theology can Ilyin's thought be considered as one of the components of the ideological guise surrounding the 2013 law. The human awareness of the existence of the law and the necessity of obedience to it was understood by Ilyin as dependent on individual morality and the religious foundations of the subject. Moreover, he identified the political leader as someone who promulgates and implements the law. In his vision, the law resulted from the leader's individual order and was completely arbitrary; the political leader ruled with its help, but was not tied to it himself – he could not have been, because he could not act against his own law-determining will.[76] The subjects of the law, by understanding it, confirmed that they are citizens of the country ruled by the leader, and, as a result, they were striving to ultimately become one with him: 'with the redeemer in command of such a system, Russia would exhibit the metaphysical identity of all people of the same nation'.[77]

Let us now look at how Ilyin's political theology turns out to be the building block of the façade of the ideology that legitimises the Russian anti-gay law. The bill's inclusion of higher penalties for non-Russian citizens found guilty of 'homopropaganda' and Vladimir Putin's presentation of homosexuality in his 2013 speech as a Western institution transplanted to Russian soil follow Ilyin's belief that Russia is infected by Europe with decadent movements, while remaining a political organism that is itself sinless. Similarly, Putin's presentation of Europe as a place where faith in God mixes with faith in Satan, that is, his emphasis on the religious

---

75 Snyder, above n. 69, p. 90.

76 Snyder, above n. 69, p. 96; B. Bowring, *Law, Rights and Ideology in Russia: Landmarks in the Destiny of a Great Power*, Routledge, New York 2017, p. 49.

77 Snyder, above n. 69, p. 91.

dimension of the law – albeit indefensible on a rational level, should be seen as the aftermath of Ilyin's political theology and his thinking on the Russian issue in religious terms. The emphasis on the links between the human body of the leader and his power, which researchers see in Putin's public relations stunts, can also be traced back to Ilyin's characteristics of the Russian leader.

6. CONCLUSION

In the introduction to this chapter, I quoted Kathryn Stoner's assertion that Russian populism is different from European or American populism because its guise of ideology remains extremely carefully constructed; after examining the three sources of this ideological façade as implications of the 2013 law, I have to agree with this statement. Both Russian populism in general and its instruments draw richly on the history of Russian political and legal thought, building both material and formal legitimacy for the state's oppression of certain social groups – in this case, LGBT communities.

On the mere façade of ideology that legitimises the law, a special place is given to the general clause on traditional values, which are carried by the common Russian and threatened by the West. Moreover, the 2013 bill also draws on the ideas of the 19th-century *Narodniki* movement and from the political theology of Ilyin, in which Russia is portrayed as a sinless body, sullied with the ideas coming from outside (but always reborn thanks to the leader acting as a *katechon*). As far as the formal aspect is concerned, one should point out the apparent rooting of the discussed law in, first, Andrei Vyshinsky's statist view of the law (according to which the interests of the state and the citizen are identical); second, in the Gorbachev-era legalist philosophy of law; and third, in Ilyin's psychosocial theory, which emphasises the aspect of understanding the law if the subject belongs to the national community.

These are the sources for the appearance of ideology in this particular instrument of Russian populism, which is the 2013 anti-gay law. This legal act is of historical importance for Putinism as it opened the era of the 'traditional values' legal clause as a key institution of the Russian state and began to define the term. Of course, the question arises as to whether Russian populism can be a permanent project if its façade is drawn from such diverse sources; however, this is a topic for another article.

BIBLIOGRAPHY

T. Aalberg, F. Esser, C. Reinemann, J. Strömbäck and C.H. de Vreese (eds), *Populist Political Communication in Europe*, Routledge, New York 2017.

J. Abromeit, Y. Norman, G. Marotta and B.M. Chesterton, 'Introduction' in J. Abromeit, Y. Norman, G. Marotta and B.M. Chesterton (eds), *Transformations of Populism in Europe and the Americas: History and recent tendencies*, Bloomsbury Publishing, London 2015.

K. Abts and S. Rummens, 'Populism versus Democracy' (2007) *Political Studies* 55, 405–24.

A. Acorn, *Compulsory compassion: A critique of restorative justice*, University of British Columbia Press, Vancouver 2004.

G. Agamben, *Creation and Anarchy. The Work of Art and the Religion of Capitalism*, tr. A. Kotsko, Stanford University Press, Stanford CA 2019.

——, 'Distanziamento sociale', <https://www.quodlibet.it/giorgio-agamben-distanziamento-sociale>.

——, *Homo Sacer II*, Kritika i humanisam, Sofia 2019.

——, *Stasis. Civil War as a Political Paradigm*, Stanford University Press, Stanford 2015.

——, *State of Exception (Homo sacer II, 1)*, tr. K. Attell, The University of Chicago Press, Chicago and London 2005.

——, 'The state of exception provoked by an unmotivated emergency' <http://positionswebsite.org/giorgio-agamben-the-state-of-exception-provoked-by-an-unmotivated-emergency/>.

J. Agnew, *Globalization and Sovereignty. Beyond the Territorial Trap*, Rowman & Littlefield, Lanham 2017.

N. Ajello, Norberto Bobbio e il Partito persona' 09.04.2008 *La Repubblica* <https://ricerca.repubblica.it/repubblica/archivio/repubblica/2008/04/09/norberto-bobbio-il-partito-persona.html>.

A. Ajnenkiel, *Historia Sejmu Polskiego*, Vol. II, part II: II Rzeczpospolita, Państwowe Wydawnictwo Naukowe, Warszawa 1989.

R. Albert, 'How Unwritten Norms Change Written Constitutions' (2015) 38 *Dublin University Law Journal* 2.

D. Albertazzi, D. McDonnell and J.L. Newell, 'Di lotta e di governo: The Lega Nord and Rifondazione Comunista in Office' (2011) 17(4) *Party Politics*, 471–87.

R. Alexy, *Theorie der Grundrechte*, Suhrkamp, Frankfurt am Main 1994.

Y. Algan, E. Beasley and M. Foucault, *Les Origines du Populism*, Seuil, Paris 2019.

A. Algostino, 'Participatory Democracy and its Dark Sides' (2020) 12 *Federalismi.*

G. Allegri, 'Pluralismo solidale, innovazione sociale e processi federali per un nuovo garantismo costituzionale' in G. Allegri, A. Sterpa and N. Viceconte (eds), *Questioni costituzionali al tempo del populismo e del sovranismo*, Editoriale scientifica, Napoli 2019.

J.G. Allen and R.M. Lastra, 'Border Problems: Mapping the Third Border' (2020) *The Modern Law Review* 9.

D. Amirante (ed.), *«Altre» democrazie. Problemi e prospettive del consolidamento democratico nel sub-continente indiano*, FrancoAngeli, Milano 2010.

D. Andress, 'Jacobinism as Heroic Narrative: Understanding the Terror as the Experience of Melodrama' (2014) 5 *French History and Civilisation* 6, 18.

——, 'Living the Revolutionary Melodrama: Robespierre's Sensibility and the Construction of Political Commitment in the French Revolution' (2011) *Representations* 103, 107.

O. Angeli, 'Global constitutionalism and constitutional imagination' (2017) 6 *Global Constitutionalism* 3.

A. Applebaum, *Iron Curtain: The Crushing of Eastern Europe, 1944–1956*, Anchor Books, New York 2013.

A. Arato, 'How we got here? Transition failures, their causes and the populist interest in the Constitution' (2019) 45 *Philosophy and Social Criticism* 9–10, 1106–15.

——, *Post Sovereign Constitutional Making: Learning and Legitimacy*, Oxford University Press, Oxford 2016.

B. Arditi, *Politics on the Edges of Liberalism: Difference, Populism, Revolution, Agitation*, Edinburgh University Press, Edinburgh 2007.

H. Arendt, *On Revolution*, Penguin, London and New York 1963.

——, *The Human Condition*, Chicago University Press, Chicago 1958.

——, *The Human Condition*, 2nd ed., The University of Chicago Press, Chicago and London 1998.

S.A. Arjomand, 'Law, Political Reconstruction and Constitutional Politics' (2003) 18 *International Sociology* 1.

P. Aslanidis, 'Is Populism an Ideology? A Refutation and a New Perspective' (2016) 64 *Political Studies* 1, 88–104.

——, 'Populism and Social Movements' in C. Rovira Kaltwasser, P. Taggart, P. Ochoa Espejo and P. Ostiguy (eds), *The Oxford Handbook of Populism*, Oxford University Press, Oxford 2017.

M. Avbelj and J. Letnar Černič, *The Impact of European Institutions on the Rule of Law and Democracy: Slovenia and Beyond*, Hart Publishing, Oxford 2020.

R. Axtmann, 'The State of the State: The Model of the Modern State and Its Contemporary Transformation' (2004) 25 *International Political Science Review/Revue internationale de science politique* 3, 259–79.

G. Azzariti, 'Passato e presente. Cittadini, partiti e gruppi parlamentari: esiste ancora il divieto di mandato imperativo?' (2009) III/IV *Democrazia e Diritto* 311–64.

M. Babińska, J. Matera and M. Bilewicz, Zaraza ponad podziałami. Związki poglądów politycznych z postawami wobec epidemii SARS-CoV-2, Warszawa March 2020, <http://cbu.psychologia.pl/uploads/f_bulska/Polityka_COVID.pdf?fbclid=IwAR1vVyh-DBQwhQYBMUDER-0H1wGRTW7pC_hTOI5q6qCXpd9thlTzVflX0OQ>.

M.L. Bailey, 'Most Hevynesse and Sorowe The Presence of Emotions in the Late Medieval and Early Modern Court of Chancery' (2019) 37 *Law and History Review* 1, 1–28.

T. Baldwin, *Ctrl Alt Delete: How Politics and the Media Crashed Our Democracy*, Hurst & Company, London 2018.

J.M. Balkin, 'Populism and Progressivism as Constitutional Categories' (1991) *Yale Law Journal* 104.

H. Bang and D. Marsh, 'Populism: a major threat to democracy?' (2018) 39 *Policy Studies*, 3, 352–63.

A. Barak, 'Unconstitutional Constitutional Amendments' (2011) 44 *Israeli Law Review* 322.

A. Barbashin, 'Ivan Ilyin: A Fashionable Fascist', <https://www.ridl.io/en/ivan-ilyin-a-fashionable-fascist/>.

N.W. Barber, 'Populist leaders and political parties' (2019) 20 *German Law Journal* 129–40.

A. Barbera and A. Morrone, *La Repubblica dei referendum*, Il Mulino, Bologna 2003.

P. Bárd, 'The Hungarian "Lex NGO" before the CJEU: Calling an Abuse of State Power by its Name', *VerfBlog*, 27.01.2020, <https://verfassungsblog.de/the-hungarian-lex-ngo-before-the-cjeu-calling-an-abuse-of-state-power-by-its-name/>.

P. Bárd and K. Bárd, 'The European Convention on Human Rights and the Hungarian Legal System', <http://real.mtak.hu/65944/1/Bard_Bard_Comparative_study_on_the_implementation_of_the_ECHR_at_the_national_level_ENG_149_168_u.pdf>.

R.R. Barr, 'Populism as a political strategy', in C. de la Torre (ed.), *The Routledge International Handbook of Global Populism*, Routledge, London and New York 2019.

M. Bassini, 'Rise of populism and the Five Star Movement model: an Italian case study' (2019) 11 *Italian Journal of Public Law* 1, 302–33.

A. Batory, 'Populists in government? Hungary's system of national cooperation' (2016) 23 *Democratization* 2, 283–303.

A. Batory and S. Svensson, 'The use and abuse of participatory governance by populist governments' (2019) 47 *Policy and Politics* 2, 227–44.

K. Baynes, 'The Liberal/Communitarian Controversy and Communicative Ethics' in D. Rasmussen (ed.), *Universalism vs. Communitarianism, Contemporary Debates in Ethics*, The MIT Press, Cambridge 1995.

P. Becchi, *Manifesto sovranista. Per la liberazione dei popoli europei*. Giubilei Regnani, Rome 2019.

D. Bell, *The End of Ideology: On the Exhaustion of Political Ideas in the Fifties*, Harvard University Press, Cambridge 2000.

R. Bellamy, 'Constitutionalism' (2019) *Encyclopaedia Britannica*, <www.britannica.com/topic/constitutionalism>.

——, *Political Constitutionalism*, Cambridge University Press, Cambridge 2007.

M. Belov, 'Direct Democracy and European Integration' in S. Knezevic and M. Nastic (eds), *Globalisation and Law*, Faculty of Law–University of Niš, Niš 2017.

——, 'Rule of Law in Space of Flows' in M. Belov (ed.), *Rule of Law at the Beginning of the Twenty-First Century*, Eleven, The Hague 2018.

C. Berlet and M. Lyons, *Right-wing Populism in America*, Guilford Press, New York 2014.

P. Berretta, 'I poteri di democrazia diretta' in G. Amato and A. Barbera (eds), *Manuale di diritto pubblico. II. L'organizzazione costituzionale*, 5th ed., Il Mulino, Bologna 1984.

J.M. Bessette, 'Deliberative Democracy: The Majority Principle in Republican Government' in R.A. Goldwin and W.A, Schambra (eds), *How democratic is the constitution?* American Enterprise Institute for Public Policy Research, Washington D.C. 1980.

H.-G. Betz, 'A Distant Mirror: Nineteenth-Century Populism, Nativism, and Contemporary Right-Wing Radical Politics' (2013) 9 *Democracy and Security* 3, 201.

S. Bianchini, *Eastern Europe and the Challenges of Modernity, 1800–2000,* New York, Routledge 2009, p. 19.

A. Bickel, *The least dangerous branch: the Supreme Court at the bar of politics*, Yale University Press, New Haven 1986.

R. Bienvenu, *The Ninth of Thermidor: The Fall of Robespierre*, Oxford University Press, Oxford 1970.

A Bień-Kacała, 'Illiberal democracy in action: Polish kind of symbolic legislation' (2019) *European Studies. The Review of European Law, Economics and Politics* 6, 268–78.

——, 'Polexit is Coming or is it Already Here? Comments on the Judicial Independence Decisions of the Polish Constitutional Tribunal', *International Journal of Constitutional Law Blog*, 28.04.2020, at: <http://www.iconnectblog.com/2020/04/polexit-is-coming-or-is-it-already-here-comments-on-the-judicial-independence-decisions-of-the-polish-constitutional-tribunal>.

A. Bień-Kacała and A. Tarnowska, 'Power of Authority. A few words on the Chief of State one hundred years ago and the present' (2019) 46 *Przegląd Prawa Konstytucyjnego*, 6, 124–35.

A. Bień-Kacała, A. Tarnowska and W. Włoch, 'The nation, delegation, and constitutional change in Poland' (2018) 59 *Hungarian Journal of Legal Studies* 4, 355–77.

F. Bilancia, 'Constitutional Roots of Democracy' (2019) *Costituzionalismo.it* 3, 33–46.

——, 'The constitutional dimension of democracy within a democratic society' (2019) 11 *Italian Journal of Public Law* 1, 8–21.

E. Bindi, 'Calamandrei e la questione sociale' in (2012) 3 *Gruppo di Pisa. La Rivista.*

A. Bíró-Nagy, 'Illiberal democracy in Hungary: the social background and practical steps of building an illiberal state', Barcelona Centre for International Affairs, 2017, <https://www.cidob.org/en/articulos/monografias/illiberals/illiberal_democracy_in_hungary_the_social_background_and_practical_steps_of_building_an_illiberal_state>.

A. Bíró-Nagy and G. Laki, *Orbán 10. Az elmúlt évtized a Magyar társadalom szemével*, Budapest 2020.

P. Biscaretti di Ruffia, 'Democrazia' in AA.VV., *Enciclopedia del Diritto*, XII, Giuffrè, Milano 1964.

P. Blokker, 'Building democracy by legal means? The contestation of human rights and constitutionalism in East-Central Europe' (2020) 18 *Journal of Modern European History* 3.

——, 'Il costituzionalismo populista' in M. Anselmi, P. Blokker and N. Urbinati (eds), *Populismo di lotta e di governo*, Fondazione Feltrinelli, Milano 2018.

——, *New Democracies in Crisis? A Comparative Constitutional Study of the Czech Republic, Hungary, Poland, Romania and Slovakia*, Routledge, London/New York 2013.

——, 'Political and Constitutional Imaginaries' in S. Adams and J. Smith (eds), *Social Imaginaries: Critical Interventions in a Paradigm-in-the-Making*, Rowman and Littlefield, Lanham, Maryland 2019.

——, 'Populism as a constitutional project' (2019), 17 *International Journal of Constitutional Law* 2, 536–553.

——, 'Populist Constitutionalism', in C. de la Torre (ed.), *Routledge Handbook of Global Populism*, Routledge, New York 2018.

——, 'Populist Counter-Constitutionalism, Conservatism, and Legal Fundamentalism' (2019) 15 *European Constitutional Law Review* 3.

——, 'Populist Nationalism, Anti-Europeanism, Post-nationalism, and the East-West Distinction' (2005) 6 *German Law Journal* 2, 371–89.

——, 'Populist Understandings of the Law: A Conservative Backlash?' (forthcoming) *Participation and Conflict (PaCo)*.

——, 'The Populist Assault on the Constitution' in P. Blokker and M. Anselmi (eds), *Multiple populisms. Italy as democracy's mirror*, Routledge, London 2020.

——, 'Varieties of Populist Constitutionalism: The Transnational Dimension' (2019) 20 *German Law Journal* 332–50.

P. Blokker, B. Bugaric and G. Halmai, 'Introduction: Populist Constitutionalism: Varieties, Complexities, and Contradictions (2019) 20 *German Law Journal*, 291–95.

A. Bloom, C. Butterworth and C. Kelly (eds), *Rousseau: Letter to d'Alembert and Writings for the Theatre*, University Press of New England, Dartmouth 2004.

J. Blount, 'Participation in constitutional design' in T. Ginsburg and R. Dixon (eds), *Comparative Constitutional Law*, Edward Elgar, Cheltenham, Northampton, MA 2011.

C. Blum, *Rousseau and the Republic of Virtue; The Language of Politics in the French Revolution*, Cornell University Press, Ithaca 1986.

N. Bobbio, 'Democrazia' in N. Bobbio, N. Matteucci and G. Pasquino (eds), *Dizionario di politica*, Tea, Torino 1990.

——, *Ideological Profile of Twentieth-Century Italy*, Princeton University Press, Princeton 2014.

G. Bognetti, *Dividing Powers. A Theory of the Separation of Powers* (A. Baraggia and L.P. Vanoni, English eds; K. Bailey trans), Wolters Kluwer Cedam, Milan 2017.

D. Bonansinga, 'Who Thinks, Feels. The Relationship Between Emotions, Politics and Populism' (2020) 13 *Partecipazione e conflitto* 1, 83.

B. Bonikowski, 'Three Lessons of Contemporary Populism in Europe and the United States' (2016) 23 *The Brown Journal of World Affairs* 1, 9–24.

B.H. Bornstein and R.L. Wiener (eds), *Emotion and the law: Psychological perspectives*, Springer, New York 2009.

T. Boros, M. Freitas, G. Laki and E. Stetter, *State of Populism in Europe*, Foundation for European Progressive Studies, Brussels and Budapest 2018.

G. Borradori, *Philosophy in times of terror. Conversations with Jürgen Habermas and Jacques Derrida*, The University of Chicago Press, Chicago 2008.

O. Bowcott, 'Judge questions coronavirus case against "homeless" London man', <https://www.theguardian.com/uk-news/2020/may/12/judge-questions-coronavirus-case-against-homeless-london-man?CMP=Share_iOSApp_Other&fbclid=IwAR1lstN-4_vkj5INVeWXV5Kc5c_XBZV33kpWuI_dIU2KPClRe8cWe-bSPaA>.

B. Bowring, *Law, Rights and Ideology in Russia: Landmarks in the Destiny of a Great Power*, Routledge, New York 2017.

A. Bozóki, *The Roundtable Talks of 1989. The Genesys of Hungarian Democracy*, CEU Press, Budapest 2002.

A. Bozóki and D. Hegedűs, 'An externally constrained hybrid regime: Hungary in the European Union' (2018) 7 *Democratization* 1173–1189.

B. Bremer, 'The missing left? Economic crisis and the programmatic response of social democratic parties in Europe' (2018) 24 *Party Politics* 1, 23–38.

Z. Brzeziński, *The Grand Failure. The Birth and Death of Communism in the Twentieth Century*, MacDonald, London 1989.

M. Bucholc, 'Commemorative Lawmaking: Memory Frames of the Democratic Backsliding in Poland After 2015' (2019) 11 *Hague Journal on the Rule of Law*, 86–105.

B. Bugaric, 'Could Populism Be Good for Constitutional Democracy?' (2019) *Annual Review of Law and Social Science* 15, 41–58.

——, 'The Populist Backlash Against Europe: Why Only Alternative Economic and Social Policies Can Stop the Rise of Populism in Europe' in F. Bignami (ed.), *EU Law in Populist Times*, Cambridge University Press, Cambridge 2018.

——, 'The two faces of populism: Between authoritarian and democratic populism' (2019) 20 *German Law Journal* 3, 390–400.

B. Bugaric and M. Tushnet, 'Populism and constitutionalism: an essay on definitions and their implications' (in press) *Cardozo Law Review*.

B. Bugarič, 'A crisis of constitutional democracy in post-Communist Europe: "Lands in-between" democracy and authoritarianism' (2015) 13 *International Journal of Constitutional Law* 1.

——, 'Central Europe's descent into autocracy: a constitutional analysis of authoritarian populism' (2019) 17 *International Journal of Constitutional Law* 2.

——, 'Protecting Democracy and the Rule of Law in the European Union: The Hungarian Challenge' (2014) 79 *LSE 'Europe in Question' Discussion Paper Series*, 7–14.

B. Bugarič, A. Kuhelj, 'Varieties of Populism in Europe: Is the Rule of Law in Danger?' (2018) 10 *Hague Journal of the Rule of Law* 22.

M.J. Bull and J.L. Newell, 'Still the Anomalous Democracy? Politics and Institutions in Italy' (2009) 44 *Government and Opposition* 1, 42–67.

G. De Búrca, J. Morijn and M. Steinbeis, *Stand with Wojciech Sadurski: his freedom of expression is (y)ours, VerfBlog*, 18.11.2019, <https://verfassungsblog.de/stand-with-wojciech-sadurski-his-freedom-of-expression-is-yours/>.

M. Burgess, *Federalism and the European Union: The Building of Europe 1950–2000*, Routledge, London 2000.

L. Bustikova and P. Guasti, 'The State as a Firm: Understanding the Autocratic Roots of Technocratic Populism' (2019) 33 *East European Politics and Societies and Cultures* 2, 302–30.

C. Buzzacchi, *La solidarietà tributaria. Funzione fiscale e principi costituzionali*, Giuffré, Milano 2011.

——, *Il lavoro da diritto a bene*, Franco Angeli, Milano 2019.

P. Calamandrei, 'Appunti sul professionismo parlamentare' in P. Calamandrei, (N. Bobbio ed), *Scritti e discorsi politici*, Vol. II, La Nuova Italia, Firenze 1966.

——, 'Cenni introduttivi sulla Costituente e i suoi lavori' in P. Calamandrei (N. Bobbio ed), *Scritti e discorsi politici*, Vol. II, La Nuova Italia, Firenze 1966, p. 421.

——, 'La Costituzione e le leggi per attuarla' in P. Calamandrei (ed.), *Opere giuridiche*, Morano, Napoli 1965.

M. Calise, *La democrazia del leader*, Laterza, Roma-Bari 2016.

J. Callaghan, *The Retreat of Social Democracy*, Manchester University Press, Manchester, New York 2000.

M. Canovan, 'Trust the People! Populism and the Two Faces of Democracy' (1999) 47 *Political Studies* 1, 2.

E. Carolan, *The New Separation of Powers. A Theory for the Modern State*, Oxford University Press, Oxford and New York 2009.

T. Carothers, 'The end of the transition paradigm' (2002) 13 *Journal of Democracy* 1.

F. Carreira da Silva and M. Brito Vieira, 'Populism and the politics of redemption' (2018) 149 *Thesis Eleven* 1, 10–30.

C. Castoriadis, *The imaginary institution of society*, MIT Press, Cambridge, Massachusetts 1997.

P. Casula, 'Sovereign Democracy, Populism, and Depoliticization in Russia. Power and Discourse During Putin's First Presidency', (2013) 60 *Problems of Post-Communism* 3, 8.

M. Ceccorulli, 'The EU and Covid-19: Overcoming the lockdown mindset on migration', <https://www.globus.uio.no/resources/global-justice-blog/covid-19-series/ceccorulli-corona-migration-may20.html?fbclid=IwAR0155fXWv01r-jxYIaM9zC3F9iDeeY5iE_B0pHJiLgMht7BehgHZ_shslU>.

A. Cento Dull, *Italian Neofascism The Strategy of Tension and the Politics of Nonreconciliation*, Berghahn Books, New York and Oxford 2012.

C. Cercel, 'The Destruction of Legal Reason: Lessons from the Past' (2019) 89 *Folia Iuridica*, 15–30.

G. Cerrina Feroni, 'Ripensare la democrazia rappresentativa. Aldilà del "mito" populista' (2019) *Osservatorio sulle Fonti* 2, 1–13.

L. Chamberlain, *Lenin's Private War: The Voyage of the Philosophy Steamer and the Exile of the Intelligentsia*, St Martin's Press, New York 2015.

S. Chambers, 'Afterword, Populist Constitutionalism v. Deliberative Constitutionalism'. in R. Levy et al. (eds), *The Cambridge Handbook of Deliberative Constitutionalism*, Cambridge University Press, Cambridge 2018.

——, 'Democracy and constitutional reform: Deliberative versus populist constitutionalism' (2019) 45 *Philosophy and Social Criticism* 9–10, 1116–31.

E. Cheli, 'La sovranità, la funzione di governo, l'indirizzo politico' in G. Amato and A. Barbera (eds), *Manuale di diritto pubblico. II. L'organizzazione costituzionale*, 5th ed., Il Mulino, Bologna 1984.

C. Chen, *The Return of Ideology: The Search for Regime Identities in Postcommunist Russia and China*, Ann Arbor, University of Michigan Press 2016.

C. Chimenti, 'I partiti politici' in G. Amato and A. Barbera (eds), *Manuale di diritto pubblico. II. L'organizzazione costituzionale*, 5th ed., Il Mulino, Bologna 1984.

I. Chopin and C. Germaine, *A comparative analysis of non-discrimination law in Europe 2017*, European Commission, Brussels 2017.

A. Cichocka and A. Cislak, 'Nationalism as collective narcissism' (2020) *ScienceDirect Current Opinion in Behavioral Sciences* 34, 69–74.

S. Clifford, *The CEO Pay Machine: How It Trashes America and How to Stop It*, Penguin Random House, New York 2017.

J. Cohen, 'Deliberation and Democratic Legitimacy' in J. Bohman and W. Rehg (eds), *Deliberative Democracy. Essays on Reason and Politics*, MIT Press, Cambridge MA and London 1997.

——, *Globalization and Sovereignty. Rethinking Legality, Legitimacy and Constitutionalism*, Cambridge University Press, Cambridge 2012.

J.L. Cohen 'Hollow parties and their movementization: The populist conundrum' (2019) 45 *Philosophy and Social Criticism* 9–10, 1084–1105.

J. Colón-Ríos, 'Five Conceptions of Constituent Power' (2014) 13 *Law Quarterly Review* 2, 306.

——, *Weak Constitutionalism, Democratic Legitimacy and the Question of Constituent Power*, Routledge, London/New York 2012.

X. Contiades and A. Fontiadou, 'Models of Constitutional Change' in X. Contiades (ed.), *Engineering Constitutional Change. A Comparative Perspective on Europe, Canada and the USA*, Routledge, London and New York 2013.

L. Corrias, 'Populism in a Constitutional Key: Constituent Power, Popular Sovereignty and Constitutional Identity' (2016) 12 *European Constitutional Law Review* 1, 6–26.

L. Corso, 'What does Populism have to do with Constitutional Law? Discussing Populist Constitutionalism and Its Assumptions' (2014) *Rivista di filosofia del diritto* 2.

R. Cotterell, 'Law, Emotion and Affective Community' Queen Mary University of London, School of Law Legal Studies Research Paper No. 282/2018.

S. Cowan, V.E. Munro and H. Baillot, 'Second-hand emotion? Exploring the contagion and impact of trauma and distress in the asylum law context' (2013) 40 *Journal of Law and Society* 4, 509–540.

B. Crick, 'Populism, politics and democracy' (2005) 12 *Democratization* 5, 625–32.

Z.S. Csaky, *Nations in transition. Dropping the democratic façade*, Freedom House 2020.

E. Csatlós, 'The Application of International Law as an Instrument of Interpretation in Hungary – the Practice of the Constitutional Court and Ordinary Courts in a Comparative Approach', <http://publicatio.bibl.u-szeged.hu/7049/8/2961433.pdf>.

D. Curtin, 'Accountable independence of the European Central Bank: seeing the logics of transparency' (2017) 23 *European Law Journal* 1–2, 28–44.

R. Dahl, *Democracy and its Critics*, Yale University Press, New Haven 1989.

R.A. Dahl, 'Efficiency of the "versus" effective citizenship order: a dilemma of democracy', Dahl-Ferrara-Haberle, New-Rusconi, in M. Luciani (ed.), *Democracy at the end of the century*, Laterza, Bari 1994.

——, *Polyarchy, participation and opposition*, Yale University Press, New Haven, CT 1971.

J. Daley, 'There's no such thing as Left and Right any more – can we all agree on that?' in *The Telegraph*, 10.10.2015.

T.G. Daly, 'Democratic Decay: Conceptualising an Emerging Research Field' (2019) 11 *Hague Journal on the Rule of Law*, 10–26.

——, 'Illiberal Democracy: Pinning Down a Problematic Term', International Association of Constitutional Law (IACL) World Congress, Seoul, June 2018.

——, 'The Democratic Recession and the "New" Public Law: Toward Systematic Analysis', *International Journal of Constitutional Law Blog*, 22.04.2016.

G. Debord, *The Society of the Spectacle*, tr. D. Nicholson-Smith, Zone Books, New York 1994.

B. De Cleen and Y. Stavrakakis, 'Distinctions and Articulations: A Discourse Theoretical Framework for the Study of Populism and Nationalism' (2017) 24 *Javnost-The Public*, 301–19.

B. De Cleen, J. Glynos and A. Mondon, 'Critical Research on Populism: Nine Rules of Engagement' (2018) 25 *Organization*, 649–61.

J. De Haan, 'The European Central Bank: Independence, Accountability and Strategy: A Review' (1997) 93 *Public Choice* 3–4, 395–426.

C. De La Torre, 'Populism Revived: Donald Trump and the Latin American Leftist Populists' (2018), 75 *The Americas* 4, 733–753.

—— (ed.), *The promise and perils of populism: Global perspectives*, University Press of Kentucky, Lexington 2014.

F. Del Luchesse, 'Machiavelli and constituent power: The revolutionary foundation of modern political thought' (2017) 16 *European Journal of Political Theory* 3, 6.

G. Delledonne, G. Martinico, M. Monti and F. Pacini, 'Introduction: A Constitutional Viewpoint on Italian Populism' in G. Delledonne, G. Martinico, M. Monti and F. Pacini (eds), *Italian Populism and Constitutional Law*, Palgrave Macmillan, London 2020.

N. Demertzis, 'Emotions and populism' in S. Clarke, P. Hogett and S. Thompson (eds), *Emotion, politics and society*, Palgrave Macmillan, London 2006.

A. de Tocqueville, *Democracy in America*, The Lawbook Exchange, Clark, New Jersey 2003.

J. Dewey, 'A Common Faith', in J.A. Boydston (ed.), *Collected Works of John Dewey. The Later Works: 1925–1953*, Southern Illinois Press, Carbondale-Edwardsville 1991.

——, 'Challenge to Liberal Thought', in J.A. Boydston (ed.), *Collected Works of John Dewey. The Later Works: 1925–1953*, Southern Illinois Press, Carbondale-Edwardsville 1991.

——, 'Creative Democracy — The Task Before Us', in J.A. Boydston (ed.), *Collected Works of John Dewey. The Later Works: 1925–1953*, Southern Illinois Press, Carbondale-Edwardsville 1991.

——, 'Democracy and Education', in J.A. Boydston (ed.), *Collected Works of John Dewey. The Middle Works: 1899–1924*, Southern Illinois Press, Carbondale-Edwardsville 1991.

——, 'Ethics', in J.A. Boydston (ed.), *Collected Works of John Dewey. The Later Works: 1925–1953*, Southern Illinois Press, Carbondale-Edwardsville 1991.

——, 'Individualism, Old and New', in J.A. Boydston (ed.), *Collected Works of John Dewey. The Later Works: 1925–1953*, Southern Illinois Press, Carbondale-Edwardsville 1991.

——, 'Liberalism and the Social Action', in J.A. Boydston (ed.), *Collected Works of John Dewey. The Later Works: 1925–1953*, Southern Illinois Press, Carbondale-Edwardsville 1991.

——, 'Reconstruction in Philosophy and Essays, in J.A. Boydston (ed.), *Collected Works of John Dewey. The Later Works: 1925–1953*, Southern Illinois Press, Carbondale-Edwardsville 1991.

——, 'The Public and its Problems', in J.A. Boydston (ed.), *Collected Works of John Dewey. The Later Works: 1925–1953*, Southern Illinois Press, Carbondale-Edwardsville 1991.

G. de Vergottini, *Diritto costituzionale comparato*, Cedam, Padova 1999.

B. de Witte, 'The Pillar Structure and the Nature of the European Union: Greek Temple or French Gothic Cathedral?' in T. Heukels, N. Blokker and M. Brus (eds), *The European Union after Amsterdam: A Legal Analysis*, Kluwer Law International, The Hague 1998.

J.W. de Zwaan, 'The Legal Personality of the European Communities and the European Union' (1999) *Netherlands Yearbook of International Law* 30, 75–113.

G. Di Cosimo, 'Personale e digitale: le metamorfosi del partito' (2019) *Forum di Quaderni costituzionali*.

A. Di Giovine, 'Forme di Stato' in L. Pegoraro (ed.), *Glossario di Diritto pubblico comparato*, Carocci, Roma 2009.

A. Di Giovine and S. Sicardi (eds), *Democrazie imperfette*, Giappichelli, Torino 2005.

A. Di Gregorio, 'Constitutional Courts in the Context of Constitutional Regression. Some Comparative Remarks' in M. Belov (ed.), *Courts, Politics, and Constitutional Law*, Routledge, London 2019.

——, 'I fenomeni di degenerazione delle democrazie contemporanee: qualche spunto di riflessione sullo sfondo delle contrapposizioni dottrinali' (2019) *Nuovi Autoritarismi e Democrazie (NAD)* 2, 2.

——, 'L'Ungheria e i valori europei: un matrimonio impossibile' (2018) *Rassegna parlamentare* 2.

A. Di Gregorio (ed.), *The Constitutional Systems of Central-Eastern, Baltic and Balkan Europe*, Eleven International Publishing, The Hague 2019.

I. Diamanti, 'Alla periferia della crisi. Il populismo e il disagio della democrazia rappresentativa' (2018) 1 *Stato e mercato* 117–25, 117–119.

R. Diaz-Bone, 'Institutionalist and methodological perspectives on law – Contributions of the economics of convention' (2015) *Historical Social Research/ Historische Sozialforschung*, 23–41.

B. Dima, 'The European models of semi-presidentialism: the peculiarity of Romania's post-communist system of government' (2014) *Romanian Journal of Comparative Law* 1.

J. Dirix, W. Peeters, J. Eyckmans, P.T. Jones and S. Sterckx, 'Strengthening bottom-up and top-down climate governance' (2013) 13 *Climate Policy* 3, 363–83.

R. Dixon and D. Landau, '1989–2019: From democratic to abusive constitutional borrowing' (2019) 17 *International Journal of Constitutional Law* 2.

P. Dobner and M. Loughlin (eds), *The twilight of constitutionalism?*, Oxford University Press, Oxford 2010.

R. Douglass, *Rousseau and Hobbes: Nature, Free Will and the Passions*, Oxford University Press, Oxford 2016.

O. Doyle, 'Populist constitutionalism and constituent power' (2019) 20 *German Law Journal*, 161–80.

T. Drinóczi, 'Concept of quality in legislation – revisited: matter of perspective and a general overview', (2015) *Statute Law Review* 3, 211–27.

——, 'Constitutional Identity in Europe: The Identity of the Constitution. A Regional Approach' (2020) 21 *German Law Journal* 2, 105–30.

——, 'Constitutional politics in contemporary Hungary' (2016) *Vienna Journal or International Constitutional Law* 1, 63–98.

——, 'Dialogic interaction and legislation on parliamentary election in Hungary 2010–2014' (2016) *Osteuropa Recht* 4, 452–467.

——, 'Hungarian Abuse of Constitutional Emergency Regimes – Also in the Light of the COVID-19 Crisis', *MTA WLP* 2020/13.

——, 'Hungarian Democratic Backsliding in light of the recent emergency coronavirus legislation' Public Jurist, Hong Kong University Political Science Magazine, June, 2020.

——, 'Legislation in Hungary', in H. Xanthaki and U. Karpen (eds), *Legislation in Europe-A Country to Country Guide*, Hart Publishing, Oxford forthcoming.

T. Drinóczi and A. Bień-Kacała, 'COVID-19 in Hungary and Poland: extraordinary situation and illiberal constitutionalism', in Theory and Practice of Legislation (2020) <https://www.tandfonline.com/doi/full/10.1080/20508840.2020.1782109>.

——, 'Extra-legal particularities and illiberal constitutionalism. The case of Hungary and Poland' (2018) *Hungarian Journal of Legal Studies* 4, 346–47.

——, 'Illiberal Constitutionalism: The Case of Hungary and Poland' (2019) 20 *German Law Journal* 8, 1140–66.

—— (eds), *Rule of Law, Common Values and Illiberal Constitutionalism. Poland and Hungary within the European Union*, Routledge 2020.

T. Drinóczi, F. Gárdos-Orosz and Z. Pozsár-Szentmiklósy, 'Formal and Informal Constitutional Amendment in Hungary' (2019) MTA Law Working Papers 18.

M. Duverger, *Les parties politiques*, Colin, Paris 1954.

R. Dworkin, *Taking Rights Seriously*, Harvard University Press, Cambridge MA 1977.

D. Dyzenhaus, 'Canada the Good?', <https://verfassungsblog.de/canada-the-good/>.

A. Dzur and C. Hendriks, 'Thick populism: democracy-enhancing popular participation' (2018) 39 *Policy Studies* 3, 334–51.

S. Earle, 'The terrifying rehabilitation of Nazi scholar Carl Schmitt', *New Statesman* 10.04.2019, <https://www.newstatesman.com/2019/04/terrifying-rehabilitation-nazi-scholar-carl-schmitt>.

U. Eco, *Il fascismo eterno*, La nave di Teseo, Milano 2017.

D. Edelstein, *The Terror of Natural Right: Republicanism, the Cult of Nature, and the French Revolution*, Chicago University Press, Chicago 2009.

L. Elia, *La Costituzione aggredita: forma di governo e devolution ai tempi della destra*, Il Mulino, Bologna 2005.

——, 'La peculiarietà e l'evoluzione del Sistema italiano riguardo ai partiti politici', in Idem, *Costituzione, partiti, istituzioni*, Il Mulino, Bologna 2009.

C. Elliott, *French Criminal Law*, Routledge, New York 2011.

J. Elster, 'Introduction' in J J. Elster (ed.), *Deliberative Democracy*, Cambridge University Press, Cambridge, 1998.

M. Eltchaninoff, *Inside the Mind of Vladimir Putin*, C. Hurst and Co. Publishers Ltd., London 2018, p. 5.

P. English, M.T. Grasso and B. Buraczynska, 'Convergence on crisis? Comparing Labour and Conservative Party framing of the economic crisis in Britain, 2008–14' (2016) 44 *Politics & Policy* 3, 577–603.

European Commission for Democracy through Law (Venice Commission), '*Opinion on the Fourth Amendment to the Fundamental Law of Hungary*' Opinion 720/2013 (2013).

Y. Ezrahi, *Imagined democracies, necessary political fictions*, Cambridge University Press, Cambridge 2012.

S. Fabbrini, 'Quella santa alleanza fra populismo e nazionalismo' (2017) 22 January, *Il Sole 24 Ore*.

——, 'When Media and Politics Overlap: Interferences from the Italian Case' (2011) 46 *Government and Opposition* 3, 345–64.

L. Favoreu, *Les Cours constitutionelles*, Presses Universitaires de France, Paris 1992.

L. Fazzi, 'Social work, exclusionary populism and xenophobia in Italy' (2015) 58 *International Social Work* 4, 595–605.

J. Fernandez, T. Fleury Graff and A. Marie, 'La crise sanitaire, prétexte à une fragilisation du droit d'asile' <https://www.leclubdesjuristes.com/blog-du-coronavirus/que-dit-le-droit/la-crise-sanitaire-pretexte-a-une-fragilisation-du-droit-dasile/?fbclid=IwAR34KHus0ggvFmkke9gowXIVneWbIP4X5uuKtbwG_IVbOMuYPXxz-VD6BNw>.

M. Ferraresi, *Solitudine*, Einaudi, Torino 2020.

F. Ferraresi, *Threats to Democracy. The Radical Right in Italy after the War*, Princeton University Press, Princeton 2012.

P. Filipek, 'The New National Council of the Judiciary and Its Impact on the Supreme Court in the Light of the Principle of Judicial Independence' (2018) XVI *Problemy Współczesnego Prawa Międzynarodowego, Europejskiego i Porównawczego* 177–96.

A. Floridia, 'Il 'caso' italiano: il circuito perverso del populismo' (2013) 78 *Ábaco* 67–72.

J.P. Forgas and D. Lantos, 'Understanding Populism: Collective Narcissism and the Collapse of Democracy in Hungary', <http://www.sydneysymposium.unsw.edu.au/2019/chapters/ForgasSSSP2019%20.pdf>.

J.E. Fossum, 'The crisis, a challenge to representative democracy in the European Union?' in J.E. Fossum and A.J. Menéndez (eds), *The European Union in crises or the European Union as crises?* Arena Centre for European Studies, Oslo 2014.

M. Foucault, *The Birth of Biopolitics: Lectures at the Collège de France, 1978–1979: Lectures at the College De France, 1978–1979*, Palgrave Macmillan, London 2008.

T. Fournier, 'From Rhetoric to Action – a Constitutional Analysis of Populism' (2018) 08 *EUI Working Papers*, 1–18.

——, 'From rhetoric to action, a constitutional analysis of populism' (2019) 20 *German Law Journal* 3, 362–81.

M.R. Fowler and J.M. Bunck, 'What Constitutes the Sovereign State?' (1996) 22 *Review of International Studies* 4, 381–404.

A. Foxall, 'Photographing Vladimir Putin: Masculinity, Nationalism and Visuality in Russian Political Culture', (2013) 18 *Geopolitics* 132.

E. Fraenkel, *The Dual State*, Oxford University Press, Oxford 1941.

G. Frankenberg, 'COVID-19 und der juristische Umgang mit Ungewissheit' <https://verfassungsblog.de/covid-19-und-der-juristische-umgang-mit-ungewissheit/?fbclid=IwAR124mNjX5XLFVp6v1pl4NAzl-PBa9O5eqR1UWkNHow5Blcrv-Dc6vBdzKQ>.

M. Fratianni and H. Huang, 'Reputation, Central Bank Independence and the ECB' in P.L. Siklos (ed.), *Varieties of Monetary Reforms. Lessons and Experiences on the Road to Monetary Union*, Springer, Cham 1994.

M. Freedman, *Capitalism and Freedom*, The University of Chicago Press, Cambridge 1962.

U. FREVERT, *Emotions in History ? Lost and Found*, Central European University Press, Budapest 2011.

M. FRIEDMAN, 'The Social Responsibility of Business Is to Increase Its Profits' in W.C. ZIMMERLI, M. HOLZINGER and K. RICHTER (eds), *Corporate Ethics and Corporate Governance*, Springer, Berlin and Heidelberg 2007.

C. FROST, 'Summoning Sovereignty: Constituent Power and Poetic Prophecy in Ireland's 1916 Proclamation of the Republic' (2017) 24 *Constellations* 76, 77.

F. FUKUYAMA, '30 Years of World Politics: What Has Changed?' (2020) 31 *Journal of Democracy* 1, 13.

F. FUREDI, *Populism and the European culture wars: the conflict of values between Hungary and the EU*, Routledge, London 2017.

É. FÜLÖP et al., 'Emotional Elaboration of Collective Traumas in Historical Narratives' (2014), <http://real.mtak.hu/20201/3/emotional_elaboration_of_collective_traumas.pdf>.

M. GANINO, 'Appunti e spunti per una ricerca di diritto costituzionale su paesi "altri"' in AA.VV., *Alle frontiere del diritto costituzionale. Scritti in onore di Valerio Onida*, Giuffré, Milano 2011.

S. GANTY, 'Belgium and COVID-19: When a Health Crisis Replaces a Political Crisis', <https://verfassungsblog.de/belgium-and-covid-19-when-a-health-crisis-replaces-a-political-crisis/>.

J. GAVIRIA-MIRA and E. HOYOS-CEBALLOS, 'Pandemic and Executive Powers in Colombia: A Problem and a Modest Proposal', <https://verfassungsblog.de/pandemic-and-executive-powers-in-colombia-a-problem-and-a-modest-proposal/>.

M. GDULA, *Nowy autorytaryzm, [The New Authoritarianism]*, Wydawnictwo Krytyki Politycznej, Warsaw 2018.

J. GERHARDS, H. LENGFELD, Z. IGNÁCZ, F.K. KLEY and M. PRIEM, *European Solidarity in Times of Crisis: Insights from a Thirteen-Country Survey*, Routledge, New York 2019.

D. GEWIRTZMAN, 'Our founding feelings: emotion, commitment, and imagination in constitutional culture' (2008) 43 *University of Richmond Law Review* 623, 323–339.

T. GINSBURG, 'Thirty years after the fall: An academic perspective' (2019) 17 *International Journal of Constitutional Law* 2.

T. GINSBURG and A.Z. HUQ, *How to Save a Constitutional Democracy*, The University of Chicago Press, Chicago and London 2018.

T. GINSBURG, A. HUQ and M. VERSTEEG, 'The Coming Demise of Liberal Constitutionalism' (2018) 85 *University of Chicago Law Review* 239.

F. GIUFFRÉ, *La solidarietà nell'ordinamento costituzionale*, Giuffré, Milano 2002.

B. GLASSNER, *The Culture of Fear: Why Americans Are Afraid of the Wrong Things: Crime, Drugs, Minorities, Teen Moms, Killer Kids, Mutant Microbes, Plane Crashes, Road Rage, & So Much More*, Basic Books, New York 2010.

M.A. GLENDON, *Rights Talk: The Impoverishment of Political Discourse*, The Free Press, New York 1991.

A. Golec De Zavala, K. Dyduch-Hazar and D. Lantos, 'Collective Narcissism: Political Consequences of Investing Self-Worth in the Ingroup's Image' (2019) 40 *Advances in Political Psychology* 1, 46.

J. Grant, 'Justifying Constituent Power in an Age of Populism' (2020) 52 *Polity* 1.

J. Gray, *Two Faces of Liberalism*, Polity, Cambridge 1995.

J. Greenwood, 'Organized civil society and democratic legitimacy in the European Union' (2007) 37 *British Journal of Political Science* 2, 333–57.

L.E. Grinin, 'New Basics of State Order or Why do States Lose Their Sovereignty in the Age of Globalization' (2012) 3 *Journal of Globalization Studies* 1, 3–38.

C.H. Guilluy, *Twilight of the Elites: Prosperity, the Periphery, and the Future of France*, Yale University Press, New Haven and London 2019.

G. Guins, 'Soviet Law-Terra Incognita', (1950) 9 *The Russian Review* 1, 17.

T. Győrfi, *Against the New Constitutionalism*, Edward Elgar, Cheltenham 2016.

——, 'Democracy' [Demokrácia], in P. Takács, I.H. Szilágyi and B. Fekete, *State theory. Chapters and lectures on the general theory of the state [Államelmélet. Fejezetek és előadások az állam általános elmélete köréből]*, Szent István Társulat, Budapest 2012.

——, 'Limitations on majority decision-making and constitutional adjudication' [A többségi döntés korlátai és az alkotmánybíráskodás], in A. Jakab and A. Körösényi (eds), *Constitution in Hungary and elsewhere. Political science and constitutional law approaches [Alkotmányozás Magyarországon és máshol. Politikatudományi és alkotmányjogi megközelítések]*, MTA TK PTI, 2012.

K. Gözler, *Judicial Review of Constitutional Amendments*, Ekin Press, Bursa 2008.

D. Habermas, *A World of Struggle: How Power, Law, and Expertise Shape Global Political Economy*, Princeton University Press, New Haven 2016.

J. Habermas, *Die nachholende revolution*, Suhrkamp, Frankfurt 1990.

——, *The Theory of Communicative Action*, vol. 1 & vol. 2, Polity Press, Oxford 1991.

——, 'Three Normative Models of Democracy' in S. Benhabib (ed.), *Democracy and Difference. Contesting the Boundaries of the Political*, Princeton University Press, Princeton 1996.

J. Habermas and K. Günther, 'Kein Grundrecht gilt grenzenlos' <https://www.zeit.de/2020/20/grundrechte-lebensschutz-freiheit-juergen-habermas-klaus-guenther?fbclid=IwAR1sy4JcLGo5UNLYu4pDSxglvPCf4ce4Lbdg4lW5CC6amPCyGS2O27oADXM>.

J. Hage, 'Philosophy of Law', in J. Hage, A. Waltermann and B. Akkermans (eds), *Introduction to Law*, 2nd ed., Springer, 2017.

G. Halmai, 'Populism, authoritarianism and constitutionalism' (2019) 20 *German Law Journal* 3, 296–313.

——, 'Silence of transitional constitutions: The "invisible constitution" concept of the Hungarian Constitutional Court' (2018) 16 *International Journal of Constitutional Law* 3.

——, 'The Rise and Fall of Constitutionalism in Hungary' in P. Blokker (ed.), *Constitutional Acceleration within the European Union and Beyond*, Routledge, London/New York 2017.

O. Hamilak, M. Sulyok and L.N. Kiss, 'Measuring the "EU"-clidean distance between EU law and the Hungarian Constitutional Court – focusing on the position of the EU Charter of Fundamental Rights', (2019) *Czech Yearbook of Public & Private International Law* 10, 145–48.

A. Hamilton, J. Madison and J. Jay, *The Federalist with The Letters of 'Brutus'*, ed. T. Ball, Cambridge University Press, Cambridge 2003.

N. Hammerstein, *Die Deutsche Forschungsgemeinschaft in der Weimarer Republik und im Dritten Reich; Wissenschaftspolitik in Republik und Diktatur, 1920–1945*, C.H. Beck, Munich 1999.

J. Hanson and K. Hanson, 'The Blame Frame: Justifying (Racial) Injustice in America' (2006) 2 *Harvard Civil Rights Civil Liberties Law Review* 41, 413–80.

J.N. Hazard, 'Soviet Law: An Introduction' (1936) 36 *Columbia Law Review* 8, 1236.

D. Healey, 'Untraditional Sex and the Simple Russian' in: T. Lahusen (ed.), *What is Soviet Now?: Identities, Legacies, Memories*, Lit Verlag, Berlin 2008.

M. Hein: 'Do Constitutional Entrenchment Clauses Matter? Constitutional Review of Constitutional Amendments in Europe' (2020) 18 *International Journal of Constitutional Law* 1.

H.M. Heinig, 'Gottesdienstverbot auf Grundlage des Infektionsschutzgesetzes Verfassungsrechtliche Rechtfertigung und Grenzen' <https://verfassungsblog.de/gottesdienstverbot-auf-grundlage-des-infektionsschutzgesetzes/>.

C.M. Herrera, 'Le populisme constitutionnel' (2018) *Annuaire International de Justice Constitutionnelle* XXXIV.

F. Hill and C.G. Gaddy, *Mr. Putin: Operative in the Kremlin*, Brookings Institution Press, Washington D.C. 2015.

A.O. Hirschman, *The rhetoric of reaction*, Harvard University Press, Cambridge Massachusetts 1991.

T. Hobbes, *Leviathan*, CreateSpace Independent Publishing Platform, 2011.

E. Hobsbawm, *Primitive Rebels*, University of Manchester Press, Manchester 1959.

A. Honneth, *The Struggle for Recognition. The Moral Grammar of Social Conflicts*, tr. J. Anderson, The MIT Press, Cambridge 1995.

J. Hopkin and M. Blyth, 'The Global Economics of European Populism: Growth Regimes and Party System Change in Europe' (2018) 54 *Government and Opposition* 2, 193–225.

D. Howarth and P. Loedel, *The European Central Bank. The New European Leviathian?* Palgrave Macmillan, London 2005.

P. Howell O'neill, T. Ryan-Mosley and B. Johnson, 'A flood of coronavirus apps are tracking us. Now it's time to keep track of them', MIT Technology Review, <https://www.technologyreview.com/2020/05/07/1000961/launching-mittr-covid-tracing-tracker/>.

M. Hunter-Henin, 'The Legal Face of Populism: From the Classroom to the Courtroom', Jean Monnet Working Paper 9/17.

A. Huq and T. Ginsburg, 'How to Lose a Constitutional Democracy' (2018) *University of Chicago Law Review* 78.

E. Huskey, 'A Framework for the Analysis of Soviet Law' (1991) 50 *The Russian Review* 1, 68–69.

——, 'Vyshinski, Krylenko, and the Shaping of the Soviet Legal Order' (1987) 46 *Slavic Review* 3/4, 416.

G. Hálmai, 'A Coup Against Constitutional Democracy. The Case of Hungary' in: M. A. Graber, S. Levinson and M. Tushnet (eds), *Constitutional Democracy in Crisis?* Oxford University Press, Oxford 2018.

——, 'Is there Such Thing as 'Populist Constitutionalism'? The Case of Hungary' (2018) 11 *Fudan Journal of the Humanities and Social Sciences*, 7–8.

P. Häberle, 'Die offene Gesellschaft der Verfassungsinterpreten: Ein Beitrag zur pluralistischen und "prozessualen" Verfassungsinterpretation' (1975) 30 *JuristenZeitung* 10.

B. Iancu, 'Separation of Powers and the Rule of Law in Romania: the Crisis in Concepts and Contexts' in A. Von Bogdandy and P. Sonnevend (eds), *Constitutional Crisis in the European Constitutional Area. Theory, Law and Politics in Hungary and Romania*, Hart Publishing, Oxford 2015.

R. Inglehart and P. Norris, *Trump, Brexit and the Rise of Populism: Economic Have Nots and Cultural Backlash*, Harvard Kennedy School, John F. Kennedy School of Government, 2016.

International Institute for Democracy and Electoral Assistance, *Optional Referendum in the World*, 17.08.2015, <http://www.idea.int/news-media/media/optional-referendum-world>.

K. Jacobs, A. Akkerman and A. Zaslove, 'The voice of populist people? Referendum preferences, practices and populist attitudes' (2018) 53 *Acta Politica* 4, 517–41.

G. Jacobsohn, 'Anchoring and sailing: contrasting imperatives of constitutional revolution' in G. Jacobsohn and M. Schor, *Comparative Constitutional Theory*, Edward Elgar, Cheltenham, Northampton, MA 2018.

——, *Constitutional identity*, Harvard University Press, Cambridge MA 2010.

S. Jankovic, 'Polish Democracy Under Threat? An Issue of Mere Politics or a Real Danger?' (2016) 9 *Baltic Journal of Law & Politics* 49–68.

R.S. Jansen, 'Populist Mobilization: A New Theoretical Approach to Populism' (2011) 29 *Sociological Theory* 2, 75–96.

P. Johnson, *Homosexuality and the European Court of Human Rights*, Routledge, New York 2013.

K. János, *Constitutional democracy [Alkotmányos demokrácia]*, Indok, 2000.

——, *Do we have human rights? [Vannak-e emberi jogaink?]*, Dialogues Européens, Paris 1988.

S. Jürgensen and F. Orlowski, 'Critique and Crisis: The German Struggle with Pandemic Control Measures and the State of Emergency, <https://verfassungsblog.de/critique-and-crisis-the-german-struggle-with-pandemic-control-measures-and-the-state-of-emergency/>.

E. Kamenka and A. Erh-Soon Tay, 'Social Traditions, Legal Traditions' in E. Kamenka (ed.), *Law and Social Control*, St. Martin's Press, New York 1980.

I. Kant, 'Toward Perpetual Peace: A Philosophical Sketch' in I. Kant (ed.), *Toward Perpetual Peace and Other Writings on Politics, Peace, and History*, tr. D.L. Colclasure, Yale University Press, New Haven and London 2006.

S. Karstedt, I. Loader and H. Strang, *Emotions, Crime and Justice* (Onati International Series in Law and Society), Bloomsbury Publishing, London 2011.

A. Kavanagh, 'The Constitutional Separation of Powers' in D. Dyzenhaus and M. Thorburn (eds), *Philosophical Foundations of Constitutional Law*, Oxford University Press, Oxford and New York, 2016.

V. Kazai, 'The Illiberal Challenge to the Rule of Law Principle: The Neglected Procedural Aspect (With Special Focus on Hungary)' 2019 ESIL Annual Research Forum, Göttingen (4–5 April 2019), available at <https://ssrn.com/abstract=3513204>.

M. Kazin, *The populist persuasion: An American history*, Cornell University Press, Ithaca 1998.

R.D. Kelemen, 'Europe's Other Democratic Deficit: National Authoritarianism in Europe's Democratic Union' (2017) 52 *Government and Opposition* 2, 211–38.

K. Kelland, 'U.N. warns of global mental health crisis due to COVID-19 pandemic' <https://uk.reuters.com/article/us-health-coronavirus-mentalhealth/u-n-warns-of-global-mental-health-crisis-due-to-covid-19-pandemic-idUKKBN22Q0AO?fbclid=IwAR0OgvkLxWMzEqsN-cm0KM-N33zxfckE5gZe2RddR0oScKDQHe5kX1P-ri4>.

D. Kelly, 'Populism and the History of Popular Sovereignty' in C. Rovira Kaltwasser, P. Taggart, P. Ochoa Espejo and P. Ostiguy (eds), *The Oxford Handbook of Populism*, Oxford University Press, Oxford 2017.

H. Kelsen, 'Das Problem der Parlamentarismus' in H. R. Klecatsky, R. Marcic and H. Schambeck (eds), *Die Wiener rechtstheoretische Schule*, Franz Steiner Verlag, Wien 2010.

——, *General Theory of Law and the State*, Harvard University Press, Cambridge MA 1945.

——, *The Essence and Value of Democracy*, tr. B. Graf, Rowman and Littlefield Publishers, Lanham and New York 2013.

D. Kennedy, *A World of Struggle: How Power, Law, and Expertise Shape Global Political Economy*, Princeton University Press, New Haven 2016.

——, *Legal Education and the Reproduction of Hierarchy: A Polemic Against the System*, New York University Press, New York 2007.

C. Klein, *Théorie et pratique du pouvoir constituant*, Presses Universitaires de France, Paris 1996.

D.B. Knight, 'Territory and People or People and Territory? Thoughts on Postcolonial Self-Determination' (1985) *International Political Science Review* 248–72.

T.T. Koncewicz, 'The Capture of the Polish Constitutional Tribunal and Beyond: Of institution(s), Fidelities and the Rule of Law in Flux', (2018) 43 *Review of Central and East European Law* 116ff.

A. Kondyakov, 'Resisting the silence: The use of tolerance and equality arguments by gay and lesbian activist groups in Russia', (2013) *Canadian Journal of Law and Society* 403.

M.S. Konstantin, *USSR: The Corrupt Society: The Secret World of Soviet Capitalism*, Simon & Schuster, New York 1982.

D. Kosar and J. Petrov, 'The Architecture of the Strasbourg System of Human Rights: The Crucial Role of the Domestic Level and the Constitutional Courts in Particular' (2017) *ZaöRV* 77.

D. Kosař, J. Baroš and P. Dufek, 'The Twin Challenges to Separation of Powers in Central Europe: Technocratic Governance and Populism' (2019) 15 *European Constitutional Law Review* 3.

M. Koskenniemi, 'Between Impunity and Show Trial' (2002) 6 *Max Planck Yearbook of United Nations Law* 1, 1–32.

——, 'International law and the far right: reflections on law and cynicism' (2019) Fourth T.M.C. Asser Lecture.

J. Kossoff, 'Medical detection dogs able to sniff 750 people an hour could help identify coronavirus cases, researchers say', <https://www.businessinsider.com/sniffer-dogs-answer-to-the-covid-19-testing-crisis-mirror-2020-4>.

M. Kotwas and J. Kubik, 'Symbolic Thickening of Public Culture and the Rise of Right-Wing Populism in Poland' (2019) 33 *East European Politics and Societies and Cultures* 435–71.

L. Kounine, 'Emotions, mind, and body on trial: a cross-cultural perspective' (2017) 51 *Journal of Social History* 2, 219–230.

K. Kovács, 'Hungary's Orbánistan: A Complete Arsenal of Emergency Powers', <https://verfassungsblog.de/hungarys-orbanistan-a-complete-arsenal-of-emergency-powers/>.

E. Kowalewska, 'Competing visions of Constitutionalism in Post-Socialist Poland' ('New constitutionalism? New forms of democracy and rule of law beyond liberalism' conference, International Institute for the Sociology of Law, Oñati, Spain, July 2018).

L. Kramer, 'Popular Constitutionalism' (2004) 92 *California Law Review* 4.

I. Krastev and S. Holmes, 'Explaining Eastern Europe: Imitation and Its Discontents' (2018) 29 *Journal of Democracy* 3, 120.

P. Krekó and Z. Enyedi, 'Explaining Eastern Europe: Orbán's Laboratory of Illiberalism' (2018) 29 *Journal of Democracy* 3.

H. Kriesi, 'Populism. Concepts and conditions for its rise in Europe' (2015) *Comunicazione politica* 2, 175–93.

N. Krisch, '*Pouvoir constituant* and *pouvoir irritant* in the postnational order' (2016) 14 *I•CON*, 657.

E. Kriza, 'From utopia to dystopia? Bukharin and the Soviet Constitution of 1936' in K-M. Simonsen and J. S. Kjærgård (eds), *Discursive Framings of Human Rights: Negotiating agency and victimhood*, Routledge, New York 2017.

I. Kukorelli (ed.), *Constitutional theory I. Basic concepts, constitutional institutions [Alkotmánytan I. Alapfogalmak, alkotmányos intézmények]*, Osiris, Budapest 2007.

M. Kumm, J. Havercroft, J. Dunoff and A. Wiener, 'Editorial. The end of "the West" and the future of global constitutionalism' (2017) 6 *Global Constitutionalism* 1.

A. Kustra-Rogaska and O. Hamulak, 'Keeping distance: chapters from randomized (non)application of the European Court of Human Rights before the Polish Constitutional Tribunal' (2019) 9 *Baltic Journal of European Studies* 4, 90.

A. Kúria, 'Az Alaptörvény követelményeinek érvényesülése a bírósági ítélkezésben' Joggyakorlat-elemző Csoportja2016.El.II.JGY.K.1. <https://kuria-birosag.hu/sites/default/files/joggyak/alaptorveny_osszefoglalo_velemeny.pdf>.

La Costituzione della Repubblica nei lavori preparatori della Assemblea costituente, (I), Camera dei Deputati – Segretariato Generale, Roma 1970.

N. Lacey, 'Populism and the Rule of Law' (2019) *Annual Review of Law and Social Science* 15, 79–96.

K. Lachmayer, 'Austria: Rule of Law Lacking in Times of Crisis' <https://verfassungsblog.de/rule-of-law-lacking-in-times-of-crisis/>.

E. Laclau, *La raison populiste*, Seuil, Paris 2008.

——, *On Populist Reason*, Verso, London and New York 2005.

K. Łakomiec, 'Academic freedom(s) in the drift towards authoritarianism (4/4) – Poland', 15.11.2019, <https://ds.hypotheses.org/6391>.

J. Lambaerts, 'The Plague was Already Present (Critique in Times of Coronavirus)', <https://criticallegalthinking.com/2020/04/29/the-plague-was-already-present-critique-in-times-of-coronavirus/>.

D. Landau, 'Abusive Constitutionalism' (2013) 47 *UC Davis Law Review* 189–260.

——, 'Populist Constitutions' (2018) *The University of Chicago Law Review* 85.

D. Landau and H. Ferner, *Comparative Constitutional Making*, Edward Elgar, Cheltenham, Northampton, MA 2019.

A.F. Lang jr., M. Kumm, A. Wiener, J. Tully and M. Poiares Maduro, 'Interdisciplinarity: Challenges and opportunities' (2013) 2 *Global Constitutionalism* 1.

K.C. Langdon and V. Tismaneanu, *Putin's Totalitarian Democracy. Ideology, Myth, and Violence in the Twenty-First Century*, Palgrave Macmilllan, New York 2019.

V. Laopodis, 'DEMOS: Democratic evaluation of multiple options in society', in J. Berleur and D. Whitehouse (eds), *An Ethical Global Information Society. IFIP – The International Federation for Information Processing*, Springer, Boston 1997.

W. Laquer, *Putinism. Russia and Its Future With the West*, St Martin's Press, New York 2015.

M. Laruelle, 'In Search of Putin's Philosopher', *Intersection Project* 03.03.2017, <http://intersectionproject.eu/article/politics/search-putins-philosopher>.

M. Laruffa, 'The absolutist dream of democracies in crisis. The political culture inspiring soft and hard populism' (2019) *Politica e Società* 2, 269–82.

C. Lash, *The Revolt of the élites and the Betrayal of Democracy*, W.W. Norton, New York 1995.

T. Laue, 'The Fate of Capitalism in Russia: The Narodnik Version' (1954) 13 *The American Slavic and East European Review* 1, 17.

S. Laulhé Shaelou and A. Manoli, 'A Tale of Two: The COVID-19 Pandemic and the Rule of Law in Cyprus', <https://verfassungsblog.de/a-tale-of-two-the-covid-19-pandemic-and-the-rule-of-law-in-cyprus/>.

J. Leaman, 'Reversing the neoliberal deformation of Europe' in J.E. Fossum and A.J. Menéndez (eds), *The European Union in crises or the European Union as crises?*, Arena Centre for European Studies, Oslo 2014.

L. Lessig, *They Don't Represent US*, Dey Street Books, New York 2019.

S. Levitsky and D. Ziblatt, *How Democracies Die*, Crown, New York 2018.

H. Lindahl, 'Constituent Power and Reflexive Identity: Towards an Ontology of Collective Selfhood' in M. Loughlin and N. Walker (eds), *The Paradox of Constitutionalism: Constituent Power and Constitutional Form*, Oxford University Press, Oxford 2008.

J. Linz and A. Stepan, *Problems of Democratic Transition and Consolidation*, Johns Hopkins Press, Baltimore and London 1996.

T. Lochocki, *The Rise of Populism in Western Europe*, Springer, Cham 2018.

M. Loughlin, 'The Concept of Constituent Power' (2014) 13 *European Journal of Political Theory* 2, 218.

——, 'The constitutional imagination', (2015) 78 *The Modern Law Review* 1.

M. Luciani, 'Il referendum abrogativo. Commento dell'art. 75' in G. Branca and A. Pizzorusso (eds), *Commentario della Costituzione*, N. Zanichelli-Soc. Ed. del Foro italiano, Bologna-Roma 2005.

J.-F. Lyotard, *The Postmodern Condition*, Manchester University Press, Manchester 1984.

T. Macdonald, 'Sovereignty, Democracy, and Global Political Legitimacy' in C. Brown and R. Eckersley (eds), *The Oxford Handbook of International Political Theory*, Oxford University Press, Oxford 2018.

M. Madsen, P. Cebulak and M. Wiebusch, 'Backlash against international courts: explaining the forms and patterns of resistance to international courts' (2018) 14 *International Journal of Law in Context* 2.

P. Magnette, 'Towards Accountable Independence? Parliamentary Controls of the European Central Bank and the Rise of a New Democratic Model' (2000) 6 *European Law Journal* 4, 326–40.

B. Magyar, *Post-Communist Mafia State – The Case of Hungary*, CEU Press and Noran Libro, Budapest 2016.

C.S. Maier, *Once Within Borders. Territories of Power, Wealth, and Belonging since 1500*, The President and Fellows of Harvard College, Harvard University Press, Cambridge, Massachusetts 2016.

P. Mair, 'Political Opposition and the European Union' (2007) 42 *Government and Opposition* 1, 1–17.

M. Manetti, 'Costituzione, partecipazione democratica, populismo' (2018) 3 *Rivista AIC*.

M. Manetti and B. Arditi, *Politics on the Edges of Liberalism*, Edinburgh University Press Ltd., Edinburgh 2007.

B. Manin, *The Principles of Representative Government*, Cambridge University Press, Cambridge and New York 1997.

A. Manzella, 'Il Parlamento' in G. Amato and A. Barbera (eds), *Manuale di diritto pubblico. II. L'organizzazione costituzionale*, 5th ed., Il Mulino, Bologna 1984.

A. Manzella et al., 'Artt. 64-69. Le Camere' in G. Branca and A. Pizzorusso (eds), *Commentario della Costituzione*, N. Zanichelli-Soc. Ed. del Foro italiano, Bologna-Roma 1986.

R. Markowski, 'Creating Authoritarian Clientelism: Poland After 2015' (2019) 11 *Hague Journal on the Rule of Law* 130–31.

T.A. Maroney, 'A Field Evolves: Introduction to the Special Section on Law and Emotion' (2015) 8 *Emotion Review* 1, 4.

——, 'Law and emotion: A proposed taxonomy of an emerging field' (2006) 30 *Law and Human Behavior* 2, 119.

J. S. Martinez, 'Horizontal Structuring' in M. Rosenfeld and A. Sajó (eds), *The Oxford Handbook of Comparative Constitutional Law*, Oxford University Press, Oxford and New York 2012.

G. Martinico, 'Fra mimetismo e parassitismo. Brevi considerazioni a proposito del complesso rapporto tra populismo e costituzionalismo' (2019) *Questione giustizia* 1, 74.

——, *Il diritto costituzionale come speranza. Secessione, democrazia e populismo alla luce delle Reference Re Secession of Quebec*, Giappichelli, Torino 2019.

E. Mavrozacharakis, 'Populism and Democracy: An Ambiguous Relationship' (2018) 7 *European Quarterly of Political Attitudes and Mentalities* 4, 19–35.

D. McDonnell, 'Eviction Canceled: The 2006 Local Elections', in J.L. Briquet and A. Mastropaolo (eds), *Italian Politics: the Centre-left Poisoned Victory*, Berghahn, New York 2007.

J. Mccormick, 'Pocock, Machiavelli and Political Contingency in Foreign Affairs: Republican Existentialism Outside (and Within) the City' (2017) 43 *History of European Ideas* 171, 173.

R. Mehring, 'Carl Schmitt und die Pandemie. Teil I', <https://verfassungsblog.de/carl-schmitt-und-die-pandemie-teil-i/?fbclid=IwAR0oLewmdX13rFYCdOSDS7T1wSy7Usc6yF_unAW7m5WxMlDDyrbSwu8_32g>.

I. Melnykovska and R. Schweickert, 'Bottom-up or top-down: what drives the convergence of Ukraine's institutions towards European standards?' (2008) 8 *Southern European and Black Sea Studies* 4, 445–68.

Y. Mény, *Populismo e democrazia*, Il Mulino, Bologna 2004.

Y. Mény and Y. Surel, 'The Constitutive Ambiguity of Populism' in Y. Mény and Y. Surel (eds), *Democracies and the populist challenge*, Palgrave, London 2002.

A. Mercescu, 'The COVID-19 Crisis in Romania, or on How One Cannot Escape (Bad, Legal) Culture', <http://exceptions.eu/2020/05/11/the-covid-19-crisis-in-romania-or-on-how-one-cannot-escape-bad-legal-culture/?fbclid=IwAR3hTyciWC-Kiei2r9KFjHVN0KjGzx6aepFuZ9VYlnDz89Jr94dWUydAh_Y>.

L. Mezzetti, *Le democrazie incerte. Transizioni costituzionali e consolidamento della democrazia in Europa orientale, Africa, America latina, Asia*, Giappichelli, Torino 2000.

I. Michel, 'Le paradigme de la transition: chronique d'une fine annonceé. Le cas de l'Europe centrale et orientale' (2006) *Revue d'études politiques et constitutionnelles Est-Européennes* Numéro spéciale.

B. Milanovic, *Global Inequality: A New Approach for the Age of Globalization*, Harvard University Press, Cambridge 2016.

K.P. Miller, 'Constraining Populism: The Real Challenge of Initiative Reform' (2001) *Santa Clara Law Review* 41, 1037–84.

M.K. Miller and B.H. Bornstein, *Stress, Trauma, and Wellbeing in the Legal System*, Oxford University Press, Oxford 2013.

S. Moeckli, 'Direct democracy and political participation from a cross-national perspective' in T. Zittel and D. Fuchs (eds), *Participatory Democracy and Political Participation: Can Participatory Engineering Bring Citizens Back In?* Routledge, Abingdon 2007.

B. Moffitt and S. Tormey, 'Rethinking Populism: Politics, Mediatisation and Political Style' (2014) *Political Studies* 62, 381–97.

K. Möller, 'Popular Sovereignty, Populism and Deliberative Democracy' (2018) 42 *Philosophical Inquiry* 17.

C. Möllers, 'Pouvoir Constituant – Constitution – Constitutionalisation' in J. Bast and A. von Bogdandy (eds), *Principles of European Constitutional Law*, Hart Publishing, Oxford 2010.

——, *The Three Branches: A Comparative Model of Separation of Powers*, Oxford University Press, Oxford and New York 2013.

M. Molyneux and T. Osborne, 'Populism: a deflationary view' (2014) 46 *Economy and Society* 1.

L. Morel, 'Referendum' in M. Rosenfeld and A. Sajó (eds), *The Oxford Handbook of Comparative Constitutional Law*, Oxford University Press, Oxford and New York 2012.

C. Mortati, *Le forme di governo*, Cedam, Padova 1973.

——, 'Sulla posizione del partito nello Stato' in C. Mortati (ed.), *Problemi di politica costituzionale*, Vol. 4, Giuffré, Milano 1972.

C. Mortati et al., 'Principi fondamentali, artt. 1-12', in G. Branca and A. Pizzorusso (eds), *Commentario della Costituzione*, N. Zanichelli-Soc. Ed. del Foro italiano, Bologna-Roma 1975.

L. Mosca and F. Tronconi, 'Beyond left and right: the eclectic populism of the Five Star Movement' (2019) 42 *West European Politics* 6, 1258–83.

Ch. Mouffe, *The Democratic Paradox*, Verso, London and New York 2000.

Y. Mounk, *The People Versus Democracy: Why Our Freedom Is in Danger and How to Save It*, Harvard University Press, Cambridge Massachusetts 2018.

C. Mudde, *An Ideational approach*, in C. Rovira Kaltwasser, P.A. Taggart, P. Ochoa Espejo and P. Ostiguy (eds), *The Oxford Handbook of Populism*, Oxford University Press, Oxford 2017.

——, *Populist radical right parties in Europe*, Cambridge University Press, Cambridge 2007.

——, 'The paradox of the anti-party party: Insights from the extreme right, (1996) 2 *Party Politics* 2.

——, 'The Populist Zeitgeist' (2004) 39 *Government and Opposition* 4, 541–63.

C. Mudde and C. Rovira Kaltwasser, 'Exclusionary vs. Inclusionary Populism: Comparing Contemporary Europe and Latin America' (2013) 48 *Government and Opposition* 2, 147–74.

——, *Populism: A Very Short Introduction*, Oxford University Press, Oxford 2017.
——, 'Populism' in M. Freeden and M. Stears (eds), *The Oxford Handbook of Political Ideologies*, Oxford University Press, Oxford 2013.
A. Mueller, 'The meaning of populism' (2019) 45 *Philosophy and Social Criticism* 9–10, 1025–57.
H. Muir-Watt, 'Conflicts of laws unbounded: the case for a legal-pluralist revival' (2016) 7 *Transnational Legal Theory* 3, 313–53.
——, 'Private International Law Beyond the Schism' (2011) 2 *Transnational Legal Theory* 3, 347–428.
J. Muis and T. Immerzeel, 'Causes and consequences of the rise of populist radical right parties and movements in Europe' (2017) 65 *Current Sociology Review* 6, 914.
Y.W. Muller, 'The People must be extracted from within the people. Reflections on populism', *Constellations, Vol. 21, n. 4*, 2014.
J.-W. Müller, *Che cos'è il populismo?* Università Bocconi Ed., Milano 2017.
——, *Democracia cristiana o democracia illiberal?* in *El Pais* 09.02.2020.
——, 'Populism and Constitutionalism' in C.R. Kaltwasser et al. (eds), *The Oxford Handbook of Populism*, Oxford University Press, Oxford 2018.
——, 'Should the EU Protect Democracy and the Rule of Law inside Member States? (2015) 21 No. 2 *European Law Journal* 141–60.
——, '"The People Must be Extracted from Within the People": Reflections on Populism' (2014) 21 *Constellations* 4.
——, *What Is Populism?*, University of Pennsylvania Press, Philadelphia 2016.
M. Naim, *How to be a populist. Power and populism in a new world*, in Ipsos MORI Social Research Institute's Understanding Society – *Beyond Populism*, 2017, <https://www.ipsos.com/sites/default/files/2017-07/Understanding_society-beyond_populism-2017.pdf>.
F. Neumann, 'Rule of law and sovereignty' [Jogállamiság és szuverenitás], in T. Péter (ed.), *An anthology from the literature of the Rule of Law and the Rechtsstaat [Joguralom és jogállam. Antológia a Rule of Law és a Rechtsstaat irodalmának köréből]*, ELTE, 1995.
——, *The Rule of Law. Political Theory and the Legal System in Modern Society*, Berg Publishers, Oxford 1986.
J.L. Newell, 'Italy: The Extreme Right Comes in from the Cold' (2000) 53 *Parliamentary Affairs*, 469–85.
S. Newton, *Law and the Making of the Soviet World: The Red Demiurge*, Routledge, New York 2015.
C. Noble and G. Ottmann, 'National Populism and Social Work' (2018) 3 *Journal of Human Rights and Social Work* 3, 112–20.
N. Nugent, *The Government and Politics of the European Union*, Palgrave Macmillan, London 2010.
G. O'Donnell, L. Whitehead and P.C. Schmitter (eds), *Transitions from Authoritarian Rule: Tentative Conclusions about Uncertain Democracies*, Johns Hopkins University Press, Baltimore and London 1986.

Z. Oklopcic, *Beyond the people: Social imaginary and constituent imagination*, Oxford University Press, Oxford 2018.

——, 'Imagined ideologies: Populist figures, liberalist projections, and the horizons of constitutionalism' (2019) 20 *German Law Journal* 201–06.

M. Olivetti, 'Partiti e regime parlamentare in Italia nella riflessione di Leopoldo Elia' in G. D'Andrea, F. Marini, S. Mattarella, M. Olivetti, F. Pizzetti, P. Ridola and A. Silvestrini (eds), *Leopoldo Elia. Costituzionalista e uomo politico rigoroso e innovatore*, Diabasis, Reggio Emilia 2009.

V. Onida, 'Le Costituzioni. I principi fondamentali della Costituzione italiana' in G. Amato and A. Barbera (eds), *Manuale di diritto pubblico. I. Diritto pubblico generale*, 5th ed., Il Mulino, Bologna 1984.

D. Orso, N. Federici, R. Copetti, L. Vetrugno and T. Bove, 'Infodemic and the spread of fake news in the COVID-19-era' (2020) *European journal of emergency medicine: official journal of the European Society for Emergency Medicine*, 10.1097/MEJ.0000000000000713.

M. Orłowski, 'PiS kontratakuje ws. sądów. Rządowe billboardy zawisną w całej Polsce', *Gazeta Wyborcza*, 7.09.2017, available at: <http://wyborcza.pl/7,75398,22335331,pis-kontratakuje-ws-sadow-rzadowe-billboardy-zawisna-w-calej.html>.

A. Pace, 'Diritti di libertà e diritti sociali nel pensiero di Calamandrei' in P. Barile (ed.), *Piero Calamandrei*, Giuffré, Milano 1990.

P. Paczolay, *Constitutional adjudication – constitutional interpretation [Alkotmánybíráskodás – alkotmányértelmezés]*, Rejtjel, 2003.

——, 'Constitutional adjudication on the border of politics and law' [Alkotmánybíráskodás a politika és jog határán] in P. Paczolay (ed.), *Constitutional adjudication – constitutional interpretation [Alkotmánybíráskodás – alkotmányértelmezés]*, Rejtjel, 2003.

F. Pallante, *Contro la democrazia diretta*, Einaudi, Torino 2020.

G. Pallaver, M. Gehler, M. Cau (eds), *Populism, Populists, and the Crisis of Political Parties: A Comparison of Italy, Austria, and Germany 1990–2015*, Bologna Il Mulino, Duncker/Humboldt 2018.

E. Palonen, 'Transition to Crisis in Hungary: Whistle-Blowing on the Naked Emperor' (2012) 40 *Policy & Politics* 5.

S. Panunzio (ed.), *I costituzionalisti e le riforme: una discussione sul progetto della Commissione bicamerale per le riforme costituzionali*, Giuffrè, Milano 1998.

T.S. Pappas, 'Populist Democracies: Post-Authoritarian Greece and Post-Communist Hungary' (2014) 49 *Government and Opposition* 1, 1–23, 2.

R. Parker, *Here, the People Rule, A Constitutional Populist Manifesto*, Harvard University Press, Cambridge 1998.

R.D. Parker, '"Here, the people rule": A constitutional populist manifesto' (1993) 27 *Valparaiso University Law Review* 3.

G. Pasquino, *1945–1996: profilo della politica in Italia*, Laterza, Roma 1996.

——, 'Der unerwartete Machtwechsel. Die italienischen Wahlen vom März 1994 und ihre Folgen' (1994) 35 *Politische Vierteljahresschrift* 3, 383–401.

——, 'La transizione politica italiana. Da Tangentopoli ad oggi' (2015) 20 *Journal of Modern Italian Studies* 1, 155–57.

——, *Minima politica. Sei Lezioni di Democrazia,* Utet, Torino 2020.

G. Pasquino and C.M. O'Neill, 'A Postmortem of The Bicamerale' (1998) 14 *Italian Politics* 101–20.

P. Pasquino, 'Dalla democrazia della paura alla democrazia dell'alternanza' (2015) 3 *Quaderni costituzionali* 731–34.

——, 'Le Gouvernement Berlusconi: une année après' (2002) 103 *Pouvoirs* 4, 13–28.

C.J. Patrick, 'A new synthesis for law and emotions: insights from the behavioral sciences' (2015) 47 *Arizona State Law Journal* 47, 1239.

T. Pauwels, *Populism in Western Europe: Comparing Belgium, Germany and the Netherlands*, Routledge, London and New York 2014.

L. Pech and D. Kochenov, *Strengthening the Rule of Law Within the European Union: Diagnoses, Recommendations, and What to Avoid*, Policy Brief, European Commission, June 2019.

L. Pech and K.L. Scheppele, 'Illiberalism Within: Rule of Law Backsliding in the EU' (2017) 19 *Cambridge Yearbook of European Legal Studies* 4.

——, 'Poland and the European Commission, Part I: A Dialogue of the Deaf?', *Verfassungsblog*, 03.01.2017.

A. Pedler, 'Going to the People. The Russian Narodniki in 1874-5', (1927) 6 *The Slavonic Review* 16,137.

E. Peluso, N. Meyer and T. Bustamante, 'Authoritarianism Without Emergency Powers: Brazil Under COVID-19', <https://verfassungsblog.de/authoritarianism-without-emergency-powers-brazil-under-covid-19/>.

E. Peruzzotti, 'Populism as Democratization's Nemesis: The Politics of Regime Hybridization' (2017) 2 *Chinese Political Science Review* 320.

J. Petrétei, *Hungarian constitutional law I. [Magyar alkotmányjog I.],* Dialog Campus, 2002.

J. Petrétei and T. Péter: *Bases of Hungary's constitutional law [Magyarország alkotmányjogának alapjai]*, Kodifikátor Foundation, Pécs 2013.

B. Pezzini, 'Attualità della Resistenza: la matrice antifascista della Costituzione repubblicana' in B. Pezzini and S. Rossi (eds), *I giuristi e la Resistenza. Una biografia intellettuale del Paese*, Franco Angeli, Milano 2016.

X. Philippe, 'La légitimation constitutionnelle des démocratures' (2019) *Pouvoirs* 2, 35–37.

T. Piketty, *Capital and Ideology*, Harvard University Press, Cambridge 2020.

——, *Capital in the Twenty-First Century*, Harvard University Press, Cambridge 2017.

——, 'Social-fédéralisme contre national-libéralisme', in *Le Monde*, 10.02.2020.

R.H. Pildes, 'The Inherent Authoritarianism in Democratic Regimes' in A. Sajo (ed.), *Out of and Into Authoritarian Law*, Kluwer Law International, New York 2003.

A. Pin, 'The transnational drivers of populist backlash in Europe: The role of courts' (2019) 20 *German Law Journal* 225–44.

C. Pinelli, 'Illiberal regimes in the perspective of comparative constitutionalism' (2017) *Rivista di Diritti Comparati* 1, 7–9.

——, 'L'Europa democratica nella strettoia fra populismo e tecnocrazia', (2013) *Meridiana* 77, 101.

——, 'The Populist Challenge to Constitutional Democracy' (2011) 7 *European Constitutional Law Review* 5–16.

M.S. Piretti, *Le elezioni politiche in Italia dal 1848 ad oggi*, Laterza, Roma-Bari 1996.

A. Pirro, 'The polyvalent populism of the 5 Star Movement' (2018) 26 *Journal of Contemporary European Studies* 4, 443–58.

F. Pizzolato, *I sentieri costituzionali della democrazia*, Carocci editore, Roma 2019.

A. Pizzorusso et al., 'Disposizioni transitorie e finali, 1-18. Leggi costituzionali e di revisione costituzionale (1948-1993)', in G. Branca and A. Pizzorusso (eds), *Commentario della Costituzione*, N. Zanichelli-Soc. Ed. del Foro italiano, Bologna-Roma 1995.

S. Platon, 'From One State of Emergency to Another – Emergency Powers in France' <https://verfassungsblog.de/from-one-state-of-emergency-to-another-emergency-powers-in-france/>.

M.F. Plattner, 'Illiberal democracy and the struggle on the right' (2019) 30 *Journal of Democracy* 1.

K. Polanyi, *Origins of our time. The great transformation*, Farrar & Rinehart, New York 1944, London 1954.

G. Pollock, T. Brock and M. Ellison, 'Populism, ideology and contradiction: mapping young people's political views' (2015) 63 *The Sociological Review* 2, 141–66.

P. Pombeni, 'I partiti. La 'costituzione' che c'è e quella che verrà' in D. Verdini (ed.), *Popolo e leader. Il tempo dei partiti nuovi*, Fondazione Magna Carta, Roma 2008.

E. Posner, 'Liberal Internationalism and the Populist Backlash' (2017) 49 *Arizona State Law Journal* 795–819.

——, *The perils of global legalism*, The University of Chicago Press, Chicago 2009.

Z. Pozsár-Szentmiklósy, 'The hyper-judicialisation of politics of Moldova: Opportunities for constitutional reform', *constitutionnet.org*, <http://constitutionnet.org/news/hyper-judicialisation-politics-moldova-opportunities-constitutional-reform>.

Z. Pozsár-Szentmiklósy and Y. Roznai, 'The Timing of Judicial Review of Constitutional Amendments – Towards a "Time Sensivity Test" Following the Moldovan Constitutional Court's Decision on the Modality of Electing the President' in S. Ranchordás and Y. Roznai (eds), *Time, Law and Change. An Interdisciplinary Study*, Hart, Oxford, London, New York 2019.

A. Przeworski, *Democracy and the Limits of Self-Government*, Cambridge University Press, New York 2010.

A. Puddington, 'Breaking down democracy: global strategies, and methods of modern authoritarians', June 2017, <https://freedomhouse.org/sites/default/files/June2017_FH_Report_Breaking_Down_Democracy.pdf>.

C.M. Pulido, B. Villarejo-Carballido, G. Redondo-Sama and A. Gómez, 'COVID-19 infodemic: More retweets for science-based information on coronavirus than for false information', (2020) 35 *International Sociology* 4, 377–92.

V. Puscas, 'Dezvoltarea constitutionala a Republicii Moldova. 20 de ani de la adoptarea Constiutiei' (2014) *Revista Institutului National al Justitiei* 2.

E. Putterman, 'Rousseau on the people as legislative gatekeepers, not framers' (2005) 99 *American Political Science Review* 145.

Sz. Péter and T. Péter: *The theory of the rule of law [A jogállamiság jogelmélete]*, Napvilág, Budapest 2004.

J. Přibáň and W. Sadurski, 'The Role of Political Rights in the Democratization of Central and Eastern Europe' in W. Sadurski (ed.), *Political Rights under Stress in 21st Century Europe*, Oxford University Press, Oxford 2006.

G. Radbruch, 'Gesetzliches Unrecht und übergesetzliches Recht', *Süddeutsche Juristen-Zeitung*, Jahrg. 1, Nr. 5 (August 1946).

K. Ragnarsson, 'The counter-majoritarian difficulty in a neoliberal world: Socio-economic rights and deference in post-2008 austerity cases' (2019) 8 *Global Constitutionalism* 3.

B. Randazzo, 'Populismo e diritto. Dialogando con Enrico Scoditti' (2019) *Questione Giustizia* 1, 70.

R. Rawlings, P. Leyland and A. Young (eds), *Sovereignty and the Law. Domestic, European, and International Perspectives*, Oxford University Press, Oxford 2013.

J. Rawls, *A Theory of Justice*, The Belknap Press of Harvard University Press, Cambridge 1999.

L.K. Ray, 'Judicial personality: Rhetoric and emotion in Supreme Court opinions' (2002) 59 *Washington & Lee Law Review* 193.

C. Rega, *Ecological Rationality in Spatial Planning*. Springer Nature Publishing, New York 2020.

G.U. Rescigno, *Corso di diritto pubblico*, Zanichelli, Bologna 1994.

F. Rescigno, 'La gestione del coronavirus e l'impianto costituzionale' (2020) 3 *Osservatorio AIC*.

G. Rico, M. Guinjoan and E. Anduiza, 'The Emotional Underpinnings of Populism: How Anger and Fear Affect Populist Attitudes' (2017) 23 *Swiss Political Science Review* 4, 444–61.

D. Ritleng (ed.), *Independence and Legitimacy in the Institutional System of the European Union*, Oxford University Press, Oxford 2016.

K.M. Roberts, 'Populism and Political Representation', in C. Lancaster and N. Van de Walle (eds), *The Oxford Handbook of the Politics of Development*, Oxford University Press, Oxford 2018.

P. Robinson, 'On Resistance to Evil by Force: Ivan Il'in and the Necessity of War' (2003) 2 *Journal of Military Ethics* 2, 150.

D. Rodrik, 'Populism and the economics of globalization' (2018) *Journal of International Business Policy* 2.

M. Rooduijn, S.L. de Lange and W. van der Brug, 'A populist Zeitgeist? Programmatic contagion by populist parties in Western Europe' (2014) 20 *Party politics* 4, 563–74.

P. ROSANVALLON, *La légitimité démocratique. Impartialité, reflexivité, proximité*, Éditions du Seuil, Paris 2008.
——, *Penser le populisme*, in *La vie des idèes*. Collège de France, September 2011.
——, *The Society of Equals*, tr. A. GOLDHAMMER, Harvard University Press, Cambridge and London 2013.
M. ROSENFELD, 'Constitutional Identity' in M. ROSENFELD and A. SAJÓ (eds), *The Oxford Handbook of Comparative Constitutional Law*, Oxford University Press, Oxford 2012.
F. ROSS, 'Beyond left and right": the new partisan politics of welfare' (2000) 13 *Governance* 2 155–83.
J.J. ROUSSEAU, 'Considerations on the Government of Poland', in F. WATKINS (ed.), *Jean-Jacques Rousseau: Political Writings*, Thomas Yelsen, New York 1953.
——, *Du Contrat Social: Principes de Droit Politique*, ENAG, Paris 1998/1762, Book II.
——, *Lettre à d'Alembert* (1758).
——, 'Letters Written from the Mountain' in C. KELLY, and E. GRACE (eds), *Letter to Beaumont, Letters Written from the Mountain, and Related Writings*, Dartmouth College Press, Dartmouth 2001.
——, *Projet de Constitution pour la Corse*, Nautilus, Paris 2000.
C. ROVIRA KALTWASSER, 'The ambivalence of populism: threat and corrective for democracy' (2012) 19 *Democratization* 2, 184–208.
Y. ROZNAI, *Unconstitutional Constitutional Amendments. The Limits of Amendment Powers*, Oxford University Press, Oxford 2017.
——, *Unconstitional Constitutional Amendments. The Limits if Amendment Powers*, Oxford University Press, Oxford and New York 2017.
D. RUNCIMAN, *Così finisce la democrazia*, Bollati boringhieri, Torino 2019.
——, *How Democracy Ends*, Profile Books London 2018.
P. SADURA and S. SIERAKOWSKI, 'Political cynicism: The Case of Poland', <http://politicalcritique.org/cee/poland/2019/poles-political-cynicism-research-report/>.
W. SADURSKI, 'How Democracy Dies (in Poland): A Case Study of Anti-Constitutional Populist Backsliding' (2018) *Sydney Law School Research Paper* No. 18/01.
——, *Poland's Constitutional Breakdown*, Oxford University Press, Oxford 2019.
——, 'Polish Constitutional Tribunal Under PiS: From an Activist Court, to a Paralysed Tribunal, to a Governmental Enabler' (2019) 11 *Hague Journal on the Rule of Law* 63–84.
A. SAJÓ, 'Constitutional sentiments' (2006) 47 *Acta Juridica Hungarica* 1, 1–13.
——, 'Emotions in constitutional design' (2010) 8 *International Journal of Constitutional Law* 3, 354.
——, 'Emotions in constitutional institutions' (2016) 8 *Emotion Review* 1, 44.
——, 'The Constitution of Illiberal Democracy as a Theory About Society' (2018) *Polish sociological review* 4, 405–10.
——, 'The Rule of Law as Legal Despotism: Concerned Remarks on the Use of "*Rule of Law*" in Illiberal Democracies' (2019) 11 *Hague Journal on the Rule of Law* 376.

A. Sajó and R. Uitz, *The Constitution of Freedom: An Introduction to Legal Constitutionalism*, Oxford University Press, Oxford 2017.

W. Sandholtz and R. Taagepera, 'Corruption, Culture, and Communism' (2005) 15 *International Review of Sociology* 1, 109–31.

G. Sartori, *Democrazia: cosa è*, Rizzoli, Milano 1993.

——, *Democrazia e definizioni*, il Mulino, Bologna 1957.

——, *Democracy [Demokrácia]*, Osiris, 1999.

——, 'European Political Parties: The Case of Polarized Pluralism', in J. La Palombara and M. Weiner (eds), *Political Parties and Political Development*, Princeton University Press, Princeton 1966.

——, *Parties and Party System: A Framework Analysis*, ECPR Press, Colchester 2005.

C. Sartwell, 'The Left-Right Political Spectrum Is Bogus' in *The Atlantic*, 20.06.2014.

J. Schafer, 'Behind Trump's Strange "Invisible Enemy" Rhetoric', <https://www.politico.com/news/magazine/2020/04/09/trump-coronavirus-invisible-enemy-177894>.

M. Saward, *Democracy*, Polity Press, Cambridge 2003.

A. Schedler and R. Sarsfield, 'Democrats with adjectives: Linking direct and indirect measures of democratic support' in (2007) 46 *European Journal of Political Research* 639.

K.L. Scheppele, 'Autocratic legalism' (2018) 85 *The University of Chicago Law Review* 2.

——, 'The opportunism of populists and the defense of constitutional liberalism' (2019) 20 *German Law Journal* 3.

——, 'The Social Lives of Constitutions', in P. Blokker and C. Thornhill (eds), *Sociological Constitutionalism*, Cambridge University Press, Cambridge 2017.

——, 'Underreaction in a Time of Emergency: America as a Nearly Failed State', <https://verfassungsblog.de/underreaction-in-a-time-of-emergency-america-as-a-nearly-failed-state/>.

——, 'Understanding Hungary's Constitutional Revolution' in A. von Bogdandy and P. Sonervend (eds), *Constitutional Crisis in the European Constitutional Area. Theory, Law and Politics in Hungary and Romania*, Beck, Hart & Nomos, München 2014.

A. Schillaci, 'Dalla crisi economica alla crisi democratica: la sfida populista alla solidarietà e l'identità europea' (2020) 4 May 2020, *Federalismi.it* 15–39.

A. Schmidt, 'Challenges of the illiberal democracy in Hungary. Some aspects to the 2018 elections', (2018) 6 *Polski Przegląd Politologiczny* 2, 88.

C. Schmitt, *Constitutional Theory*, tr. J. Seitzer, Duke University Press, Durham 2008.

——, *Der Begriff des Politischen*, Duncker & Humblot, Berlin 2015.

——, *Dictatorship. From the origin of the modern concept of sovereignty to proletarian class struggle*, tr. M. Hoelzl and G. Ward, Polity Press, Cambridge and Molden, MA 2014.

——, *Political Theology: Four Chapters on the Concept of Sovereignty*, The University of Chicago Press, Chicago 2006.

——, *The Crisis of Parliamentary Democracy*, tr. E. Kennedy, MIT Press, Cambridge and London 2000.

P.C. SCHMITTER, 'Reflections on "Transitology" – Before and After' in D.M. BRINKS, M. LEIRAS and S. MAINWARING (eds), *Reflections on uneven democracies: the legacy of Guillermo O'Donnell*, Johns Hopkins University Press, Baltimore 2014.

F. SCHORKOPF, 'The European Union as An Association of Sovereign States: Karlsruhe's Ruling on the Treaty of Lisbon' (2009) 10 *German Law Journal* 8, 1219–40.

S.F. SCHRAM, *The Return of Ordinary Capitalism: Neoliberalism, Precarity, Occupy*, Oxford University Press, Oxford 2015.

M.A. SCHREURS, 'From the Bottom Up: Local and Subnational Climate Change Politics' (2008) 17 *The Journal of Environment & Development* 4.

J. SCHUMPETER, *Capitalism, Socialism and Democracy*, 2nd ed., Allen & Unwin, London and New York 1947.

C.A. SCHWARTZ, 'Corruption and Political Development in the U. S. S. R.' (1979) 11 *Comparative Politics* 4, 425–43.

S.H. SCHWARTZ and A. BARDI, 'Influences of adaptation to communist rule on value priorities in Eastern Europe' (1997) *Political Psychology* 2, 407–08.

J. SCIPIONI, 'White House advisor Dr. Fauci says handshaking needs to stop even when pandemic ends – other experts agree', <https://www.cnbc.com/2020/04/09/dr-anthony-fauci-handshaking-needs-to-stop-even-after-pandemic.html>.

J. SCOTT, 'Politics as the Imitation of the Divine in Rousseau's "Social Contract"' (1994) 26 *Polity* 473.

J.T. SCOTT, 'Rousseau's Anti–Agenda-Setting Agenda and Contemporary Democratic Theory' (2005) 99 *The American Political Science Review* 137.

A. SCRIBANO, M.E. KORSTANJE and F.A.T. LOPEZ, *Populism and Postcolonialism*, Routledge, London 2019.

B. SELEJAN-GUTAN, 'Informal Constitutional Changes in Romania' (2015) 1 *Romanian Journal of Comparative Law* 35–53.

M.N. SELLERS, 'Law, Reason, and Emotion' in M.N. SELLERS (ed.), *Law, Reason and Emotion*, Cambridge University Press, Cambridge 2017.

K. SENGUL, 'Populism, democracy, political style and post-truth: issues for communication research' (2019) 5 *Communication Research and Practice* 1, 88–101.

R. SENNET, *Building* and *Dwelling. Ethics for the City*, Ferrar, Strauss and Giroux, New York 2018.

R. SERVICE, *Kremlin Winter: Russia and the Second Coming of Putin*, Picador, New York 2019.

W.H. SEWELL, 'Historical Events as Transformations of Structures: Inventing Revolution at the Bastille' (1996) 25 *Theory and Society* 854–55.

J. SHKLAR, *Legalism*, Harvard University Press, Cambridge 1964.

——, *Men and Citizens: A Study of Rousseau's Social Theory*, Cambridge University Press, Cambridge 1985.

J.N. SHKLAR, *Legalism. Law, Morals and Political Trials*, Cambridge, Harvard University Press 1964.

E.J. SIEYÈS, 'What Is the Third Estate?', in E.J. SIEYÈS, *Political Writings. Including the Debate between Sieyès and Tom Paine in 1791*, tr. M. SONENSCHER, Hackett Publishing Company Inc., Indianapolis and Cambridge 2003.

G. Silvestri, 'La Commissione di inchiesta su Tangentopoli. Considerazioni ingenue di un costituzionalista' (2000) 1 *Quaderni costituzionali* 121–122.

Z. Simon, 'Orban's Hungary Is No Longer a Democracy, Freedom House Says', <https://www.bloomberg.com/news/articles/2020-05-06/orban-s-hungary-is-no-longer-a-democracy-freedom-house-says>.

B. Singer, 'Reconciling liberalism and communitarianism' in B. Singer (ed.), *Pragmatism, Rights and Democracy*, New York University Press, New York 1999.

G. Skąpska, 'Law and society in a natural laboratory: the case of Poland in the broader context of East-Central Europe' in M. Kaase, V. Sparschuh and A. Wenninger (eds), *Three social science disciplines in Central and Eastern Europe: handbook on economics, political science and sociology (1989–2001)*, Informationszentrum Sozialwissenschaften; GESIS Servicestelle Osteuropa; Collegium Budapest, Institute for Advanced Study, Berlin 2002.

A. Śledzińska-Simon, 'The Rise and Fall of Judicial Self-Government in Poland: On Judicial Reform Reversing Democratic Transition' (2018) 19 *German Law Journal*, 1839–69.

D.A. Smith, D.J. Solinger and S.C. Topik (eds), *States and Sovereignty in the Global Economy*, Routledge, London–New York 1999.

T. Snyder, *Bloodlands: Europe Between Hitler and Stalin*, Basic Books, New York 2012.

——, *The Road to Unfreedom. Russia-Europe-America*, Alfred A. Knopf, New York 2017.

G. Soares and J. Collins, 'The Idiocy of Rural Life' (1982) 32 *Civilisations* 1, 31.

V. Sozayev, *Russia in the 21st century: A culture war caused by traditionalist revanchism*, in: *The Situation Of Lesbian, Gay, Bisexual And Transgender People In The Russian Federation (Last Three Months 2011 – First Half 2012)*, Moscow Helsinki Group, Moscow 2013.

G.Y. Spiró, *Két középkelet-európai mentalitás az államiság szempontjából*, 2000 Irodalmi és Társadalmi havi lap 6 (2007).

P.A. Stadter, 'Herodotus and the Athenian "arche"' in *Annali della Scuola Normale Superiore di Pisa. Classe di Lettere e Filosofia*, Serie III, Vol. 22, No. 3, 1992.

B. Stanley, 'Populism in Central and Eastern Europe', in C. Rovira Kaltwasser, P. Taggart, P. Ochoa Espejo and P. Ostiguy (eds), *The Oxford Handbook of Populism*, Oxford University Press, Oxford 2017.

——, 'The Thin Ideology of Populism', (2008) 13 *Journal of Political Ideologies* 1, 95.

Y. Stavrakakis, 'Populism and Hegemony', in C. Rovira Kaltwasser, P. Taggart, P. Ochoa Espejo and P. Ostiguy (eds), *The Oxford Handbook of Populism*, Oxford University Press, Oxford 2017.

S. Civitarese Matteucci, 'The Italian Response to Coronavirus and Constitutional Disagreement' <https://ukconstitutionallaw.org/2020/04/30/stefano-civitarese-matteucci-the-italian-response-to-coronavirus-and-constitutional-disagreement/?fbclid=IwAR1XiPp-IRpNgbPh1ZXLHZVe0O_BSL0ZfhY0KKy6k3P2hHmTmnZuDW1Eql4>.

P. Steinberger, 'Hobbes, Rousseau and the Modern Conception of the State' (2008) 70 *The Journal of Politics* 595.

J. Stiglitz, *People, Power and Profits: Progressive Capitalism for the Age of Discontent*, Penguin Books, New York 2019.

A. Stille, 'How Matteo Salvini pulled Italy to the Far Right' (2018) *The Guardian* <https://www.theguardian.com/news/2018/aug/09/how-matteo-salvini-pulled-italy-to-the-far-right>.

J. St. Mill, 'Considerations of Representative Government' in J. St. Mill, *Essays on Politics and Society*, J. M. Robson (ed.), University of Toronto Press, Toronto 1977.

D. Stockemer (ed.), *Populism Around the World. A Comparative Perspective*, Springer, Cham 2019.

K. Stoner, 'Russia in Retrospect and in Prospect' (2018) 50 *Comparative Politics* 3, 302.

E. Stoppioni, 'The Protection of Health Must Take Precedence: Testing the Constitutional State of Crisis in Luxembourg' <https://verfassungsblog.de/the-protection-of-health-must-take-precedence-testing-the-constitutional-state-of-crisis-in-luxembourg/>.

K. Strøm, W.C. Müller and T. Bergman, 'Parliamentary Democracy: Promise and Problems' in K Strøm, W.C. Müller and T. Bergman (eds), *Delegation and Accountability in Parliamentary Democracies*, Oxford University Press, Oxford and New York 2006.

C.R. Sunstein, *Republic.com*, Princeton University Press, Princeton and Harvard 2001.

F. Sureau, *Sans la Liberté*, Gallimard, Paris 2019.

D. Swank and H.G. Betz, 'Globalization, the welfare state and right-wing populism in Western Europe' (2003) 1 *Socio-Economic Review* 2, 215–45.

A. Stone Sweet, 'Constitutional Courts' in M. Rosenfeld and A. Sajó (eds), *The Oxford Handbook of Comparative Constitutional Law*, Oxford University Press, Oxford 2012.

——, 'Constitutions and Judicial Power' in D. Caramani (ed.), *Comparative Politics*, Oxford University Press, Oxford 2007.

J. Swenson, *On Jean-Jacques Rousseau: Considered as One of the First Authors of the Revolution*, Stanford University Press, Stanford 2000.

SWR Aktuell 'Menschenleben versus Menschenwürde?' <https://www.swr.de/swraktuell/schaueble-wertediskussion-zu-corona-100.html?fbclid=IwAR1xfhaSvsTRSEhzrYQqZsbEDPdffmtoANvUhI8McuWyXASqiFQE_E5ge-o>.

Z.S. Szabó, 'Többpólusú alapjogvédelmi rendszer a gyakorlatban – a kormánytisztviselők indokolás nélküli felmentésének tükrében [Multilevel protection of human rights in practice – in the light of dismissal of government officials without justification]', (2015) *Pro Futuro* 1, 138.

M.E. Szatlach, 'European identity and populism' (2007) *Polish Political Science* 36, 69–90.

Z. Szente, '*Az Alkotmánybíróság döntése Magyarország Alaptörvényének Átmeneti rendelkezései alkotmányosságáról. Az Alaptörvény integritása és az alkotmányozó hatalom korlátai*' (2013).

L. Sólyom, *Az alkotmánybíráskodás kezdetei Magyarországon*, Osiris, Budapest 2001.
——, 'The Hungarian Constitutional Court and Social Change' (1994) 19 *Yale Law Journal* 1.
P. Taggart, 'Populism in Western Europe' in C. Rovira Kaltwasser, P. Taggart, P. Ochoa Espejo and P. Ostiguy (eds), *The Oxford Handbook of Populism*, Oxford University Press, Oxford 2017.
P.A. Taguieff, 'Political science confronts populism: from a conceptual mirage to a real problem' (1995) *Telos* 103.
M. Tarchi, 'Italy: the promised land of populism?' (2015) 7 *Contemporary Italian Politics* 3, 273–85.
A. Tarnowska, 'The Sovereignty Issue in the Public Discussion in the Era of the Polish 3rd May Constitution (1788–1792)' in U. Müssig (ed.), *Reconsidering Constitutional Formation I National Sovereignty*, Springer Open, 2016.
C. Taylor, *Modern social imaginaries*, Duke University Press, Durham/London 2004.
L.A. Thio, 'Constitutionalism in Illiberal Polities' in M. Rosenfeld and A. Sajó (eds), *The Oxford Handbook of Comparative Constitutional Law*, Oxford University Press, Oxford 2012.
G.F. Thompson, 'Populisms and liberal democracy – business as usual?' (2017) 46 *Economy and Society*, 1, 43–59.
N.S. Timasheff, 'Soviet Law', (1952) 38 *Virginia Law Review* 7, 871.
C. Timmerman, G. Verschraegen, K. Hemmerechts and R. Willems, 'Europe and the Human Rights Imaginary' in: H. Alma and G. Vanheeswijck (eds), *Social Imaginaries in a Globalizing World*, De Gruyter, Berlin 2018.
V. Tolstykh, 'The Nature of Russian Discourses on International Law' in P. Morris (ed.), *Russian Discourses on International Law: Sociological and Philosophical*, Routledge, New York, 2019.
M. Troper, 'Sovereignty' in M. Rosenfeld and A. Sajò (eds), *The Oxford Handbook of Comparative Constitutional Law*, Oxford University Press, Oxford 2012.
L. Trócsányi and B. Schanda (eds), *Introduction into the constitutional law [Bevezetés az alkotmányjogba]*, HVG-ORAC, 2012.
A. Tsyganov and P. Tsygankov, 'Pluralism or isolation of Civilisations? Russia's foreign policy discourse and the reception of Huntington's paradigm of the post-cold war world', (1999) 4 *Geopolitics* 3, 51.
R. Tuck, 'Democratic sovereignty and democratic government' in R. Bourke and Q. Skinner (eds), *Popular Sovereignty in Historical Context*, Cambridge University Press, Cambridge 2016.
T. Tulich, M. Rizzi and F. Mcgaughey, 'Cooperative Federalism, Soft Governance and Hard Laws in Australia's State of Emergency', <https://verfassungsblog.de/fighting-covid-19-legal-powers-and-risks-australia/>.
J. Tully, *Public Philosophy in a New Key*, Cambridge University Press, Cambridge 2008.
M. Tushnet, *Advanced Introduction to Comparative Constitutional Law*, Edward Elgar, Cheltenham, Northampton, MA 2014.

——, 'Authoritarian Constitutionalism' in T. Ginsburg and A. Simpser (eds), *Constitutions in Authoritarian Regimes*, Cambridge University Press, New York 2014.

——, 'Authoritarian Constitutionalism' (2015) 100 *Cornell Law Review* 391, 438.

——, 'Popular Constitutionalism as political law' (2006) *Chicago-Kent Law Review* 81.

——, 'Varieties of Populism' (2019) 20 *German Law Journal* 382–89.

W. Twining, *Globalisation and Legal Theory*, Cambridge University Press, Cambridge 2000.

G.A. Tóth, 'Authoritarianism', *Max Planck Encyclopedia of Comparative Constitutional Law*, February 2017.

——, 'Constitutional Markers of Authoritarianism' (2019) 11 *Hague Journal on the Rule of Law* 41–42.

G.A. Tóth (ed.), *Constitution for a Disunited Nation: On Hungary's 2011 Fundamental Law*, CEU Press, Budapest 2012.

R.M. Unger, *Democracy Realized: The Progressive Alternative*, Verso, New York 2001.

——, *False Necessity: Anti-necessitarian Social Theory in the Service of Radical Democracy*, Verso, New York 2004.

——, *Free Trade Reimagined: The World Division of Labor and the Method of Economics*, Princeton University Press, New Haven 2010.

——, *Knowledge Economy*, Verso, New York 2019.

——, *The Left Alternative*, Verso, New York 2009.

——, *The Religion of the Future*, Harvard University Press, Cambridge 2014.

——, *The Self Awakened. Pragmatism Unbound*, Harvard University Press, Cambridge 2009.

N. Urbinati, 'Democracy and Populism' (1998) 5 *Constellations* 1, 110–24.

——, *Democracy Disfigured*, Harvard University Press, Cambridge, Massachusetts 2014.

——, 'Liquid parties, dense populism' (2019) 45 *Philosophy and Social Criticism* 9–10, 1069–83.

——, *Me the People. How Populism Transforms Democracy*, Harvard University Press, Cambridge MA 2019.

——, 'Political Theory of Populism' (2019) *Annual Review of Political Sciences* 22, 111–27.

——, 'Populism and the Principle of Majority', in C. Rovira Kaltwasser, P. Taggart, P. Ochoa Espejo and P. Ostiguy (eds), *The Oxford Handbook of Populism*, Oxford University Press, Oxford 2017.

E. Várnay, 'Az Alkotmánybíróság és az Európai Bíróság. Együttműködő alkotmánybíráskodás?' (2019) *Állam és Jogtudomány* 2, 66–70.

B. van Klink, 'Symbolic Legislation: An Essentially Political Concept' in B. van Klink, B. van Beers and L. Poort (eds), *Symbolic Legislation Theory and Developments in Biolaw*, Springer International Publishing, Switzerland 2016.

B. Verbeek and A. Zaslove, 'Italy: a case of mutating populism?' (2016) 23 *Democratization* 2, 304–23.

A. Verdun, 'Political Leadership of the European Central Bank' (2017) 39 *Journal of European Integration* 2, 207–21.

S. Vertovec, 'Covid-19 and enduring stigma. The corona pandemic increases xenophobia and exclusion worldwide', <https://www.mpg.de/14741776/covid-19-and-enduring-stigma?fbclid=IwAR1tjr5Zqjjj3YZ0lDt39IKWm3KvoD_KiXcqrcMpSWvLiAYZlxzETw8Kk1I>.

G.E. Vigevani, 'Origine e attualità del dibattito sulla XII disposizione finale della Costituzione: i limiti della tutela della democrazia' (2019) 1 *Media Laws*.

M.J.C. Vile, *Constitutionalism and the Separation of Powers*, 2nd ed., Liberty Fund, Indianapolis 1998.

S. Vinciguerra, 'Fascismo (sanzioni)' *Enciclopedia del Diritto*, Giuffrè, Milano 1967.

K. von Beyme, 'Judicial review' [Alkotmánybíráskodás] in P. Paczolay (ed.), *Constitutional adjudication – constitutional interpretation [Alkotmánybíráskodás – alkotmányértelmezés]*, Rejtjel, 2003.

A. Von Bogdandy and L.D. Spieker, 'Countering the Judicial Silencing of Critics: Article 2 TEU Values, Reverse Solange, and the Responsibilities of National Judges' (2019) *European Constitutional Law Review*.

P. Wagner, 'The Political Form of Europe, Europe as a Political Form' (2005) 80 *Thesis Eleven* 1, 47–73.

J. Waldron, 'Separation of Powers in Thought and Practice' (2013) 54 *British Columba Law Review* 2, 438.

A. Walicki, *The controversy over capitalism: studies in the social philosophy of the Russian populists*, Clarendon Press, New York 1968.

N. Walker, 'Populism and constitutional tension' (2019) 17 *International Journal of Constitutional Law* 2.

——, 'Sovereignty and Beyond: The Double Edge of External Constitutionalism' (2018) *Virginia Journal of International Law* 58, 799–820.

M. Walzer, 'Philosophy and Democracy' (1981) *Political Theory* 379.

T. Warczok and H. Dębska, 'Sacred Law and Profane Politics: The Symbolic Construction of the Constitutional Tribunal' (2014) 188 *Polish Sociological Review* 462.

M. Weber, 'Economy and Society. An outline of interpretive sociology' in G. Roth and G. Wittich (eds), University of California Press, Berkeley 1978.

J.H.H. Weiler, 'The Political and Legal Culture of European Integration: An Exploratory Essay' (2011) 9 *International Journal of Constitutional Law* 3–4, 678–94.

M. Weisberger, 'Dogs are being trained to sniff out COVID-19 in humans' <https://www.livescience.com/dogs-smell-covid-19.html>.

R.A. Wessel, 'Revisiting the International Legal Status of the EU' (2000) *European Foreign Affairs Review* 5, 507–37.

J. Westaway, 'Globalization, Sovereignty and Social Unrest' (2012) 5 *Journal of Politics and Law* 2, 132–39.

K. Weyland, 'Populism: A Political-Strategic Approach' in C. Rovira Kaltwasser, P. Taggart, P. Ochoa Espejo and P. Ostiguy (eds), *The Oxford Handbook of Populism*, Oxford University Press, Oxford 2017.

A. WIELOMSKI, *W poszukiwaniu katechona. Teologia polityczna Carla Schmitta*, von borowiecky, Warszawa 2018.

C. WILKINSON, 'Putting "Traditional Values" Into Practice: The Rise and Contestation of Anti-Homopropaganda Laws in Russia', (2014) 13 *Journal of Human Rights* 3, 367.

M.A. WILKINSON, 'Authoritarian liberalism as authoritarian constitutionalism' in H.A. GARCÍA and G. FRANKENBERG (eds), *Authoritarian Constitutionalism. Comparative Analysis and Critique*, Edward Elgar Publishing, Cheltenham 2019.

——, 'The Specter of Authoritarian Liberalism: Reflections on the Constitutional Crisis of the European Union' (2013) 14 *German Law Journal* 5, 527–60.

A. WINKLER, *We the Corporations: How American Businesses Won Their Civil Rights*, Liveright Publishing Corporation, New York and London 2018.

C. WOLFE, *Judicial activism. Bulwark of freedom or precarious security?* Brooks/Cole Publishing Company, California 1991.

——, 'Judicial review and democracy' [Alkotmánybíráskodás és demokrácia], in: P. PACZOLAY (ed.), *Constitutional adjudication - constitutional interpretation [Alkotmánybíráskodás - alkotmányértelmezés]*, Rejtjel, 2003.

S. WOLIN, *Democracy Inc. Managed Democracy and the Specter of Inverted Totalitarianism*, Princeton University Press, Princeton 2008.

P. WROŃSKI, 'PiS chce zmienić konstytucję. Będzie odwołanie do Boga i likwidacja autonomii państwa i Kościoła?', *Gazeta Wyborcza*, 04.05.2017.

W. WRZESIŃSKI, *Charakter narodowy Polaków. Z rozważań historyka [National character of Poles. From the historian's reflections]*, Wrocław 2004.

B. YACK, 'Of Scribes and Tribes: Progressive Politics and the Populist Challenge' (2019) 1 *Critical Review* 14, 6.

G. YEUNG, 'Fear of Unaccountability vs Fear of a Pandemic: COVID-19 in Hong Kong', <https://verfassungsblog.de/fear-of-unaccountability-vs-fear-of-a-pandemic-covid-19-in-hong-kong/>.

F. ZAKARIA, *The Future of Freedom: Illiberal Democracy at Home and Abroad*, W.W. Norton and Company, New York 2007.

——, 'The Rise of Illiberal Democracy' (1997) 76 *Foreign Affairs* 6, 22.

J. ZIELONKA, *Counter-revolution: Liberal Europe in retreat*, Oxford University Press, Oxford 2018.

C. ZILIOLI and M. SELMAYR, *The Law of the European Central Bank*, Hart, Oxford 2001.

S. ŽIŽEK, 'Introduction: Remembering, Repeating and Working Through' in S. ŽIŽEK (ed.), *Lenin. The Day after the Revolution*, Verso, London and New York 2018.

S. ZUBOFF, *The Age of Surveillance Capitalism. The Fight for a Human Future at the New Frontier of Power*, Public Affairs, New York 2019.

INDEX

ABOUT THE EDITOR

Dr Martin Belov is Professor in Constitutional and Comparative Constitutional Law at the University of Sofia 'St. Kliment Ohridski', Bulgaria. He is also Vice Dean of the Faculty of Law and is responsible for international relations and digitalisation of the education and scientific activities in the Faculty. Martin Belov has been a visiting professor at University Paris II Pantheon-Assas, France (2019), University Roma Tre, Rome, Italy (2019), Goethe-University Frankfurt am Main, Germany (2019), University of Girona, Spain (2019), University 'Pompeu Fabra', Barcelona, Spain (2019), Europa-University Viadrina, Frankfurt/Oder, Germany (2017 and 2018), University of Bari, Italy (2018), European Law and Governance School, Athens, Greece (2017–2018), University of Södertorn, Stockholm, Sweden (2017), Scuolla Superiore Sant'Anna, Pisa, Italy (2016), University of Warsaw, Poland (2015), University of Lisbon, Portugal (2012), State University of Milan, Italy (2011) and University of Cologne, Germany (2007–2009), amongst others. Previously, he has been a project researcher at the Max-Planck Institute for European Legal History, Frankfurt am Main, Germany (2010–2012) and a visiting researcher at the Institute for Federalism, Fribourg, Switzerland (2014). He has specialised at the University of Oxford, UK (2017), Max-Planck Institute for Comparative Public Law and International Law, Heidelberg, Germany (2009) and many other academic institutions. Martin Belov is a member of the European Group of Public Law, International Association of Legislation, Advisory Board of the Central and Eastern European Forum of Young Legal, Political and Social Theorist, and other scientific and academic organisations. He is also a member of the scientific boards of many academic journals and has published 18 books and more than 80 scientific papers.

www.ingramcontent.com/pod-product-compliance
Ingram Content Group UK Ltd.
Pitfield, Milton Keynes, MK11 3LW, UK
UKHW021008120926
8556IPUK00028B/192

9 781839 700606